THE GREAT GUNS LIKE THUNDER
THE CANNON FROM THE CITY OF DERRY

B.G. Scott, R.R. Brown, A.G. Leacock & C.J. Salter

The great Guns like Thunder, have shaken our Walls; the small Shot hath poured upon us like a shower of Hail; and the Bombs, like Lightning, have ruin'd our Houses; we have seen Death in all its horrible shapes, and we are at every Moment entertain'd with spectacles of Misery and Mortality.

'A Sermon Preached before the Garrison of London-Derry in 1689'
The Reverend Seth Whittle, Minister of Bellaghy

In Memoriam

R.J. Hunter

22 October 1938 – 24 September 2007

First published in May 2008 by
Guildhall Press
Unit 15
Ráth Mór Business Park
Bligh's Lane
Derry BT48 0LZ
T: (028) 7136 4413 F: (028) 7137 2949
info@ghpress.com www.ghpress.com

Copyright © Derry City Council

ISBN 978 1 906271 10 7

A CIP record for this book is available from the British Library.

The authors assert their moral rights in this work in accordance with the Copyright, Designs and Patents Act 1998.

All rights reserved. No part of this publication may be reproduced or transmitted in any form or by any means, electronic or mechanical, including photocopy, recording, or any information storage or retrieval system, without permission in writing from the publisher. The book is sold subject to the condition that it shall not, by way of trade or otherwise, be lent, re-sold or otherwise circulated without the publisher's prior consent in any form of binding or cover other than that in which it is published and without a similar condition, including this condition, being imposed on the subsequent purchaser.

CONTENTS

- *iv* Forewords
- *vii* Acknowledgements
- *ix* List of Figures
- *x* List of Plates
- *xii* List of Tables
- *xiii* Conventions
- *xvii* Introduction
- *1* Chapter 1: The Conservation and Restoration Project
- *27* Chapter 2: The Historical and Technological Backgrounds to the Cannon
- *63* Chapter 3: The City Defences and the Use of Cannon
- *99* Chapter 4: The Origins of the Ordnance of the Sixteenth and Seventeenth Centuries
- *139* Chapter 5: The Elizabethan Guns
- *145* Chapter 6: The Guns of the Seventeenth Century
- *163* Chapter 7: The Guns of the Eighteenth and Nineteenth Centuries
- *179* Chapter 8: Some Observations on the Technology of the English Cannon
- *199* Chapter 9: The Cannon Founders
- *211* Appendix A: Contemporary Documents Relating to the Londonderry Ordnance
- *233* Appendix B: The Siting of the Derry Magazine in 1566
- *236* Bibliography
- *246* Index

FOREWORD

*by Arlene Foster, MLA,
Minister of the Environment*

The cannon situated upon Londonderry's Walls have for 400 years been integral to the city's defence and also to its ornamentation. As defensive objects, they were tried and tested in their early years on a number of occasions. Some, such as Roaring Meg, assumed an almost mythical status in the story of this defence. Most, however, played a more general role and have stood through the years as a reminder – along with the Walls themselves – of an important part of the city's history.

Their recent restoration has added to this interest. For the first time in many years, their makers' marks have been clearly revealed. Historically accurate carriages and plaques explaining their origins have also contributed to increasing their importance. The cannon are now displayed as the major collection that they are and this is to the great credit of their owners at the City Council.

The work has complemented the efforts of the Environment and Heritage Service – an agency within my Department – who, particularly over the last ten years, have put much time into restoring the fabric of the City Walls. The monument is once again open to all and an important focus for the heritage offering of Northern Ireland.

The recent collaborative work between the City Council, the Northern Ireland Tourist Board, EHS, the Department of Social Development and Ilex, the urban regeneration company for the city, to increase the prominence of the walled city as a heritage destination has built upon these efforts. There is now new signage, a Conservation Plan, improved museum facilities and the ongoing restoration of nearby historic buildings. Improved lighting and management arrangements are also in development.

This publication will only add to these efforts – adding another layer of interest and helping to increase the reasons why a visitor should linger. It also helps to highlight and cast new light upon the important history of the monument. For this reason my Department is happy to contribute to the funding of this book. Our heritage is often bound up in quick summaries and received impressions and it is important to remind ourselves, and perhaps surprise ourselves, through detailed research, of the quality and rarity of some of our surviving historic structures.

I commend this publication.

FOREWORD

*by Alderman Drew Thompson,
Mayor, Derry City Council*

The cannon on Derry's Walls have witnessed the city's eventful history for 400 years. Gifted to the citizens to defend their young Plantation settlement, the cannon remain a potent symbol of our long relationship with the City of London. Today they are one of our proudest possessions.

Once they ceased to fire in anger after the relief of the siege in 1689, the cannon were not always treated with the respect they deserved. Occasionally, people were moved to write to the local press, expressing concern about their dilapidated state. Such correspondences often prompted vigorous debate between Londonderry Corporation and The Honourable The Irish Society as to which organisation was responsible for footing the bill to restore them.

Happily, there is now little risk of the cannon being taken for granted over the next 400 years. Their metalwork burnished, their paintwork gleaming, the cannon have been proudly restored to their place on the Walls in readiness for the celebration of the 400th anniversary of the Plantation of Ulster in 1613. Their restoration was achieved through a joint venture by Derry City Council and the Department of Enterprise, Trade and Investment with support from the European Union.

The Great Guns Like Thunder has been published to document the restoration work and to act as a guide for the future care of the cannon. This authoritative publication is the result of an initiative between the City Council, the Department of the Environment and The Honourable The Irish Society. This book celebrates the fascinating history of the cannon and their restoration. As its pages reveal, each of the great cannon has its own story to tell.

DERRY CITY COUNCIL

FOREWORD

*by Alderman Sir Michael Oliver, Governor,
The Honourable The Irish Society*

The Honourable The Irish Society, together with the London Companies of the Grocers, the Fishmongers, the Merchant Taylors, the Salters and the Vintners, has had the great pleasure of supporting the publication of this book, which tells the story of the Londonderry cannon from their manufacture in the sixteenth and seventeenth centuries to their eventual refurbishment and replacement on the Walls of Londonderry in 2007.

The Society, which continues to own the City Walls, has always taken a deep interest in the preservation of the historic fabric of Londonderry. The fine new work by Dr. Scott and his co-authors will enable a much wider audience to see how such an internationally significant collection of cannon came to exist in the first place and has subsequently been so well restored.

A debt of gratitude is owed by the city's inhabitants to Derry City Council, whose decision it was to restore these historic artefacts and to invite visitors from the rest of the world to view them and everything else that Londonderry has to offer. It is also a mark of the importance of the project that those London Companies mentioned above were prepared, after so many centuries, once again to offer funding and the Society is most grateful for their support.

The Society works to develop the economic, civic, cultural and social links between Londonderry and the City of London for the benefit of all sections of the community, and this will be symbolised when the current Lord Mayor of London, Alderman David Lewis, takes part in the forthcoming launch celebrations of the book.

We are proud to be associated with such an undertaking.

The Merchant Taylors' Company

The Grocers' Company

The Salters' Company

The Fishmongers' Company

The Vintners' Company

ACKNOWLEDGEMENTS

This project was conceived originally by Mark Lusby, Senior Economic Development Officer at Derry City Council and Annesley Malley, Chair of the Foyle Civic Trust. It was set in train by the Economic Development Section of Derry City Council under the project management of Dermot Harrigan, Tony Monaghan, Elaine Griffin and Terence O'Kane along with assistance from Jim Gallagher and Patricia Crossan of the City Engineer's Department. These officers were not just bystanders during its course, but offered continuous encouragement and all of the assistance and support that the authors could have wished for. Their enthusiasm and professionalism meant that we were able to work to a much wider research remit than has been usual in the previous experience of any of us. It allowed us to follow a multi-disciplinary approach to the research, covering the archaeology, history and technology of the guns and their carriages, something we believe has not been done before. Whatever the merits of this work, they are in no small part due to the Council team.

JL Ornamental Castings, under its Managing Director John Lavelle, was the contractor for the project. John and his team brought to the work a wealth of experience in the conservation and restoration of metalwork, including cast irons, and a high degree of perfectionism. R.D. (Bob) Smith, formerly Keeper of Conservation at the Tower Armouries in Leeds, created the designs for the reproductions of the gun carriages to authentic seventeenth-century patterns. The wheels for the field carriages were made to virtually original specifications by Mike and Greg Rowland of Mike Rowland, Wheelwrights and Coachbuilders, and the trails for them by JL Ornamental Castings, who also made the block carriages entirely and undertook the final assembly of all. Again, we are most grateful for all of their continuous and enthusiastic support.

Safe removal of the samples was a lengthy and laborious task that fell to Thomas Gough of JL Ornamental Castings, and that of preparing them for metallographic examination to Graeme Craig of the University of Ulster, School of Electrical and Mechanical Engineering.

The chemical analyses of the metal samples taken from the cannon were conducted by Drs Connor Murphy and Joe Foley of the State Laboratory of the Irish Republic. They gave most generously of their time and expertise, thus laying the ground for the study of the cannon technology.

Preparation for optical microscopy and preliminary work on the identification of the inclusions was done by Evan Wang, at the Oxford University, Department of Materials BegbrokeNano laboratory facilities funded by the Technology program of the United Kingdom Government, and we are grateful also to the Worshipful Company of Ironmongers for their sponsorship of him. Judith Root of Oxford Instruments gave valuable assistance in pointing to the most effective use of the particle analysis software.

Line drawings of the guns and their markings were done by Bronagh P. Murray, with photographic contributions from the authors, Gail Pollock of the Environment and Heritage Service (NI), Mark Lusby and Lorcan Doherty. Gary Bates of Big Fish Design in the City devised and drew Fig. 5. The Rev. William Morton, Dean of St. Columb's Cathedral, kindly provided panoramic views from the top of the bell tower.

The late R.J. (Bob) Hunter, W.P. (Billy) Kelly, Paul Kerrigan, Brian Lacy, John McGurk, Annesley Malley and R.D. (Bob) Smith, each of whom has made such an important contribution to the study of the City, its history and archaeology, and of post-mediaeval fortifications and ordnance in general, all gave generously of their knowledge and time, and took much trouble in reading drafts of this work in its various stages. Annesley Malley also provided much-needed assistance in helping to locate those guns that had left the immediate confines of the City and in providing information on their recent histories, as well as by locating for us images to be used in the book. All of these provided comments and suggestions that were most helpful in shaping the final form of the work. Obviously, none bears responsibility for any of its demerits.

Samuel McKean and Robert Moore most kindly allowed us to inspect and record cannon in their possession, as did Phillip and David Gilliland, who have generously donated the London

Shield saker (C25) to the City, to sit on the Artillery Bastion. We are also grateful to them for information on the former provenances of this gun and also the other two (C26 and C27) in their possession. Craig Jefferson generously presented the City with a London Shield demi-culverin in his possession (C18), now located at Guildhall Square, along with a rare example for Ireland of a late-Victorian garrison carriage.

We have also benefited greatly from discussions and correspondence with, and assistance from, a number of friends and colleagues, R. Balasubramaniam, Nico Brinck, James Curl, Kelleen Doyle, Suzanne Funnell, Winifred Glover, Steven Grenter, Robert Heslip, Lar Joye, Connie Kelleher, Paul Logue, Chris Lynn, Finbar McCormick, Simon Metcalf, Eileen Murphy, Peter Northover, James O'Neill, David Maconaghy, Trevor Parkhill, Greg and Mike Rowland, Martin Rudd, Lesley Simpson, Bob Smith, Pauljac Verhoeven, Steve Walton, Kenneth Wiggins, Arco Willeboordse, Guy Wilson and Tom Wylie.

In studying the merchants who were responsible in 1642 for the arrival of fifteen cannon, the name William Felgate stands out. It was thus a surprise and delight to find that this most interesting character not only has direct descendants, but that two of them – Don Felgate and Bunny Felgate – are active in research into their family history. The information which they have provided has helped greatly to flesh out as 'real' characters not only William, but also his brothers Tobias and Robert.

Searches of the records of the Twelve Great Companies of London were greatly assisted by the archivists of a number of them – David Beasley, Worshipful Company of Goldsmiths, Alex Buchanan, Worshipful Company of Clothworkers, Ursula Carlyle and Gary Haines, Worshipful Company of Mercers, Penny Fussell, Worshipful Company of Drapers, Katie George, Worshipful Company of Salters, and Pauline Siddall, Worshipful Company of Grocers. The staff of the Guildhall Library, London, were invariably helpful, as were those of the Bodleian Library, British Library, National Archives and Sheffield City Library. Sarah Joy Maddeaux of the National Archives of Scotland offered kind assistance in locating the manuscript of the accounting of the 1620 Culmore guns. Dr John Cherry of the National Library of Ireland provided much help with manuscript sources there.

We are grateful for the permission to reproduce images in their collections given by the British Library, London, National Archives, Kew, Staatliche Museen zu Berlin Gemäldegalerie, The Royal Collections, The Worshipful Company of Drapers, The Worshipful Company of Grocers, The Science Library, London and Trinity College, Dublin.

Production of this book was carried out by Guildhall Press in the City, with the layout and design by Joe McAllister to whom our best thanks for his skill and patience.

Funding for the restoration programme came from the Economic Development Programme of Derry City Council, the Northern Ireland Department of Enterprise, Trade and Investment and the European Regional Development Fund. The publication has been financed by the Economic Development Programme of Derry City Council and the Environment and Heritage Service of the Northern Ireland Department of the Environment, and by the generous funding provided by The Honourable The Irish Society, the Worshipful Company of Fishmongers, the Worshipful Company of Grocers, the Worshipful Company of Merchant Taylors, the Worshipful Company of Salters, and the Worshipful Company of Vintners, organised by Edward Montgomery, Esq, DL, Ireland, Representative of The Honourable The Irish Society, to whom gratitude is also due.

LIST OF FIGURES

1	Terminology of cannon and carriage parts	xiv
2	Reconstruction of a nineteenth-century garrison carriage	4
3	Block carriage from Windsor Castle	14
4	Illustration of a block carriage intended for a yacht and attributed to Willem van de Velde the Younger, 1675	15
5	The 2006 locations of the cannon throughout the City	24
6	Preparation of a cannon mould with false core	35
7	Cutting off the gun head and reaming the bore	36
8	Tools for checking the bore of a cannon	36
9	Lifting gear for cannon	45
10	Gunners' accessories	47
11	How to use a gunner's quadrant	51
12	The angular bastion and its main associated elements	64
13	Comparison of the fields of fire from angular, round and square bastions	65
14	The primary fortifications constructed by Sir Henry Docwra c 1600	71
15	Cannon mounted on a wooden gun platform	75
16	Cartographic traces of the Londonderry Citadel	78
17	Cannon mounted on the cathedral roof	89
18	Eastern elevation of Londonderry Cathedral in 1689	89
19	C7 – rose-and-crown saker of 8ft 6ins	140
20	C12 – rose-and-crown demi-culverin of 10ft, the Thomas Johnson gun	140
21	The surviving rose-and-crown emblems on C7 and C12	141
22	Tudor rose-and-crown emblems on English brass cannon	141
23	C8 – Demi-culverin of 9ft 6ins bearing the initials of John Browne	146
24	C20 – Demi-culverin of 9ft 6ins with the 'club and arrow' marks	146
25	C2 – Demi-culverin of 10ft bearing the City of London shield	149
26	C13 – Demi-culverin of 8ft bearing the City of London shield	151
27	C17 – Saker of 8ft bearing the City of London shield	151
28	C18 – Demi-culverin of 10ft bearing the City of London shield	152
29	C25 – Saker bearing the City of London shield	152
30	City of London shield on C2	152
31	C16 – Demi-culverin of 9ft	153
32	C21 – Demi-culverin of 10ft	154
33	C1 – Demi-culverin of 10ft engraved VINTNERS LONDON 1642	155
34	C3 – Demi-culverin of 10ft engraved MARCHANT TAYLERS LONDON 1642	157
35	C4 – Demi-culverin of 7ft 6ins engraved SALTERS LONDON 1642	157
36	C6 ('Roaring Meg') – Demi-culverin of 10ft engraved FISHMONGERS LONDON 1642	157
37	C9 – Demi-culverin of 10ft engraved MERCERS LONDON 1642	158
38	C10 – Demi-culverin of 10ft engraved GROCERS LONDON 1642	159
39	C11 – Demi-culverin of 10ft engraved MARCHANT TAYLERS LONDON 1642	159
40	C5 – Falcon of 5ft 6ins	160
41	C19 – 6-pdr from the Bersham works of John Wilkinson	165
42	C22 – 6-pdr from the Bersham works of John Wilkinson	165
43	C26 – 6-pdr from the Bersham works of John Wilkinson	165
44	C14 – 3- or 4-pdr with 'P' marking	171
45	C24 – 3- or 4-pdr	171
46	C27 – English 6-pdr with fleur-de-lys and 'crowned P'	171
47	The basic iron-carbon equilibrium diagram	180
48	The distribution of element burden from breech to muzzle	184
49	Average burden at breech, trunnion and muzzle areas	185
50	Approximate distribution of concentration of the most distinctive surface flaws on the underside of C8	186

51 Variation in percentage burden around the circumference of cannon at the trunnions	186
52 Distribution of micro-SG values from breech to muzzle	187
53 Variations in specific gravity from breech to muzzle	187
54 Scatter plots of average burden vs average micro-SG and SG	188
55 Distribution of graphite sizes from breech to muzzle	189
56 Variations in the average sizes of graphite flakes from breech to muzzle	189
57 Distribution of hardness values from breech to muzzle	190
58 EDS spectrum from (MnFe)S inclusions	192
59 Clustering of analytical data	194

LIST OF PLATES

1 Nineteenth-century engraving of cannon at the Double Bastion in 1837	1
2 Cannon on the Walls overlooking Guildhall Square c. 1929	2
3 Roaring Meg (C6) on a nineteenth-century garrison carriage	2
4 C12 on its decaying carriages in 2004	3
5 C18 on the nineteenth-century garrison carriage which formerly supported Roaring Meg	3
6 Garrison carriage markings (a) date stamp 1884, (b) calibre to be carried 64-pdr	3
7 (a) C7 showing the Tudor Rose and Crown obscured by overpaint, (b) C1 with the engraved name 'Vintners' obscured by overpaint	4
8 Grocers' inscription (C10) emerging during cleaning from under paint layers that had totally obscured it	5
9 Corrosion under flaking paint on the underside of C11	5
10 (a) C14 in situ in Shipquay Street in 2002 (b) after removal in 2006	5
11 (a) C15 in situ in Pump Street in 2002 (b) after removal and before it was stolen from Pennyburn depot	6
12 'Roaring Meg' (C6) being lifted from the Memorial Garden to join C17 for transport to Belfast	7
13 Removing the overpaint from C12 with paint-stripper and high pressure water jet	7
14 C8 undergoing chemical treatment	8
15 Previously unseen marks on C8 after removal of paint and chemical cleaning	9
16 Casting flaws on the muzzle of C11	10
17 Batch of cannon undercoated and partially lacquered	11
18 The inevitable response of some to improvements in civic property	11
19 The components of a field carriage as illustrated by Robert Norton in 1628	13
20 Seventeenth-century block carriage with cannon at Windsor Castle	14
21 Raven's 1622 painting of Phillips' design for a defended Market Hall in Londonderry	15
22 The storming of the Blackwater Fort	16
23 Assembling the basic components for the block carriages	17
24 Block carriage for C8 nearing completion	17
25 Ship's carriage for C19 under construction	17
26 Final fitting of cannon to their block carriages	18
27 Cannon on block carriages returned to the City Walls in 2005	18
28 (a) Hub sections ready for assembly (b) Greg Rowland constructing a hub	19
29 Fitting hub and spokes together	20
30 Mike Rowland fitting felloes and spokes together	20
31 A completed pair of wheels outside the workshop of Mike Rowland, Wheelwright and Coachbuilder, by Appointment to Her Majesty The Queen	21
32 Cheeks being fitted with their ironwork	21
33 A wheel and axle assembly complete with ironwork	22
34 Assembled field carriage for C10	22
35 C10 mounted on its carriage	22
36 The seven London Company guns on their field carriages on display in Shipquay Place, 12 May 2006	23
37 Burt Castle, Co Donegal, an O'Doherty stronghold c 1600	28
38 Pistol loop by the entrance to Burt Castle, Co Donegal	29

39 Diver working with a cannon on the sea bed	31
40 British army ordnance with A-frames at Ebrington Barracks, Londonderry, c 1890	45
41 Gun crews firing, loading and cooling their cannon	46
42 Aiming a cannon	51
43 Jacobite gunner using a quadrant to lay his mortar at the 1689 Siege of Londonderry	51
44 *The Kings Fort att Lifford*	65
45 *The Island and forte of the Derry*	66
46 The extensions to the City defences as proposed by Engineer Jean Thomas	68
47 Exchanges of small arms fire at Derry	69
48 The fortified Lough Foyle landscape in 1601	70-71
49 Plan of 'London Derry' of 1619 by Nicholas Pynnar	73
50 *The Platt of the Cittie of London Derrie as it Stand built and Fortifyed*	74
51 Access way to the Water Bastion on the Raven 1622 map	74
52 Plan of Londonderry from Tindal's *Continuation*	78
53 *A plot of ye cittie and iland of Londonderry*	80
54 Part of the map of the Siege of 1689 by Captain Thomas Neville	80
55 Ravelin at Bishop's Gate	80
56 Troops with a saker at the Battle of the Yellow Ford	82
57 The Maculloch map of the Siege of 1689	87
58 Used shot for a demi-culverin comprising lead cast around brick	90
59 The use of gabions by Jacobite troops to protect their ordnance	92
60 Cast iron saker on the town wall of Youghal, Co Cork	149
61 Cascable of a cast-iron demi-culverin in Ballymullan Barracks, Tralee, Co Kerry	149
62 Woodcut published in early 1642 showing a gunner with a small field piece	160
63 John Wilkinson cannon restored and mounted on its new carriage	163
64 Bersham marks on C19	163
65 John Wilkinson 6-pdr outside Christ Church, Limavady, Co Londonderry, and its trunnion markings	166
66 Two guns from the grounds of Glendarragh House, Termonbacca, Co Londonderry	167
67 John Wilkinson 6-pdr at Fermanagh County Museum	167
68 John Wilkinson 6-pdr from Londonderry, now in Kingston Ontario	168
69 William Shannon	168
70 John Wilkinson 6-pdr in Mozambique	169
71 Cannon at Mullenan, Co Londonderry	170
72 C23 – Russian 24-pdr from the Crimea	172
73 C23 – casting flaws in one of the carriage wheels	172
74 C23 – trunnion markings and imperial eagle	173
75 Russian 36-pdr on the Mall, Armagh City, Co Armagh	173-174
76 Russian 24-pdr outside Newry Town Hall, Newry, Co Down	174
77 Russian 24-pdr in the Castle Gardens, Lisburn, Co Antrim	175
78 Graphite types observed in polished specimens	180
79 Structures observed in the assemblage	183
80 Fragments deriving from the mould material in a void at the muzzle of C10	184
81 Remanent structures in corrosion products in the muzzle of C10	185
82 Zone of major flaws exploited by corrosion on the underside of C6 ('Roaring Meg')	186
83 Graphite flakes in C1 and the output of the image analysis software	189
84 Hardness measurements and SEM images of the microstructure from the outer surface to the interior of the powder chamber of C6	190
85 MnS and Ti(CN) inclusions	191
86 MnS and Ti-rich inclusions	192
87 Micro-crack in pearlite and phosphide eutectic	194
88 Secondary deposition on graphite flakes	195
89 Memorial slab to Anne (née Dobell), wife of George Browne	204
90 *Squire John Wilkinson* by Thomas Gainsborough	205

91 Reconstruction of the Wilkinson cannon boring machine	206
92 The Wilkinson obelisk at Lindale-in-Cartmel	208
93 The precept of 18 March 1642	214
94 The accounting for the cannon sent by the Worshipful Company of Grocers	215
95 The inventory of ordnance and accessories in Culmore on 10 July 1674	225
96 *A chapelle fortified where capt Cotes his company lyeth*	234

LIST OF TABLES

1 The types of cannon known to have been present *c* 1600–1690	xv
2 Checklist of the Londonderry cannon	xviii
3 Examples of ordnance, munitions and gunners recorded at or ordered to be sent to Culmore, Lifford and Dunalong *c.* 1600–1639	102
4 Examples of ordnance, munitions and gunners recorded at or ordered to be sent to Londonderry pre-1641	103-104
5 Examples of ordnance, munitions and gunners recorded at or ordered to be sent to Culmore and Strabane *c.* 1640–1690	110-112
6 Examples of ordnance, munitions and gunners recorded at Londonderry *c.* 1640–1690	113-117
7 The cannon recorded as purchased by the Great Companies and the Londonderry ordnance listing of the Reverend Richard Winter and the 1660 inventory	123
8 Payments for munitions, accessories and services for the Londonderry cannon in the accounts of the Great Companies for 1642–1643	124-125
9 Summary of the main features of the Elizabethan guns	139
10 The main characteristics of the cannon of *c.* 1610 – 1635	146
11 The main characteristics of the cannon of 1641–1642	154
12 The main characteristics of the eighteenth- and nineteenth-century guns	164
13 Summary of element compositions, SG and Micro-SG, inclusion levels and hardness values	181
14 Predicted densities vs observed	188

CONVENTIONS

In Britain and Ireland pre-decimalisation, all measurements on cannon were in Imperial units – i.e. lengths in feet and inches, weights in pounds, quarters (28lb) and hundredweights (112lb). In the case of the Russian 24-pdr, its weight was given in *pud*, a Russian unit of measurement equal to 36.11lb or 16.38kg, and divided into thirty-five *funt* equivalent to 1.03lb or 468gm. We shall use Imperial as the primary units in this study, although where appropriate, they are followed by the metric equivalents in brackets. In Tables 9–12, the lengths of the guns are measured from the base ring to the muzzle face.

When discussing the twelve Great London Companies, they are listed in their seventeenth-century order of precedence, as are the Minor Companies.

Throughout the text, the cannon will be referred to by their current catalogue numbers, prefixed by the letter 'C' (thus, C1, C2 etc.). In 2002, Derry City Council conducted an inventory of all known cannon and their locations. The types and locations of all of the cannon in 2002 and their current locations (2008) are given in Table 2. The conventions used for naming of the various parts of a cannon and carrriages are shown in Fig. 1. Calibres were measured using pipe-calipers and taking a series of readings as far inside the bore as possible, then averaging out the readings.

Terminology

The terminology and classification of cannon is often confused and confusing, depending on which source is being consulted. Blackmore (1977, 391) quoted from the English edition of Tartaglio's *Arte of Shooting*, printed in 1588, whose translator wrote

> ... through the intolerable fault of careless or unskilful gunfounders all our great pieces of one name are not of one length nor of one weight, nor of one height in their mouths, and therefore the gunners' books and tables which do show that all our great pieces of one name are of an equal length, and of equal weight, and of an equal height in their mouths, are erroneous.

We shall use the terminology shown in Fig. 1.

The types of cannon represented in the Derry assemblage or reported as having been in the Lough Foyle area in the seventeenth century are:

Demi-cannon	second largest of the sixteenth- and seventeenth-centuries types, with a bore averaging 6.5ins (16.5cm) and firing a shot of around 30lb (13.6kg). These were used primarily to batter defences.
Culverin	largest of a family of guns which includes those below, with a bore averaging 5.5ins (14cm) and firing a shot of around 18lb (8.2kg). With the demi-culverin, used for more accurate targetting of sections weakened by cannon.
Demi-culverin	a bore averaging 4.5ins (11.4cm) and firing a shot of 9–12lb (4.1–5.4kg).
Saker	a bore averaging 3.5ins (8.9cm) and firing shot of 5–6lb (2.3–2.7kg). Used both to loosen stonework and as an anti-personnel weapon.
Minion	a bore averaging 3.25ins (8.3cm) and firing a shot of around 4lb (1.8kg). Primarily an anti-personnel weapon for use in the field.
Falcon	a bore of 2.75ins (7cm) and firing a shot of 2.5–3lb (1.1–1.4kg). As with the falconet below, a field-piece used as an anti-personnel weapon.
Falconet	a bore averaging 2.25ins (5.7cm) and firing a shot of around 1.5lb (0.7kg).

It has been argued that for the sixteenth and seventeenth centuries, there is a broad relationship between the calibre of a cannon (the diameter of its bore) and its length from muzzle to breech, also between the calibre and the circumference measured at the touch hole. However, this is by no means universally accepted. A most useful source for detailed comparison of

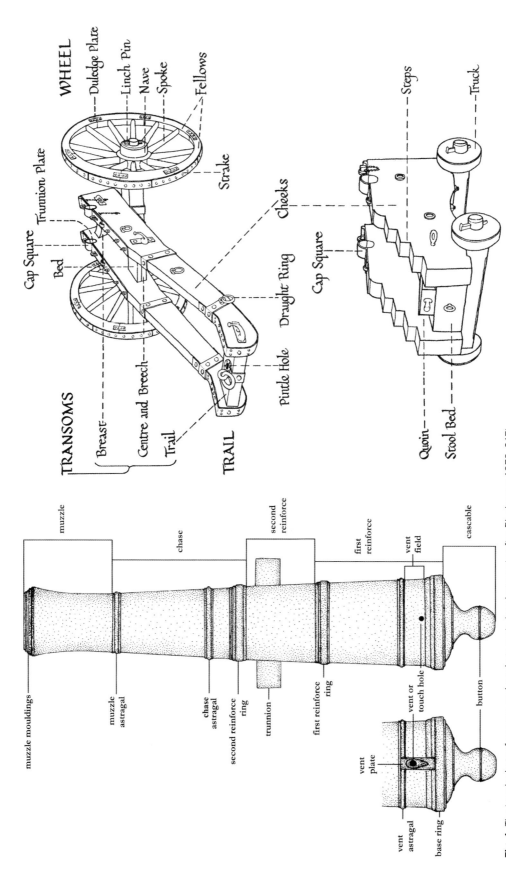

Fig. 1 The terminology of cannon and carriage parts (carriage parts after Blackmore 1976, 217).

the dimensions given by contemporary writers in the late sixteenth and seventeenth centuries is Blackmore (1977, 391*ff*). The following table shows the range of values commonly recorded during the sixteenth and seventeenth centuries.

Clearly none of these types has a single set of dimensions thus making precise identification difficult. As length varies so, obviously, does weight. Although the manuals – which usually are dealing with bronze rather than cast iron guns – all record lengths and weights, cannon came in all sorts of lengths and correspondingly weights and there was much more variety in practise than the record suggests. This is reinforced by the real weights and lengths of the Londonderry cannons. Also, both wear from use and corrosion will have increased apparent size of the bore.

Type	Bore in inches	Length in feet	Weight in lbs	Length:bore	Shot in pounds	Charge in pounds
Demi-cannon	6.5	10.0–12.0	4000–6000	18.5–22:1	30.0–33.0	18.0–23.0
Culverin	5.0–5.5	11.0–13.0	4000–5500	26.4–28.4:1	17.0–19.0	10.0–11.0
Demi-culverin	4.0–4.5	10.0–12.0	2500–3600	30.0–32.0:1	9.0–11.0	8.0–10.0
Saker	3.25–3.75	9.0–10.0	1500–1900	32.0–33.2	5.0–6.0	3.0–5.0
Minion	3.0–3.25	7.0–8.0	750–1500	28.0–29.5	3.0–4.0	2.5–3.0
Falcon	2.75	6.0–7.0	700–800	26.2–30.5:1	2.25–2.5	2.5
Falconet	2.0–2.25	5.0–6.0	400–500	30.0–36.0:1	1.25–1.5	1.25

Table 1 The types of cannon known to have been in the City *c.* 1600–1690 (Imperial units).

Putting the last carriage into Guildhall Square. Left: Jim Gallagher, Dermot Harrigan, Tony Monaghan (Derry City Council). Centre, on the carriage: Phillip Colton, John Killyleagh, Thomas Gough, Hugh O'Halloran, Gavin Walsh, Michael Robinson. In front: John Lavelle (JL Ornamental Castings). Right: Brian Scott and Ruth Brown (authors).

INTRODUCTION

As part of its Economic Development Plan 2000–2006, Derry City Council committed itself to ensuring that the Historic Walled City of London≈Derry is recognised, developed and promoted as a tourism icon both for Northern Ireland and for Ireland as a whole. The City is a potent and lasting reminder of the Plantation of Ulster, and while the modern city is officially known as 'Londonderry', it is commonly referred to as 'Derry'. 'Derry' (also the regular Elizabethan and early Stuart usage) became 'Londonderry' on 29 March 1613 when the City was granted its charter. We feel it reasonable to use 'Derry' for the period pre-1613 (and hence, preceding the building of the stone fortifications), 'Londonderry' post-1613 for the remainder of the period under study, and 'Derry' for the modern city.[1] On the grounds of accuracy, we shall always refer to 'County Londonderry', simply because there has never been a 'County Derry'.

The seventeenth-century walls represent the largest built monument in state care in Northern Ireland, encompassing the main cultural and commercial quarter of the City as well as being the hub of its two designated conservation areas. The conservation and restoration of its historic cannon was identified in 2005 as a priority tourism development project by the Economic Development Section of the City Council. With a mandate from the Council's Development Committee (known then as the 'City Marketing Committee') in that year, Economic Development officers subsequently gained both endorsement and financial assistance from the Department of Enterprise Trade and Investment and the European Union Structural Funds to undertake this important work. With the 400th anniversary of the Plantation of Ulster fast approaching, the restoration of the guns was the first key investment in making the primary stronghold of the Plantation ready for the quadricentennial celebrations.

Derry, or more precisely "Historic London≈Derry", was created as the citadel for the Plantation of Ulster, an event that has shaped the history and landscape of the northern half of the island of Ireland for the 400 years since 1610. The legacies of this remarkable occurrence of human migration, landscape and social change are of local, national and international significance. The City of Derry with its intact City Walls and heritage assets, including its seventeenth-century cannon, will provide a focal point for commemorating the Plantation of Ulster. The cannon restoration project also included historical research to identify the types and origins of the various pieces, and the results form the body of this book.

The cannon preserved in the City constitute one of the largest and most important collections in Europe of early cast-iron guns of definite provenance and dating. The main group of twenty comprises pieces of English origin which date from the later sixteenth century to the period immediately before April or May of 1642. As such, they are not merely of importance to the history of the City itself, but assume major significance for Ireland and Britain, as well as for continental Europe as a whole. The guns were placed, at various times in the earlier seventeenth century, in a city that was the focal point in the militarised landscape of the Lough Foyle area of northwestern Ulster, a result of English determination finally to bring the whole of the region under Crown control.

Overall, the assemblage falls into four main parts, the first being two guns which were cast pre-1600 and can be linked directly to the military campaigns of Sir Henry Docwra between 1600 and 1603. At least one was cast by Thomas Johnson, Gunfounder to Elizabeth I, as witnessed by his initials on the barrel. Second are those which, on stylistic grounds fall into the period *c.* 1615–1630 and quite possibly *c.* 1618–1624. Of these, two (possibly three) can be attributed with some certainty to the works of the Browne dynasty of Royal Gunfounders and, in one case, specifically to John Browne, the first of that name. They

Table 2 Checklist of the cannon in January 2008. All dimensions and weights are in imperial, with metric in square brackets.

2002 inv.	Type	Length in inches	Weight in pounds	SG	Bore in inches	Marks	Date	2002 Locations	2008 Locations
1	Demi-culverin	120 [304]	3333 [1512]	6.750	4.50 [11.43]	Vintners London 1642	1642	Double bastion	Double Bastion
2	Demi-culverin	120.1 [305]	4004 [1816]	6.985	5.20 [13.2]	London shield	c. 1615–1630	Royal Bastion	Grand Parade
3	Demi-culverin	120 [304]	3750 [1701]	6.830	4.25 [10.80]	Marchant Taylers London 1642	1642	Royal Bastion	Church Bastion
4	Demi-culverin	90 [226]	2795 [1268]	6.890	4.92 [12.50]	Salters London 1642	1642	Royal Bastion	Artillery Bastion
5	Minion?	66.1 [168]	549 [249]	6.225	2.95 [7.5]			Memorial Garden	Memorial Garden
6	Demi-culverin	120 [304]	3955 [1794]	6.900	4.71 [12.0]	Fishmongers London 1642 ('Roaring Meg')	1642	Memorial Garden	Double Bastion
7	Saker	102 [209]	2183 [990]	6.690	3.94 [10]	Tudor rose-and-crown	c. 1590	Shipquay Place	Shipquay Place
8	Demi-culverin	103 [261]	3117 [1414]	6.954	4.80 [12.2]	'club and arrow' [both cast in?], IB [around touch hole], H [on breech face]	c. 1615–1630	Shipquay Place	Shipquay Place
9	Demi-culverin	120 [304]	3977 [1804]	6.990	4.80 [12.19]	Merce's London 1642	1642	Shipquay Place	New Gate Bastion
10	Demi-culverin	120 [304]	3951 [1792]	6.950	4.92 [12.50]	Grocers London 1642	1642	Shipquay Place	New Gate Bastion
11	Demi-culverin	120.1 [307]	4034 [1830]	7.076	4.60 [11.7]	Marchant Taylers London 1642	1642	Shipquay Place	Church Bastion
12	Demi-culverin	128.1 [300]	3147 [1550]	6.860	4.50 [11.6]	Tudor rose-and-crown, initials TI [= TJ = Thomas Johnson], weight stamp [3]3 3 0, date 1590	1590	Shipquay Place	Shipquay Place
13	Demi-culverin	120 [304]	2826 [1282]	6.890	4.06 [10.3]	London shield, initials 'SB' in punched dots on the breech face.	c. 1615–1630	Shipquay Place	Shipquay Place
14	6-pdr	53 [135]	1010 [458]	6.89	3.12 [7.92]	Letter 'P' on first reinforce	c. 1727–1787	Shipquay Street	Creggan Country Park
15	Minion?							Pump Street	Believed stolen
16	Demi-culverin	108 [274]	2676 [1214]	6.937	4.33 [11.0]	Letter 'C' in punched dots like C13 between 1st and 2nd reinforces	c. 1615–1630	Guildhall	Grand Parade
17	Saker	97 [247]	2004 [909]	6.784	3.74 [9.5]	London shield	c. 1615–1630	Guildhall	Shipquay Place
18	Demi-culverin	120 [305]	2875 [1304]	6.863	4.10 [10.4]	London shield	c. 1615–1630	Jefferson's Yard	Shipquay Place
19	6-pdr	53 [135]	913 [414]	6.933	3.78 [9.6]	B [on right trunnion face.], SOLID [on left trunnion face]	c. 1775–1795	Pennyburn depot	Royal Bastion
20	Demi-culverin	102 [259]	3047 [1382]	6.876	4.45 [11.3]	'club and arrow', [arrow chiselled?]	c. 1615–1630	Pennyburn depot	Shipquay Place
21	Demi-culverin	120 [305]	3342 [1516]	6.954	3.94 [10.0]		c. 1610–1625	Pennyburn depot	Grand Parade
22	6-pdr	53 [135]	922 [418]	6.950	3.78 [9.6]	B [on right trunnion face]	c. 1775–1795	Pennyburn depot	Royal Bastion
23	Russian 24-pdr	96 [243.8]	4306 [1954.1]	7.12	5.76 [14.6]	АЛКСНД–3ВД (Alexandrovski works–Petroza-vodsk), 24–Њ (24–pdr), 120–П (120 pud = 4333 lb, 182_ (date last digit obliterated)	1820–1829	Clooney Terrace	Clooney Terrace
24	3-pdr	66 [167.5]	503 [228]	6.760	2.60 [6.6]		post-1730	Tower Museum	Memorial Garden
25	Saker	79* [201]	1667 [765]	6.892	3.50 [8.9]	London shield	c. 1615–1630	Brook Hall	Artillery Bastion
26	6-pdr	52 [132]	838 [380]	6.786	3.50 [8.9]	B [on right trunnion face.], SOLID [on left trunnion face]	c. 1775–1795	Brook Hall	Brook Hall
27	6-pdr	51 [130]	820 [317]	6.763	3.50 [8.9]	'Crowned P' on first reinforce, partly obliterated by fleur-de-lys	post-1780	Brook Hall	Brook Hall

* The muzzle of C25 is broken off.

include also pieces with the shield of the City of London cast in. Third come seven engraved guns, which were purchased by the Great Companies of London for the City between March and May of 1642, and belong to an original batch of fifteen for which there is an excellent documentary record. In fact, many of the seventeenth-century pieces again can be linked to the Browne dynasty, whose works produced thousands of cast-iron guns in the period roughly 1590–1670. They supplied both the state and private markets and, while examples of their work have been found as far afield as Australia and India, the cannon in the City represent the largest group of cast-iron survivals of the prodigious output of their works in Kent. Finally, we have a varied selection of guns dating from the last decades of the eighteenth century through possibly to the 1820s, with products of the Wilkinson Bersham works prominent.

Londonderry was perhaps the last major town in Europe to be enclosed by massive, defensive stone walls, which were built between 1614 and 1618 to the design of Sir Edward Doddington and under the supervision of Peter Benson and others. Their layout, begun initially as earthworks in 1600 by the military commander Sir Henry Docwra – the man largely responsible for obtaining for the City its first Charter, which was granted by James I on 4 July 1604 – was in line with the developments in military fortifications that had arisen from the introduction and increasing deployment of artillery across Europe. Although chiefly remembered in popular tradition for the siege of 1689, the walls earlier helped fend off attack in late 1641 and throughout 1642, and withstood a 119-day siege in 1649. In fact, from the time of their completion until well into the earlier part of the eighteenth century, they provided a continuous and relatively safe haven in turbulent times.

The guns which now grace the walls are silent witnesses to the period when the whole of historic Ulster was a battleground while, at the same time, this part of it was destined to be the focus for a capitalist enterprise of staggeringly misplaced optimism – the Plantation of Londonderry. The early pieces come also from a period of accelerating metallurgical innovation, when the development of mass production and casting of iron was in full flight, and their technology foreshadows developments leading directly to the Industrial Revolution. And, while we know little of the recent history of the eighteenth-century 6-pdrs, other than that they may have been part of an original batch now broken up and dispersed, they are representatives of the technology of boring out solid cylinders, one that not only made a major contribution to the development of gunfounding, but which made a perhaps more significant and far-reaching one to the Industrial Revolution by providing a key component for the steam engine. Finally, the 24-pdr taken in 1855 from Sevastopol at the end of the Crimean War and, like so much other captured ordnance distributed by the Victorians throughout the cities of the British Isles and Empire, is a reminder of the use of captured weaponry for propaganda purposes.

The ordnance of the late sixteenth and seventeenth centuries were types still in common use in Ireland when the struggle between William III and James II began. The earlier ones provided security during the Eleven Years War which started at the end of October 1641, while all but one probably saw service during the sieges of 1649 and 1689.[2] It is, perhaps, somehow fitting that one of their siblings provided a major turning point in the final major battle of the Williamite wars. Sometime in the late afternoon of Sunday 12 July 1691, at Aughrim County Galway, the commander of the Jacobite forces, Charles de Claremont, Marquis de St Ruth, was decapitated by a cannon ball fired from the Williamite battery.[3] Although the fog of war clouds the precise detail, it seems likely that at a critical phase of the battle, dismay at the loss of St Ruth and confusion in its aftermath contributed significantly to Ginkel's victory.

This project started out with a narrow and well-defined remit – to restore and preserve the assemblage of cannon, to remount them on authentic replicas of contemporary carriages, to identify and provenance them as far as possible, and to make the information gleaned freely available. It was grounded in the intent to preserve this part of the heritage and in so doing, to display the historic walls and their armaments to the best advantage, both for the citizens of Derry and as a tourist attraction. But the simple question 'how many of the cannon saw service in the siege of 1689' spawns a host of new ones – what are the dates of the cannon? Why these particular types? When did they arrive in the City? Where were they made, of what and by whom? How did they finish up in their 2002 locations? Finding the answers has not proved straightforward. We do have good evidence – in the form of contemporary accounts – that the demi-culverin sent to the City in 1642 by the Fishmongers Company and nicknamed 'Roaring Meg' was fired at the Jacobite besiegers in 1689. However, although there are good grounds for believing that many (if not all) of the others also saw such service, 'belief' is not proof of any sort!

One is faced immediately with different figures given for the number of guns in the City at any one time. Thus there are discrepancies between contemporary accounts of numbers of cannon available to the defenders of 1689. This is put variously by different sources as ranging from twenty (Reverend George Walker), to thirty-four (Captain Ash) or thirty-five (the anonymous author of *Remarkable Occurrences*). The statement in 1837 by Colby in *OS Londonderry* that some fifty pieces survived in the City can be explained in terms of the gathering of guns into the magazine as a repository from the start of the eighteenth century, with many being obsolete pieces.[4] It is, however, difficult to reconcile the different accounts, one reason being that guns were not simply put into defended sites and then left for all time, but could be (and were) redeployed at any time. A demi-culverin was sent to the first garrison at Derry which was established in late 1566, and after the magazine exploded in April 1567 and the troops withdrew, it eventually ended up at Caernarvon in Wales. Similarly, on 29 June 1618, the Lord Deputy wrote to the Privy Council (*Cal. SPI* 1615–1625, 202) that he had ordered five 'brass' cannon (three from Dublin and one each from Duncannon and Cork) to be sent over to the Tower of London, requesting that culverins and demi-culverins be sent over to replace them. Possibly in the earlier part of 1640, the then Lord Lieutenant Sir Thomas Wentworth, Earl of Strafford, or possibly his short-lived successor Sir Christopher Wandesford, removed most of the Londonderry ordnance, leaving the City desperately under-gunned when the Irish Rebellion broke out at the end of October of that year. And sometime after 1649, probably 1650 or 1651, Sir Charles Coote, first Earl of Mountrath, removed 'brass' ordnance from the City which, between 1675 and 1682, the City Council tried (unsuccessfully) to retrieve.

Also, it is clear that from the time when Sir Henry Docwra established a permanent English stronghold at Derry, the fort of Culmore was an integral part of the defences of the City and was provided with ordnance. Until at least 1611, garrisons supplied with cannon were stationed at Dunalong and Lifford. Further, Strabane was garrisoned and defended by at least one piece of 'brass' ordnance as late as March of 1642, when it was lost to the insurgents. While Culmore retained its importance throughout the seventeenth century, Dunalong soon fell into disrepair, and it is probable that the ordnance from there ended up in either Londonderry or Culmore.

A second reason for the difficulties of making precise attributions is the often sparse nature of what should be the primary documentary evidence. The records of the Londonderry Corporation are fragmentary, while what should have been the key source of information – the records of the Irish Society – was largely destroyed in a fire in the eighteenth century. And of course, the destruction of so many records in the Four Courts in Dublin in 1922 has left an irretrievable gap. The minutes of the Common Council of the City of London provide tantalising glimpses, with references to committees dealing specifically with Ireland and the Plantation, but little insight on cannon. Although Ireland figures regularly in the State Papers (both the State Papers Domestic and the Irish State Papers), ordnance is seldom treated as other than yet one more tool of war. The records of the English Ordnance Office do provide more detail and – as, for example, with the records of Docwra's campaign – occasionally can pinpoint particular batches of ordnance. For the later part of the seventeenth century too, the Carte collection of manuscripts provides significant information.

Happily, though, the records of the Great Companies of London are a treasure-house of information on the cannon sent to Londonderry in 1642. We have precise details of decisions to purchase and accounts listing costs which are of a detail rare indeed. While some Company records were lost in the Blitz, and others have suffered through the passage of time, we can correlate precisely the listing given by the Reverend Richard Winter in 1643 with their archives and with detailed Ordnance Office inventories including those for 1660, 1674 and 1684. Not only this, but we know the names of most of those involved in the sale of the cannon and of the carriages, gunners' accessories, powder and shot – in fact, down to the name of the otherwise anonymous engraver who put the names of the Companies on the barrels of the guns which they purchased in early 1642 for the City. In particular, we can reconstruct in some detail the activities of at least four of those named and, in the case of the merchant William Felgate, retrieve a detailed history from contemporary records, as well as from family history through the modern wonder of the internet and the genealogical researches of Don Felgate and Bunny Felgate, direct descendants.

We have not attempted to add to the voluminous literature detailing the siege of Londonderry in 1689, nor to the much smaller body of writing on the siege of 1649, or that concerning the perilous state of the City in the 1640s. Our interest here is in the cannon themselves and their parts in these events, not to add yet another account of them. Although in the seventeenth century ordnance was playing a major role in the shaping of both offensive and defensive operations across Europe and the British Isles, its role in the history of the Lough Foyle area receives little real attention from contemporary writers. Thus, for example, probably the most famous of the defenders of the City in 1689, George Walker, devotes but two lines of his chronicle to the types and location of the cannon, and the adversarial writings of Walker and Mackenzie enlighten us on sectarian doctrine, but not really at all on armaments. Even in the pseudo-historical play by Governor John Mitchelburne, which mirrors the events of 1689, the alarums and calls to arms virtually ignore ordnance. Two diarists of the siege, Captains Bennett and Ash make occasional reference to the successes of the defenders in using ordnance, but say barely anything about the ordnance itself. The situation is the same with the diary of Captain Henry Finch, one of the defenders during the siege of 1649. As to the gunners, it is left to Joseph Aickin, a physician who almost certainly survived the siege of 1689 and witnessed events at first hand, to leave the most complete set of references and list of names in the doggerel of his McGonagle-esque epic *Londerias*.

We have had the unparalleled opportunity to take significant metal samples for specific gravity measurements, metallurgical examination and chemical analysis. In addition, during the conservation of the cannon, records were taken of their weights in air and in water, so that the specific gravities of the cast irons in bulk could be recorded. To the best of our knowledge, no other single contemporary European assemblage has been subjected to such technical analysis. The information thus obtained has provided some new insights into the technology of cast iron gunfounding in the sixteenth to eighteenth centuries. However, much more work remains to be done on this material, and the archive survives for further research. We present the results here as a preliminary study only, and hope that it will stimulate others to explore this largely unknown area of the history of the exploitation of ferrous metals.

This research has taken us from the City Walls, to the laboratories of the Universities of Ulster and Oxford and the State Laboratory of the Irish Republic at Celbridge, County Kildare, from the sixteenth- and seventeenth-centuries iron smelting furnaces and foundries of southern England, as far afield as the Great Barrier Reef of Australia. We have followed the trail from the icy waters of the Baltic at Riga to Kingston, Ontario in Canada, from the Virginia and Bermuda colonial settlements to the Forbidden City of Beijing and Karatsu Castle in Japan, along the ramparts of Mehrangarh Fort at Jodhpur in India, and to Mozambique in Africa. Well-dated shipwrecks carrying comparative guns, surviving records from many sources and, of course, the cannon themselves have all played their parts in putting together this story. One can marvel at the skill, knowledge and organisation which went into their production and the elegance of their forms. But it does have to be remembered that although they could deter and save life (as in the period after early 1642), these were weapons of war whose sole purpose was to wreak death and destruction, an ugliness reflected in the often ugly history of their times.

While we were completing the final draft of this work, we were greatly saddened by the death of the historian R.J. (Bob) Hunter. During what turned out to be his last month, and despite being in great pain, Bob took infinite care in reading through the chapters and making detailed annotations and suggestions. His knowledge of the City and its history was encyclopædic, and he was generosity itself in sharing it and in allowing us access to his unpublished research. Bob's enthusiasm was wholly infectious, and the care which he took over his explanations and descriptions was proof – if any were needed – of what a good teacher and mentor he had been during his time at The University of Ulster. In dedicating this work to him, we hope in some small measure to repay all of his kindness. He will be much missed.

Notes to Introduction

1 All references to the 'Cathedral' are to Saint Columb's Church of Ireland cathedral.

2 However, an inventory of 1661 refers to a saker at Londonderry which was so damaged as to be unserviceable.

3 The gun in question was supposedly displayed in Dublin Castle in the nineteenth century, but its whereabouts are now unknown.

4 This was the situation also at the other major Ulster repository of Carrickfergus (e.g. McNeill 1981, 13).

CHAPTER 1
The Conservation and Restoration Project

When finally they were no longer needed for the defence of Londonderry, the cast-iron cannon which had stood on the Walls were neglected, some being left to lie in the open as shown by a drawing of the Double Bastion, made in 1837 (Plate 1). Two of the guns depicted were sent over by the Mercers (foreground) and Vintners (leaning against the rampart in the background).

In the pioneering *Ordinance Survey of the County of Londonderry* (from which Plate 1 is reproduced), Colonel Thomas Colby (*OS Londonderry* 100) recorded that the '. . . total number of cannon remaining in the City and suburbs is nearly fifty.' Sadly, that number has dwindled to twenty-four,[1] although some have survived in the surrounding county and further afield. However, the number recorded as being in the City from its foundation, through to the present day has ranged from a low of four in January 1642, through forty-one in an inventory of 1706, to Colby's figure of 'nearly fifty'. The history of the surviving guns from the period after the siege of 1689, and their journey to their positions in 2002, has been well documented by Annesley Malley.[2] And in pictures, the cannon – in particular 'Roaring Meg' – make frequent appearances (Plates 2–3).

Although an impressive sight on the Walls, the City Council and its Officers recognised that there were major problems both with the state of preservation of the cannon themselves and, perhaps more pressing from the point of view of public safety, with the decay of the

Plate 1 Double Bastion by George Petrie, after a sketch by Lt. Dawson R.E. (from the *O.S. Memoirs of the Parish of Templemore*, 1837).

Plate 2 Cannon on the Walls overlooking Guildhall Square c. 1929.

Plate 3 Roaring Meg (C6) on a nineteenth-century garrison carriage. (*Courtesy of Mark Lusby*)

Chapter 1 – The Conservation and Restoration Project

Plate 4 C12 on its decaying carriage in 2004.

carriages on which they were mounted (Plate 4). Many of the carriages were deteriorating visibly, to the point where they were in danger of collapse.

One cannon (C17) was found in the yard of Mr. Craig Jefferson's company, mounted on a nineteenth-century garrison carriage, which itself became a part of the conservation project. This carriage, now much deteriorated (Plate 5), had previously carried Roaring Meg (C5) as can be seen clearly in an early photograph (Plate 3). The carriage itself, designed to carry a 64-pdr can be dated to 1884 from a series of official incised marks[3] on the faces of its steps (Plate 6), and is identical to one dated to *c.* 1870 in the collections of the Tower Armouries (Blackmore 1976, Plates 48–49). Fig. 2 illustrates how it was constructed originally.

All of the mounted cannon had been painted over and over again, some to the point where all surface detail, including touch

Plate 5 C18 on the nineteenth-century garrison carriage.

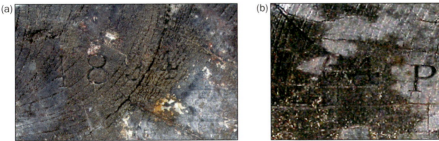

Plate 6 Garrison carriage markings (a) date mark 1884, (b) calibre of piece to be carried 64-pdr.

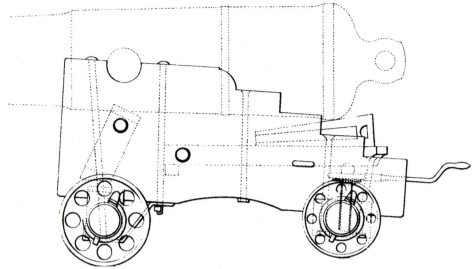

Fig. 2 Reconstruction of a nineteenth-century garrison carriage of the type on which 'Roaring Meg' and C18 were mounted at various times (after Hughes 1969, 114, Fig. 82).

holes, had become obscured in part or totally (Plates 7–8). This led to loss of information and, when this study started, it was thought that only four out of the fifteen cannon sent to the City in 1642 (see pp 118*ff*) had survived. There were, however, discrepancies between lists published at different times.[4] Stripping off overpaint revealed three more inscriptions, bringing the number of survivals of this important group up to seven.

Indeed, one of the great pleasures of this work was to see appearing for the first time in many years the inscribed names of some of the London Companies.

As might be expected, much of the overpainting had been done without any regard to ongoing deterioration, so that all showed active corrosion breaking through the paint layers, particularly on their undersides. This was particularly marked on the underside of C11 (Plate 9).

Another cause of problems was the use of some cannon as street furniture (*OS Londonderry* 100)

> *... a few are preserved as memorials ... but the greater number have been converted to the quiet purposes of peace, serving as posts for fastening cables, protecting the corners of streets &c.*

The results of this unfortunate practice can clearly be seen on C14 and C15 which were embedded in the pavements of Shipquay and Pump Streets respectively (Plates 10–11). Milligan recorded a total of eleven guns used as street furniture in 1950 when his book on the City was published (Milligan 1996, 229). At the time of this study, only two remained – one in Shipquay Street and one in Pump Street.

(a)

(b)
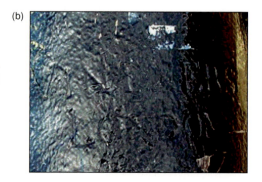

Plate 7 (a) C7 showing the Tudor Rose-and-crown obscured by overpaint, (b) C1 with the engraved name of the Vintners Company obscured by overpaint.

Chapter 1 – The Conservation and Restoration Project

Plate 8 Grocers inscription (C10) emerging during cleaning from under paint layers that had totally obscured it.

Plate 9 Corrosion under flaking paint on the underside of C11.

(a)  (b)

Plate 10 (a) C14 *in situ* in Shipquay Street in 2002, (b) after removal in 2006.

(a)

(b)

Plate 11 (a) C15 *in situ* in Pump Street in 2002, (b) after removal and before it was stolen from Pennyburn depot.

Lifting the cannon

Before treatment of any sort could begin, the cannon first had to be removed from their locations and transported to Dunmurry (Plate 12). It is not really until one is involved in an exercise of this kind that one can appreciate fully the task facing those sixteenth- and seventeenth-century soldiers who had to move these large lumps of metal – the heaviest weighing nearly two tons – for many long miles through Ireland without the benefits of modern roads, cranes, flat-bed lorries and hydraulic forklift trucks!

Plate 12 'Roaring Meg' (C6) being lifted from the Memorial Garden to join C17 for transport to Belfast.

The treatment and restoration of the cannon

Two key considerations were first to ensure that the removal of the old overpaint did not in any way damage any preserved surface detail, second that all treatments were as far as possible reversible. Bearing these in mind, the primary tasks of the treatment program for the cannon were:

- to remove the old paint and loose corrosion products to reveal fully all of the surviving surface details;
- to clear the barrels of all extraneous material (from cigarette butts and soft drink cans to heavily-concreted accumulations of earth and stones);
- to eliminate all active corrosion and to stabilise the metal surfaces to prevent further deterioration;
- to apply protective coatings that would protect the cannon from the elements and, at the same time, not obscure any of the detail revealed in the cleaning process.

The removal of the old paint and corrosion was a relatively straightforward task. Paint stripper was applied to the surfaces and the paint peeled off in layers with the assistance of a high-power water jet (Plate 13).

Plate 13 Removing the overpaint from C12 with paint stripper and high-pressure water jet.

When cleaning those cannon known to have engraved the names of the London Companies, care was taken to see if any trace of the painted legends visible in photographs from the period pre-1989 (when the cannon were given their last coats of paint) could be found. Unfortunately, the last overpaintings had obliterated these markings.

When cast iron corrodes, it develops a pitted surface, reminiscent of the texture of a lunar landscape. Old paint can cling stubbornly to the bases of these craters, requiring often strenuous effort to get out the last vestiges when using mechanical cleaning methods such as wire brushing or grit blasting. For this reason, the last traces of paint were left in place until the second stage of treatment – chemical cleaning – was applied. Once as much of the paint that could be removed easily was off, a final task was to look for patches of scale that might become detached, even though seeming secure. These were removed carefully, and the underlying surfaces cleaned back by stiff bristle brushing.

The bores of most of the pieces contained quantities of earth and stones, as well as small finds. In some cases, the filling was quite loose and could be removed with a hooked metal rod after loosening with the high-pressure water jet. In other instances, a fair degree of force was required to break up large stones and concretions. Once cleared of debris, the bores were inspected to see if they formed a continuous parallel-sided pipe back to the inside face of the breech, or if there was the degree of taper towards the powder chamber that would mark a piece out as a 'drake'. All of the cannon proved to have parallel-sided bores all the way back to the breech, thus confirming them to be 'home bored'. In terms of the overall conditions of the pieces, the bores not surprisingly were where the most evident corrosion could be seen, with much ferrous debris and scale mixed in with the intrusive material.

Chemical cleaning of any metal requires the cleaning medium to loosen or remove corrosion, whilst not itself attacking the metal surface, and so a sequestering agent was employed. The reagent does not only find use in museums, but is also widely employed in the dairy industry to clean stainless steel milk containers. It also has the advantage of being easy to wash away.

At the workshops of JL Ornamental Castings, two tanks large enough to hold three cannon at a time were constructed of breeze block and lined with heavy-duty butyl rubber sheet. One held the cleaning reagent in which the cannon spent from between ten and fifteen days after as much paint as possible had been stripped off, and they were lifted in and out by sling and crane (Plate 14). The second

Plate 14 C8 undergoing chemical treatment.

Chapter 1 – The Conservation and Restoration Project

held clean water and was used to rinse away all traces of the cleaning reagent. The cannon spent an average of five days in this and developed a very slight bloom of fresh corrosion as a result. The cast-iron carriage of the Russian 24-pdr was treated in the same way.

Once cleaned of paint and loose corrosion, the cannon were weighed using a balance accurate to 5kg. Two readings were taken – weight in air and weight in water, the resulting difference allowing the specific gravity of the metal of each to be calculated (p. 196). The object of this exercise was to determine how close the cast iron of the guns came to the modern SG range as a part of a detailed, overall assessment of the quality of the metal from which they were made. The results are discussed in Chapter 8, but it can be noted here that many of these measurements in bulk came out lower than expected.

After removal from the water tank, the cannon were dried thoroughly, by mopping off surfaces, then by soaking in acetone. To ensure that the barrels were dried thoroughly, the cannon were tilted and then filled with acetone, left over a weekend and then drained, before being dried off by an air blast over a day. The slight bloom of corrosion was loose enough to be removed with a stiff brush, leaving the metal surfaces clean and stable. When the reagent had taken effect, the stubborn paint simply brushed off along with the sludge of corrosion products. The barrels were cleared with a wad of plastic 'steel wool' mounted on a pole, rather like the sponge that would have been used to clean a cannon during use.

Although most of the markings on the cannon could be located before cleaning, a number showed up which had been completely obscured by overpaint. Of particular importance were the marks on C8 which consisted of the initials 'IB' on either side of the touchhole and the letter 'H' on the breech face (Plate 15). The significance of these is discussed below (p. 147).

Starting with Thomas Colby (*OS Londonderry* 100), through to Milligan (1996, 228) it is stated regularly in the literature that one of the cannon on the Walls bore the initials 'ER' on either side of the rose-and-crown emblem, and also showed the date 1590.[5] For this reason, it was assumed that this piece was C12. However, careful removal of the overpaint showed that neither C12, nor C7, both of which have the rose-and-crown emblem, had ever sported the letters 'ER'. However, directly below the rose-and-crown of C12, the initials 'TI', never before noted, were revealed along with the remains of a weight marking (pp 139-140) and a date of 1590. We have been unable

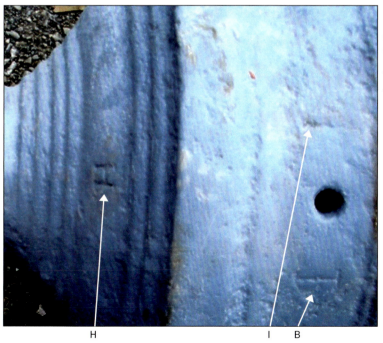

Plate 15 Previously unseen marks on C8 after removal of paint and chemical cleaning, linking this piece with the Royal Gunfounder John Browne and possibly his furnace at Horsmonden in Kent.

9

to find any illustration of the 'ER' marking and it is difficult to imagine how the 'TI' (which stands for Thomas Johnson, the predecessor of the Brownes as Royal Gunfounder) could be so misread. Further, these initials are below the rose-and-crown, not flanking it, and are much smaller than the normal letters of the 'ER' found on such guns (e.g. Blackmore 1976, 44, no. 34). We know that by 1601, Sir Henry Docwra had a number of iron cannon located in Derry, Culmore, Dunalong and Lifford (pp 107*ff*), and it thus seems quite likely that, originally, there was a third Elizabethan cannon which did have the initials of Elizabeth I and a date of 1590, but which has like so many others been lost since the nineteenth century.

Removal of the overpaint, applied with such abandon over the years, in some cases revealed traces of the moulds in which the cannon were cast. Although exceedingly faint in most cases – and thus well-nigh impossible to show in print – some of the marks and striations show clearly that the cannon were cast in two-piece moulds. Along with patterns of imperfections, their distribution raised the intriguing possibility that at least some of the cannon had been cast horizontally.

Cleaning down to the metal surface revealed serious casting flaws (Plate 16), and also that two of the cannon had suffered from botched attempts to improve their appearance. The major unsightly casting flaws on the underside of Roaring Meg (C6) had been filled in with a synthetic paste (probably car-body filler) which had come loose due to corrosion. In an attempt to increase the length of the trunnions of the small 3-pdr, C24, holes had been drilled in the faces, and large bolts and nuts inserted, with the nuts being covered over with probably the same material as was used on C6.

At this point, samples for metallographic and chemical analyses were taken using a diamond coring bit with oil cooling to prevent heating of the samples. Three samples were taken from each gun, the sites being the muzzle face, the underside between the trunnions and at the breech. The holes left by the process were filled with epoxy resin and blended to the textures of the surrounding surfaces. Two additional cores were taken from the top and mid-point from the seven Company guns, as a number of these cannon showed patterns of flaws and

Plate 16 Casting flaws on the underside of the muzzle of C11.

traces of moulds that indicated the possibility of horizontal casting. Finally, a complete core was taken from the outside of C6 through to the inside of the powder chamber. The results of the metallography and chemical analyses are presented and discussed in Chapter 8.

Having cleaned and stabilised the surfaces, the next stage was to apply the protective coatings to prevent fresh deterioration. The protective coatings had to be robust enough to withstand the Northern Ireland climate and, at the same time, thin enough so as not to obscure surface detail. A three-layer application was chosen, comprising two coats each of a phosphate-based primer followed by two of a black acrylic lacquer containing graphite. Over these were applied three thin coats of microcrystalline wax to provide both a light lustre to the finished surfaces and a further degree of water-repellence (Plate 17). The wax also makes removal of graffiti more easy than from a painted surface.

To ensure that the surfaces of the barrels were properly sealed, they were filled with the undercoat, left for twenty-four hours and then drained. The second coat and the two coats of acrylic lacquer were then applied using a sponge-head on a long pole. However, sealing of the interior surfaces is only a partial solution as rainwater (as well as rubbish inserted by the thoughtless) will always accumulate over time. Putting a wooden bung (or one of

Chapter 1 – The Conservation and Restoration Project

Plate 17 Batch of cannon undercoated and partially lacquered.

any material) in the muzzle is, at best, only a partly-effective solution as these inevitably deteriorate and allow water in. Indeed, when C6 ('Roaring Meg') was tilted so that the barrel was at a slight downwards angle, several litres of what is best described as a malodorous 'soup' leaked out around the gaps between its wooden bung and the barrel wall.

It was decided to take an approach that, we believe, has not been used before. The barrels were filled with an inert polyurethane foam to within 8cm of the mouth. This was smoothed off and covered with a thin coat of epoxy resin. To ensure a complete seal, the resin was, in turn, coated with the acrylic lacquer and microcrystalline wax. The foam has added less than 2kg to the weights of the cannon, while ensuring that fresh corrosion caused by accumulation of water and breakdown of the coatings over a long period cannot happen.

Plate 18 The inevitable response of some to improvements in cultural property.

11

The Great Guns Like Thunder

The results of the conservation program are that each cannon has been restored to a stable condition, one in which all of the surviving surface features are clearly visible. But this is not the end of the process, as the City Council has initiated a monitoring and maintenance program to deal with the inevitable graffiti and to ensure that any future problems are detected rapidly and dealt with immediately. Unhappily, as Plate 18 (taken only a few weeks after these cannon had been returned to the Walls) shows, it seems destined that vandalism by the feeble-minded will be a greater cause of deterioration over the coming years than wind and weather.

Finds from the cannon barrels

Most of the cannon had their bores blocked with an assortment of debris, ranging from compacted sand, gravel and lumps of concrete, through to loose accumulations of rubbish inserted by the thoughtless. The heavily blocked barrels were cleared by hand and the contents sifted, producing a small assemblage[6] of material, including a cannon ball in C19, musket balls, coins of George III and a Victorian pocket watch in Roaring Meg, musket balls, clay pipe fragments, one with the name 'Doherty' on the stem and a ceramic bottle. The guns also yielded the bones of small mammals (e.g. the skull of a rat from C13) and, from C12, what appears to be the skeletal remains of cuts of pork, sheep/goat and cow, found right at the back of the powder chamber!

The reconstructions of the carriages

The Russian 24-pdr is mounted on its original cast-iron carriage, while the English pieces displayed throughout the City were mounted in the nineteenth century on replica ships' carriages (see Plates 2–4 above). While these are appropriate for the late eighteenth and early nineteenth centuries cannon in the assemblage (C14, C19, C22 and C23 – see Chapter 7 below), they were not for the earlier pieces. The primary problem in deciding what would be the most historically accurate form of carriage for the earliest cannon was the fact that in the sixteenth and seventeenth centuries, guns could be mounted on more than one form of carriage, depending on whether they were in transit, in the field, mounted on fortifications, or for maritime service. Thus, for Ireland in 1684, a comprehensive inventory (from which has been abstracted Appendix A14.3) includes references to 'marching', 'platform' 'ship's', 'standing', 'travelling' and 'block' carriages.[7] And in reference to seventeenth-century carriages for naval ordnance, Caruana (1994, 181) notes the use of the terms 'whole truck' and 'half truck', referring to carriages with 'trucks' – solid wheels.

A superficial look at published reproductions of contemporary depictions of cannon, not just at Londonderry, but at other fortifications of similar date, suggests that all were mounted[8] on two-wheeled carriages. However, a gun to be used in the field had to have a carriage that allowed it to be transported as easily as possible, while one that was to be mounted on defences required a different form that was short enough to allow for recoil in a limited space. It is clear from the surviving records of purchase that in most instances at least, the cannon that were purchased for Londonderry by the Great Companies (see pp 118*ff*) were sent over with field carriages – two-wheeled carriages with long trails. The decision was made, therefore, to mount the surviving Company guns and the minion and falcon on replica field carriages. The general form of such carriages is well known, and remained basically unchanged over several centuries. A good model is found in an illustration from the 1692 publication *An epitome of the whole art of war* which offers an image of a cannon of the type purported to be of the form used in the Williamite siege train at Athlone, Galway and Limerick (*Epitome* Plate opposite p. 66).

Here we can see the large, spoked wheels with metal strengthening, the long body bearing the weight of the cannon, and the extended tail.[9] A clearer picture of construction was given in an engraving in Norton (*Gunner* Fig. 19, opposite p. 130), showing the form of the train and wheels, and the positioning of the iron fastenings and heavy nails through the rim (Plate 19). The accounts of several of the London Companies who sent artillery to Londonderry in 1642 detail payments to a wheelwright, carpenter and blacksmith – the complement of craftsmen required to construct a carriage like this. Thus, this was the form chosen for the mounting of the guns which can be linked to individual Companies.

But it was clear that while land carriages could have been set on the bastions, they could not have been set on the ramparts. Equally, it was clear that the nineteenth-century ships' carriages were inappropriate for all but the late eighteenth-century guns. So what form of carriage for cannon on the ramparts was authentic for the period?

When fired, all cannon would recoil and, in a narrow or confined space – such as the rampart of a fort or the gun-deck of a warship – it was imperative that the distance of travel be kept to a minimum. Use of rope and block-and-tackle was one solution, and another which appears in the 1630s was to build in a source of friction to act as a brake against the backward movement. The crucial study here is that by Smith (2001) who reported a previously unrecorded cannon of earlier seventeenth-century date in the Curfew Tower at Windsor Castle, still mounted on its original carriage (Plate 20 and Fig. 3).

Although similar in general form to the nineteenth-century ship's carriage, the feature most

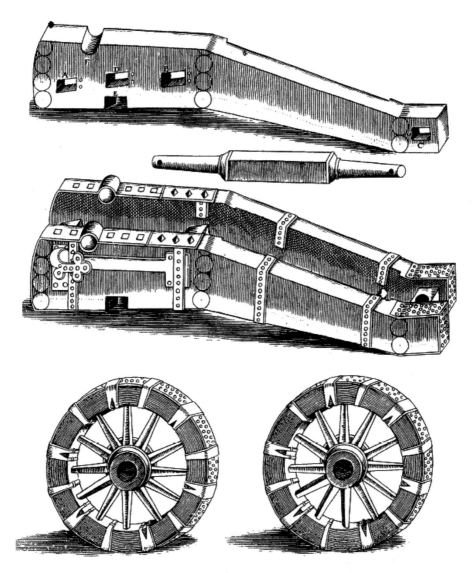

Plate 19 The components of a field carriage as illustrated by Robert Norton in 1628 (*Gunner* 130).

immediately obvious is the large block of wood which replaces a rear set of wheels. A carriage of very similar design, sketched by a Lieutenant Thomas James of the Ordnance (Caruana 1994, 181, Fig. 83), and supposedly used in the warship *Sovereign of the Seas* in 1637, also had a block in place of rear wheels.[10]

Two Dutch depictions of sea carriages, both identical in principle to the Windsor Castle and *Sovereign of the Seas* carriages, in documents dating to *c.* 1660 and 1675 were noted by Puype (1991, 15–16, Figs 9–10). In particular, the parallel with the overly ornate carriage design (Fig. 4) attributed to the Dutch artist Willem van de Velde the Younger (1633–1707), who specialised in seascapes and ships, is of interest.

The balancing of a cannon on trunnions placed above the centre of gravity meant that since weight was being exerted on the rear of the carriage, firing exerted a downwards force there. Thus, replacing the back wheels with a solid block maximised the braking effect that could be applied to curtail recoil. This was par-

Plate 20 Seventeenth-century block carriage with cannon at Windsor Castle. (*The Royal Collection* © 2008 Her Majesty Queen Elizabeth II)

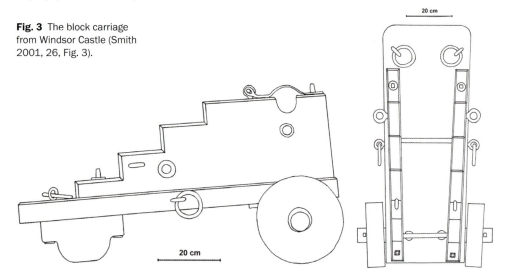

Fig. 3 The block carriage from Windsor Castle (Smith 2001, 26, Fig. 3).

Chapter 1 – The Conservation and Restoration Project

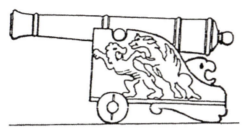

Fig. 4 Block carriage intended for a yacht and attributed to Willem van de Velde the Younger, 1675 (after Puype 1991, 16, Fig. 10).

ticularly relevant for ship-board use as Puype (*ibid.* 17) notes, pointing out that this design – which gave the additional bonus of increasing range – is also known from the nineteenth century.[11]

As part of his survey of the Plantation in 1622, Sir Thomas Phillips offered a coloured drawing (Plate 21) of a fortified Market Hall (never, in fact, built) which he proposed should be placed in what is now the Diamond (e.g. *Phillips MSS* Plate 2). Two versions of this are known – one in the Archiepiscopal Library at Lambeth Palace, the other in the archives of the Worshipful Company of Drapers at Drapers Hall in London. When reproduced in black and white (e.g. Curl 1986, 77, Fig. 22), even the fine detail of the Drapers Company manuscript loses detail. Although the two wheels are shown as large and spoked, this is a general convention that is found in contemporary depictions from across Europe. When we look at the carriages shown on the map of Culmore, also drawn by Raven (e.g. Curl 2000, 128, Fig. 31), it is clear that the wheels of all thirteen depicted there are solid.

The important point to note here is that while it could be argued that the rather stylised perspective is distorting the detail, these carriages do not have the trails of land carriages.

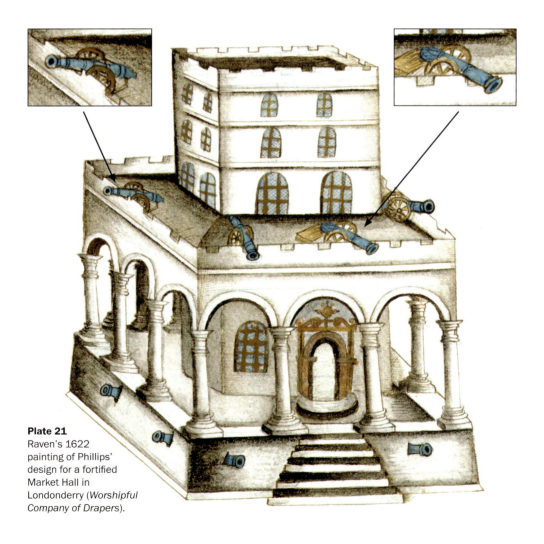

Plate 21
Raven's 1622 painting of Phillips' design for a fortified Market Hall in Londonderry (*Worshipful Company of Drapers*).

Rather, the breech ends are depicted as resting on blocks of wood. And one detail which is crucial here is the way in which the ends of the wooden blocks are clearly shown.

An earlier piece of evidence comes from the depiction of the storming of the Blackwater Fort in 1597 by the forces of Thomas, Lord Burgh (Plate 22).

Here, the defences are depicted as comprising an enclosing rectangle with one face being the river Blackwater. At the two angles are round bastions, each shown with a mounted cannon, a pile of shot and a barrel of powder. Placed centrally and directly opposite the troops breaking through the palisade along the river bank, is a third cannon. While the cannon on the bastions are shown as mounted on carriages with the typical long trails of field pieces, that on the joining wall has no trail and would appear to have a block behind the two wheels which are fitted to a splayed bed, thus making it a block carriage. Such depictions of two-wheeled carriages with a bed wider at the back are not uncommon (as, for example in *Compleat Gunner* 66), although in many cases it may be that they are poor depictions of a short trail.

C5 and C24, seventeenth- and eighteenth-century pieces respectively, would have been used primarily as anti-personnel pieces in the field, and so it was felt that the best mounts for them were field carriages. These were made by scaling down the design of the carriages for the guns of the Companies of the City of London.

Building the carriages

Construction of the block carriages began with the turning of the wheels and axle components, and the shaping of the bed and cheeks (Plates 23–24). The ships carriages for the eighteenth-century guns were constructed in the same way, but with four wheels instead of two (Plate 25).

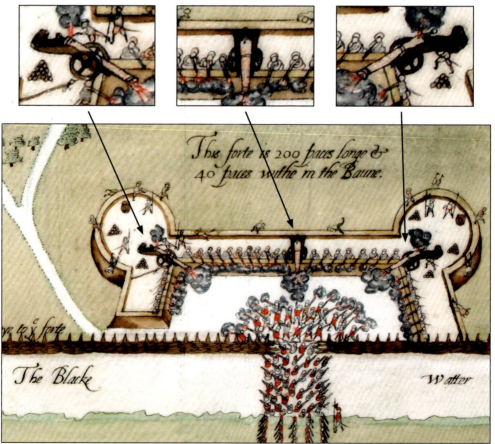

Plate 22 The storming of the Blackwater Fort (*TCD* MS 1209/34).

Plate 23 Assembling the basic components for the block carriages at the workshops of JL Ornamental Castings Ltd.

Plate 24 Block carriage for C8 nearing completion.

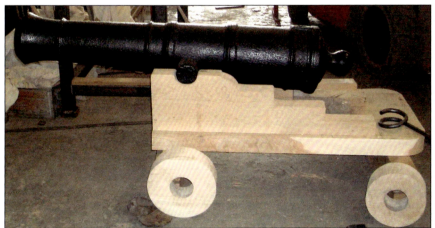

Plate 25 Ship's carriage for C19 under construction.

After the wooden components had been assembled and fitted to each carriage (Plate 26), the iron tyres for the wheels, the attachment rings and the capsquares were fitted. Finally, the cannon were transported back to the City Walls and mounted there once again (Plate 27).

All of the components for the bodies of the field carriages were made and assembled at the workshops of JL Ornamental Castings using oak timber. However, construction of these was a much more complex task, and construction of the carriage wheels was contracted out to the firm of Mike Rowland, Wheelwrights and Coachbuilders, Coylton, Devon (Plates 28–31). The design of the carriages was done by Robert Smith[12] and, as far as possible, the modern reconstructions conform to the original. There were, however, several deviations in the construction of the wheels,[13] resulting primarily from the need to ensure maximum proof against the elements.[14] Thus, for example, it is likely that

Plate 26 Final fitting of cannon to their block carriages.

Plate 27 Cannon on block carriages returned to the City Walls in 2005.

Chapter 1 – The Conservation and Restoration Project

in the seventeenth century, the iron rims for the wheels would have been shrunk on. Because it was felt necessary that the metal be galvanised to protect against corrosion, this was not possible as the coating would have been destroyed by heat.[15]

The spokes were sawn square, a concession to modern tooling and speed, although the originals would have been cleft from oak and taper driven into the hub. Because it was not possible to put a continuous bond on the wheels because of the galvanising, it was decided to strake the tyres. Straking is where a tyre is put on to the wheel in sections, each spanning from centre of felloe to centre of felloe. The spokes are cramped together to close any gaps at the joints between felloes. This would have been done hot originally, and nails driven while the plates were hot. In fact, it seems clear that the originals were straked so that in fact, the only deviation has been the lack of heat. Straking was still in use by rural wheelwrights until well into the twentieth century, farmers preferring it because of the extra grip that it provided. Greg Rowland (*pers. comm.* 2005) has noted that the step-down in hub profile removes some of its strength and that an optimum probably would have been

Plate 28 (a) Hub sections ready for assembly, **(b)** Greg Rowland constructing a hub.

Plate 29 Fitting hub and spokes together.

Plate 30 Mike Rowland fitting felloes and spokes together.

egg-shaped in cross-section (front to back). Nevertheless, contemporary illustrations such as Plate 19, indicate that such stepping was not uncommon in the seventeenth century. Finally, the wheels were given an overall dish of 3ins (7.6cm). This is a construction technique that goes back a long way, and Biringuccio (*Pirotechnia* Book VII.8, 315) wrote in 1540 for the makers of field carriages

> *Be careful when you put the cavities* [i.e. sockets] *for fixing the spokes in the hub to do it so that they throw the ends outwards by at least the thickness of the felloe, so that the wheel does not press squarely on the spoke . . . it has been observed that when one marches with guns, some stone may be encountered that knocks against the wheels, or the road may be found to slope very much and the carriage be thrown on one side. Then the wheels made in this way adapt their spokes so that they are straight and make an effort to hold up the weight much more powerfully than those which have vertical spokes. For when the roads are steep and sloping and the wheels are bent, the carriage easily turns over and the wheels break in the spokes or felloes.*

The cheeks were constructed in Belfast (Plate 32) and then joined up to the wheel assemblages (Plate 33) ready for the final adjustments required for each individual cannon (Plates 34–35).

On 12 May 2006, all seven surviving Company guns on their carriages were mounted in Shipquay Place, below the seven already placed on the Walls in 2005. This was certainly the first time since the 1690s that so many of the seventeenth-century cannon had been presented together for inspection by the Mayor, Councillors and citizens (Plate 36).

Plate 31 Complete wheels outside the workshop of Mike Rowland, Wheelwright and Coachbuilder, by Appointment to Her Majesty The Queen.

Plate 32 Cheeks being fitted with their ironwork.

Plate 33 A wheel and axle assembly complete with ironwork having its protective coating applied.

Plate 34 Assembled carriage for C10 (Grocers Company).

Plate 35 C10 mounted on its carriage.

Plate 36 All seven Company guns on display in Shipquay Place. May 2006.

The Great Guns Like Thunder

Relocating the cannon

There is no record of how the surviving cannon were placed at any point in the recorded history of Londonderry, and so decision on the placement of the restored cannon was a matter of how best to present them. After much discussion, it was decided by the City Council that those cannon on field carriages should be placed on the bastions, while those seventeenth-century guns mounted on block carriages would be distributed along the Walls. The two 6-pdrs, C19 and C22, were placed on Royal Bastion on the Walls. The Russian 24-pdr was returned to its original location at Clooney Terrace in the Waterside. The locations are shown in Fig. 5.

Notes to Chapter 1

1 Colby of course was writing before the Russian 24-pdr was presented to the City in 1860, and the rediscovery in 1864 at the old North Quay of one of the guns presented by the Salters Company. At the start of this study, twenty-four cannon were known to have survived, but the probable minion which had been embedded in the pavement of Pump Street has since, regrettably, been stolen from the Pennyburn Depot where it was being stored. However, early in 2007, another saker bearing the London shield and a further two 6-pdrs were drawn to the attention of the Council and the authors by Phillip and David Gilliland of Brook Hall, and these have been included in the report. We are most grateful to them for permission to describe and include these pieces.

2 Unpublished report to Derry City Council, November 2002. We are indebted to Annesley Malley for much information on the recent history of the assemblage and for his unstinting help throughout the course of this work.

3 Other marks visible on the step faces are '56 Cwt' and 'WD'.

4 Thus, in the 2002 inventory taken by the City Council, the four Company guns known were those of the Salters, Merchant Taylors, Vintners and Fishmongers. The Ordnance Survey Memoirs in 1837 (*OS Londonderry* 100), and Simpson (1847, 40–41) listed five Company guns as those of the Vintners and Mercers on the Double Bastion, and those of the Fishmongers, Merchant Taylors and Grocers on the Royal Bastion. However, in 1853, Reid (1853, I, 337 note 14) listed the survivals as being those 'granted by the Vintners, Mercers, Grocers and Merchant-tailors'. A useful summary of the different catalogues is given by Milligan (1996, 225*ff*).

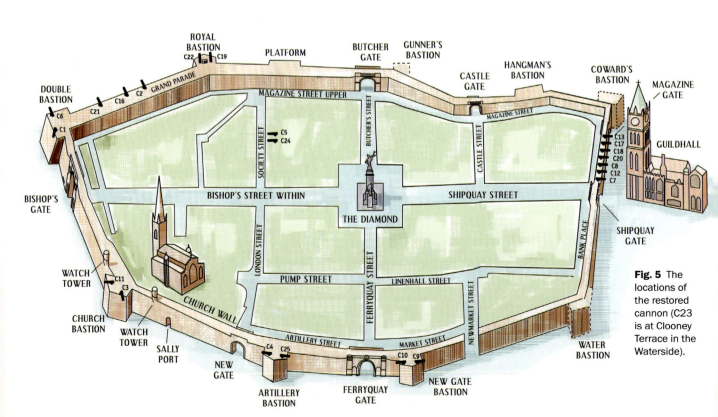

Fig. 5 The locations of the restored cannon (C23 is at Clooney Terrace in the Waterside).

Chapter 1 – The Conservation and Restoration Project

5 The gun illustrated by Milligan (1996) in Plate XV is not one of the Elizabethan cannon, but one of those bearing the shield of the City of London (most likely C2).

6 Now in the collections of Derry City Museum. Identifications of ceramics and clay tobacco pipes were done by Lesley Simpson, Down County Museum, of coins by Robert Heslip, Department of Local History, Ulster Museum and of bone by Drs Eileen Murray and Finbar McCormick, School of Archaeology and Palaeoecology, The Queen's University Belfast, to whom our thanks. The ball retrieved from C19 is 3.1ins (7.8cm) in diameter and weighs 4.04lb (1.832kg). Unless this is a case of excessive windage, it is likely that this ball was originally intended for a smaller calibre piece.

7 It is of particular interest to note that at Cork (*Ormond MSS* I, 370), Limerick (*ibid.* 381–382), Galway (*ibid.* 385–286) and Carrickfergus (*ibid.* 395), cannon are described as mounted on, or having in store for them, 'ship's carriages'. Indeed, the entry for Galway notes a total of 42 ship's carriages in 'unserviceable' condition.

8 The very first mounts for cannon were essentially large blocks of wood to which the gun was lashed, with rudimentary wheels at the front (Smith 2001). The earliest depiction of this type in Ireland comes from an indenture, dated 1543, from the Earl of Ormond to Martin Poterchelo, a gunner in Kilkenny (de hÓir 1983, 81 Plate 7).

9 Note also in Plate 41 the depiction of wooden planks under the wheels, required to prevent them from digging into soft ground when the cannon was fired. One of the complaints levelled against the Great Companies was that the bastions of Londonderry (which were earthen constructions faced by stonework) were not provided with proper platforms for the ordnance (see p.75 *f*).

10 Caruana (1994, 181) notes that the carriages for the *Sovereign of the Seas* were made by Matthew Banks, Master Carpenter for the Ordnance, to whom a debenture was issued on 1 May 1639. Banks was the predecessor at the Board of Ordnance of John Pitt who made the carriages for the guns sent over in 1642 by the London companies (pp 130-131).

11 As shown by the mounting of carronades on carriages with a pair of front wheels and a block at the rear (ffoulkes 1937, Plate XIIIA facing p.109; Blackmore 1976, Plate 44).

12 Robert Smith, formerly Keeper of Conservation at the Tower Armouries, is one of the foremost international authorities on the subject.

13 We are most grateful to Greg Rowland of Mike Rowland, Wheelwrights and Coachbuilders, for his detailed and expert input in preparing this section of the work.

14 In the inventory of 1660 (Appendix 14.1a), it is noteworthy that the carriages constructed in 1642 for the Company guns are regularly described as 'Carridge and wheels rotten'. It is intended that these carriages will last a great deal longer than eighteen years!

15 Paradoxically, this way of ensuring against corrosion of the rims meant that a venerable method of preserving structural wood was lost. Charring of wood – which would have resulted from shrinking on the iron tyres at heat – was used as a preservative since at least Iron Age times (for example, to help seal the bases of palisade uprights against various forms of organic attack).

CHAPTER 2
The Historical and Technological Backgrounds to the Cannon

Ireland 1566–1691

A century and a quarter of increasingly bitter strife, interrupted by a period of relative peace and prosperity in the earlier seventeenth century, opened in October 1566 with moves by the Crown to eliminate the threat of Shane O'Neill in Ulster. It ended on 3 October 1691, with the surrender of Limerick by Patrick Sarsfield to the forces of William III under Godert de Ginkel, an event which saw the final end to Irish hopes for an independent nation and completed the subjugation of the whole of the island to English rule. Across Europe, this period saw a terrible brutalisation of conflict, with widespread destruction and the commission of appalling atrocities, with civilians and combatants alike finding mercy at a premium.[1]

All sides felt unconstrained in inflicting on the others what was termed bluntly 'frightfulness' by some English commanders, and practised with vigour, even enthusiasm – by, amongst others, Sir Richard Bingham, Sir William St Leger and Sir Charles Coote, Snr and Jnr. Thus, in 1625, the Dutch humanist, theologian and jurist Hugo Grotius, seeking to formulate encompassing rules to govern the conduct of contemporary warfare, felt obliged to consider circumstances under which the killing of prisoners of war, even of civilians of all ages and sexes, could be deemed to be justified.[2] No stranger to the horrors of contemporary warfare in Europe, the Confederate commander Owen Roe O'Neill on returning in 1642 to his native Ulster from Flanders, lamented that the region 'not only looks like a desert, but like hell if there could be a hell upon earth', observing bitterly that 'on both sides there is nothing but burning, robbery in cold blood, and cruelties such as are not usual even among the Moors and Arabs.' (Casway 1984, 64). And in the broader European context, increasing expertise in the use of cannon improved greatly the return against expenditure in terms of enemy casualties and destruction of resources.[3]

This was a time of shifting conflicts between the English and Irish factions, amongst the Irish themselves, between Scots and Irish, between Royalist and Parliamentarian, Parliamentarian and the Catholic Confederacy and, finally, between the rival Kings James II and William III. War was overlaid upon war with, for example, the Eleven Years War in Ireland (which began with the uprising of 1641) becoming inextricably intertwined with the English Civil Wars of 1642–1649. Armies marched and counter-marched with ever-changing objectives so that, for example, in 1644 no fewer than four distinct sets of military forces – the Scots in north-eastern Ulster, various 'British' forces in Ulster and Munster including the so-called Laggan Army (McKenny 2005), troops under the Marquis of Ormond, and those of the Catholic Confederacy – were operating with a variety of intents and purposes (Wheeler 1995, 43*ff*). Allegiance and loyalties were not immutable either. Just one example of how quickly and how far alliances could shift is provided by the agreement of July 1649 between Sir Charles Coote Jnr who was holding Londonderry under siege for Parliament against an unlikely alliance of Covenanters and Royalists, Protestant and Catholic, and Owen Roe O'Neill (e.g. Kelly, W.P. 2001a, 35*f*) who, until a few months before, had been leading his troops in the Royalist cause, but now brought them to the relief of the City.

But the conflicts that made one large battlefield of much of Ireland, were not a purely insular affair, rather a part of the intricate ornamentation of the bloody pavane performed across the Atlantic archipelago. Ireland was embroiled in the conflict between England and Scotland in the 'Bishops' Wars' of 1639–1640, and was a battleground between supporters of

Crown and Parliament between 1642 and 1651. It was the stage on which the last struggle for power between two English Kings was played out between 1689 and 1691. Further afield, under successive sovereigns, England engaged in European conflicts, while European powers – Spain and France – sought to gain influence and advantage through intervention in Irish affairs. Always viewing Ireland as the potential springboard for the opening of another front against the English, they sought this either through the supply of money and weaponry to those opposed to English rule there, or through direct intervention as with the landings of Spanish forces at Smerwick in 1580 and at Kinsale in 1601.

As Fissell (2001, 206) notes, this period was not one when a backward and laggard English military establishment on the fringe of innovative Europe fought Irish primitives who used anachronistic tactics.[4] All of the key elements of Michael Roberts' 'military revolution' (Roberts, M. 1967) were embraced by the Tudors, and had reached Ireland at least by the time that Elizabeth I turned the full force of her attention on the island. Thus, gun loops and ports for small cannon can be found on Irish castles from the earlier decades of the sixteenth century (Kerrigan 1995, 24ff). And on the Irish side, as part of his tactics against the English, Hugh O'Neill in the early 1590s (Hayes-McCoy 1969, 110f) introduced small arms in numbers to his followers, encouraging practice and increasing standards through training – another component of the 'military revolution' – so that they were 'infinitely belaboured with training in all parts of Ulster.' (Hayes-McCoy 1976, 125). He was successful to the point where Lord Deputy Mountjoy in 1602 could comment of Irish fighters, (Hayes-McCoy 1969, 110–112) that they were

generally better armed than we, knew better the use of their weapons than our men and even exceeded us in discipline . . . being very many and expert shot.

This sentiment was echoed by Fynes Moryson who wrote (Kew 1998, 70)

Their shott, which I said to be so rude in the beginning of the Rebellion, as three men were used to shoote off one peece not without feare, became in fewe yeares most active, bold and expert in the use of these peeces.

Although sixteenth- and seventeenth-centuries innovations in military architecture are thought to be primarily the realm of the English, there is evidence that the Irish too were absorbing ideas from Europe as shown, for example, in the layout of the O'Doherty castle at Burt in County Donegal, in two drawings of around 1600 (*NA* MPF/1-335/1 and MPF/1-335/2). Here are depicted cannon mounted defensively (Plate 37), albeit not on 'proper' bastions, but

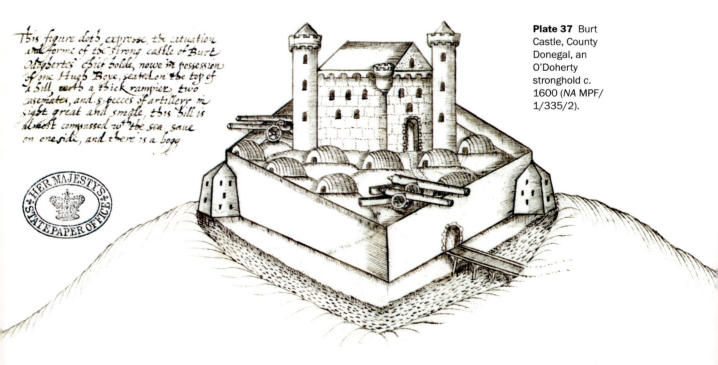

Plate 37 Burt Castle, County Donegal, an O'Doherty stronghold c. 1600 (*NA* MPF/1/335/2).

there are casemates allowing for small-arms fire to be directed along the whole perimeter.[5] And several true gun loops can still be seen in the fabric of the now-ruined castle (Plate 38). Constructed before 1587 (Lacy 1983, 370), it is clear from a contemporary depiction of the militarised landscape in north-western Ulster that the builders had an eye for area defence.

The legend to Plate 37 reads

This figure doth express the cituation and forme of the strong castle of Burt Odoghertes [O'Doherty's] chiefe holde, now in possession of one Hugh Boye, seated on the top of a hill, with a thick rampier, two casemates, and 5 peeces of artillery in sight, great and smale, this hill is almost compassed wth the sea, save on one side, and there is a bogg. (reproduced by kind permission of the National Archives).

Equally, from at least the earlier sixteenth century onwards, the English were adopting the lessons of continental Europe and applying them in Ireland as can be seen, for example, from the 1530s when Lord Deputy Skeffington used a substantial artillery train to deal with the uprising of Silken Thomas, the first major use of an artillery train on land in Ireland. Similarly, the construction of artillery forts from the later sixteenth century onwards, culminated in the significant expansion of such structures after 1600 (e.g. Kerrigan 1995). Notable for this study are those built as part of the militarization by Sir Henry Docwra of the Lough Foyle area, where he brought to bear his considerable knowledge of continental warfare, and of conditions in Ireland gained while serving under Sir Richard Bingham in Connaught (McGurk 2006a, 24*ff*).

In the seventeenth century in particular, all sides brought to the Irish conflicts experience gained in the various European theatres of war. The most famous of the Irish commanders, Owen Roe O'Neill, Thomas Preston and Garret Barry had all served with distinction in the Spanish Army of Flanders, and they and those who returned with them in 1642 from the various European campaigns brought with them their experience of the most modern techniques of warfare (e.g. Loeber and Parker 1995, 71*ff*; Murtagh 1996; McKenny 2005, 40). On the Planter side, for example, two key leaders of the Laggan Army in Ulster, Sir Robert Stewart and his brother William, had seen service in the armies of Sweden and Poland. And comrades in arms from Europe could find themselves distanced one from the other. Thus, Alexander Leslie, Robert Monro and Sir Arthur Aston all fought in the army of Gustavus Adolphus of Sweden until his death at the Battle of Lützen in November 1632. Subsequently, Leslie led forces against Charles I at the start of the Civil War and Monro commanded Covenanter forces in Ulster while Aston, a devout Royalist, led the defence of Drogheda and was killed by Cromwellian forces at its fall in 1649.

Studies of the contorted and confusing history of this unhappy period have filled great lengths of library shelf, and it is not the intention here to do more than bring out those episodes and events of direct relevance to Londonderry and its ordnance.[6] The focus of this chapter is thus on the background to the cannon which defended the City in the seventeenth century. Chapter 3 will take a brief overview of the development of the fortifications, while the pivotal role of the London Companies in the provision of ordnance in the first half of the seventeenth century will be dealt with in Chapter 4.

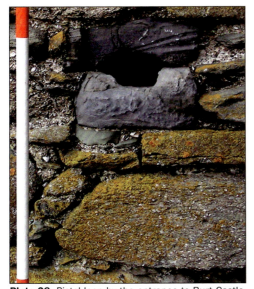

Plate 38 Pistol loop by the entrance to Burt Castle, County Donegal.

Background

Certainly, radical changes in the ways in which warfare was conducted by all sides in Ireland were initiated in the sixteenth century by the introduction in numbers of gunpowder weapons, first the caliver and arquebus, later artillery. This was an inevitable overspill from the broader European scene, where it seems not unreasonable to argue that the advent of missile-firing weapons powered by gunpowder had the same profundity of effect on warfare and society as that argued by White for the stirrup from the eighth century A.D. onwards (White 1962, 1*ff*).

For the purposes of this study, it is the deployment and management of artillery in sieges, and the defence against them, that is the most important. The fact that Londonderry does not appear to have suffered any sustained siege or series of direct assaults from the outbreak of the Irish Rebellion of 1641, right through to 1649, shows how good defences deterred all but the strongest and best equipped of adversaries. And the period from November 1641 to perhaps May or June of 1642, when the insurgents scored many successes elsewhere in Ulster, was one when the City was desperately short of weaponry, particularly artillery. Similarly, the sieges of 1649 and in 1689 demonstrate that strong fortifications manned by determined defenders could frustrate significant forces equipped with artillery. But these episodes show also the difference in capabilities between forces with and without artillery in a country where the majority of fortifications predated its introduction. In November 1641, insurgents began a siege of Drogheda which lasted until March 1642 and ultimately failed because the besieging troops lacked cannon. But eight years later, on 10 September 1649, the guns of the Parliamentary army under Oliver Cromwell blasted the mediaeval walls of the city, creating in a day a breach through which troops poured to perpetrate their infamous massacre of the garrison and so many of the inhabitants. It is one of the 'what if?' questions of Irish history to speculate on the outcome in 1649 had Londonderry been held by Royalists, and thus been forced to face the awesome power of the Cromwellian siege train.

Up to the end of the sixteenth century, Spain was a significant source of ordnance and munitions for the Irish, followed in importance by cannon captured from the English, such as those taken at the Yellow Ford and Blackwater, County Armagh in 1597 (Hayes-McCoy 1969, 130–131). But not all foreign guns came from seizure, trade or gift. The disastrous gales of September 1588 wrecked some fourteen ships of *La Felicissima Armada* of Phillip II of Spain along the Irish coast (Flanagan 1988, 16*ff*), some of which were salvaged by the Irish, some by the English. In June 1589 Sir George Carew, Master of the Ordnance in Ireland under Elizabeth (subsequently in England under both James I and Charles I), was ordered (*Carew MSS* 1589–1600, 2, 8 June 1589) by Lord Deputy Sir William Fitzwilliam to

repair unto that part of Tomond upon the sea where some of the Spanish fleet perished and where there are certain pieces of ordnance meet to be recovered . . .

He reported subsequently (*ibid.* 8, 8 June) that

Since our coming hither . . . we have spent our time to good purpose, for already we have weighed three pieces of artillery of brass . . . Yesterday we fastened our haullsers to a cannon of battery or basylyske, as we suppose by the length, for they lie at four fathom and a half of water [= 27 feet, 8.23m]; which was so huge that it brake our cables. Our diver was nearly drowned, but Irish aqua vitae hath such virtue as I hope of his recovery. If the diver from Dublin were here with his instruments, I would not doubt to bring good store of artillery from hence . . . And yet I cannot find any small pieces of brass or iron. I think the inhabitants of this country have gotten them.[7]

Divers[8] were employed to recover guns (Plate 39) and the process, including the use of air bags, was described by Norton (*Gunner* 125–127). And these were the forerunners of the techniques used by divers of the City of Derry Sub-Aqua club during the marine excavation of *La Trinidad Valancera* in Kinnegoe Bay in County Donegal. Shortly after, on 1 August

1589, Carew was despatched (*Carew MSS* 1589–1600, 11, 1 August 1589) to

> ... *that part of Ulster where some of the Spanish fleet perished and where there are certain pieces of ordnance meet to be recovered* ...

He was too late, however, to prevent the salvage of a number of (almost certainly bronze) pieces from the wreck of the galleass *Girona* at Lacada Point on the coast of County Antrim, which the local warlord Sorley Boy MacDonald mounted at his nearby stronghold of Dunluce Castle. A vessel, *The Popinjay* under a Captain Thornton (p. 81), which could have been used for retrieving these and other guns, had been sent to Chester (*ibid*. 12, 24 August 1589). Indeed, as late as 1612, the English government was still paying for 'Spanish ordnance ... cast away in the year 1588 upon the coast of Ireland' and recently recovered from the Armada wrecks (*NA* WO 49/38, f. 94r). Later in the 1640s, the Spanish supplied small arms, munitions and ordnance to the Irish (e.g. Loeber and Parker 1995, 75–76).

In the seventeenth century, the armaments industries throughout Europe increased output, and an arms trade – both legal and illegal – supplied weaponry and munitions to those prepared to pay the prices asked.[9] For example, at least some of the guns now preserved at Portumna Castle, County Galway, said by tradition to have been used by Jacobite forces at the Battle of Aughrim in 1691, came probably from Sweden via France, and from Dutch sources. Guns were also captured from Crown forces, for example at Culmore in 1608, at Newry, County Down and Strabane, County Tyrone in November 1641, at Limerick in June 1642, from the pinnace *Confidence* off Wexford in July 1642 (*Ormond MSS* II, 174), and at Benburb in June 1646. During the Nine Years War, Hugh O'Neill imported powder from unscrupulous merchants in Glasgow and Birmingham (McGurk 2006b,158), but also trawled as far afield as Danzig (modern Gdánsk) on the Baltic (Hayes-McCoy 1976, 126).

What is noticeable is the exceedingly low level of gunfounding in Ireland up to 1641, and the exceeding sparse evidence for any subsequent to that. Ordnance was supplied primarily from England, and those ironworks which were involved in cannon manufacture in Ireland belonged to a handful of English loyal to the Crown. Thus, one of the signal failures of the Irish insurgents in 1641 was to seize Dublin and its arsenal. Had this been achieved and

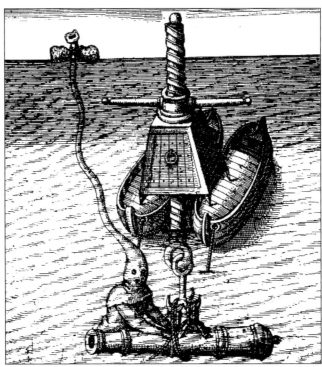

Plate 39 Diver working with a cannon on the sea bed (*Gunner*, plate facing p. 128).

significant numbers of cannon been captured, the outcome of the struggle might well have been significantly influenced.[10] Similarly, the lack of heavy ordnance led the besiegers of King John's Castle, Limerick to use mining to create breaches in the defences (Wiggins 2001). But lack of foundry facilities affected not just the Irish as can be seen, for example, in the Commissioners at Star Chamber being instructed as late as 1648 (*Cal. SPI Addenda 1625–1660*, 780, 5 May 1648)

> *... to find out a skilful founder and discover and report upon what terms he will go over to Dublin and there to cast three pieces which are not so useful for the present service of the Kingdom into pieces which may be more useful.*

Equally, much of the evidence (e.g. Lenihan 2001, 53*f*) points to a situation in which the Irish were almost wholly reliant on outside suppliers for powder. Shortages of this vital commodity were exposed at the end of 1641 and in the earlier part of 1642 when, in some instances, Confederate forces felt compelled to go to what today seem extremes to procure saltpetre for gunpowder (see pp41-42 below). The author of the *Aphorismical Discovery* wrote (Gilbert 1879, I, 25)

> *Great and exceeding penurious was ammunition with the Irish ... this penurie was generall in all the four provinces amonge the royalists ... neither armes or ordinance had they to prevent further distruction in the north ...*

Set against this, English forces drew on a well-established (though often under-resourced) system of production and distribution and always held numerical superiority in terms of artillery. It should be noted, however, that the outbreak of the Civil War in England left a not dissimilar situation to that in Ireland, with only the Brownes in Kent being significant producers.[11] That the authorities in Dublin were caught wholly unawares in October 1641 is evident from the frantic correspondence between various centres, Dublin and London. But after the initial confusions from the end of 1641 through to the middle of 1642, the English Ordnance Office managed to keep up at least part of the supplies required by the forces loyal to both Crown and Parliament while the conflicts lasted.

And when Cromwell landed at Dublin with his army on 15 August 1649, his siege train had more firepower than that of all of the other forces operating in Ireland combined (*cf.* Roberts, K. 2005, 234). Nevertheless, the lack of serious gunfounding in Ireland for Crown interests proved a weakness from December 1641 on. If any of the foundries in operation in Ulster prior to the Irish Rebellion (see McCracken 1957, 1965) had been geared up to produce ordnance, Londonderry and other centres in the north might not have been so dangerously under-provisioned with defensive artillery at this perilous time. The logistics were fragile, as illustrated by the inability of the Ordnance Office to meet demands for the Bishops' Wars in 1639 and 1640 (Fissell 1994, 90*ff*) and, quite dramatically, by the problems caused by the interruption in supplies, not just of ordnance, but of *matériel* in general, brought about by the start of the English Civil War in August 1642.

Bringing the elements together

1 CANNON PRODUCTION

As with armaments in the modern world, cannon were the products of interaction between a number of industries. Ores had to be mined and charcoal manufactured to fuel the blast furnaces which converted iron ore into cast iron and those which produced the copper and tin which were then alloyed to make bronze.[12] The furnaces themselves had to be constructed, operated and maintained, requiring a skilled labour force. Thus, just to obtain and transport the raw materials for gun founding and to construct and maintain the metallurgical facility involved a complex of interdependencies, sometimes with competition for resources as, for example, between charcoal burning, manufacture of barrel staves and ship building (Scott 1985, 293–294). And, of course, there were the skilled founders who constructed complex moulds into which large volumes of molten metal were poured.

Guns of this period, both cast iron and bronze, were cast individually in one-off moulds and the technology of gunfounding is discussed further in Chapter 8. Mould making required great skill on the part of the pattern makers and founders, and the making of these moulds required special clays and loams which again had to be mined, prepared, transported and formed. Foundries producing cannon were at the centre of a complex web of industry and commerce, requiring major investment for their establishment and incurring significant overheads in terms of both labour and materials (e.g. Schubert 1957, 246*ff*; Crossley 1997). Thus, for example, for the Royal Gunfounder, John Browne (pp 201*ff*) to construct a new furnace at Brenchley in Kent over the winter of 1637-1638 (and for which he was paid between 1641 and 1642[13]), most likely for the casting of bronze ordnance for the vessel *Sovereign of the Seas*, was estimated (*NA* WO 49/75, 219r; 10 Feb 1641) as being in the region of the princely sum of £1000.[14]

Charge of a newe Fowndery in Kent
. . . A Debenture made unto John Browne Esqe, his M^(ates) Founder of Ordnance and shott, for the some of One Thousand Pounds (directed to bee paid upon the Estimate of 1000 l for the charge of making a newe Fowndrey for his Mats Service.) vizt: For the building and forming of a newe Fowndrey and Furnace, beeing made of purpose in the Parish of Branchley in the County of Kent, for the said Mr Browne to cast divers peeces of Brass Ordnance for his M^(atie) newe Shipp called the Soveraigne of the Seas for making a Vault, and for Iron and woodoen Tooles, and other necessaries requisite and usefull for a Founder of Brass Ordnance, together with all Instruments fitting thereunto to perform this present, and all other such like Service, as his M^(atie) shalbe pleased hereafter to employ and Comaund to bee done. Amounting to the some of m li.

The situation as regards the production of ordnance and shot in Ireland in the seventeenth century is unclear,[15] not least because of the contradictory evidence for Crown attitudes to the trade that can be observed in official documents of the time. Thus, for example in 1614, the Privy Council wrote to Sir Oliver St John on this subject (*APC* 1613–1614, 440, 18 May 1614), stating that

. . . wee are informed there are some that goe aboute to errect furnasses in that kingdome of Ireland for the casting of iron ordnance: we have thought it very expedient hereby to pray and require your lordship not to give way to the erecting of such furnasses, but to make a speciall restrainte and prohibicion of the same in all parts of that kingdome, untill you receive further order from us.

Nevertheless, Richard Boyle, first Earl of Cork, had extensive ironworks in Munster, and invested thousands of pounds in his operations. These included double furnaces at Cappoquin and Lisfinny in County Waterford (*Lismore* I(1), 91 and I(2), 6). Cannon and shot were certainly being cast at Cappoquin as shown by Boyle's entry in his journal for 22–25 March 1626 (*Lismore* I(2), 179), which reads

. . . My lo president [Sir Edward Villiers, Lord President of Munster] *cam from Moallo* [Mallow, Co. Cork] *to Lismoor and staied with me till the 25th, and then we sawe a peec of ordenance caste at Cappoquin and some shott . . .*

Boyle, who had strong contacts with the financier Philip Burlamachi, also a major player in the European arms market, later went into partnership with Sir Charles Coote Snr in ironworks capable of producing ordnance at Mountrath, Co Laois. And the Lord Deputy of Ireland, Sir Thomas Wentworth, was a major shareholder in ironworks at Ballynakill, County Laois, where ordnance was cast. These works were run by Richard Blacknall[16] a former employee of Boyle, and in 1633 minions produced there were proofed at Kilmainham, County Dublin.

The accurate preparation of moulds, using the right materials, was crucial to the production of functional, reliable and safe cannon. Thus, it is not surprising that practical writers on artillery like John Smith (*Grammar* 71–72) and Robert Norton (*Gunner* 70–73) devoted detailed attention to the subject. The mould[17] was made up by building up layers of clay over a rope-covered wooden spindle (Fig. 6a), shaping to the desired form of the cannon using a strickle board cut to the desired profile (Fig. 6b). The breech is depicted usually as being prepared as a separate piece, as were the trunnions. Once the mould had been built up to the desired thickness, it was reinforced with iron banding (Fig. 6c). Fig. 6d illustrates the cross-section through the mould with the core in place to form the bore of the gun. The muzzle end was extended with a 'gun head' into which, when the molten metal was poured, impurities would rise and be removed when the head was cut off (Fig. 7a). This methodology obviously requires that the guns were cast vertically, although as we shall see in Chapter 8, some of the evidence presented by the chemical and metallographic analyses indicates the possibility of some casting in a horizontal position.

The actual casting of cannon was a highly-skilled art, representing the development of expertise in the production and handling of molten metal in bulk, in quantities that could be as high as many tonnes at a time. Obviously, the larger the size of the cannon to be cast, the more molten iron was required, so that by the earlier part of the seventeenth century, founders were building double furnaces, such as those of Boyle at Cappoquin and Lisfinny, to ensure that they were smelting enough metal to fill the moulds. From the evidence, cannon founders cast a number of cannon in each campaign. Thus there was an intimate relationship between the numbers which they wished to cast at one time, the size of the guns to be cast and the capacity of the foundry to produce molten metal in bulk. This placed an obvious limitation on casting of cast-iron pieces, since in the sixteenth and earlier seventeenth centuries, the molten metal was tapped straight from the smelting furnace. The obvious solution was to increase the number of furnaces operating for the casting campaign, but this was expensive.

It was of the greatest importance that the mould material and that of the pit surrounding it was completely dry, otherwise small pockets of superheated steam would form, causing flaws on the surface[18] as can be seen, for example, around the muzzle of C11 (Plate 16). Although the founder of many of the Londonderry guns, John Browne I, had a highly-skilled workforce at his foundries, the surface flaws evident on C6 and C11 suggest that in some cases at least, complete drying of their moulds was not achieved, although this may have been due also to the orientation of the guns when cast (p. 186). Equally, gas evolution within the body of the metal could cause voids and blowholes. Another regular problem was that of the core moving during the casting process, meaning that the bore was not true. This was addressed by attempting to adjust by boring (Fig. 7b), using cutting heads with hardened steel teeth (Fig. 7c), although it was not until the eighteenth century that the problem was finally solved by the casting of cannon as solid blocks, with the barrel then being bored out (pp 205-206).

Measuring the bore, and determining how true was its alignment was carried out using a variety of instruments, including those illustrated by Norton (Fig. 8).

The quality of castings exercised the minds at the Ordnance Office, since metal with significant flaws would not withstand the pressures generated when a gun was fired.[19] A common reference is to 'honeycombed' iron guns (as, for example, in the Londonderry inventories for 1674 and 1684, where a saker is described as 'honeycombed and clogged' – Appendix 14.2a and 14.3a). Francis Povey, who became 'Surveyor General and Controller of the Ordnance in Ireland' in 1683 described it (Barter Bailey 2000, 80) as

The thing call'd a Hony-Comb, derives its name from the Comb of Bees, which is full of holes. The occasion is often by the Noel [=newel] which makes the Concave [=bore] *of the Gun. If it be not well wrought and Neal'd from any Moisture, your Mettle running hot, and meeting with any sort of Moistness, causes a sort of Convulsion in the Mettle; which cooling, leaves great holes which cannot be bored out, especially if your Noel be made to high: which is often done to save the trouble of Boreing.*

Although this was a significant casting fault, it is clear that as a subsurface flaw, it could be exposed and developed by wear. Thus, in 1627, John Smith in *A Sea Grammar* wrote (Goell 1970, 85)

Chapter 2 – The Historical and Technological Backgrounds to the Cannon

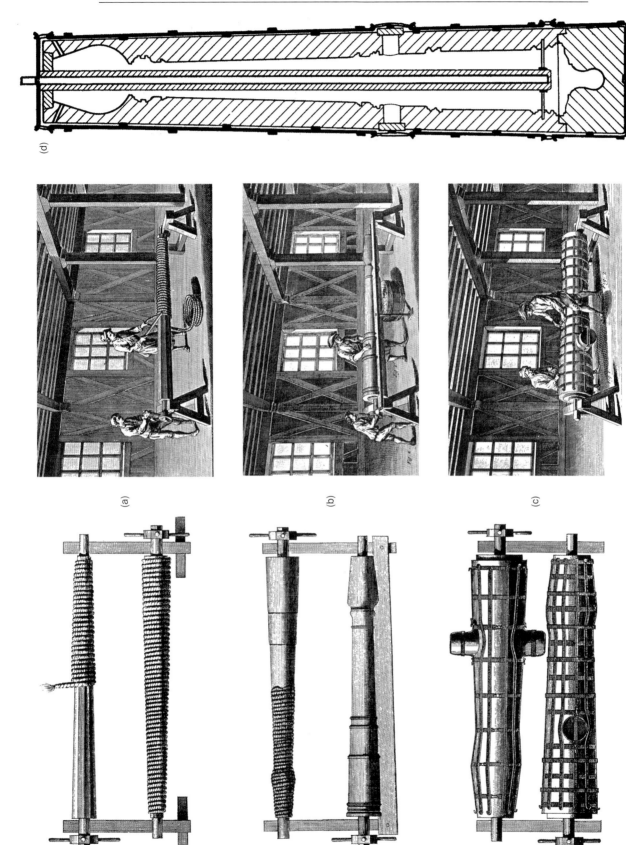

Fig. 6 Preparation of a cannon mould with false core (a–c after ffoulkes 1937, d after *Pirotechnia* 452, Fig. VI).

The Great Guns Like Thunder

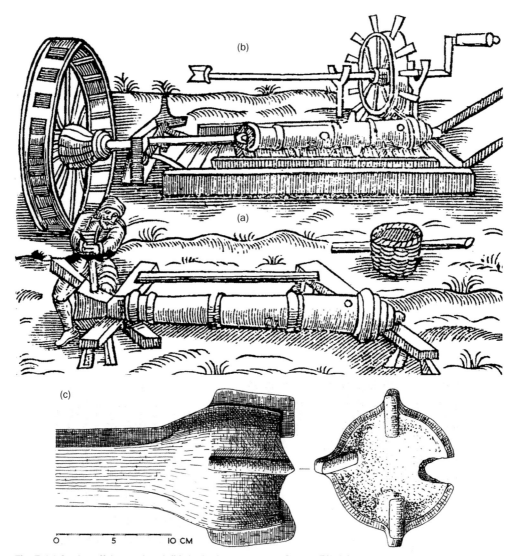

Fig. 7 (a) Cutting off the gun head, **(b)** the boring apparatus (*Gunner* 71), **(c)** seventeenth-century cutting head from Chiddingley, Sussex with three of its four steel teeth still in place, (after Butler and Tebbutt 1975).

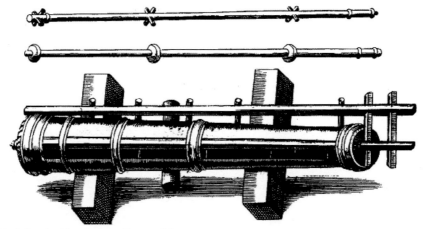

Fig. 8 Tools for checking the bore (*Gunner* 81).

Honicombed is when shee is ill cast or overmuch worne, shee will be rugged [rough] *within . . .*

The metallographic evidence from Roaring Meg (C6) in particular (pp 183*ff*) shows that while a piece might appear sound on the surface, significant voids in the metal – either empty or with a slag filling – could be present. While, as with Roaring Meg and the Merchant Taylors' C11, the outer surface appearance of casting flaws might be somewhat unsightly, it was on the inside of the bore that they could cause real problems, as Smith went on to describe (*ibid.*):

. . . which is dangerous for a crosse barre shot to catch hold by, or any ragge of her wadding, being a fire and sticking there, may fire the next charge you put in her;

What Smith brings out is that sub-surface flaws not detectable in the as-cast condition could be exposed by wear and that it was thus necessary for the gunner to check the bore of his gun regularly, using a tool called a 'searcher'. Smith (*Grammar* 109) also advocated a method used until comparatively recently as a qualitative check for defects in working castings, namely to strike the metal part to be checked and listen to the sound produced.

If upon the outside of the Metal of any Piece of Ordnance, you strike a smart blow with an Iron Hammer; if you hear a hoarse sound, doubtless there are Honeycombs, *or such like* Flaws.

In fact, examination of the Londonderry cannon has shown significant surface flaws, some of which when probed have proved to be more than 2cm in depth. Smith (*Grammar* 109–110) took as normal the fact that flaws could go right through the metal, writing

As soon as you have discharged any Piece of Ordnance, let one be ready to cover the Mouth of the Piece close, and stop the Touch-hole at the same time; by which means you may know if any Cracks or Flaws do go through the Metal, for if any such be, a visible smoke will come through those Flaws *or* Cracks.

2 GUNPOWDER

Gunpowder is a mixture comprising three substances, saltpetre, sulphur and charcoal, and the majority of authorities see the optimum proportions as being 75% saltpetre (ideally potassium nitrate[20] – KNO_3), 10% sulphur and 15% charcoal.[21] Without it, a cannon was merely an expensive and inert lump of metal. The production of gunpowder was another complex industry, involving the collection of saltpetre efflorescence on stone- and brickwork,[22] more importantly from decaying animal and vegetable matter,[23] the mining and transport of sulphur and the burning of charcoal.[24] The British Isles have no natural deposits of sulphur, so that all had to be imported, primarily in the seventeenth century from Sicily.

As with cannon founding, the gunpowder industry involved a complex set of trade relationships, as well as competitions. Thus, saltpetre was not just an ingredient of gunpowder but found use, amongst other industries, in the refining of gold and silver.[25] On 5 August 1624, the Privy Council was informed (*APC* 1623–1625, 294) of a petition

. . . in the name of the refyners or parters of gold and silver humbly complayning that in regard of some late orders for the speedie provision of greate quantities of gunpowder for the furnishing of his Majestie's store and defence of the kingdome they can by noe meanes (as heretofore they were accustomed) buye or procure any saltpeeter at all, wherby as well his Majestie's Mynte as the Company of Goldsmiths are hindred and sustaine much prejudice, for that without a certaine water proceeding from salt-peeter the refyners of gold and silver (who are of necessarie use both to the Mynte and trade of goldsmiths) cann doe nothing in their mysterie.[26]

The matter was passed on to Lord Carew, Master of the Ordnance, with the recommendation (*APC* 1623–1625, 301–302, 10 August 1624) that three 'refyners' – Simon Owen, John Wollastone and William Gibbes be allowed to buy saltpetre from the Ordnance as they

. . . are verie fitt and experienced men in that misterie[27] *and that the quantity of five*

tonne of salt-peeter by the yeare wilbe requisite to the uses abovesaid.

By the early 1600s, the cutting down of timber for charcoal (also for barrel staves[28]) had caused such a loss of timber that on 1 January 1611, the Privy Council (*Cal. SPI* 1611–1614, 1) ordered Lord Deputy Chichester to '. . . take measures to preserve the timber in His Majesty's woods in Ireland for the use of His Majesty's navy.' Some thirty years later, this concern was still evident, as in his address to the Irish parliament of 16 March 1640, Charles I proposed (*Commons J. Ireland* I, 124, 127) that an act be passed to the effect that

> . . . *timber shall not be felled to make Coals for the burning of Iron, Glas or for burning of Lime or Bricks.*

In Ulster, primary use of charcoal was in the blast furnaces that were in operation (McCracken 1957, 1965), elsewhere at least a proportion would have gone into gunpowder making. And as late as 1685, as a result of the effects of charcoal production on the lands of the Vintners and Salters Companies, the Irish Society requested the inclusion of new provisions in their leases to prevent further destruction of woodland (Curl 2000, 158).

Gunpowder is a mixture, not a single chemical compound like the commercial explosives of today and, if the ingredients were not thoroughly mixed, or the powder was mishandled, they could separate out. A further problem for the gunpowder maker (and user) was the fact that nitrates of magnesium and calcium in particular are highly hygroscopic – that is, they readily absorb moisture from the atmosphere. By the later sixteenth century, treatment with ashes (which contain significant levels of potassium hydroxide – KOH) of the liquor created by the leaching of the piles of noxious waste, allowed for significant reductions in the levels of all but potassium and sodium nitrates. Nevertheless, before the development of a systematic chemical approach in the eighteenth century, this was the best that the producers of saltpetre could do.

The ingredients had to be mixed safely and thoroughly, so that the ingredients were intimately intermingled (the process known as 'incorporation'), and the size of the particles of gunpowder that were produced had a profound effect on its properties. The earliest powders were made by mixing the dry powders together, producing the fine powder in the seventeenth century called *serpentine*. Later, ingredients were mixed together wet and forced through sieves to produce coarse grains, the product being known as *corned* powder. Apart from considerations of performance, serpentine suffered from two major faults. First, it presented a large surface area to the atmosphere, allowing the hygroscopic nitrates to absorb moisture. Moisture could be absorbed from the barrel staves, opening them to allow in more water. Second, because the ingredients were mixed dry, they had a tendency to separate out thus rendering the powder unserviceable. Thus, it is not surprising to find regular references in contemporary records of 'spoiled' powder which had to be returned to powder makers to be 'repaired', sometimes by simply remixing the ingredients, sometimes by extracting the saltpetre with water and starting anew (e.g. Kelly, J. 2004, 120). Thus in 1598, 'wet and unserviceable' powder was returned to the powder maker Robert Evelyn to be 'new boiled' (*NA* WO 49/22, f. 104v) and, of course, famously, we have reference to the removal of the 'decayed powder' from the Houses of Parliament in November 1605 (*NA* WO 49/31, f. 100r). Norton (*Gunner* 145–147) and Nye (*Gunnery* 23–25), amongst many others, described several methods for 'renewing' powder, which Norton stated that every gunner should know. Sir Henry Docwra had regularly to contend with unserviceable powder and match in his campaigning in the Lough Foyle area (McGurk 2006a, 133–134), and nearly eighty years later, an inventory of June 1678, recorded that out of the eight hundred and fifty-one barrels of powder in the various stores in Ireland, one hundred and seven (nearly 13% of the current stock) were 'unserviceable' (*Carte MSS* 54, f. 608, dated 5 June 1678).

Saltpetre also found use in the preparation of 'match' – a cord that was used both by gunners to fire their cannon, and the arquebusier to fire his weapon. The cord was soaked in a solution of saltpetre, providing when dry a slow-burning source of ignition for the priming powder. As with powder, the hygroscopic saltpetre could absorb water and make the match unserviceable. In an incident which very evidently embarrassed and exasperated Sir Henry Docwra, when called on in July 1601 to rendezvous with Mountjoy, he found that the stock of match in Derry on which he relied was unusable (*Docwra* 58–59; McGurk 2006a, 111–112). On this occasion, Docwra suffered from civil service literalism of a type that would have delighted Sir Humphrey Appleby. Thinking that his clerk had confirmed that there were sufficient supplies, he was horrified to find that the match he required was 'rotten and much had been wasted'. One can almost see the smoke rising from his quill pen as he recorded

> . . . I called for the Clarke and asked him the reason . . . said I, did yow not tell Mee the other day that yow had 60 barrels? I tould you said hee that I had 60 barrels of Powder and soe I had, but of match yow asked me nothing.

There is a crucial difference in performance between fine- and coarse-grained powders. Modern 'high' explosives – such as the infamous Semtex – are said to 'detonate', while the gunpowder of the seventeenth century, a 'low' explosive, 'deflagrates', the difference being simplistically explained as that between a very fast rate of burning and decomposition and a very slow one.[29] Speed of deflagration in gunpowder depends on grain size, and the rate was critical to the performances of gunpowder weapons.[30] Gunpowder burns at a fairly uniform rate at the surface of its individual grains and the flame front is propagated by a fine spray of molten salts. Uncompressed, a fine powder will burn more rapidly than a coarse one, because a much greater surface area is exposed for combustion. However, when confined within the barrel of a weapon, a fine powder has much less space between grains to allow the salt spray to develop with maximum efficiency, and thus a serpentine charge overall burns from end to end. A charge of corned powder, where a significant proportion of the volume of the charge is empty space, will burn much faster. The more rapid evolution of gas meant that a much higher proportion of the energy produced was translated into the forward motion of the projectile than with serpentine powder. This more powerful propellant had its disadvantages, however, in that the gunner had to be aware of the need to use smaller charges, if catastrophic bursts were to be avoided. We have evidence to show that the gunners in the Lough Foyle area were being supplied with corn powder from at least 1601 (Table 4).

Gunpowder was dangerous to friend and foe alike if not treated with respect.[31] In 1549, Diarmuid O'Sullivan Beare was killed by an gunpowder explosion in his castle (de hÓir 1983, 86). The very first English garrison at Derry was forced to decamp after the catastrophic explosion in 1567 of the powder magazine which caused heavy casualties (Appendix B), an accident attributed to divine vengeance for the desecration of holy ground. During the shambolic attempt by Sir Henry Bagenal to reinforce the Blackwater Fort, which resulted in his defeat at the Battle of the Yellow Ford in County Armagh on 14 August 1598, a soldier managed to let his match ignite the contents of one barrel of powder (Plate 56) which, in turn, set off a second, so that he 'spoiled many men and disordered the battle' (Hayes-McCoy 1969, 124–125). Showing that against stupidity, the Gods themselves truly strive in vain, in September of 1630, the small warship the *7th Whelp* under the command of Captain Dawtrey Cooper, was engaged with the *Mary Rose* in action against a Dutch warship. She was sunk when a careless member of the crew, holding a lit candle, ignited the powder in the magazine.[32] After the lifting of the siege of Londonderry in 1649, the defences at Charles Fort close to the City were surrendered, along with arms and ammunition. The diarist of the siege, Captain Henry Finch,[33] recorded (*Finch Journal* 14) that after the surrender of Charles Fort on 11 August,

> The souldiers left all their armes: but their powder-bags, hornes, bandaleeres &c. being laid upon a heap (through accident or negligence) blew up and burnt severall of our officers and some souldiers very sore, and some horses, one or two in danger of death.

And, demonstrating that smoking around gunpowder is unwise,[34] another diarist, Captain Ash, recounted (*Ash Journal* 97) that in Londonderry on 25 July 1689

> ... the prisoners which we took to-day in the main guard, as some of them were smoking tobacco near some powder, a spark fell out of the pipe on the floor where some grains had been scattered, which took fire, and ran along to where half a barrel stood and blew it up. It has much disfigured the three prisoners and three men of the garrison;

One of the best documented accounts of a major accident in Ireland is that which occurred in Dublin and was described in a letter dated 16 March 1597, from Sir George Bourchier, then Master of the Ordnance, to Lord Burliegh (Lennon 1988). That this was caused by negligence on the quayside, compounded by the fact that the powder had been packed in single- and not double-skinned casks as was normal, would have been no consolation to the families of the casualties who included over one hundred and twenty dead.[35]

Detonation of powder through enemy action was always a major hazard too. English troops of Sir Henry Docwra, under the command of Captain Lewis Oriell (Orrell), were garrisoned in Donegal Abbey in September 1600. Although possibly accidental (Docwra was undecided: Kelly, W.P. 2003, 60), while they were under attack their powder stock blew up, although casualties were not heavy.[36] An attack by the forces of Sir Charles Coote on those laying siege to Londonderry in 1649 resulted in an explosion of powder which caused at least one death (*Finch Journal* 6, 8 June 1649). And although the defenders of Londonderry in 1689 made strenuous efforts to disperse their stocks against the Jacobite bombardments, on 27 June a mortar bomb landed on the house of one Joseph Gallagher in Bishop Street where two barrels were stored. The resulting blast killed some fourteen people, soldiers and civilians alike (*Ash Journal* 81).

From the time that Hugh O'Neill made serious introduction of firearms to his troops in the Nine Years War, through to the final Cromwellian subjugation of Ireland, non-English forces in Ireland were almost totally reliant on imports of gunpowder.[37] While in late sixteenth and seventeenth-centuries England, denunciations of the intrusive activities of the 'petermen', those who collected organics-rich earth from all possible locations under State licence, are not uncommon in historic records (e.g. Bull 1990), they do not appear to have had Irish counterparts, apart from a brief period in the 1640s. Lenihan (2001, 54) suggests that the first industrial production of powder in Ireland was an enterprise established at Kilkenny around 1647[38] by a French engineer called Nicholas La Laloue or Lalloe. But, in fact, in a petition of 1646 presented to no less a personage than the Papal Nuncio Rinuccini (Gilbert 1882, VI, 75–76), Lalloe sought payment of moneys owed from 1644 to

> your suppliant ... at the earnest request of generall Thomas Preston, the supreme councell, and divers others of note and qualitie, left his native countrie ... to reside in Kilkenny ... building a howse for two forges to make all sorts of instruments fit for warr both of iron and brasse workes, a salt-peeter house and two powder mills.

And, as Wiggins has shown (2001, 73), at least some powder was being produced by 1642 in mills at Limerick, Castleconnell and Kilmallock, all of which were owned by one Dr. Daniel Higgins,[39] by then a member of the Confederate Assembly in Kilkenny (*TCD MS 866*, f.130, lines 28–33)

> The s[ai]d Higgins hath three gun-powder houses, one at Lymick, another at Kilmallock & another at Castle-Connell which sev[er]all houses made weeckly fiftie pounds of powder each. But it is of smale use and imp[er]fecte, for the knave is not his craftes maister.

There is, however, a discrepancy between this account of the quality of the powder produced by Higgins,[40] and that contained in the account of the siege by John Rastall (reprinted in *Good and Bad Newes from Ireland*) where we find that

> ... the Enemy hath excellent powder it gives but small reports, but drives a bullet with extraordinary force. Powder is made in towne by Doctor Higgins ...

There seems no reason to believe that the potential for gunpowder production in Ireland in the earlier seventeenth century was any less than that for England. Production of charcoal would not have been a problem, and in theory at least, saltpetre could have been produced from the same sources and by the same methods practised there, while sulphur would have had to be imported. On 28 January 1589, Elizabeth I granted a licence (*Cal. Pat. Close Rolls* II, 188) to George and John Evelynn and Richard Hyll (or Hilles), giving them 'full power, licence and authority to dig, open and work for saltpetre in England and Ireland'. The Evelyns and Hyll, in turn, sub-licensed to

William Awcher, Arnold Haddys, Thomas Harnon and Richard Hatton, gentlemen, of approved skill and knowledge, to dig open and work for saltpetre in Ireland, and manufacture powder for the space of 11 years.

Whether or not they proceeded is unknown.

On 6 December 1625, Lord Carew wrote to the Privy Council on the subject of the monopoly on powder production held by the Evelyn family (*Cal. SPD* 1625–1626, 171). He suggested increasing the supply of saltpetre 'especially in Ireland where knowledge of manufacture is kept from the common people.' Indeed, sometime around 1627, the courtier Endymion Porter petitioned Charles I for the monopoly of gunpowder production in Ireland (*Cal. SPI Additional* 1625–1660, 91), although what became of this is again unknown.[41] Also on 21 December 1627, another petition to the King, this time by one Hugh Grove, suggested that sources of English saltpetre were suffering from exploitation and that he should be allowed to attempt its manufacture in Ireland (*Cal. SPI* 1625–1632, 296). Amongst the benefits put forward were avoidance of the hazards and expense of purchasing saltpetre abroad and providing employment, while allowing saltpetre grounds in England to regenerate. As the Irish Commissioners noted, such a venture would 'save the King from being dependent on outside sources' (*ibid.* 308).

Correspondence between Sir Henry Vane and Lord Deputy Wentworth in 1637 suggested the possibility of 'advantage to His Majesty' through the establishment of Irish production (*Strafford* Str P10(A) ff 27–28, 30 April and 12 June 1637). But according to a survey in the same year by two gentlemen, named as Milton and Stevenson, there was a 'lack' of saltpetre in Ireland, and they offered the conclusion that its production would not be economically viable (*Cal. SPI* 1633–1647, 161, 13 June 1637). This is highly surprising, given that sources of rotting, nitrogenous waste can hardly have been scarce, and it is possible that they were referring only to that found as an efflorescence on brick and stone. However, here again, there seems no reason to believe that the conditions for its occurrence found in England were any less common in Ireland, at least in urban contexts. Whether or not Milton and/or Stevenson had any relationship with the gunpowder monopolists of the time in England is an interesting but unresolved question!

It is clear that until well into early 1643, forces of the Catholic Confederacy were seriously lacking in gunpowder,[42] relying like their opponents almost entirely on external supplies. Thus, Lenihan (2001, 54) points out that insurgents seem to have had but one barrel of powder[43] at the Battle of Kilrush in early 1642. And in a letter dated 1 August 1642, Geoffrey Barron wrote to Fr Luke Wadding bemoaning the fact that the insurgents were unable to mount a serious assault on Londonderry and other centres because of a lack of powder and ordnance (*HMC Franciscans* 168):

Your letters of the taking of Kinsale, Drohedagh, Cork and Youghal were not right; for those places, together with Dublin, Knockfergus, and Londonderry, are still in the enemy's hand. But they stand but as mortgaged from us for a little powder and ordnance, which with the first we shall get, we will, God willing, easily redeem.

To overcome this shortage – thanks in no small part to the policy of Lord Deputy Wentworth[44] after 1639 of licensing and restricting purchases in Ireland (Lenihan 2001, 53: *cf. Cal. SPI* 1633–1647, 318, 16 July 1641) – even human remains were pressed into service as a source of saltpetre. Bizarre as it may seem at first, it was broadcast at the time that the nitrogenous products of rotting Protestant corpses provided some small amounts of saltpetre, allowing Confederates in Kilkenny and Waterford to augment meagre supplies.

In the aftermath of the outbreak of the Irish Rebellion in 1641, lurid reports of the maltreatment of, and atrocities against, Protestants in Ireland quickly began to circulate. Among these were claims the Catholics were deliberately desecrating their graves out of hatred (e.g. Canny 1997). Had the only source for such accusations been those of Sir John Temple (*Irish Rebellion* 119), one could be content to dismiss them as just another example of his bitter, black propaganda.[45] However, Canny (*ibid*. 57–58) identified the deposition from Kilkenny[46] from which Temple quoted (*TCD* MS 812, f. 202) and another from Waterford (*TCD* MS 820, ff 29–31), the detail of the latter at least leaving little doubt that such happened. This deposition,[47] taken in May 1643 from one Lawrence Hoey, a grocer, who arrived in Waterford from Duncannon Fort on 1 December 1641, has the deponent testifying to the disinterment in 1642 of Protestant corpses to be used as a source of saltpetre:

> *. . . about Candlemas then following the undernamed Persons, to wit Wm Woodcock Sheriffe of ye sd Cittie . . . began wth force of arm[s] to stripp and robb all ye protestants there; . . . especially aboute whitsun tide 1642 then ensuing, these persons last menconed (among others) in a most unchristian and barbarous [–] began to dig the graves where protestants were [–] buried in, caused to be digged to make gunpowder . . .*

> *. . . examinant observed that Richard Neyler of ye afd Cittie Apothecary, Peeter Morgan of ye same [–] and [–] formerly a protestant but now turned papist an Engineer and m^{str} of their ordenance digged up four corps of protestants (but their names he doth not remember) or at least caused them to be digged up wh^{ch} corpes had some bones and flesh aboute them, and those they boyled in greate furnisses till they came to salt peeter and made of them gunpowder there four pounds or thereabouts, and continued ye same course till they were provided from Dungarvan . . .*

Wiggins (2001, 90, note 30) records that during the siege of Limerick in 1642, there was excavation of the grounds of Saint Munchin's and Saint John's churches for nitrogenous earth. Further, the commander of the Irish forces, General Garrett Barry, sanctioned the digging up of Saint Mary's churchyard to obtain earth for the extraction of saltpetre. In the account by John Rastall of events in Limerick, we find

> *Powder is made in towne by Doctor Higgins, Nich: Power, Jo. Arthur Fitz-John, Hackett an Apothecary*[48] *and all St. Munction's and St. John's Church dig[e]d up 3 or four foot deep for saltpetre and some say they make a 100lb a weeke, some say lesse the certainty of that he know[e]th not.*

Bizarre, even repulsive, as it might seem,[49] neither the exploitation of burial soils nor the use of corpses in making saltpetre were an insular phenomenon. Indeed, English petermen in the 1620s and 1630s regularly dug in graveyards and church interiors, one excavating in Saint Paul's in London, and in some cases they were accused of undermining buildings[50] by their activities (Bull 1990, 7–8). In April of 1630, for example, serious complaints were laid (*Cal. SPD* 1625–1649, 245, 30 April 1630) against Thomas Hilliard and Nicholas Stevens (or Stephens), including that they were

> *digging in all places without distinction as in parlours, bedchambers, threshing and malting floors, yea, God's own house they have not forborne . . .*

while in June of that year, Stevens replied to the authorities (*ibid*. 291, 26 June 1630) in a petition stating that

> *At a time of great want of saltpetre he removed only some waste and unnecessary part of the soil of the church of Chipping Norton, as, with the concurrence of the parishioners and ministers, he had done in the churches of Coventry, Warwick and Oxford. Other digging was done in his absence by his servant whom he cast into Oxford gaol.*

In *Compleat Gunner*, the author writes that 'Salt-Peter is found commonly in great abundance, in obscured shadowed places . . . where there has been laid up together many dead bodies, and earth thrown upon them' (*Compleat Gunner* 11). Further, Canny (1997, 70) notes seventeenth-century Swedish use of 'clay' from graveyards, while J. Kelly (2004, 34) draws attention to the rendering down of military corpses in Russia in the 1670s. Thus, although really a historical oddity, use of human remains as a source of saltpetre underscores the shortages of gunpowder that very frequently arose in Ireland in the seventeenth century.[51]

3 SHOT

Solid shot could be produced from stone, from cast iron and from lead, although when circumstances demanded other materials could be pressed into service. Thus, during the Londonderry siege of 1689, when iron shot had been expended, the defenders substituted it with roofing lead cast around brick. Although stone balls, each laboriously crafted by hand, were still in use in the late sixteenth century,[52] cast iron was taking over. In fact, in the sixteenth century stone and iron shot were being used for specific cannon types – thus, perriers fired stone shot. The English Ordnance Office was still buying stone shot into the late sixteenth century and using perriers into the 1620s, though not often enough to have to buy new ammunition. Nevertheless, as late as 1684, there were stone shot in the Londonderry magazine (Appendix A14.3: Table 6). The primary value of the heavier shot fired by cannon and culverins was in battering stonework to weaken it, while rounds fired from culverins and demi-culverins could be used more surgically to concentrate on weakened sections, and sakers aimed at the parapets of fortifications to 'annoy' the defenders.[53] This is explained well in a report of 8 July 1642, by the Lords Justices in Dublin (*Letters and Papers* 73) in which, amongst other things, they requested full cannon for the Crown forces, saying

We now find the great necessity of sending hither two whole cannon . . . and if we have not other ordnance then culvering the service will be much the more difficult and the longer in doing, and the expence and charge of powder will be much more, by reason of the many shotts that culverings are forced to make before they can make a breach, whereas cannon cleares and rents the walls at first and leaves them so shaken as a few shotts afterwards from the culvering breakes down all that the cannon had shaken:

In addition to battering walls, shot also caused structural damage inside fortifications. One tactic to maximise this, and used particularly in Europe, was to heat cast-iron shot to red heat just prior to firing, so that if it ended up in contact with flammable material it would start a fire (e.g. *Compleat Gunner* cap. XIV, 11; Hughes 1969, 51–52).

Although in the earlier seventeenth century, artillery usually was less important in battles than in assaults on fortified places, the effects on infantry and cavalry could be terrible to behold.[54] George Creichtonn, chaplain to the regiment of the Duke of Ormond, wrote of the effects of artillery fire on Confederate troops at the battle of Ross in Wexford in March 1643 (Gilbert 1882, II, 258), saying

. . . they did see what terrible work the ordnance had made, what goodlie men and hors lay there all torn and their guttes lying on the ground, arms cast away, and strewed over the field.

One can only imagine the effects on the first ranks to break into the Blackwater Fort in 1597 if the depiction of enfilading small arms and cannon fire in Plate 22 is in any way accurate!

While cannon balls of all calibres could wreak appalling havoc amongst troop formations, some forms of ammunition were specifically designed as anti-personnel and anti-property munitions. Cannon could be used to fire case- or canister-shot, a container filled with fragments rather like modern shrapnel or with lead bullets.[55] Another form of shot consisted of two iron balls joined together by a length of chain, hence the name 'chain shot'. It was normally deployed by seaborne gunners both to destroy the rigging of an enemy vessel, as well as an anti-personnel munitions,[56] although as with canister shot, could be used on land. Thus, for example, Roger Boyle (*Art of War* 57) wrote that

> *I think it very advisable on the flanks of every Bastion, to have the Cannon of it, which is next to the Curtain, still loaden with Chain-shot, and so pointed, as when it is fired, the Chain-shot may cut off all the Ladders, which on an intended surprised by Scallado* [=escalade]*, may be fastened with iron Crooks to the top of the Parropet* [=parapet] *of the Curtain. The City of Geneva was once preserved by this Caution . . .*

Both types of ammunition saw use during the siege of 1689, with Jacobite troops using chain shot against the Butcher Gate defences. Mortars hurled hollow spheres – shells – usually of cast iron, filled with powder. And it was the mortar that caused more casualties and damage to buildings in Londonderry in 1689 than any other weapon.

Cast-iron shot was generally supplied from central stores, although it was not uncommon for gunners on both land and sea to cast round shot into moulds made specially for use when immediate needs had to be met (e.g. Simmons 1991). This practice required little skill compared with the casting of ordnance. Such munitions as canister shot would have been produced by specialists commissioned by the Ordnance Office. Some cast-iron round shot was produced in Ireland, including at Kilrea, County Londonderry (Annesley Malley *pers. comm.* 2005), and at the ironworks of Richard Boyle at Cappoquin, County Waterford. Sir Thomas Wentworth claimed in 1634 that he could provide shot 'at one-sixth less than what the King now pays.' (*Cal. SPI* 1633–1647, 84, 3 November 1634), possibly obtaining it from the works at Ballynakill, County Laois.

4 GUNNERS' ACCESSORIES

Ordnance required some form of carriage both for transport, as well as for when it was to be fired and this, in turn, required skilled carpenters and blacksmiths. Finally, when the cannon, its carriage, and the powder and shot were assembled, a number of accessories were needed so that it could actually be fired. Apart from anything else, a gun had to be loaded onto its carriage, and this required an A-frame structure (Fig. 9) of the type illustrated, for example, by Norton and Hexham (*Gunner* 119; *Art Military* 11). The generic term for a device to lift and position a cannon was a 'gin' or 'gynne', and an inventory of 1627 for Culmore (Table 3) includes a 'gynne, 2 ropes, one block head, one gynne pole', this quite probably being the one supplied in the consignment delivered to the castle in 1620 (p. 212).

It is fascinating to compare the illustrations by Norton and Hexham (published in 1628 and 1643 respectively) with a picture of British army ordnance at Ebrington Barracks, Londonderry, sometime at the end of the nineteenth century (Plate 40). As can be seen, some 300 years after Norton described lifting gear, the same simple A-frame was still in service.

An illustration from the 1684 work *Les Travaux de Mars* by Mallet (Plate 41) shows gun crews in action, complete with tools for loading. Powder was not simply poured down the barrel of the cannon, but was packed in weighed quantities into bags made from cloth such as canvas or paper[57] (referred to as 'cartridges' or 'cartouches') to be loaded. This was done with a small scoop or shovel of non-ferrous metal to avoid creating sparks. Also used were brass or tin measures called 'cases of plate' which held the right amount of powder to fill the appropriate cartridge for each type of gun, and allowed charges of powder to be carried round safely.

Getting the powder right down the barrel was done using a ladle made of copper, non-ferrous metal being used to ensure against accidental striking of sparks (Fig. 10). The powder charge was put on it, turned over in the barrel to drop it into place and withdrawn. A rammer was then used to put the shot and wadding in place. Since the powder was in a bag, it was necessary to burst this to allow it to come into contact with the priming powder when this was ignited. A thin spike or 'pricker' was another essential accessory. After a gun was fired, it was good practice to assist with cooling, by draping wet material over the breech. There were always some smouldering residues from the powder bags and wadding, as well as burning particles of powder, and trying to recharge without first

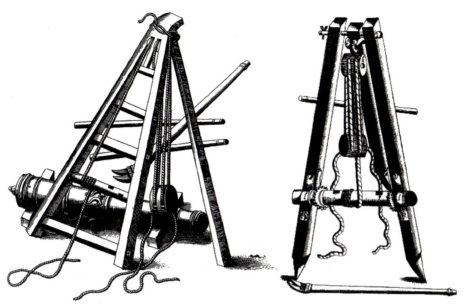

Fig. 9 Lifting gear for cannon (from *Gunner* facing p. 118 and *Art Military* 12).

clearing the barrel and dousing any sparks using a 'sponge' – a sheepskin, often wrapped round the ramrod – was not a good idea, and so a sponge and water bucket were vital.

As John Smith noted, particles of burning powder adhering to the wall of the bore, or lodged in honeycombing, could cause premature ignition of the next charge to be loaded. Should it be necessary to remove an unfired charge, the gunner needed a 'worm' or 'wadhook', a long wooden pole with two metal prongs, twisted into a spiral, which was inserted and twisted in the barrel to pull out remaining debris. Some twenty-nine 'worms, ladles and sponges' are listed as being in the ordnance stock of Culmore in 1627 (Table 3). Ladles, sponges and wadhooks accompanied at least those cannon sent in 1642 by the cannon sent by the Grocers,

Plate 40 British army ordnance with A-frames at Ebrington Barracks, Londonderry, c. 1900.

Ironmongers and Vintners (Table 8). The 1660 inventory for Londonderry (Appendix A14.1a) ends with 'Item Three old Demy Culverin Ladles one saker Ladle four sponges, 1 worme'.

Casting flaws would have been evident on the outside surfaces, but obviously were difficult to detect inside the bore and so a tool called a 'searcher' was employed. This comprised a long rod with a head with sprung points that was inserted into the bore and turned. The points sank into any soft area of honeycomb, leaving traces on them when the searcher was withdrawn.[58] Thus, it is interesting to note that one of the costs to the Grocers Company[59] was for 'searching' the demi-culverins sent to Londonderry in 1642 (Table 8). However, as noted above, searching was not a one-off operation after the cannon was cast,

Plate 41 Gun crews firing, loading and cooling their cannon (after Mallet 1684).

Chapter 2 – The Historical and Technological Backgrounds to the Cannon

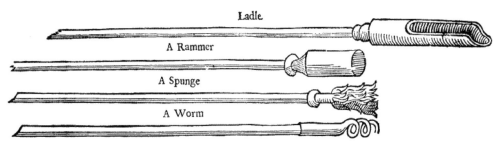

Fig. 10 Gunners' accessories (after Moretti *Treatise* Fig. 34).

but evidently throughout its life was an essential part of the routine of the gunner.

Another difficulty for gun crews was that while there were distinct calibres – and thus diameters – of ball, there were also significant variations within the products of different foundries. Thus, no gun crew could afford to be without a set of shot gauges, a series of rings which they could use to grade the shot supplied to them, and also check that the balls were truly spherical. The question was not whether a ball would be too big to fit, but rather that it would be too small! A degree of clearance between the shot and the bore – known as 'windage' – was essential, usually with the diameter of the ball being between 1% and 5% smaller than that of the bore.[60] Even before they reached Londonderry in 1689, the Jacobites had problems with their shot since, according to d'Avaux (*Négociations* 221)

Le desordre n'a pas esté moins grand dans son artillerie, car de cent cinquante boulletz qu'on a envoyé, il ne s'en est trouvé que vingt cinq qui pussent servir à une des pieces.

The chaos was no less great in his ordnance for, of one hundred and fifty rounds delivered, there turned out to be only twenty-five which could used in one of the pieces.

And the anonymous author of one tract published in June 1689, spoke of the problems encountered by Rosen with the poor quality of ammunition (*Letter from Dublin* 413)

. . . I hear the bullets both for field pieces and muskets were found to have been too big, which caused General Rosen to storm horribly.

It was also essential to know the weight of shot, as this was a major factor governing the size of the powder charge to be used. For this, a gunner required his 'rule'. Quite how precisely this was used to determine weight is not fully agreed, but Hildred (2003) argues convincingly for it being from a direct measurement of the diameter of the shot. Wooden shot gauges and gunners' rules were retrieved from the wreck of the Armada vessel *La Trinididad Valancera*, located by members of the City of Derry Sub-Aqua Club who participated in its excavation (Flanagan 1988, 81–82).

To fire the cannon, a source of ignition for the priming powder was necessary and this was provided by a length of slow-burning cord impregnated with saltpetre, a 'match', which was often held at the end of a stick or linstock to put some space between the gunner and his gun. These were often personalised and ornately carved,[61] as with that from *La Trinidad Valancera* (Flanagan 1988, 80, no. 6.15) in which a short length of match survived. The gunner at the top of Plate 41 is touching off his piece with match held in a linstock, as are the gunners depicted on the ramparts in the storming of the Blackwater Fort (Plate 22).

5 SUPPLY AND DISTRIBUTION

Cannon, powder and shot had to be placed with the troops who would use them, and the logistics of supply and transport became, in itself, a significant arm of warfare. In England, the Office of Ordnance developed over more than two centuries, until the time of Elizabeth I whose Privy Council in 1569 consolidated and reorganised it into a centralised bureaucracy responsible for the management of all of the branches necessary to acquire, maintain and distribute ordnance and munitions where required (e.g. Fissell 2001, 43*ff*). Dealing both with weaponry for land and sea, the Office

– based in the Tower of London – sought to control the distribution of arms to royal arsenals, oversaw the production of and trade in weaponry, and had its own army of craftsmen responsible for maintaining the stock of the Crown. It even had its own 'ratkatcher' in 1639, one William Wixley (*NA* WO 49/75 f. 142v)! But high office was purchased,[62] and the primary production privatised, with individual contractors in the earlier seventeenth century striving to create monopolies, as did the Browne dynasty of gunfounders, and the powder manufacturers Sir John Evelyn, later Samuel Cordwell and George Collins (Edwards, P. 2000, 109). Although it is fair to say that often the technology and industry were often operating at the edge of what was possible, this seventeenth-century military-industrial complex suffered from the primary defects of its modern counterparts – corruption, incompetence and a tendency for suppliers to gouge the State for as much as they could – while senior officials of the Ordnance Office[63] could become wealthy on the proceeds of graft and kickbacks.[64]

An extension of the English organisation was the creation in the 1530s of an Irish branch, based in Dublin Castle.[65] The first holder of the title of Master General of Ordnance for Ireland was Sir John Travers who was appointed in January 1550 (*Lib. Mun.* II, 101), and records of this year refer to the 'edifying of an ordnance house' (*Cal. Pat. Close Rolls* I, 225), while in 1551, the appointments of

Thomas Elyot of Balrusk . . . to the office and "roome" of gunner with a fee of 20d a day, viz. 12d per day for himself and 8d per day for a man to attend him . . .

and of

Peter Fourde, clerk, to the office of Comptroller and Surveyor of the Ordnance artificers and workmen, for constructing, maintenance and reparation of the ordnance, artillery and stores within the castle of Dublin.

are noted (*Cal. Pat. Close Rolls* I, 234–235). The Master of Ordnance was responsible for ensuring not only an adequate supply of arms and armour for the troops, and for their maintenance, but also for provisioning and clothing.[66] And he was responsible for the oversight of the Master Gunner whose responsibility it was to ensure training and adequate standards of gunnery amongst Crown forces. His office controlled not just the distribution of weaponry and munitions, but from 1612 onwards everything from the surveying of fortifications[67] through to the supply of general provisions, food and clothing.[68] And the Irish ordnance office not only had its clerks and administrators, but also smiths, carpenters and even a horse-trace maker. On 5 November 1597, one John Miles (*Cal. Pat. Close Rolls* II, 435) was appointed to

the Office of Smith of her Majesty's Ordnance, with authority to make, repair and amend, when occasion shall require, all ordnance and other iron works in the realm; . . . Fee 1s a day and 8d for his man.

Just two examples relating to supply, include munitions to be sent to Derry (*Cal. SPI* 1509–1573, 317, 10 November 1566) for the ill-fated garrison of 1566–1567 (Appendix B)

Memorandum of a proportion of powder and other munition be sent from England to Col. Randolfe, at the Derry

and the requirement (*Ormond MSS* I, 321) of 12 January 1665

. . . To the master of the ordnance: To cause to be sent, with all convenient speed, to his majesty's garrison of Londonderry 50 barrels of powder with match and ball proportionable, to be laid up in store there.

The keeping of detailed accounts and inventories[69] was also a duty of the Ordnance Office, so that not only was the cost of supplies noted, but also that for transport, as in accounts (*Ormond MSS* 7, 197) for 22 February 1683

Charge for carriage of ammunition. 1683, February 22.
To Londonderry twenty ditto [barrels of powder] and ten of match £4 10s 00d

It can be seen from Tables 3–6 that the regularity of detailed accounts increased after the Restoration, while those inventories pre-1641 are usually sketchy.

Testing or 'proofing' was a crucial process to ensure that guns did not blow up when the attempt was made to fire them, and the post of Proof Master was established in the early seventeenth century to ensure that ordnance met official standards and were 'safe' to use. This did not simply involving firing guns to see if they survived, but also included the creation of the range and the 'carrying in of Earth and making up the Butts' (e.g. *NA* WO 49/75 f. 22v, debenture of 27 April 1638 to William Franklin). But even with such checks, references to guns exploding in use are not uncommon.[70] For example, in a deposition dated 21 July 1643, a Francis Sacheverell (Gilbert 1879, I(2), 546–548), who was taken prisoner to Charlemont Fort in Co, Armagh, deposed that he

> *did see one great iron piece ... which the said Owen caused to be charged to trie her against the steeple* [of the Protestant church] *before they would carrie her to Dungannon, wherewith she was burste and killed their gunner, whereat they were very sorry both for the loss of the gun and the man.*

Most proofing of guns produced within the sphere of Crown influence was done normally either on Tower Hill or at the Tower of London, or at the foundry itself (Brown 2005a, 43), and also at Millhall on the river Medway in Kent, where ordnance originating in the Weald was shipped upriver to London. However, there is at least one instance where guns manufactured in Ireland were tested at Kilmainham, outside Dublin. In 1633, Lord Deputy Wentworth witnessed the test firing of four iron minions there, noting (Knowler 1739, I, 163) that they were

> *very good, and doubtless as good Mine* [i.e. metal] *as is in the World, it casts the closest and smoothest, and with the closest Grain I ever saw, and the workmen are passing good:*

His papers also make passing mention of the proofing of 'some twenty iron minions', probably at Ballynakill, County Laois (*ibid.* 123). This, of course, is perfectly logical since it would have constituted a major cost to any founder in Ireland had it been necessary to send cannon to London for proofing. And this, of course, provides us with some evidence for some production of ordnance in Ireland.

Unfortunately, the records of where ordnance was to be sent within Ireland are most sketchy. Thus, although the Debenture Books of the Ordnance Office in Elizabethan times show annual purchases for, and transport of, ordnance and munitions to Ireland, they are usually unspecific over destination.[71] For example, in 1619 and 1621, the books record lists of munitions and other provisions sent 'into the Relme of Ireland' and to 'Dublin' (*NA* WO 49/48, ff 257–262 dated May 1619, and *NA* WO 49/50, ff 138–141 dated 7 August 1621). Later, the royal gunfounder John Browne (first of that name) received an order in December 1619 for three whole culverins and three demi-culverins 'for Ireland' (*NA* WO 49/48, f. 139r), but with no more detail of the end user. Given both that this is the period when Londonderry was being supplied with ordnance, and that up to at least 1642 Browne appears to have been the principal supplier of guns destined for Ireland – and for Londonderry in particular – it is a pity that we have no indication of a destination in Ireland, or indeed where these pieces finally ended up.

6 GUNNERS

Even with carriage, powder, shot and all accessories, cannon were not of the greatest use unless operated by skilled gun crews, and it was the task of the Master Gunner of the Office of Ordnance to ensure that forces deploying artillery included competent gunners within their ranks. In England, gunners were expected to have attended a course of gunnery at the Artillery Garden in London under the tutelage of the Master Gunner of England (e.g. Walton 2003). They were expected to be able to read and to work out their accounts, as well as deal with the complicated calculations involved in the gunnery of the time.[72] Thus, for example, most seventeenth-century manuals, like that of Robert Norton (*Gunner* 17*ff*) included a long section on arithmetic and geometry. The gunner had to be able to calculate the weight of his shot and know that of the charge to propel it, as well as the angles of elevation required for different distances.

A Master Gunner was an individual normally regarded with respect, but Thomas Cave who was described as Master Gunner of Ireland, was listed (*Cal. SPI* 1633–1647, 111, 30 September 1635) as not having received his *per diem* of 1s 8d since his appointment in 1623. No less a personage than Charles I ordered payment in full on 30 September 1635! Less drastic was the failure to pay two gunners brought to Derry by Sir Humphrey Covert in 1601 (McGurk 2006b, 163). *Lib. Mun.* II, 107, lists five Master Gunners for Ireland between 1604 and 1614,[73] and we know that specific provisions were made at different times for professional gunners at Londonderry, including one John Horne in 1601.[74] McGurk (2006, 133) identifies the two gunners who served Docwra at Derry as John Redworth and Thomas Brewton. An account of payments to the military establishment of Ireland of 1 April 1666, amongst other things lists all of the gunners employed in Ulster, at Londonderry, Culmore and Carrickfergus (*Cal. SPI* 1666–1669, 1 April 1666, 70: Table 6), with their total pay being £136 17s 6d. In negotiations with Lord Mountjoy, following the closure by the Apprentice Boys of the gates of Londonderry on 7 December 1688, one of the persons to be pardoned in the event of surrender was Alexander Watson, gunner (p. 88: Milligan 1951, 46), possibly the gunner listed in the military establishment for Ireland in 1687 (Table 6).

As we have seen, even guns of supposedly the same type could vary significantly in bore and length and, as William Eldred, Master Gunner at Dover Castle, wrote in his *Gunners Glasse* of 1646 (1646, a2)

The Gunner must observe three things, firstly to know his Peece, and secondly her execution, and thirdly the distance to the mark. Without this it is impossible ever to make a good shot, except it be by chance, as the blind man hit the crow.

Aiming a cannon accurately was not just a matter of pointing it in the direction of the target. Smooth-bore weapons, large and small, project a round ball that acquires a degree of spin as it travels up the barrel. Thus, as a pace bowler in cricket or a pitcher in baseball obtains swing, so the projectile will follow a curved trajectory that must be compensated for (e.g. Hall, B.S. 1997, 135*f*). Another factor is that the body of the cannon tapers towards the muzzle, while the bore is straight, something which is illustrated in Plate 42.

Here, the gunner is sighting along the barrel using a small sighting aid called a 'dispart' by William Eldred, to aim at his target,[75] and is making allowance for the taper. Different distances required different angles of elevation of the barrel, and a tool used to calculate this was the quadrant, the use of which was illustrated by, amongst others, the author of *Compleat Gunner* (Fig. 11).

An example of this can be seen in the engraving of the 1689 siege by de Hooghe (Plate 43). Over the last fifty years or more, there has been a fair degree of disagreement amongst scholars as to the level of accuracy over distance that could be achieved by a skilled gunner (see for example Hall, A.R. 1952; Hall, B.S. 1997, 134*ff*; Guilmartin 2003, 167*ff*), but it is clear that under the right direction, gun crews were capable of hitting many of their targets.

Hale (1985, 48) notes the importance of skilled (to which one could add 'and consistent') gunners – and the consequences of their lack, drawing attention to the resistance in 1571 of Famagusta to continuous bombardment by the Ottoman Turks, and to the failure of the English forces in 1591/2 to reduce Rouen, despite heavy cannonade. One can note too, for example, the contrast between the taking of Mont San Giovanni in 1495 by Charles VIII and the situation when the same artillery train failed to impress at Castel Nuovo in Naples (Black 2002, 38). In terms of defence also, gunners had to be reliable. John Beech, the gunner in charge of ordnance at King John's Castle, Limerick had a reputation for being neither a good shot nor reliable in terms of allegiance. His inability to hit his targets – 'he comonly shott over and was supposed to be corrupt' – was a factor in demoralising the defenders at the start

Chapter 2 – The Historical and Technological Backgrounds to the Cannon

Plate 42 Aiming a cannon (*Gunner* facing p. 97).

of the siege (Wiggins 2001, 99 and 117 note 23). At the battle of Liscarrol, County Cork, fought on 3 September 1642 (*Memorable Passages* 6–7), the inaccuracy of the artillery fire from both sides stood out

> ... on the left hand we placed our horse to counter theirs ... In this posture we stoode about halfe an houre, in which time they made fourteene shot at our horse, but without any execution, ours plai'd as fast upon them, and not with much better successe, for only one shot hit which slew five of them;

Owen Roe O'Neill brought his own expertise in gunnery to the conflict, personally directing fire in the assault on Portlester Castle, County Westmeath (Casway 1984, 87) when his own gunners failed to impress (Gilbert 1879, I, 71–72), and killing Lord Moore in the process with a direct shot.

Plate 43 Jacobite gunner using a gunner's quadrant to lay his mortar at the 1689 siege (see Plate 59).

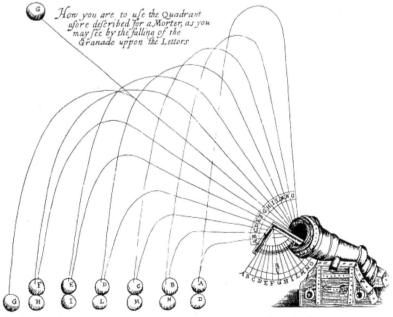

Fig. 11 How to use a gunner's quadrant (*Compleat Gunner* facing p. 84).

51

The Generall was not well pleased with his gunner, of he perceived that he shooted too high and did little hurte . . . the Generall did level . . . against Moore, gave fire, his aime was so neere, that he hitted him.

In the 1649 Siege of Londonderry, although both sides possessed ordnance, neither seems to have been able to make effective use of it. And even the mighty 'New Model Army' created by Oliver Cromwell was not immune to gunnery failures. On 25 August 1651, Lord Muskerry wrote to the Duke of Ormond concerning the sieges of Limerick and Galway (*Ormond MSS* I, 187). Concerning that of Limerick, he stated

The siege hath lain before Limerick these three months . . . they [Ireton's forces] *have spent, as I am credibly informed, 3,000 piece of cannon* [shot] *and 500 bombasses* [mortar shells] *against the town and have not done worth 5l. of hurt nor killed 7 men.*

Notes to Chapter 2

1 For a discussion of the further brutalisation of Renaissance warfare in Europe as a whole, see for example M. Roberts (1995, 27–29), Hale (1985, esp. 83*ff*) and Black (2002, 19*f*). For the British Isles during the mid-seventeenth century, see for example Carlton (1998), also for graphic descriptions of battlefield conditions during the English Civil Wars. For Ireland in general, see for example Whelan (2001, 320*ff*), for Ulster in particular Hayes-McCoy (1976, 131*f*) and McGurk (1997, 226–227; 2006,180*f*). Hale (1983, 335*ff*) discusses contemporary seventeenth-century European views of violence.

2 *De Jure Belli ac Pacis Libri Tres*. In Book III, Chapter 4 'On the Right of killing Enemies', he cites, amongst others, the strikingly modern view of Cyprian that 'Murder committed by individuals is a crime; when accomplished by public authority it is called a virtue.' (Kelsey 1925, 645*f*).

3 Although nowhere explicitly stated, it is clear that monarchs and military commanders – like their modern counterparts in the military-industrial complex – regarded cannon as providing the most 'bang for bucks' achievable!

4 Eltis (1998, 100*ff*) gives a somewhat less complimentary assessment of later sixteenth century English engagement with contemporary military developments on the Continent.

5 There are now no traces of the outer wall, although one angle may be preserved in a field boundary. Traces of the original surrounding ditch, well ploughed out, are visible in the surrounding fields.

6 The reader interested in the wars and warfare of this period in Ireland can consult profitably the works of (amongst others) Falls (1950), Hayes-McCoy (1969), Parker (1996), McGurk (1997), Ó Siochrú (1999), Fissel (1994, 2001), Lenihan (2001) and McKenny (2005), along with the papers in ed. Mac Cuarta (1993), ed. Ohlmeyer (1995), eds Bartlett and Jeffery (1996), eds Kenyon and Ohlmeyer (1998), ed. W.P. Kelly (2001), ed. Lenihan (2001), and references therein. For an all-encompassing treatment of Sir Henry Docwra's Lough Foyle campaigning, see McGurk (2006a). Wiggins' admirable study (2001) of the Confederate siege of King John's Castle, Limerick combines historical and archaeological evidence to great effect to trace the course of the action and the tactics of the protagonists.

7 Interestingly, an iron piece from the *Duquesa Santa Anna* was abandoned in 1588 by the Spanish commander Don Alonzo de Leiva at Kiltoorish Lake in County Donegal, as he and his men set off for Killybegs harbour. It was not retrieved by the English, but remained *in situ* until recognised by Sténuit in 1968 (1974, 120 and Plate 13). It is now in the collections of the Ulster Museum (acquisition no. BDSA 1), Belfast. According to an account by Thomas Fagan of the Ordnance Survey in 1857/8 (cited in Lacy 1983, 371), there were in fact three iron pieces at the site, two of which were lost in an attempt to get them across the lake in the eighteenth century. That the English did not recover them, coupled with the account of only one cannon having been removed from the *Duquesa Santa Anna* (Sténuit 1974, 117), indicates that the others came from another wreck and were brought

to augment the defences at the castle. We are most grateful to Winifred Glover, Curator of World Cultures, Department of Archaeology and Ethnography, Ulster Museum, for drawing this to our attention.

8 As depositions to the High Court of Admiralty show, salvage of ordnance (and other valuables) from wrecked vessels by professional divers, not surprisingly, was a regular occurrence (e.g. Appleby 1992, 146, deposition of Jacob Johnson dated 19 July 1622, also 194–195 and *passim*).

9 For treatment of the European arms trade, see for example the contributions in eds Puype and van der Hoeven (1996). The Netherlands was a major centre, and Fr Luke Wadding, Guardian of the Irish Franciscan Convent in Rome and a member of the Curia, deposited funds in a bank in Antwerp in 1642 for the purchase there of *matériel* (*HMC Franciscans* 128).

10 Following the outbreak of the Irish Rebellion, the Catholic Church made strenuous efforts to channel funds to purchase armaments for the insurgents. Thus, on 22 March 1642, Fr Luke Wadding, in a letter to Fr Hugh Bourke (*HMC Franciscans* 128), General of the Irish Franciscans in France and Germany, informed him that

> *I sent you 10,000 crowns to be laid out with the advice and concurrence of Don Eugenio* [Owen Roe O'Neill] *and Preston in artillery and munitions.*

11 In London, the founders Richard and Thomas Pitt worked at the Tower and leather guns were produced at Vauxhall, while the operation set up by some of John Browne's workmen in Oxford produced only small drakes, as did that in Edinburgh.

12 By the mid-sixteenth century, cannon were being cast regularly in two distinct metals – 'iron' which was what today we term 'cast iron' (an alloy of iron and carbon where the content of carbon exceeds 4%) and 'bronze' (an alloy of copper and tin in an approximate ratio of 80:20). Confusingly, contemporary documents speak of 'brass' cannon (brass primarily being an alloy of copper and zinc). This may have arisen from the fact that small quantities of 'latten' (an old word for brass) or of *lapis calaminaris* (calamine, ZnO) were often melted into the furnace charge, giving rise to zinc contents almost always less than 2% (e.g. Blackmore 1977, 408–409). And to add a little more confusion, at the end of the sixteenth century, the founder Peter Gill was described in Ordnance Office documents as 'one of her Ma^{ts} gonnefounders of Brasse and Copper Ordynance' (e.g. *NA* WO 51/1, Quarter Book December 1595, unpaginated). The author of *Compleat Gunner* noted that calamine (ZnO) or 'latten' (brass) was added to the melt 'to cause the Piece to be of a good colour.' (*Compleat Gunner* 3).

13 The delays in payments which become apparent in the late 1630s presumably reflect the mounting financial problems facing the government of Charles I.

14 *pace* P. Edwards (2000, 93–95), the sum of £1700 which he ascribes to construction costs appears, in fact, to refer to a cancelled bill for £1,688 4s 6d (*NA* WO 49/75, f. 220r) presented by Thomas Pitt for the casting of six cannon and subsumed into Browne's accounts, along with that from Browne for the remaining guns.

15 For a review of the evidence, see Scott forthcoming.

16 Richard Blacknall was one of the Members of Parliament for Queen's County (i.e. County Laois) in 1634 (*Cal. SPI 1633–1647*, 65, 14 July 1634: Kearney 1989, 233). In 1626, he and his partner Henry Wright petitioned the Crown for the right to mine ore, burn charcoal and smelt iron to produce ordnance (*Cal. SPI Addenda 1625–1660*, 74f). They had a royal patent to produce ordnance in Ireland as early as 1628 (*Cal. SPI 1625–1632*, 381, 26 August 1628). In 1631 Blacknall described himself in a letter to Lord Dorchester as '. . . not a mere idle projector, but have spent 26 years learning ironwork in Spain, France and Ireland.' (*ibid.* 619, 30 June 1631). As early as 1620, Wright had been in dispute with Boyle over the works at Cappoquin (*APC 1619–1621* 302–313, 15 November 1620). Interestingly, Wright and Blacknall were for a time in partnership with Sir Sackville Crowe who was one of the principal business rivals of the Browne family in the earlier seventeenth century (p. 203), and at that time Treasurer of the Navy. Blacknall

and Boyle had a major falling out, with Boyle having had Blacknall arrested in January 1628 for debts of £7000 which he claimed were owed (*Cal. SPI* 1625–1632, 306, 23 January 1628: *cf. APC* 1628–1629, 72, 31 July 1628). In the resulting case, Blacknall and Wright were exonerated and Charles I himself intervened in November of that year, instructing the Lord Deputy to renew their patent, and describing them as 'sole makers of iron ordnance, shot and bar iron in Ireland.' (*ibid.* 399, 8 November 1628). However, the case brought by Boyle dragged on until 1631, stretching the resources of the partners and preventing them from fulfilling their contracts. Thomas Wentworth became interested and, somewhat tactlessly, in August 1633 interviewed Blacknall in the presence of Boyle and Sir William Parsons '. . .to see what safety there might be to contract to him.' In a letter of 26 August 1633, to Lord Cottingham, he detailed what he perceived as the benefits of the proposals regarding the production of iron ordnance and recorded his decision that '. . . I will become a partner myself, and venture something of my own money, and draw others in wth more if I can.' (*Strafford* Str P3 ff 9–10). This is something that he apparently came to regret quite quickly, writing on 4 November of that year (Knowler 1739, I, 144–145) that

> *I am in great Streights how to carry my- self in the two Businesses of Ormond Plantation and Blagnal's* [=Blacknall's] *Works . . . The later is a continual Charge unto me, on my Faith I am two hundred pounds out of Purse enforced thereto; for if I did not by these Means keep the workmen together, they would all run away for want of Work, which were a great Pity; for, as I hear, they are the best of Christendom, and civil and orderly Men: they have cast some half a Score of Minions which, upon Trial, prove passing smart and fine Pieces.*

17 The illustrations in Fig. 6 are taken from eighteenth-century works, although the principles employed would have varied little from the period when the bulk of the Londonderry guns were cast.

18 A mould that had been dried imperfectly could also cause disastrous accidents. On 10 May 1716, at the recasting of a bronze gun, molten metal was spewed out from the mould with a force likened to that at 'the mouth of a *Vulcano*, or a little *Vesuvius*', resulting in the deaths of seventeen people, including the founder and his son (Blackmore 1976, 16). Amongst the injured was Col. Albert Borgard, Chief Firemaster, later to be the first Colonel of the Royal Artillery. The cause of this was certainly a build up of steam which created pressures that forcibly and catastrophically reversed the flow of the molten metal. This particular piece is still on display at the Arsenal at Woolwich.

19 There are no obvious references to a Proof Master at the Irish Ordnance Office, although this is hardly surprising given the lack of evidence for consistent cannon founding in Ireland. The dangers of honeycombing were not confined to early cast-iron ordnance. In 1882, the railway bridge at Inverythan in Aberdeenshire collapsed as a train was passing over, killing five passengers. The cause was determined to be the failure of a cast-iron beam which was described as 'honeycombed' (Day 2000).

20 *sensu stricto*, saltpetre is potassium nitrate (KOH), but until well into the seventeenth century effectively was a mix of nitrates including those of sodium and calcium. At the start of the seventeenth century, the East India Company began to import it in bulk from northern India where there were significant deposits.

21 De hÓir (1983, 85) noted an Irish manuscript of *c.* 1580 in which a marginal note gives a recipe for gunpowder '*Do dhenam an phúdair fhínailte ann so .i. seacht cuid don ts-alpíotar 7 énchuid don raibh 7 énchuid don ghual.*' 'To make fine gunpowder thus seven parts of saltpetre and one of sulphur and one of charcoal'.

22 This was rather a limited resource. Norton (*Practice* 142) regarded the efflorescence of saltpetre as

> *. . . The Naturall Salpetre is that which groweth in continued Mynes of the Earth, or upon Rockes, or in Vaults, on Walls, and by Natures worke becommeth perfect Salpetre, whereof the store is too small to depend upon.*

23 The process – highly unpleasant to modern sensibilities – involved the stockpiling and

subsequent processing of rotting organic matter, something that J. Kelly (2004, 33) graphically describes as 'the stinking fundament of the human environment'. For the underlying chemistry of the process, see B.S. Hall (1997, 74), while for detailed descriptions, see for example B.S. Hall (*ibid. 75ff*) and J. Kelly (2004). For a succinct overview of gunpowder production in England in the seventeenth and eighteenth centuries, see Crocker and Crocker (2000, 5*ff*) and Buchanan (2005).

24 For example, the anonymous author of *Compleat Gunner* recommended (p. 17) charcoal made from wands of hazel and ash, while Whithorne (*Certaine Ways* 28) offered willow.

25 Saltpetre was used as a source of nitric acid (HNO_3), as described for example in Book X of the *De Re Metallica* of Georgius Agricola (Hoover and Hoover 1950, 439*f*), also one of the constituents (with hydrochloric acid, HCl) of *aqua regia*. In his work *A Treatise of the Art of War* published in 1677, Roger Boyle, First Earl of Orrery (son of Richard Boyle, Earl of Cork, the great ironmaster and brother of Robert, one of the fathers of modern chemistry), paid little attention to ordnance. However, in one interesting paragraph (*Art of War* 57), when describing precautions to be taken against sabotage of gun batteries, he refers to a mysterious 'corroding liquor' that could be used to so damage guns that

> . . . *a Cannon so eaten into, that when she came to be fired, she split, and kill'd some of those she should have defended against the enemy.*

It is not impossible that the 'corroding liquor' was, in fact, either concentrated nitric acid or *aqua regia*. In this case, saltpetre could be seen as supplying the means both to power cannon and to destroy them!

26 The term 'mysterie' here means 'craft' and not, as is sometimes suggested in such contexts, the practice of some form of arcane knowledge. It derives from the Latin *misteria* 'craft, craft-guild' (Latham 1965, 299).

27 Buchanan (2005, 241) notes the fact that a goldsmith headed the manufacture of gunpowder in 1642 in Gloucester, the works there including a 'saltpetre house'. This is hardly surprising since goldsmiths evidently had their own reasons for being as familiar with saltpetre production as manufacturers of gunpowder.

28 The volume of timber used for barrel staves in the period Michaelmas (29 September) 1635 and Lady Day (25 March) 1640 may be seen from a report of 1641 listing the export from Ireland of 3,759,450 hogshead staves and 2,153,650 pipe staves, taxed at 4s and 3s per thousand respectively (*Cal. SPI 1633–1647*, 312, 1 July 1641).

29 'detonation' can be defined as a supersonic process of combustion where a shock wave compresses the material, raising its temperature to ignition point. Behind the shock wave the material burns, releasing energy that promotes the propagation of the wave. 'Deflagration' is a subsonic process where a flame front of hot, burning material heats adjacent, cold material past ignition point.

30 For a detailed description of the ways in which gunpowders of different grain size burn, see B.S. Hall (1997, 80*ff*).

31 e.g. Carlton (1992, 207–208); Hall, B.S. (1997, 69*ff*). Records of gunpowder makers blowing themselves up are not uncommon. Thus, for example, the powder mills of the East India Company at Chilworth in Surrey, erected in 1626, had by 1630 blown up twice (Crocker and Crocker 2000, 11). In 1649, the stock of a ship's chandler in Tower Street, in All Hallows, Barking, in central London, comprising some twenty-seven barrels, ignited as it was being packed. The resulting explosion demolished his premises and damaged All Hallowes Barking. It destroyed some fifty dwelling houses and a crowded pub, the Crown Tavern, with very many casualties (e.g. Kelly, J. 2004, 121). And on 24 January 1650, The Merchant Taylors gave £10 to assist its victims (*Merchant Taylors* CM 7, f. 337).

> *This day at the request of Mr. Alsupp a brother of this Company and one of the liv^{ry} on ye behalfe of divers poore people of the parish of Allhallowes Barking in Tower Streete London who suffered much losse and damage by reason of the late sudden and lamentable fire and devastacon by Gunpowder there. This Court out of a fonder compassion thereof doth freely give and bestowe the summe of Tenne pounds*

to be distributed amongst the poore people there towards their said losses.

The incident is recorded in a compilation by an anonymous author entitled *Tavern Anecdotes* which recounts casualties and survival in the disaster (*Anon.* 1825, 113–114).

The Great Companies were accustomed to keeping their own stocks of arms and ammunition and, prompted probably by the same incident, on 18 January 1650, the Court of Assistants of the Grocers Company (*Grocers CM* 4, f. 229), obviously concerned about storage and safety, decided that

Upon a sad consid^{er}acon of the lamentable accident wch lately happened by gunpowder, and the danger of frequent and careles goeing where it lyes, it is agreed and ordered that the Companies store of powder in the Turrett house being old and of long continuance there, shalbe wth as convenient speed as may bee put away and sold for the best advantage and benefitt of the Company, and the provision of a new supply deferred till the C^{oy} shall give further order and direccion about the same. And it is furth^{r} ordered that those members of the Companie or oth^{rs} that have any gunpowder in the Turret house upon their own accompt shall remove and take away the same from this hall and shalbe accordingly spoken to by the Beadle of this Company for that purpose. And that neith^{er} the Wardens nor Officers of this Company shall hereafter give leave or way for the lodging of any more gunpowder in the Turret house or elsewhere about the hall without the approbation and ord^{er} of this Court.

32 The report of Francis Sydenham, captain of the *Mary Rose*, to the Lords of the Admiralty (*NA* SP16/173, 25 September 1630) included his account of the incident

I gave order to the 7th Whelp to assist them and withall told him (Captain Cooper) that I would stand with the Dutchman a war to bring him under my command. In the meantime that I stood off with the Dutchman of war an unfortunate fellow went down to the powder room with a candle in his hand without a lanthorn and took hold of the powder and blew her up and she sank down in an instant.

We are most grateful to John Wassall for this transcription.

33 The version of his diary cited throughout this work is Thomason E.573[4]. Another is *Captain Henry Finch's Relation of the siege of London-derry, by the Scotch, Irish, and dis-affected English*. in Gilbert (1879, II(2), 440–446).

34 McGurk (2006, 134) draws attention to an order from the Privy Council of 1601 that those supervising the loading of gunpowder onto vessels should 'restrayne the use of taking tobacco in any of the ships wherein the powder and munition is loden', noting that this is perhaps the earliest recorded warning of the health hazards of tobacco! Smoking prisoners seem to have been a not uncommon hazard! On 4 July 1643, for example, a prisoner at the battle of Lansdowne, near Bath, let burning ash fall into an open powder barrel, resulting in the deaths of several Royalist officers (Gentles 1998, 136; Roberts, K. 2005, 76–77).

35 Lennon (1988, 8) puts the level of casualties into perspective by noting that the population of Dublin at that time was probably significantly less than 10,000 and that is thus likely that up to 1% of the population died in the blast – the equivalent of around 10,000 of the current population of the city! Explosions in arsenals could cause devastation in urban areas (Anon. 1875). And in Europe, 1654 was a bad year for accidents, with the arsenal at Gravelines in Belgium detonating, reputedly with very great loss of life, and the explosion at Delft killing at least one hundred – including the artist Carel Fabritius who died of his wounds – and injuring many. The devastation at Delft was captured in scenes by Egbert van der Poel, one of whose daughters may also have been a victim.

36 As with the catastrophe in Derry in 1566, *AFM* VI, 2252–2253 (*sub anno* 1601) repeats the theme of divine retribution for desecration of holy ground, this time an explosion at Donegal Abbey in 1601 which was occupied by English troops.

. . . the vengeance which God wreaked upon them was this, however it came to pass, viz; fire fell among the powder which they had in the monastery of Dun-na-n-gall for carrying on the war; so that the

boarded apartments, and all the stone and wooden buildings of the entire monastery were burned.

37 But forces loyal to the Crown too suffered shortages, as seen by the very limited supplies available to the defenders of King John's Castle in Limerick in 1642 (Wiggins 2001, 84–85). In fact, this was a general problem in the earlier seventeenth century, one that was not alleviated until significant quantities began to arrive from India by way of the East India Company.

38 Nicholas La Laloue or Lalloe directed siege operations under Thomas Preston at Duncannon Fort, County Wexford in 1645, famously described by James Touchet, Earl of Castlehaven, as the only genuine siege of his time in Ireland.

39 It is possible that this is the same 'Dr. Higgins' who is listed as an army 'Physitian' in a muster list of 1640 (*Carte MSS* I, f. 182r).

40 We are most grateful to Dr. Kenneth Wiggins for this transcription from the work entitled *A Relation or Dyary of ye Siege of ye Castle of Limerick by ye Irish from May 18 until June 23, 1642* and for the next reference, (taken from TCD MS 840) *John Rastall his relation to Mr Henry Hart* (Wiggins 2001, 51–52).

41 Porter had commercial interests in Ireland which included non-ferrous metals, and his family also held monopolies on the production of paper and soap. This latter is of interest, since potash was a common factor in the manufacture of both soap and saltpetre, and the company of which Porter was a part was charged in 1635 by the Admiralty of endangering supplies of saltpetre by buying up all of the wood ash for its soap making activities (Huxley 1959, 204).

42 Various sources, such as the tract (*Reasons delivered in Ireland against the cessation of armes there . . .*) railing against the Ormond Cessation of 1643, which claimed, more than a little optimistically (*Extracts* 6, article 11) that '. . . the Irish are every where beaten, they are distressed in Victuals and Ammunition.'), reinforce this impression. Another pamphlet, *A true relation of such passages and proceedings of the Army of Dublin*, published in August 1642, claimed on p. 3 for 14 July 1642

. . . it is credibly reported that the Rebels want powder in these parts [Co. Dublin] *which if our shipping guard the Sea that none come to them, we hope in God's mercy they will not be able to stand against us. But we heare that out of France a great store is coming to them.*

Hazlett (1938, I, 115–116) recounted the deception practised by O'Neill in setting up a fake powder works, complete with staff working away with useless ingredients, but with small amounts of real powder there to persuade visitors that his forces were not suffering shortages! The overall capacity to produce gunpowder in Ireland seems not to have improved much, right through to the Williamite war, since Le Comte d'Avaux (*Négociations* 279–280), felt it necessary to recommend that saltpetre be imported to Ireland to facilitate supplies to the Jacobites. However, the idea of making powder here was rejected by Commissaire Fumeron on the grounds that it would be extremely difficult not only to find sulphur, but also skilled persons to carry out the work (Mulloy 1984, III, 85–86).

43 Against this is the comment by Borlase (*Execrable Irish Rebellion* 75) that at Kilrush 'the enemy lost all their powder and ammunition', suggesting that one barrel is perhaps an underestimate of the stock of the insurgents at the battle.

44 It is likely that Wentworth was the author of a bill to limit the import of powder to Ireland, which received its second reading on 1 April 1635 (*Commons J. Ireland* I, 113). Restrictions had been in place as early as 1625 (*Cal. SPI 1625–1632*, 53, no. 157, 29 November 1625), and in 1627, the then Lord Deputy, Viscount Falkland, reported to the Privy Council that the prohibition of private trade in powder, creating a monopoly, had made the State a profit and was a policy to be continued (*ibid.* 239, no. 692, dated May 1627). But not just policy in Ireland, but also Crown monopolist policy in England caused shortages (e.g. Edwards, P. 2000, 109). As a result, in 1638, illegal powder making was bringing in as much as 2s 6d per lb (*Cal. SPD 1625–1649*, 595–596). In October 1637, William Felgate was buying powder from the Tower at 18d per lb (*Cal. SPD 1637*,

491, 21 October 1637), and on 22 May 1639, it was ordered that the price of corned powder sold from the Tower of London be fixed at this price, the same price as it was delivered by the Royal gunpowder maker, Samuel Cordwell (*Cal. SPD* 1639, 204). Interestingly, in his submission to the Lord Deputy of 11 March 1639, concerning his budget for mounting an invasion of Scotland in support of the Crown (e.g. Stevenson 1981, 28*f*), Sir Randall MacDonnell quoted a price of 20d per pound (*Strafford* Str P24–25, no. 270), suggesting a possible touch of profiteering! Probably quite unrelated, in the first half of 1642, Scottish merchants were selling powder at Culmore between £8 0s 10d per barrel and £10/cwt – around 19.3–21.4d per lb (Carte 3, f. 333; *True and Breife Account* 301).

45 *The Irish Rebellion*, first published in 1646 by the violently anti-catholic Temple, was responsible for the dissemination of grotesquely over-inflated figures of Protestant deaths at the hands of the insurgents in the period 1641–1643. Unhappily, despite results to the contrary from modern research by objective historians of both traditions (e.g. Barnard 1997, 178*f*), Temple's figures of 200,000–250,000 deaths are still bandied about by those whose preference is the comfort of mythology over fact. Nevertheless, his was by no means the only contemporary broadcast of horror, and pamphlets such as *Ireland's Lamentation* by Sir Chidley Coote, disseminated the view that the slaughter of Protestants was totally one-sided. The barbarity of the insurgents was depicted as encompassing cannibalism '. . . they eate their children, and one another, a just judgement of God upon them for their cruelties.' (*Extract* 3). But the credibility of tales of atrocity upon atrocity by those specifically identified first as 'Catholics' did feed on memory of such events as the massacres by the Duke of Alva in the Netherlands in the period 1572–1574 (and reported back by soldiers from the British Isles serving abroad) and more recently, horrors such as the slaughter of up to 20,000 of the inhabitants of Magdeburg by the Imperial and Catholic League armies on 31 May 1631.

46 In the deposition, taken from some inhabitants of County Kilkenny, it is stated that

One Uncil Grace, and divers other Rebels in Kilkenny, broke open the doors of the Cathedral Church there . . . and made gunpowder in St. Patrick's Church, and digged up the Tombs and Graves in Kilkenny, under colour of getting up molds whereon to make Gunpowder:

47 Unfortunately, the original is badly damaged, and the microfilm taken from it cuts off areas of the margins, so that it in many cases it is not possible to read all of a line with confidence.

48 The medical profession had a strong representation – on the Confederate side at least – in powder production in the years immediately after the outbreak of the Irish Rebellion. In addition to the references above, Hunter (1981, 68) has drawn attention to one Dr. Hodges who was pressed by Sir Phelim O'Neill into attempting (unsuccessfully) to make gunpowder at Charlemont at the end of 1641.

49 *pace* Canny (1997, 58), these cases of desecration at Kilkenny, Limerick and Waterford seem to bespeak not only of hatred, but also of a total lack of emotional involvement. The remains of the dead had ceased to have any human connection, having been reduced to the status of the rest of the organic detritus from which saltpetre was produced normally.

50 One Thomas Thornhill was accused of undermining the foundations and causing the collapse of the pigeon house belonging to the Dean of Windsor! It is not impossible that the proposed act for Ireland of 1640, to 'preserve pigeon houses' (*Commons J. Ireland* I, 128), was motivated in part at least by a desire to protect this potential source of saltpetre.

51 Thus, for example, in July 1669, John, Lord Robartes, was instructed (*Cal. SPI* 1660–1662, 16 and 1666–1669, 741) as part of his new duties as Lord Deputy, that he should

. . . forthwith take an account of the state of our military stores and, for better providing them, shall endeavour to set up the art of making gunpowder in Ireland.

indicating that no significant production had yet been established to meet Crown needs.

52 Thus, for example, stone balls were still in use by the Spanish when ships of the Armada were wrecked on the Irish coast, as witnessed by

finds from the vessels *Girona* and *La Trinidad Valancera* (Flanagan 1988, 74). And nearly one hundred years later, stone shot were still to be found in the Londonderry magazine.

53 A ball from a demi-culverin is preserved embedded in the stonework at Caher Castle, County Tipperary, presumably dating from the siege in 1599 by the Earl of Essex (Johnston, D.N. 1976, Plate 9 facing p. 114).

54 The carnage that could be caused by artillery in set-piece battles is discussed in Carlton (1992, 139*ff*). Just one example of how devastating it could be is the description from the Battle of Newbury by Captain John Gwynne of 'a whole file of men, six deep, with their heads struck off with one cannon shot of ours.' (*ibid.*). The capacity of human beings to set their ingenuity to devise more effective ways of maiming and killing each other may be seen yet again in the inventory of projectile types for cannon of the sixteenth and seventeenth centuries (e.g. Blackmore 1976, 191*ff* ; Caruana 1994, 192*ff*).

55 The gunner in King John's Castle, Limerick, was killed in an incident while preparing to use canister shot against the besiegers (Wiggins 2001, 114). John Smith (*Sea Grammar* 66) described it as

> any kind of small Bullets, Nailes, old iron or the like . . . to shoot out of the Ordnances . . . these will doe much mischiefe.

56 *Grammar* 86 gives a brief definition of different types, concluding with the statement that

> All these are used when you are neere a ship, to shoot down Masts, Yards, teare the sailes, spoile the men, or anything that is above the decks.

57 Earlier in the seventeenth century, 'cartouche' or 'cartridge' referred to canister shot.

58 John Smith in 1627 described the method of 'searching' a gun for honeycomb thus (Goeller 1970, 75):

> Honicombed . . . and you may finde if she be Taper boared [sic: honey combed] either with a crooked wyer [wire] at the end of a long staffe, by scratching up amd downe to see where you can catch any hold; or a light candle at the end of a staffe, thrust up and down, to see if you can see any fault . . .

In 1643, Robert Norton (*The Gunner's Dialogue* 76) described

> . . . within her Chase or Chamber, put in an usuall Searcher, made with two or three springs with points like great pinnes heads, bending outwards, which being bended together with your hand, untill it will enter into the mouth of the Peece and that put up to the bottome of the bore, and turned round in the motion of pulling it in and out of the chase; so if any Honycombe be therein, it will stike with the points . . .

59 Possibly also the Drapers, but the terms used are less clear (Table 8).

60 Writing in his *Platica manual de artilleria* published in Milan in 1592 (tr. 3, cap. 30, fo. 15), Luis Collado ruled that shot should weigh 90% of that which would fit snugly into the bore, i.e. some 3% smaller in diameter than that of the bore. In his *Grammar*, John Smith gives a similar figure, while Lewis suggested that windage used by English gunners at the time of the Spanish Armada allowed between 1% and 5% depending on calibre (Lewis 1961, 39).

61 Smith (*Grammar* 88) describes the Lint Stock (linstock) as

> a handsome carved stick, more than halfe a yard long, with a Cocke at one end to hold fast his Match, and a sharp spike in the other to stike it fast upon the Deck or platforme upright.

62 Thus, for example, in 1684, Lord Mountjoy, purchased the office of Master of the Ordnance from Lord Longford for the sum of £3500 (*Carte MSS* 169, ff 66–67: *cf* Tomlinson (1974, 67*f*).

63 The maritime counterpart was the Navy Board which for the start of the seventeenth century, has been described as a bastion of sinecurism (e.g. Peck 1990, 106*ff*). One of its principal officers in the later part of the century was the diarist Samuel Pepys who, in his time there, amassed a significant fortune through graft. How he achieved this is well described by Tomalin (2003, 139*ff*), who shows just how commonplace – and accepted as such – were bribes and blackmail.

64 See also, for example, Ashley (1994) on the Ordnance Office in the time of Elizabeth I. We are most grateful to Dr. John McGurk for drawing our attention to this reference. Also see Tomlinson (1974) for the later seventeenth and early eighteenth centuries.

65 *Lib. Mun.* Part II, 101*ff* lists many of the offices of the Irish Ordnance office.

66 The first two appointees (Sir John Travers and Jacques Wingfield) appear to have been both corrupt and incompetent and it was not really until the later seventeenth century that the state of affairs was improved (e.g. Brady 1996, 148*ff*). The problems for the Irish Office of relying on supplies from England is graphically illustrated by the increasingly frantic letters from the Lords Justices in Dublin to the Lord Deputy during the early months of the Irish Rebellion in November 1641 to mid-1642, when supplies of all sorts – from shoes to cannon – were in desperately short supply (*Ormond MSS* II *passim*). Towards the end of the century, however, it was operating reasonably efficiently, at least in terms of the accounting procedures that led to the production in 1684 of nationwide inventories.

67 One of the first Surveyors General of Fortifications was Sir Josias Bodley, appointed in 1612.

68 Thus, for example, the complaint in 1599 about a defective axle for the carriage of a full cannon at the siege of Caher Castle (*Carew MSS* 1589–1600, 303) came under his purview.

69 *cf.* the detailed inventory of cannon at Londonderry in 1660, Appendix A14.1.

70 Perhaps the most famous casualty of a bursting cannon in Britain was James II of Scotland, who was killed at the siege of Roxburgh in 1460 by 'ane misformed gune that brake in the shuting' (ffoulkes 1937, 23). The gunner at King John's Castle, Limerick in the siege there in 1642 was John Beech, who was killed in circumstances which suggested at the time that he was actively trying to sabotage one of the guns of the defenders (Wiggins 2001, 115). Since three others were killed also, and several wounded, it is not impossible that the piece failed when fired, although an accident with canister shot is also a strong possibility.

71 But see the situation regarding cannon for Docwra's 1600 expedition – pp142-143.

72 For example, see A.R. Hall (1952, 59*ff*).

73 William Willams 1604, Thomas Horne 1606, William Holland 1609, Richard St George 1612 and Thomas Cave 1615. Cave petitioned the King on 30 September 1635, claiming payment of 1s 8d per day from 1623 onwards, totalling arrears of £319 19s 3d (*Cal. SPI* 1633–1647, 111).

74 R.J. Hunter *pers. comm.* 2005.

75 Eldred described the 'dispart' as
a little stick or straw of the length difference between the height of the mouth and the mettal, and the cylinder and its mettal; and fasten it upon the muzzle-ring with wax or clay – and this is called the Dispart.
The differences in 'heights' refers to that between the diameters of the breech and muzzle.

Chapter 2 – The Historical and Technological Backgrounds to the Cannon

CHAPTER 3
The City Defences and the Use of Cannon

Londonderry was one of the very last cities in Europe to be provided with a surrounding protective stone wall. As can be seen from its width and the positioning of angular bastions, it was designed with the specific purposes of mounting artillery and providing a defence against it.

In the days before gunpowder artillery, the primary requirements of fortifications were to enclose a suitable area with walls that were thick enough to withstand missiles hurled by aid of the forces of gravity and tension, and high enough to make scaling ('escalade') as forbidding a prospect as possible. Breastworks at the tops of ramparts protected the defenders from arrows and shot from small arms, while defenders could make the lives of the besieging forces a misery. Fortresses and fortified towns which were well-provisioned and garrisoned could sit out protracted sieges, while attackers either had to rely on overwhelming force, starvation, the fear of the defenders of reprisals in the event of the site being taken or, of course, treachery. And, while conducting a siege, attackers had to be assured of the supplies required to sustain them and to be able to defend themselves against forces sent to relieve the beleaguered. But the advent in the later fifteenth century of batteries of cannon as an effective instrument to breach massive stonework brought about radical changes that altered thinking in military architecture throughout Europe and the British Isles.

The introduction of the siege train as a 'weapon of mass destruction' is usually attributed to Charles VIII of France, in his Italian campaign of 1494–1495. Near its start, his artillery – comprising some forty pieces of heavy ordnance – took mere hours to breach the walls of the frontier fortress of Monte San Giovanni, one which had once endured a siege of seven years, allowing his troops storm in and massacre its garrison (Duffy 1979, 9*ff*: Hale 1985, 48).[1] In Ireland in 1426, John Fitzgerald, sixth Earl of Kildare, remodelled his castle at Maynooth in the old style. With its thick curtain walls, and massive gate and central keep, it epitomised the ideals of pre-gunpowder fortification. Later, a degree of new building took place to allow for the placement of cannon, including those 'borrowed' by Kildare from Dublin. But in the early sixteenth century, a regular supply of heavy artillery had reached Crown forces in Ireland (Ellis 1996, 130). Following the abortive rebellion in 1534 of Thomas Fitzgerald ('Silken Thomas'), son of the ninth Earl, the Lord Deputy, Sir William Skeffington, used heavy cannon to batter the castle into submission, before executing the garrison, despite the promise of pardon. And in 1649, the guns of the Cromwellian army took less than a day to breach the walls of Drogheda. Thus from the earlier sixteenth century, from Italy to Ireland, the advent of artillery with its power to break down even the strongest stone walls, forced military architects to develop ways of countering the new menace.[2] The Londonderry stone defences, preceded by earthen versions, represent the new style which allowed for the deployment of and defence against artillery.

The primary aim of a force attacking fortifications with cannon – fortifications which the defenders were determined to hold – was to create a breach wide enough to allow troops to pour through *en masse* to overwhelm the defenders. Even the most massive of plain stone walls would give way to a protracted battering from heavy ordnance, as witnessed by Maynooth and Drogheda, almost a century apart. Mediaeval stone fortifications also were not designed for the mounting of cannon and required modification. Earth could be banked up on the inside of walls ('rampiring') to provide a platform for guns, but this exerted outwards pressure, in fact often weakening them. Just prior to 1534, the ninth Earl of Kildare had bolstered the defences of Maynooth, adding gun platforms and, at the time of Skeffington's assault, no less than sixty of the defenders were 'gunners' (Kerrigan 1995, 22), although certainly the majority were using small arms. Similarly, the walls of Drogheda had been rampired prior to 1649, but in each case, to no avail. To withstand determined assault by cannonade, defences had to be strong enough to absorb a battering from projectiles which, in the case of those fired from the largest ordnance, impacted with energies not far removed from those of the modern demolition wrecking-ball. And if defenders were unable to respond effectively, most surrendered or fled with little or no fight. Thus in May of 1601, for example, what is today known as 'Harry Avery's Castle' at Newtownstewart in County Tyrone surrendered to Sir Henry Docwra after bombardment over a day by 'two Iron peeces', probably of saker or demi-culverin calibre, while in June of that year – after what he admitted to be a day of ineffectual use of a demi-cannon – the garrison of Enagh Castle, just outside Derry, fled when the piece was redeployed close to the Walls (*Docwra* 57–58).

As will be clear, when faced with cannon, two of the main problems with 'traditional' mediaeval fortifications were that their high profiles presented a very large target, while their stone walls were poor shock absorbers. This was addressed – as one part of an evolutionary process in military architecture that took place across Europe in the sixteenth and seventeenth centuries – by lowering significantly the heights of walls to give gunners less to aim at, and by providing a thick bracing of earth[3] behind the stonework to dampen the shocks of missile impacts. When suitably paved, these provided a wide and solid base for platforms on which ordnance could be mounted, something lacking in the earlier, unmodified fortifications. The thick parapets afforded also a reasonably protected platform for the gunners, as well as those using small arms.

But lowering the heights of walls reduced the ability of defenders to see what was going on directly below and to bring fire to bear on an enemy, rendering them more vulnerable to a sneak attack. In fact, to depress steeply the angle of ordnance on the walls (so-called 'plunging fire') to deal with attackers trying to exploit this not only exposed the gunners to enemy fire, but also made their own fire less likely to be accurate. Further, a miss would embed itself harmlessly in the earth, unlike low-angled fire, which was aimed at troop formations deliberately to skip off the ground on impact, rather like a flat stone on water. Too steep an angle could even lead, embarrassingly, to shot rolling out of the barrel before the piece could be fired! Thus, another key development was that of the bastion. Both round and rectangular bastions were tried initially, but these still left dead ground, and it was the angular bastion which proved to be the answer (e.g. Pepper and Adams 1986, 3–7; Kerrigan 1995, 5*ff*; Duffy 1996, 25*ff*; Parker 2001, 10–11). This was an arrowhead-shaped projection that provided a good all-round field of vision, as well as firm platforms for cannon and men with firearms, thus allowing the whole of the perimeter to be swept with fire during an assault (Figs 12 and 13) or attempts to mine the walls.

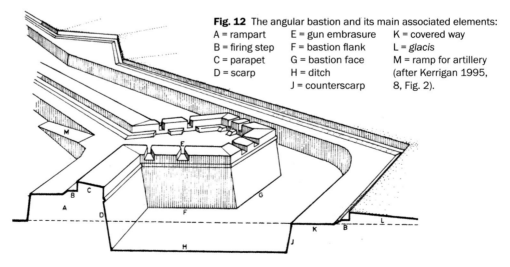

Fig. 12 The angular bastion and its main associated elements:
A = rampart   E = gun embrasure   K = covered way
B = firing step   F = bastion flank   L = *glacis*
C = parapet   G = bastion face   M = ramp for artillery
D = scarp   H = ditch   (after Kerrigan 1995,
   J = counterscarp   8, Fig. 2).

Chapter 3 – The City Defences and the Use of Cannon

Fig. 13 Comparison of the fields of fire from angular, round and square bastions. Stippled areas represent ditches, while shaded areas indicate 'dead ground' that could be exploited by an enemy. Solid lines show lines of fire (after Pepper and Adams 1986, 4, Fig. 1).

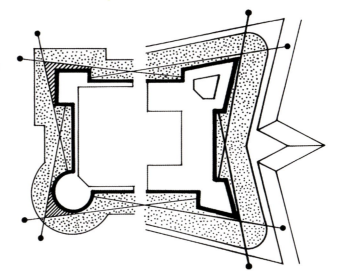

Developed in Italy in the later fifteenth and earlier sixteenth centuries, the general combination of a low, thick wall, an outer ditch and projecting angular bastions – the *trace italienne* – became the standard basis of design for fortifications across Europe and the British Isles.

The angular bastion appears in Ireland in the late sixteenth and early seventeenth centuries, in new fortifications built by both English and Irish, the earliest example being the English fort at Corkbeg, by Cork harbour, which dates to the 1550s (Kerrigan 1996, 35*ff*). Certainly, by the time that Sir Henry Docwra landed in Lough Foyle in 1600, the construction of defences designed around the use of artillery was commonplace (*ibid*. 55–56, and Figs 28 and 29). This is seen well in a map of 1607–1608 showing the fort erected by Sir Richard Hansard at Lifford, County Donegal (Plate 44).

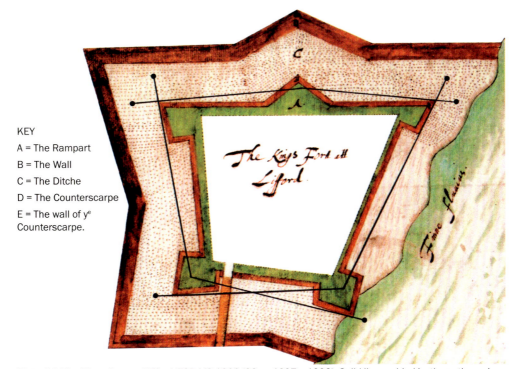

KEY
A = The Rampart
B = The Wall
C = The Ditche
D = The Counterscarpe
E = The wall of y^e Counterscarpe.

Plate 44 *The Kings Fort att Lifford* (*TCD* MS 1209/30, *c*. 1607 – 1608). Solid lines added by the authors show lines of fire.

The development of the City defences

From the first arrival of English forces, the topography of the area around Derry dictated the positioning and layout of defences. When Sir Henry Sidney arrived in 1566, *Doire Choluim Cille* was, for all practical purposes, an island (e.g. Lacy 1990, 24). Originally, the Foyle branched to the south of the site with the main branch on the east, and a narrower stream on the west, with the two rejoining to the north (Plate 45). Although by the sixteenth century, the western branch was no more than a stream flowing through an expanse of bog, there was still a fairly formidable barrier, one which could only be crossed at a couple of places. In his memoirs, Sir Henry Docwra (*Docwra* 43–44) described the land in 1600 as

> ... the River called loughfoyle encompassing it all on one side, and a bogg most comonlie wett and not easilie passable except in two or three places dividing it from the main land.

There has been regular criticism of the defences, in particular of the siting of the City, since at least 1627, when a commission of enquiry, set up to investigate charges of negligence brought by Sir Thomas Phillips against the City of London, observed (*Phillips MSS* 98) that

> ... we have viewed all the fortifications in and about the City of Londonderry, and we do find a stone wall of 20 foot high, well rampired with earth and 8 bulwarks, but the City itself is so ill situated that both the walls, houses and streets lie open to the command of any shipping that shall come to the harbour, and also to divers hills about the town ... so as in our judgement it is not a place of defence nor tenable if any foreign enemy should come before it.

although this assessment was not shared by Colonel William Legge in 1662 (Appendix A15), who wrote

> Londonderry ... is a City strongly seated by the great River of Lough foyle compassing the same on three sydes making a Goodly Capacious and Safe Haven. That ground to the landward is Marrish [=marsh] and with small cost may be cutt to bring the water quite round the towne. It is walled

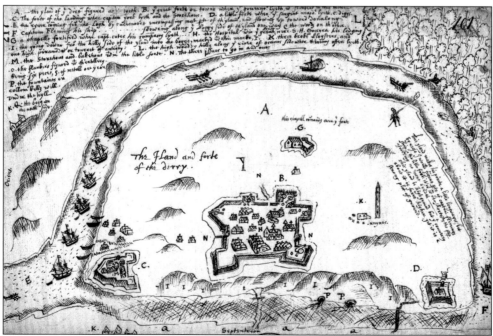

Plate 45 Sketch of the layout of *The Island and forte of the derry* in late 1600, showing the defences established by Sir Henry Docwra. It is labelled 'A Platt of LoghFoyle broght over by Capt. Covert' (*NA* SP 63/207, pt VI, no. 84/1).

with a good Stone wall, Rampired and well Flankered in Good Repair, the Defects nothing considerable, save the want of Platformes upon the Bullwarkes.

In 1685, another Thomas Phillips, Captain and surveyor (*Ormond MSS* II, 318), wrote

Londonderry hath the appearance of a place of strength, it being capable of being made an island . . . the hills overlook it so on all sides, that there could be no rest for the inhabitants, whensoever an enemy should attempt it . . . His Majesty hath a magazine there, with a small quantity of stores, as many as are fit to be trusted in a place of such indifferent force or strength to secure them; this place being incapable of being fortified, and having no way of relieving it but by the river, out of the Lough Foyle, which is commanded by a small fort called Culmore.

And references, often contemptuous, to the standards to which the defences were built have been common since then. Thus in the nineteenth century, Lord Macauley when writing of the defeatism (or treachery or incompetence, or all three) of the Governor, Robert Lundy, in 1689, noted (Lucy 1989, 28) that

He [Lundy] *seems to have thought resistance hopeless: and, in truth, to a military eye, the defences of Londonderry seemed contemptible . . . the parapets and towers were built after a fashion which might well move disciples of Vauban*[4] *to laughter; and these feeble defences were on almost every side commanded by heights.*

The initial attitudes of the French and their military charged with taking Londonderry were indeed scornful. But Macauley was on the right track (*ibid.*) when he commented, albeit with characteristic condescension, that

Indeed, those who laid out the city had never meant that it should be able to stand a regular siege and had contented themselves with throwing up works sufficient to protect the inhabitants against a tumultuary attack of the Celtic peasantry.

A European perspective on the defences, and how they required modification to bring them up to contemporary standards, is provided by plans (Plate 46: Milligan 1996, 161*ff*) drawn up around 1705 by the French engineer Jean Thomas (*Memoires*) for extensive outworks and a remodelling of sections of the existing walls.[5] Had this been undertaken, the whole form of the modern City could have been so much different.

And it should be noted that although there was a surrounding ditch for much of its circumference,[6] overall the counterscarp and outworks that were a feature of seventeenth-century fortifications in Europe were lacking. Many scholars today believe that the walls themselves would have been breached rapidly by concerted fire from a 'real' siege train (Paul Kerrigan *pers. comm.* 2007). Also, the narrow parapets did not provide the level of protection to those on the walls afforded by contemporary European fortifications, thus requiring the defenders to make extensive use of gabions. Nevertheless, one of the defenders in 1689, Joseph Bennett (*True and Impartial Account* 27–28), considered that the defences were proof against cannon fire, describing them as comprising

. . . the outward Wall being about 21 or 22 Foot high, and of a great thickness, and the inward Wall rising as high or near the heighth of a man of the outward Wall, and between these two, Earth filled up in the middle, whereon eight or ten men may walk in Breast, so that no Gun can batter it to make a Breach to storm.

The truth must lie somewhere between these two seemingly irreconcilable sets of views. The besiegers of 1649 and 1689 both had cannon, but singularly failed to breach the walls. But then in neither case did they have the calibres or organisation required to subject the walls to the expert ferocity of bombardment that could be unleashed by the siege trains at the disposal of Cromwell or Vauban with their heavy-calibre ordnance. Perhaps we can best draw the conclusion that while the walls would not have withstood the rigours of warfare in seventeenth-century Europe, in the Irish context they were found to be more than fit for

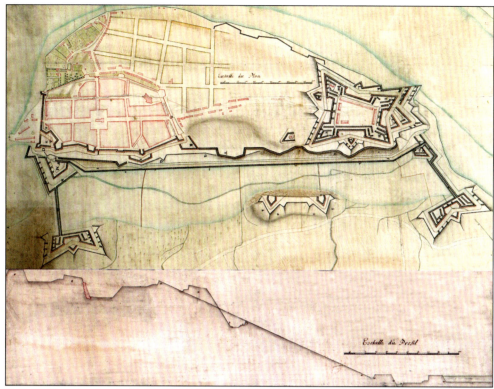

Plate 46 The extensions to the City defences as proposed by Engineer Jean Thomas (NA MPHH 1/282).

purpose. Again, this is not an original view, but one expressed by Jean Thomas (*Memoires* f. 1) who wrote (anticipating Macauley) that while Londonderry had a simple circumvallation that would have been of little use against an enemy with serious artillery

> ... *par un Ingenieur Moderne elle etait neanmoins dans ces termes la Suffisante pour lusage auquel elles fut destinee cest a dire pour couvrir la Colonnie des Bourgeois contre les Insultes des Raparies et des Papistes envieux et mecontens* ...

> ... for a modern engineer it was nevertheless in these terms sufficient for the use for which it was intended, that is to say for shielding the colony of merchants against the assaults of rapparees and of envious and malcontent papists ...

Although, at the start of the seventeenth century, the Irish were acquainted well with gunpowder weaponry, they primarily employed small arms. It was not until the turmoil of the 1640s that they began to make any significant use of ordnance, and then not on a regular basis. Even in terms of the siege warfare with which many of its commanders were familiar from their continental experiences, Irish forces did not practice 'siege warfare' in the seventeenth-century European sense, except at Duncannon, County Wexford[7] in 1645, where what was described (Gilbert 1879, I(1), 103) as

> ... the verie best siedge that was yett in Ireland, most plentifull of all necessaries, both of pay, ammunition, shuttlers, all kinds of liquor.

was directed for the Confederate General Thomas Preston by the French engineer, Nicholas La Lalloe (p. 40).

In fact, the defences erected by Docwra, and those that followed were designed as fortified enclosures, surrounded by a protective platform from which both small arms and ordnance could be deployed against forces with little or no heavy firepower. Indeed, the Everard and Rookewood map of 1600 (Plate 45) illustrates the degree of primary threat recognised – that posed by small arms as opposed to cannon (Plate 47), and there is the annotation

> ... this yland is high ground but yᵉ countrey about it is farre higher, yet it is a strong plot of ground.

showing that the engineers in 1600 perceived no problems from Irish batteries sited overlooking the town. To be sure, had the same layout on the same general topography been located in one of the many seventeenth-century theatres of war in Europe, the City would have been taken with comparative ease by any of the commanders of the time. But the fact remains that the defences remained unbreached from their completion in 1618, having on two occasions at least been subject to significantly more than 'a tumultuary attack of the Celtic peasantry'! In fact, when looking at the criticisms from 1627 onwards in their entirety, the constant theme is that the plans to provide provisions and *matériel* were so inadequate as to render the City likely to fall through lack of armaments and munitions and/or starvation (as, of course, so easily could have happened in 1689), rather than assault.

The development of the fortifications can be considered as falling into five phases, three minor, two major. First there are the short-lived works erected on the highest ground by Sidney in October 1566 and rendered indefensible by a gunpowder explosion in April 1567. No trace survives, and they almost certainly had little lasting influence on what came after.[8] Second are the defences established by Docwra, creating new bastioned earthworks and modifying existing structures, and exploiting the topography both to provide access to the river on the east, and to use it and the morass to the west as natural lines of defence. As with the Sidney defences, no archaeological traces have survived above ground (Brian Lacey *pers. comm.* 2005), although maps produced from 1600 onwards show the original as the nucleus of the later Plantation fortifications. These were taken in the short-lived rebellion of Sir Cahir O'Doherty in 1608, falling to treachery and not through force. The impressive stone walls that we see today were constructed at the cost of the City of London between 1614 and 1618 and represent

Plate 47 Exchanges of small arms fire at Derry as depicted on *NA* SP 63/207 Part VI, 84.i, dated 29 December 1601.

the third and main phase of building. Fourth – and although short-lived and obscure, but significant in its own right – is the construction of a citadel sometime around 1653, probably a stone-built structure, incorporating one wall of the Cathedral. Fifth and last, we must take into account the outworks constructed in 1642 and again in 1689 prior to the Jacobite siege, since they represent extensions, albeit temporary, of the main defences.

Sir Henry Docwra's fortifications

In 1600, in the sixth year of the 'Nine Year's War', the English strategy to confront effectively the rebellion of Hugh O'Neill included the establishment of a strong military presence, based in the Foyle estuary. The man chosen to secure the Lough Foyle area was Sir Henry Docwra, at thirty-six a veteran of campaigns in the Netherlands (Fissel 2001, 170) and Connacht (*Docwra* 7; McGurk 2006). He arrived at Culmore Point on 16 May 1600, with only one 'brass' demi-cannon and two iron culverins (*Docwra* 43), but by the end of the year, he had fortified Derry and established garrisons at Culmore, Dunalong, Lifford, Strabane and Elagh (Plate 48), and the number of pieces at his disposal had increased to at least twelve (Tables 3–4). It is clear from Plate 49, and from other contemporary maps, that Docwra designed these fortifications with the deployment of artillery and small arms firmly in mind (Fig.14). And when considering the number of cannon, we must bear in mind

that those pieces in outlying forts formed a part of the artillery park of the City.

Positioned at the mouth of the Foyle Estuary, on a spit of land narrowing the river, the fort of Culmore commanded entry from the sea. Its strategic position in controlling access to the interior is clear from the fact that it was deemed crucial to the defences of the area throughout the seventeenth century. When he landed at Culmore, Docwra described finding 'the Butt end of the old broken castle', probably belonging to the O'Dohertys. In the earliest maps, it is shown as having a central tower surrounded by a roughly triangular earthwork with bastions (Fig. 14a). In 1611, a brass robinet and one saker and two falcons, all of iron are recorded, while in 1627 between ten and fourteen pieces are referred to (Table 3). In step with the construction of the Londonderry Walls, Culmore was strengthened also by the stone facing of the rampart.[9]

Dunalong seems initially to have been the most substantial of Docwra's first outpost garrisons, as can be seen from a depiction on a map drawn in 1600 (*NA* SP 63/207, pt VI, no. 84.2: Fig. 14c) with five bastions and two 'yron' cannon. A roughly contemporary depiction (*TCD* MS 1209.14: Kerrrigan 1995, 51, Fig. 25) shows four bastions, two furnished with cannon, and a brewery at the

Chapter 3 – The City Defences and the Use of Cannon

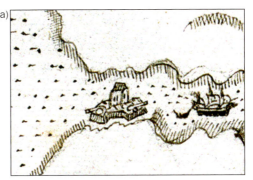

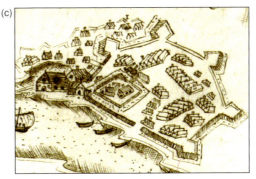

Plate 48 The fortified Lough Foyle landscape in 1601 (*NA* MPF 1/335/1).

Fig. 14 The primary fortifications constructed by Sir Henry Docwra c. 1600: (a) Culmore, (b) Derry, (c) Dunalong and (d) Lifford.

waterfront.[10] Whatever the actual form of the defences, the garrison certainly did fulfill its initial role as a centre for attacks on the surrounding countryside. It was overrun during the short-lived revolt by Cahir O'Doherty in 1608, and on 5 September in that same year, Josias Bodley (Buckley 1910, 63) described its condition as dilapidated, suggesting that 'the great entre[n]chment at Dunalonge is more fitt to be raised [razed] than repaired', while noting that it would not cost too much to bring back into service. Although there is an inventory listing five sakers at the fort in 1611 (*Carew MSS* 1603–1623, 95, dated 30 September 1611), Dunalong seems to have fallen out of use by the time that work commenced on the walls, and this evidently once-impressive fort is not referred to at all in the survey by Pynnar of 1618–1619.[11]

Lifford was provided with fortifications including one designed for artillery (Fig. 12d), and the map of *c.* 1601–1602 (Kerrrigan 1995, 51, Fig. 25) shows it as a triangular enclosure including a fort with two bastions and two probably earlier Irish forts. Subsequently, Sir Richard Hansard built the King's Fort (Plate 44), and in 1610 Thomas Blennerhasset reported the presence of some 100 troops there (Gilbert 1879, I(1), 321). A report of 1611 (*Carew MSS* 1603–1623, 221) said of Lifford that it had

> *A good and strong fort built of lime and stone with bulwarks, a parapet and a large ditch of good depth cast about it on the river side . . . There is another small fort in the town, rampiered and ditched about.*

However, on 30 January 1621, The Privy Council wrote to the Irish authorities noting a report that the defences of Lifford were in an extremely bad way, but stating their conclusion that (as with other fortifications) they could not see any purpose in repairing them without strong justification (*APC* 1619–1621, 338: see also *APC* 1617–1619, 403). Nevertheless, in 1624 it was recommended that it be 'repaired . . . and made tenable.' (*Cal. SPI* 1615–1625, 512). It was evidently back in use and garrisoned following the outbreak of the Irish Rebellion, since Richard Winter (*Newes* 2) described the town as

> *wholly fortified with Trenches and Worked by the charges of the Major of Derry, some of the Merchants being out this way a thousand pounds.*

Strabane was garrisoned[12] and and appears on maps from 1600 onwards paired with Lifford, though depicted as smaller in extent. It is much less prominent in records than Lifford, seeming to have had troops there only intermittently after the early years of the seventeenth century. In 1642 it was overrun and had one piece of ordnance removed by insurgents.

The Plantation defences

An integral part of the design of the new City of Londonderry,[13] which received its charter on 29 March 1613, were the defences designed by Sir Edward Doddington, with the work carried out by a Londoner Peter Benson, and overseen at various times by Sir John Vaughan and Captains Baker and Panton (*q.v.* Loeber 1979). The brief for the walls has not survived, but the progress can be traced through several sources. In 1614, Sir Josias Bodley, Director-General of Fortifications in Ireland, reported that the old earthen ramparts had been demolished to make way for houses, while Alderman Peter Proby and Mathias Springham noted the purchase of 500 tons of lime for use in the construction of stone wall defences, and progress in the building work (Milligan 1996, 27*ff*). By the time that Nicholas Pynnar completed his survey, the report which he submitted on 28 March 1619 stated (*Cal. SPI* 1615–1625, 378–379) that

> *The Cittie of London Derry is now compassed about with a verie strong wall, excellentlie made and neatlie wrought, being all of good lyme and stone . . . and in everie place of the wall it is 24 foot high and 6 foot thicke . . . The Bullwarks are verie large and good, being in number 9; besides two halfe-bullwarkes, and in fower of them there may be placed 4 cannons or other great pieces, the rest are not so large, but wanteth verie little. The Rampart within the Cittie is 12 foot thicke of earth; all things are verie well and substantially donne . . .*

Eltis (1998, 80) draws attention to the mid-seventeenth century calculation that earthen ramparts 20ft thick (6.10m) were 'effectively cannon-proof'. With the thick external wall, earthen backing and inner stonework, the Londonderry defences can hardly be regarded as 'weak' in this regard. It should be noted also that the designers of the walls also allowed for a slight batter to the outer facing on most of the circuit, although nothing like as pronounced as those to be observed on contemporary European fortifications.

The map which accompanies the Pynnar survey (Plate 49) includes a wealth of detail.

Chapter 3 – The City Defences and the Use of Cannon

Plate 49 Plan of 'London Derry' of 1619 by Nicholas Pynnar (*TCD* MS 1209/22*).

One of the interesting features is that it shows the internal stone facing to the ramparts. Also, inside the walls, top right, is depicted a tower house with four cannon. This is the 'old castle', an O'Doherty tower house,[14] which existed on the site when Docwra arrived (*Docwra* 45), and which figures in a number of seventeenth-century illustrations of the period. On the Thomas Raven map of 1622 (Plate 50), it is marked by the letter 'O' and described as 'the ould Castle wherein the Kinges store is kept', in other words the magazine. Indeed, this area still preserves the name 'Magazine'. This indicates a flexible approach to the deployment of artillery, with the creation of a magazine and 'artillery park' from which cannon and munitions could be moved as required – either within the City or to and from outlying garrisons.

The absence of proper access ways to the walls – and there is no such indication on the Pynnar map – was one of the many criticisms made of the work of the City of London. On the Raven map, however, access ways leading to the bastions are indicated (Plate 51), the comparative sizes suggesting possibly four ramps and two stairways. However, we must bear in mind that this almost certainly is a blueprint incorporating existing structures with proposals for others.[15]

The names of the various bastions constructed at that time were recorded by Phillips (*Cal. SPI* 1615–1625, 367: Milligan 1996, 41*ff*). Later, in the aftermath of the outbreak of the Irish Rebellion of 1641, a contemporary account describes the steps taken to organise the defence of the City. A group of Captains ('The League of Captains') took responsibility for stretches of the walls, and one of them – Captain Kilner – was to take charge of the section 'from Master Wabions Bulwarke to Chichesters Bulwark' (*Doe Castle* 4; Simpson 1847, 68). Looking at the order in which the various sections were listed, Milligan (1996, 77) made a reasonable identification with the Water Bastion, otherwise known as the Governor's Bastion. He spent some time considering possibilities for the identification of 'Master Wabion', offering some interesting etymological possibilities including a possible link to the name 'Wappin, Wapping' which survives as Wapping Lane.[16] Who Master Wabion was and why he should have had a bastion named after him is unknown. However, an isolated entry in the accounts of the Vintners Company (*Vintners AC* 3, unpaginated accounts for 1620–1621) records under 'Extraordinary payments' £6 0s 0d given 'To Thomas Wabion for money by him disbursed formerly towards the Irish plantacon'. As far as can be determined,

73

The Great Guns Like Thunder

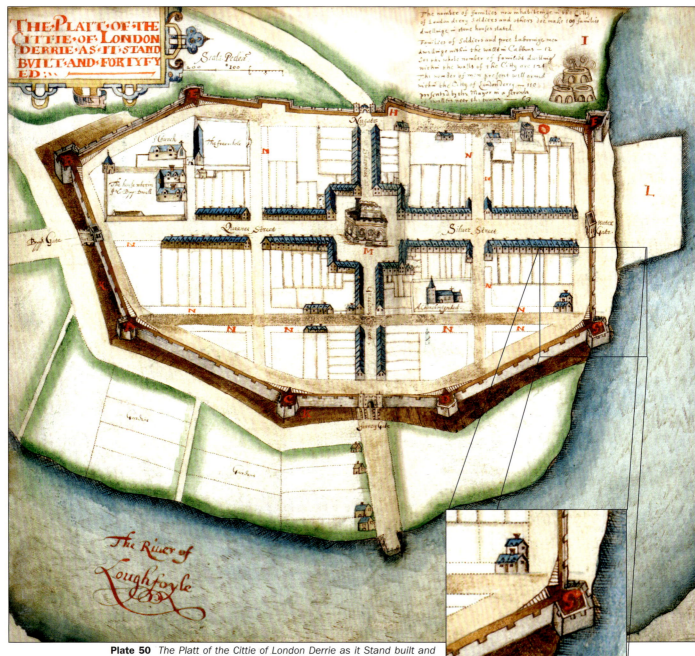

Plate 50 *The Platt of the Cittie of London Derrie as it Stand built and Fortifyed*, 1622, by Thomas Raven, for Sir Thomas Phillips (*Worshipful Company of Drapers*).

Plate 51 Access way to the Water Bastion on the Raven 1622 map.

Thomas Wabion was not a liveryman of the Vintners and we know nothing more about him, or for what he disbursed money.

The defences c. 1625–1689

The London Companies, those responsible for the building of the City, were criticised on a number of occasions for failing to provide the special platforms on the ramparts and bastions necessary for the placement of ordnance. The Phillips and Hadsor report of 1622 (*Cal. SPI 1615–1625*, 368) noted that

> *There wants great ordnance for the bulwarks, and platforms for them, and munition answerable.*

On 24 April 1624, the Lord Deputy, Lord Falkland, wrote to the Privy Council, noting that despite direction, the Londonderry defences lacked platforms for its ordnance (*Cal. SPI 1615–1625*, 487 no. 1199). The agent for the Londoners, John Rowley, had declined to initiate the work, stating that he was 'wanting power to dispose of the rents due unto the Londoner there without their allowance.' Although later in 1624 the City stated the intention to rectify this defect, in the Commissioners' report of 1627 (*Phillips MSS* 99) we find under Article 10

> *For now most of the bulwarks neither were nor are fit for platforms, and to make them fit and open to plant ordnance on the Wall must be altered, for in some places it is lower than the platforms, which we think should be speedily amended.*

There were frank exchanges with the Crown over such alleged deficiencies, but what is important is that these show that the disposition of cannon on the walls was being discussed by those familiar with the technology.

The repeated emphasis on the lack of proper platforms was not nit-picking, as sound platforms were essential for good performance. Writing in 1646, the Master Gunner William Eldred singled out the gun platform as a 'speciall thing' and declared (*Gunners Glasse* 33) that

> *The Platformes are to be well considered in a Castle or Fort, without the which, a man cannot make a good or perfect shot, and a man had as good have no peeces, as to do no good with them when we have them.*

In one of his many submissions critical of the Londoners efforts, Phillips referred to the desirability of ordnance being mounted on carriages with 'unshod wheels' (*Cal. SPI 1625–1632*, 85). Since the platforms on which they would rest were to be constructed from oak planks, it is easy to see how these could get torn up if carriage wheels had the kind of heavy studding shown in contemporary illustrations. But Norton (*Gunner* 103) illustrated a cannon on its timber platform (Fig. 15), and here the wheels are clearly studded, obviously for purchase.

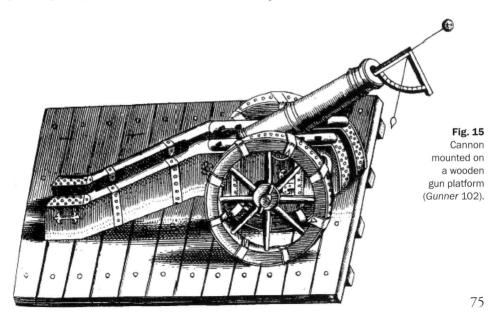

Fig. 15 Cannon mounted on a wooden gun platform (*Gunner* 102).

Eldred devoted most of one chapter to the proper construction of gun platforms, stating a preference for stone as opposed to timber on the grounds of both durability and cost (*Gunners Glasse* 33–36), backing up his case by giving costs for the laying of platforms at Dover Castle. Nevertheless, the theme of inadequate or non-existent stands for guns runs throughout seventeenth-century correspondence on the City defences. Thus, for example, in 1663, possibly on the heels of the report by Legge who noted in 1662 '... the Defects nothing considerable, save the want of Platformes upon the Bullwarkes' (Appendix A15), estimates were prepared for repairs (*Carte MSS* 54, f. 594), which included expenditure of £60 for 'Platformes new and to be repaired for 28 guns', while £20 was to be spent on providing platforms for ten guns at Culmore. And again, in October 1677, it was noted (*Carte MSS* 59, f. 636r) that

The walls in this Citty are in goode repaire, kept at the Citty's charge, but there is wanting stone Platformes in 6 bastions wch comes to 60^{li}: –:–

while two bastions at Culmore were without platforms.

In terms of the defences overall, effectively they were to stay in the form developed by the early 1620s, with minor additions such as guard houses and access ways to the ramparts. And, with the City of London having decided by that time that enough was enough in the way of expenditure that was not absolutely forced upon them, so the situation remained, although the walls themselves seem to have been reasonably maintained throughout.[17] The ongoing lack of willingness all round to lay out hard cash to maintain the defences is noticeable with the outbreak of the Irish Rebellion of 1641, where urgent repairs had to be initiated, and in the hurried outworks put in place in 1642 and 1689. And later, when the Council took over, the situation was not much better. There are regular references throughout the seventeenth century to the poor state of the ordnance and its carriages, even to a total lack of serviceable carriages. For example, in the 1660 inventory (Appendix A14.1a) carriages are described regularly as 'rotten'. In 1662,

Legge reported (Appendix A15) that there were no guns mounted at all, although an inventory of the same year did state that two demi-culverins out of a total ordnance complement of eighteen pieces were on carriages (*Carte MSS* 54, f. 517, 6 August 1662)! In 1666, Ormond issued a warrant to the Master of the Ordnance requiring him to find out how many guns required carriages and to have them made and sent to the City (*Carte MSS* 163, f. 5, 18 July 1666). The minutes of the Londonderry Corporation for July 1677 show an order for the repair of carriages (Appendix A17), and again in October 1677, standing carriages were required for twenty guns at a cost of £130 (*Carte MSS* 59, f. 636r).

Concerns over a possible amphibious assault by Dutch forces towards the close of the Second Dutch War (1664–1667) seem to have prompted some rapid consideration of the defects of the Londonderry defences, albeit tardy. In articles of a memorandum of June 1667 entitled *Considerations humbly proposed concerning ye Garrison of Londonderry* (*Carte MSS* 35, f. 510, 24 June 1667), possibly inspired by the raid on the Medway in the early part of that month when Dutch marines were landed on Canvey Island in Essex, the writer noted that

the present strength is insufficient to defend it . . . in time of imminent danger at ye gates, at ye Citadell, at Culmore . . .

recommending that 'ye guns be forthwith remounted.' And dating to a few days later, another report (*ibid.* f. 506, 28 June 1667), *Concerning ye Garrison of Derry*, stated

. . . here are not 240 souldiers (supposing that they doe stand to their Arms) to man ye Citadell, Culmore . . . neither is there one gun mounted (though so many brave ones lye on ye ground).

A recurrent theme in the charges laid in the 1620s against the City for poor performance was a lack of gunners at Londonderry and Culmore, as well as at Coleraine. In 1611, the Master of the Ordnance agreed to the retention of a gunner at Derry at a cost of 12d per day[18] (*Carew MSS* 1603–1623, 217). However, just as

Chapter 3 – The City Defences and the Use of Cannon

in the modern world, it was the bureaucrats who won out over the professional practitioners, and in 1611 the clerks were paid 2s 6d per day, while in the latter part of the seventeenth century at Londonderry (*Ormond MSS* II, 235), a gunner was still paid 12d per day and gunners' mates at the City and at Culmore got between 8d and 10d, although the clerk of the stores now was getting 20d! Indeed, the pay of the gunner in Londonderry in 1687 (Table 6) was given as £16 16s 0d *per annum*, fractionally over 11d per day, and that of the matross in Culmore at £14 *per annum*, just over 9d per day! One reason for this shortage of gunners may have been the pay differential with Dublin[19] where, in 1663, a gunner was being paid 3s per day as opposed to the 12d being paid in Londonderry (*Carte MSS* 165, f. 235r, 18 August 1663)!

The Citadel

Sir Thomas Phillips proposed a fortified market house for The Diamond, which some have seen as akin to a citadel. The depiction bristles with ordnance, (Plate 21), but the structure was never built. However, there was work carried out around 1653 towards the building of a citadel, at the same time that such structures were being built in Coleraine, Limerick, Galway and Clonmel, something that Kerrigan (1995, 100–101 and Fig. 51.7–9) notes as a feature of Commonwealth fortifications in Ireland. The inventory of the Londonderry ordnance of 1660 referred specifically to its being 'in the Citidell' (Appendix A14.1a), while the report on Londonderry by Colonel Legge in 1662 (Appendix A15) stated that

> *the late Usurpers made a Kinde of Cittadell including the Church and part of the Churchyard, making the Steeple the Magazine.*

It is perhaps a little strange that the magazine should have been placed in the most prominent target presented by such a structure, namely the steeple,[20] indeed that the citadel itself should have been placed here at all. However, we know that guns were mounted on top of the Cathedral during the siege of 1689 (p. 89), and that this is the highest point within the City, so that the choice of this area is perhaps not as odd as it might at first seem. A combination of the desires for a clear field of fire and a thumbing of the Republican nose at the old establishment – as suggested by Ormond (*infra*) – could well account for its positioning.

The various documentary references make no reference as to the form of the citadel. However, plans drawn up by Captain Thomas Phillips made in 1685 (including *BL* Maps K Top 54.31 and *NLI* MS 3137 no. 43) show the outline of an L-shaped enclosure of the Cathedral area (Fig. 16), superimposed over that of a bastioned structure[21] that enclosed the cathedral and used part of its northern wall as a face, also exploiting the Church Bastion to complete its defences. Another map (*BL* Maps K Top 54. 30) which bears a strong familial relationship to these, but is less finished in its detail, indicates the same configuration, as does a sketch map (*BL* Maps K Top 54.29) on tracing paper, which also includes a number of annotations in French.[22] Of particular interest are the annotations on *BL* Maps K Top 54.29 (Fig. 15) and *NLI* MS 3137 no. 43 (Thomas 2005, Plate 12; Ferguson 2005, 13) 'The Church formerly a Cittidell' and 'the church for merly a Citadel'.

One other map,[23] published in 1751, but in a volume that contains illustrations of places and events going back as early as the Battle of the Boyne in 1690 (Plate 52), shows virtually the same 'ghost' of the citadel as appears on the Phillips maps.

In 1664, Captain William Webb prepared a list of works on military installations, which included the record that 'The Citadel, in the City of London Derry, hath cost in building the sum of . . .' (*Ormond MSS* n.s. III, 155, dated 26 March 1664). No specific sum was cited, as for the citadels at Coleraine, Clonmel and Galway, although repairs to Raphoe and Doe Castles in County Donegal (Lacy 1983, 376*ff* and 356*ff*) are given as costing £25 and £100 respectively. A letter of 23 March 1656, from Webb[24] to Henry Cromwell refers to 'the finishing of the citadels of Londonderry and Coleraine' (British Museum *Landsdown MSS* 822, f. 212). There was a need to conduct repairs as shown by an order from Ormond to the City Governor, Sir John Gorges, dated 26 March 1664 (*Carte MSS* 165, f. 184v), instructing that the 'said ffort and

The Great Guns Like Thunder

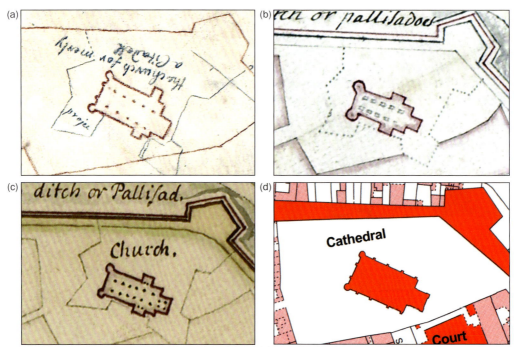

Fig. 16 Cartographic traces of the Londonderry Citadel: (a) part of a sketch map possibly by Jean Thomas, showing the outline of the former citadel with the legend 'the church for merly a Citadel'; (b) detail from *BL* Maps K Top 54.30, probably by Thomas Phillips and dating to 1685; (c) detail from *BL* Maps K Top 54.31, signed by Thomas Phillips and dating to 1685; (d) detail from a map of Londonderry (after Thomas 2005, Map 2) dating to 1831.

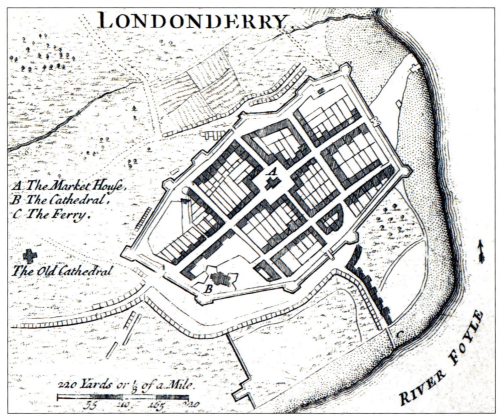

Plate 52 Plan of Londonderry from Tindal's *Continuation*, published in 1751. The Cathedral and Citadel are marked 'B' (*BL* Maps K Top 51.55).

Chapter 3 – The City Defences and the Use of Cannon

castle [of Londonderry] bee with all speed fully and substantially repaired . . .' That this work did not prove satisfactory would seem to be the reason for an Order in Council passed on 9 August 1667 (*Carte MSS* 35, f. 617) for its demolition.[25] And on 10 August the Marquess of Ormond, Lord Lieutenant of Ireland, issued a warrant for the work (*Carte MSS* 163, f. 139) which included the comment that

the citadel of Londonderry . . . erected by the late Usurpers so contiguous to the Church there, as that it is a great nuisance to the Church, and perhaps was purposely so intended by the erectors.

The order was duly acknowledged on 13 August by Viscount Dungannon (*Carte MSS* 35, f. 636), who assured Ormond that

In demolishing the Fort, not a stone of the Church shall be stirred . . . indeed, it were a pity it should, being the handsomest & best-built Church in Ireland.

However, the work seems not to have been carried out, since in 1669, the governor of the City, Sir John Gorges, requested (*Ormond MSS* n.s. III, 300) of Ormond

That your Grace will please to complete the citadel there [in Londonderry], *or give commands for its demolishing, it being now of no strength but rather an encouragement to an enemy to surprise it.*

There seem to be no references after this, so that it seems likely that whatever structure there had been was demolished in the early 1670s. Nevertheless, it must have been a fairly substantial structure with stone-faced walls like those of the City itself, which would explain why Phillips (and possibly Thomas) was able to trace its outline a number of years after it had been taken down.

The outworks

In 1625, Thomas Raven had offered suggestions for the strengthening of the Londonderry defences, including the construction of extensive bank-and-ditch outworks from a point upriver from the City (Plate 53), west-south-westwards to meet the river again downstream at the old fort known as 'Digges Fort' (shown as 'D' on Plate 47 dating back to 1600). This is accompanied by

The Ditch here intended, to be Cutt 20 foot wide 10 foot Deepe. The Earth to be Cast inwards wch will make A Rampier of good strength being made with some flankers.

This section of the defences is shown with a fortified gate with portcullis and a trail leading through to Butcher Gate. The text reads (after Milligan 1996, 66) 'A fort of stone with a drawbridge upon ye causey, the like moute be at Digges ffort'. A second line, this time seemingly of walling and from a point to the north-north-west of the Double Bastion, is shown running southwards towards the river, with a branch off to the north-east to meet the walls at the 'Lord Deputy's' bastion. The text being

A.B.C. The high Grownde lyennge nere wthout Bishopps Gate wch may be fortified with some outworks of earth as the nature of the Grownd will best afford.

These works were never built, although the lines of defences thrown up in response to the threat posed by the Jacobite army in 1689 follow quite closely the suggestions made by Raven. In fact, archaeological excavation suggests that some effort was made in 1642–1643 to enhance the defences by the addition of a substantial ditch in the area of Bishop's Gate (Logue and O'Neill 2006, 62*f* and 63, Fig. 6). The maps made by Captains Archibald Maculloch (Plate 57) and Thomas Neville (Plate 54), shown by Colonel John Mitchelburne (who commanded the defence of the City after the death of Governor Henry Baker), all have a substantial ravelin at Bishop's Gate, with outworks to the west and south cutting off the high ground around the windmill and a long section of the river frontage.

All of these works would have been of earth, and constructed by digging ditches and using the upcast for the ramparts (e.g. *Mackenzie* 34). While the ravelin depicted on plans from the period of the 1689 siege is usually attributed

The Great Guns Like Thunder

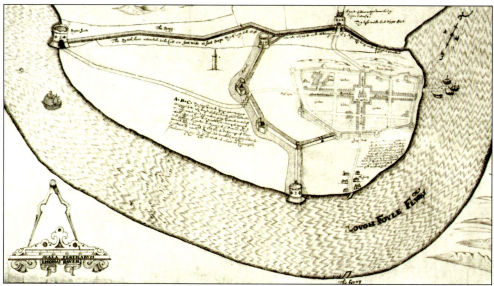

Plate 53 Part of 'A plot of ye cittie and iland of Londonderry' by Thomas Raven, 1625 (*TCD* MS 1209/22).

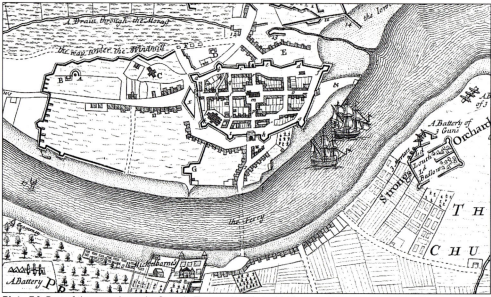

Plate 54 Part of the map drawn by Captain Thomas Neville in 1689 (*from Mitchelburne 1708*), showing the outworks constructed by the defenders, and two Jacobite batteries. The Windmill is marked as 'A', the ravelin by 'x'.

to Lundy (e.g. Logue and O'Neill 2006, 53), as part of works costed in a Royal warrant of 21 February 1689 (*Mackenzie* 54), each of the maps *BL* K Top 54.29-31, which predate this, indicate clearly a ravelin at Bishop's Gate. While it might have been intended simply to show where such a structure should be placed, it is not impossible that one had already been begun in 1685, or even that this was a much decayed defence left over from the period 1642–1649, or else associated with the construction of the citadel.[26]

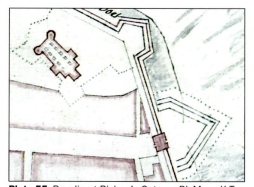

Plate 55 Ravelin at Bishop's Gate on *BL* Maps K Top 54.30.

80

Field pieces were deployed at the Windmill, the calibres not specified anywhere,[27] but the actions around the outworks primarily involved small arms and hand-to-hand fighting. Their primary purpose was to prevent the Jacobites from seizing the high ground that would have given them the opportunity to create batteries overlooking the defences from close enough to pose a very serious threat to the walls and those manning them.

The use of ordnance at Londonderry

A very early reference to cannon at Derry comes in 1589 from the then Master of the Ordnance in Ireland, Sir George Carew (*Carew MSS* 2, 18 March 1589), who described the recovery of a culverin that had formed part of the armament of the short-lived garrison there. He wrote to Lord Treasurer Burleigh

In my uncle Wyngfelde's last accompts I find that a culverin lost at the Dyrrey [=Derry], when it was burned, was afterwards recovered by George Thornton, now captain of the Queen's ship The Popingaye, *who delivered it to Sir Henry Sidney, then Lord Deputy, by whose commandment Sir Henry Pallmer, at the time his servant, transported the same in her Majesty's ship called* The Hare *into Bewmarrishe [Beaumaris in Wales], where it continued until late of years, as I understand, one William Thomas, a servant to my Lord of Leicester, carried the same to Carnarvan [Caernarfon in Wales], where it now remaineth. This culverin I think the officers of the Tower have not in their charge.*

We know that there were regular contacts between English troops and the forces of Shane O'Neill, including a decisive rout of the Irish, in which the English Commander Edward Randolph was killed. But although there is slender pictorial evidence for defences, including an angle bastion suitable for the mounting of ordnance (Appendix B), we seem to have no evidence for any cannon-fire being directed at the Irish at this time.

Despite the emphasis put in the articles of the Plantation and subsequent disputes between City and Crown on equipping the City with ordnance, the first occasion on which there was any significant defensive or offensive use of cannon was during the Royalist siege of the City in 1649. But of all of the pieces surviving today, it is possible only to point with certainty to that presented by the Fishmongers, nicknamed 'Roaring Meg' on account of the particular report, as certainly having been fired in anger at any time, and that during the siege of 1689! Prior to this, Sir Henry Docwra deployed cannon in the City, probably using the area around the 'old castle' (marked 'D' on Plate 45) as his artillery park and magazine, and as an area in which repairs were done. This facility would have been also the centre from which ordnance was drawn for deployment both at his other garrisons. Docwra never had the need to use any of the cannon at Derry itself, and in 1608, the defenders there and at Culmore had no opportunity to fire their ordnance against the forces of Sir Cahir O'Doherty.

The Irish Rebellion that erupted in October 1641 saw Londonderry with only four pieces of ordnance (calibres unspecified), something that occasioned great fear amongst the the citizens and defence forces, as can be seen from the tenor of letters sent to the authorities at the start of 1642. But despite the successes of the Irish forces across Ulster, it was their failure to capture Londonderry, Enniskillen and Dublin that weighed heavily against them in the longer term. Indeed, while the initial intention seems to have been for Sir Phelim O'Neill to take the City (Reid 1853, I, 292; Gilbert 1879, I, 510), he turned his immediate attention instead to the capture of Charlemont (which was seized through duplicity) and Dungannon. Although we have no explanation for this, it is quite probable that O'Neill felt that because of his lack of artillery, the City would be too difficult to take and that low-hanging fruit was more easily plucked. Certainly, the failure to take Drogheda can be put down to lack of ordnance and, although it seems most unlikely that he was unaware of the overall state of the Londonderry armaments, he evidently went for softer options.

Fifteen guns were sent over in early 1642 by the Great Companies (pp 121*ff*) and, added to the four already in the City, these would certainly have added greatly to the semblance of strength at a time when virtually all of the strongholds in Ulster had fallen to the insurgents. The immediate response of the garrison was to earmark houses outside the walls for demolition and orchards for cutting down, to afford clear fields of fire (*Doe Castle* 3). During 1642 and 1643, shortages of powder made the defenders nervous about their capacity to beat off a sustained attack so that, for example, they complained that they had insufficient powder for the Company guns (p. 126). Thus, on 10 January 1642, the Mayor wrote to the Lords Justices (*Letters and Papers* 3) and included the observation that

> *the whole county of Londonderry is now a prey to the rebels, and all burnt to the river side, so that the enemy braves us at the ferry, and we dare not spend a shott at him for fear of wasting our little proporcion of powder, which we keepe to defend the walls when we shall be assaulted;*

Such an attack never came, for it was the ability of the Laggan Army to clear the surrounding countryside of the enemy that was the key to the safety of Londonderry and of the refugees crowded into the City (Kenny 2005, 35*ff*). In the first years of the insurgency, the mobility and professionalism of these forces allowed them to clear a wide *cordon sanitaire*, and the use of powder weaponry was largely confined to small arms.

Docwra regularly moved ordnance in his campaigns, taking what he needed from his base in Derry, demonstrating his mastery of the tactical use of water-borne transport (McGurk 2005). But in 1642, Sir Robert Stewart and his fellow officers do not seem to have felt the same need for cannon, although it could be that a lack of suitable transport vessels may have been a factor. The movement of ordnance over land was notoriously difficult, as Sir Henry Bagenal found to his cost at the Yellow Ford in 1598 (Plate 57) when his army was forced to abandon the heaviest of his four guns, a saker, because it got bogged down.[28]

In June of 1642, when Sir Phelim O'Neill attempted to retrieve the situation by advancing on Londonderry with the twofold intention of defeating local forces and taking the City, his army was comprehensively routed by the forces under Stewart at the key battle of Glenmaquin, near Raphoe in County Donegal (McCarthy 2003). Here, neither side had ordnance, and it was musketry, cavalry and 'push of pike' that proved decisive. However, in June of the following year, when the Laggan army decisively defeated Own Roe O'Neill at Clones, County Monaghan, field pieces do

Plate 56 English troops trying to move a saker in the face of attacks from Irish skirmishers at the Battle of the Yellow Ford. Note top left, where the letter R denotes '4 barrels of powder blowne uppe' (from *TCD* MS 1209/35).

Chapter 3 – The City Defences and the Use of Cannon

seem to have played a part. On 23 June 1643, Stewart wrote to the Earl of Eglinton (*Extracts* 9–10) describing the battle, including the observation that

> ... *the rebels was routed, both Foote and Horse, and our light wings and Cannons did very good service.*

It seems likely that in this case, Stewart had taken some field ordnance from the City or from Culmore, possibly minions or falcons.

In fact, the first recorded use in anger of cannon by anyone at Londonderry itself comes in 1649. Following the execution of Charles I on 30 January of that year, the Parliamentarian Sir Charles Coote (the younger, later to be first Earl of Mountrath) seized and held the City and the fort of Culmore under siege by a coalition of forces loyal to the newly proclaimed Charles II. Rightly described by W.P. Kelly (2001a) as 'the forgotten siege', it nevertheless lasted longer than the celebrated siege of 1689 by around twenty days, although the comparatively small number of casualties on both sides is insignificant in comparison with the death-toll in the latter. A general sense of revulsion at the regicide brought together old foes – Presbyterian covenanters and Catholic and Protestant Royalists – while former comrades-in-arms became bitter enemies.[29] An account has been left by one of the defenders, Captain Henry Finch (*Finch Journal*), whose diary records events surrounding the siege.

As in 1642, Coote began his defence of the City around the end of March, later ordering the levelling of all of those buildings around the perimeter which might have provided cover for enemy forces,[30] and by a sortie in which he inflicted significant casualties on the besiegers at Carrigans in County Donegal (*ibid.* 2–3). Starting around 5 May, the investing forces dug trenches and 'laid close siedge to Derry within cannon shot of the town.' (*ibid.* 3), although it is not clear if, at this stage, they actually had any ordnance deployed. And throughout the middle of the month, they sought to develop these, but were subject to cannon fire from the defenders – '... making new works which our ordnance did annoy.' (*ibid.* 4). In the days and weeks that followed, there were regular skirmishes between the two sets of forces and, on 28 July, there seems to have been an assault on the walls which was repulsed, but Finch sheds no light on whether or not ordnance played any significant part (*ibid.* 12; Reid 1853, II, 126). In fact, the only mention of casualties caused by the guns of the City comes in his entry for 16 July (*ibid.* 10), in which he recorded that

> *They* [the besiegers] *vapoured very much all day, but approaching something too near, two of their horses, and one man was kill'd by one of our peeces of ordnance, which indeed is all the hurt I know they have done: some fault there is in platforms.*

The reference to faults in the gun platforms is of interest, since it would have been expected that such an experienced commander as Coote would have taken all possible steps to ensure that his cannon were ready for action – particularly in view not just of the perils of his own position, but also that of all of the Parliamentary forces in Ireland at that time.

According to Finch, the besieging forces were augmented in early July by the arrival of forces under Monro, bringing with them some twelve pieces of ordnance. However it is clear that at least some of these – if not all – were light field-pieces, most probably minions and small drakes, as Finch (*ibid.* 9) wrote

> ... *the enemy ... have brought to their league 12 peeces of ordnance, whereof they have shot three peeces, carrying a 4l. bullet, but being without effect, they have made no more use of them.*

In fact, this should not surprise, as in 1642 Monro himself, who had employed cannon in his campaigning (*Proceedings of the Scottish Army* 2–3), and earlier when he was defeated at the Battle of Benburb in 1646, described the great difficulties of transporting cannon in Ulster (*ibid.* 4), writing

> ... *for in this last march five of my carriages were broken, being but fielding peeces, which are the only Cannon for use in this service.*

Before coming to Londonderry, he had been involved in mopping-up operations against Parliamentary forces (McKenny 2005, 98), something requiring mobility. Presumably realising that these light pieces were of no use against the walls, the besiegers deployed them at a newly constructed fort – unsurprisingly christened 'Charles' Fort' – at the 'Knock of Ember' (*Finch Journal* 9).[31] Otherwise known as 'Crook of Ember', this is a strategically significant narrowing of the river, close to where the boom was constructed in the 1689 siege. The purpose of this battery was to interdict shipping bringing in supplies to the City, since the Royalist navy was unable to mount an effective sea blockade (McKenny 2005, 98). Coote ordered an attack by boat, but this failed 'after exchanging on both sides good store of shot both great and small' (*Finch Journal* 10). The last action involving ordnance came when two ships attempted a bombardment of Culmore. According to Finch (*ibid.* 12), the accuracy of both sets of gunners was highly questionable

> ... between them and the fort was discharged 80 pieces of ordnance, without any great hurt on either side.

As W.P. Kelly has noted (Kelly, W.P. 2001a, 45), unlike the situation in 1689, the fighting in the siege of 1649 was between professional soldiers, with commanders on both sides having seen action from the very start of the conflict in 1641 (also Miller 1996, 318*ff*). Since ordnance played a comparatively minor role in warfare in Ireland throughout the 1640s, its limited use at Londonderry is not surprising. It would seem that the cannon in the City, coupled with the mobility and aggression of the local troops, were sufficient to help to ensure that the besieging forces kept a respectful distance for most of the time, and so although not over-employed, their deterrent effect must be acknowledged. In the context of the overall military thinking of the 1640s in Ireland, it would seem that possession of numbers of heavy defensive ordnance within urban centres was in itself a significant factor in preventing direct assaults on their walls, with the quality of the gun emplacements and competence of the gunners being, perhaps, slightly lesser considerations.

In the period between the end of hostilities in 1652 and the outbreak of the war in Ireland between James II and William III, the situation evidently reverted to that of the neglect observed in earlier times of peace.[32] Cannon seem to have been removed from the City by Coote (p. 118), probably in 1650, and from entries in the inventories of 1660, 1662 and 1684 (Table 6), it is clear that there was a degree of complacency which allowed carriages and platforms to decay. The 1660 inventory for the most part indicates decay, as in the entry for the Mercers' demi-culverin 'one Demi-Culverin of Iron mounted but the Carridg and Wheeles Rotten' (Appendix A14.1a). This suggests also, that the life of a carriage would have been under twenty years. If those sent in 1642 were treated as per the method used by the 'paynter' Anthony Hancock for carriages for the Office of the Ordnance in 1639 (p. 126), it would not seem to have been particularly effective.

By the time that the famous action of the thirteen apprentices in shutting the City gates had put the inhabitants into direct conflict with James II, the inventory of armaments appeared to be as woeful as in 1641. The Reverend George Walker wrote (*Walker* 20) of the state of preparedness

> *It did beget some disorder amongst us, & confusion, when we look'd about us, and saw what we were doing; our Enemies all about us ... a Garrison we had composed of a number of poor people, frightened from their own homes, and seem'd more fit to hide themselves, than to face an Enemy ... no Engineers to instruct us in our Works; no Fire-Works, not so much as a Hand-Granado to annoy the enemy; not a Gun well mounted in the whole town ... we could not think ourselves in less danger, than the Israelites at the Red Sea.*

Evidently at least a part of these defects were remedied fairly quickly, since the defenders were able to disconcert King James and his forces with cannon fire as they approached the walls, reportedly killing one of his officers (e.g. *Mackenzie Narrative* 28).

As noted elsewhere, it is difficult to come to a conclusion as to how many cannon were

Chapter 3 – The City Defences and the Use of Cannon

available to the defenders in 1689. The evidence from surviving inventories is ambiguous, with figures varying with time – twenty-nine in March 1660, eighteen to twenty-five in 1662, down to twenty in 1685, then up to more than thirty (Table 6). The majority of contemporary and later accounts follow Walker who gave the number of guns as twenty, although at least one who participated in the defence, Captain Joseph Bennett (*True and Impartial Account* 28), put the number much higher (Table 6), noting that pieces were brought into the City from Culmore before it was surrendered to the Jacobites.[33] He described the deployment (*ibid.*) thus:

> There are four gates . . . a square in the centre of the town . . . in which Square the Market House stands . . . at every gate there is a gun planted within twenty yards . . . and four guns planted at the Market House, one directly against each Gate to clear the streets . . . There are nine Bastions about the Town, and three or four guns on each Bastion.

This account suggests a complement between thirty-five (three guns per bastion) and forty-four (four per bastion), although we should remember that guns were deployed on bastions where they were needed most at any given time. Further evidence for a figure in the thirties comes from a pamphlet[34] of 5 May 1689 (*Remarkable Occurrences* 1), reproduced 5 June 1689 (*Good News* 1) which lists the ordnance available as

> 24 mounted upon the Bastions of the Walls, upon the Tower of the Church two, and eight within the City, that is to say one at each Gate, and one at each corner of the Market-House in the middle of the City, and fronting each Gate.

a total of thirty-four. It is probable that Bennett as a military man recognised as 'ordnance' the smaller calibre weapons which appear in various inventories (Appendix A14) as part of the overall complement, while Walker who was a civilian turned warrior was not so much in tune with the niceties of artillery classification and only registered the biggest guns as being 'real' cannon. To illustrate the point, a passage in *Londerias* – 'The Exploit of the Barge of Intelligence' – describes (*Londerias* 63) the use of an armed barge used for reconnaissence

> To get intelligence we built a barge
> Of wondrous swiftness which was long and large;
> And plac'd a Drake therein or two beside,
> When we had need to sail or row with tide.

This reference to one or more drakes could be to those bronze pieces included in inventories from 1660 onwards (Appendix A14: Table 6). At around about 190lb weight (Appendix A14.1a), it is easy to see how they could be discounted as 'ordnance' when compared to weapons some twenty times heavier. Also, it is to be remembered that guns were not static within the City, but evidently were manoeuvred around to those points where they were needed most. For example, Ash (*Ash Journal* 69) recorded an incident on 27 May when five cannon – obviously moved there specifically to meet particular circumstances – were fired from the Church Bastion at the besiegers.

The ineffectual use of ordnance by the Jacobite side in 1689 has been a subject of discussion by authors over the years, most recently and usefully by Murtagh (2003). For this reason, we shall look mainly at how the defenders used their ordnance and munitions, although noting the Jacobite use of the one type of gun not found in the City, the mortar (depicted in Plate 43). While the forces under Rosen were accompanied by some well-trained artillerists, they were never properly equipped or supplied (*ibid.* 400), and indeed their ambition and determination was open to serious question. Thus, on 21 April 1689, Jacobite gunners mounted a demi-culverin

> 180 perches [around 990yds or 905m] from the Town . . . they played on the houses in the Town, but did little or no mischief only to the Market House.

For all practical purposes, at around one thousand yards a demi-culverin was outside its limits of accuracy, and so we can only view this episode as representing a certain lack of imagination on the part of Jacobite commanders, coupled with the prowess of the defenders in sweeping the ground closer to the City and forcing the besieging forces to keep a safe distance. Mackenzie (*Mackenzie Narrative* 31) augmented the account

> *The Enemy in the Afternoon brought the Cannon they had ply'd us with, down to the Point, opposite to our Men on the Strand, and play'd over warmly at them (though without any Execution) 'till one of our Guns from the Walls disabled their Gun, and kill'd the Gunner and others.*

Thomas Ash was evidently unimpressed by some of the quality of the gunnery directed against the City, writing in his diary for 9 July (*Ash Journal* 87) that

> *They played hotly against the gate* [Butcher Gate] *and shattered it much; some of the balls flew over the town and fell into the Lough (I wish they had all done so)*

In fact, neither their cannon nor their mortars came anything like close to creating a breech in the City Walls. Indeed, the defenders are reported as having taunted the besiegers, telling them that they had no need to over-exert themselves, since they would leave the gates open and thus provide a wider gap than ever they could make with their guns! And commanders of the besieging forces were less than complimentary about the skills of their own gunners, with comments to the effect that they would be unable to hit a barn if inside it (e.g. Murtagh 2003, 386). John Stevens, one of the soldiers on the Jacobite side, described with evident contempt the efforts of their gunners to hit a ship which broke through the first boom across the Foyle (Murray 1912, 71)

> *. . . a chain laid across it tied at both ends to the shores with some old ropes, which being rotted by the weather or not sound before gave way to the first small vessel that attempted the passage. Which vessel though stranded and very near our blind gunners could or would not hit, though they made several shots at her.*

The account is augmented by a letter (*Cal. SPD* 1689–1690, 161, 22 June 1689) to King Louis XIV from Jean-Bernard-Louis Desjean, Sieur de Pointis who was in charge of the artillery, who wrote

> *Our fire took no effect until the French gunners arrived. We then sent nine out of the 14 shot fired into the vessel, but she got away.*

The situation was best summarised by the commander of the Jacobite forces, General Conrad de Rosen, reported as having complained that with the resources available to him (and that included gunners), even the great Vauban himself could not have taken Londonderry (*Négociations supp.* 37; Milligan 1996, 147).

The gunnery of the defenders – for the most part civilians – was presented as being that of the untrained and not expected to be perfect. Nevertheless, Walker said of them (*Walker* 30) that they

> *. . . did not pretend to be great artists, yet they were very industrious, and scarce spent a shot without doing some remarkable execution . . .*

Certainly, they were capable of scoring direct hits on enemy emplacements and personnel. Thus, on 23 April, their retaliatory fire against a battery in Strong's Orchard killed several Jacobite troops and two monks.

> *The besiegers planted four Demi-Culverins in the lower end of Mr. Strong's Orchard, near 80 Perches* [400 yards, 366m] *. . . The besieged make due returns to their firing from the Bastions, kill'd Lieut. Fitz Patrick, Lieut. Col. O Neale, two Serjeants, and several Souldiers; and besides these, two Friars in their Habits . . .*

and on 28 April, they took out an enemy gun emplacement and killed the gunner (*Walker* 22). Ash reported (*Ash Journal* 71) that on 28 May

> *As a troop of the enemy's horse were going down to Penny-burn, our cannon from the double bastion killed three of them.*

Chapter 3 – The City Defences and the Use of Cannon

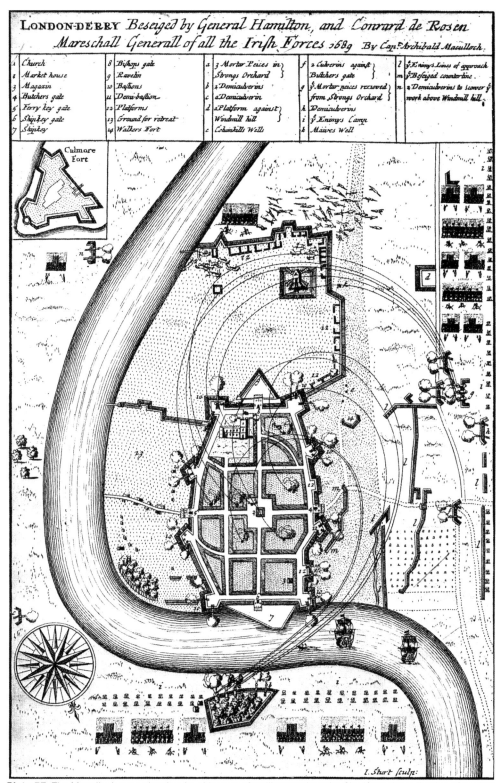

Plate 57 The Maculloch map showing Jacobite use of artillery against the City (*from the collection of the late W.S. Ferguson of Londonderry*).

Describing the prowess of the gunners firing from the Cathedral, Bennett (*True and Impartial Account* 27) wrote that they

> *exceedingly gall'd the Enemy in the Battery on the other side of the Water, insomuch that their Battery was several times broken, and at length, when they discovered a Gun to be fired from the Steeple, the Soldiers would either run out of the Works in great disorder, or fall flat on their bellies to avoid the shot.*

It is clear that despite the limited number of professional artillerists, there was enough expertise there to make reasonably effective use of the City guns. And a combination of cannon shot and small-arms fire took a disproportionately high toll on the Jacobite gunners. Le Comte d'Avaux, who kept a meticulous record of affairs during the siege, noted that of the thirty-six French gunners involved on the Jacobite side, some thirty-one were either wounded or killed (*Négociations* 338–339). It was not just rank-and-file who died, but also senior officers were lost to fire both from small arms[35] and cannon. d'Avaux reported[36] on 9 August 1689 (*ibid.* 355), in a tone less than sympathetic and intimating an opinion of *espèce d'idiot*

> *Le pauvre M. de Massé, Monsieur, a esté tué d'un coup de canon, comme il vouloit pointer un canon à une batterie qu'il avoit fait faire, faisent luy mesme l'office de commissaire d'artellerie.*

> *Poor Monsieur de Massé, Sir, was killed by a shot from a cannon, just as he was aiming a piece at a battery which he himself had had installed in his capacity as Master of the Artillery.*

Thus, it is evident that the City was not so poorly furnished with artillerymen as Walker suggested, and it is not unlikely that he underplayed this aspect to boost the image of the defenders as heroic underdogs. A list of some of those skilled in the handling of ordnance can be gleaned from the unremittingly awful doggerel of Aickin's *Londerias*.

> *Derry whose proud and stately Walls disdain,*
> *By any Foreign En'my to be t'ane,*
> *Betwixt surrounding Hills which it command*
> *On an ascending brow dos snugly stand.*
> *Against those Hills the Walls rise equally,*
> *And on strong Bastions planted Cannon lye.*
> (*Londerias* 23)

> *Watson's made Master of the Artillery,*
> *Two hundred Gunners and Montrosses* [=matrosses] *be.*
> *James Murray was Conductor of the Train,*
> *Our Ingenieur was Adams of Strabane.*
> (*ibid.* 47)

> *In all attacks our Gunners play'd their parts,*
> *For from the Walls they tamed the en'mies hearts.*
> *Eight Sakers and twelve Demiculverin*
> *Discharg'd their fury daily from within.*
> *Against the En'mies Camps on ev'ry side*
> *Which furiously amongst their forces glide.*
> *Brave Watson fir'd upon their strongest Ranks,*
> *And swept off Files from the En'mies Flanks.*
> *Lieutenant Crookshanks dismounts from our walls*
> *The En'mies Cannon which upon us falls*
> *At Pennyburn Mill. And Captain Gregory,*
> *From the Church Steeple slays the Enemy.*
> *James Murray from the Northern Bastions,*
> *Near Elah hurt the Foes Batallions.*
> *Robert Stevenson ne're mist the Enemy,*
> *But furiously amongst their troops lets fly.*
> *Lieutenant Dyell and some brave Seamen,*
> *Did from the walls slay many on the plain;*
> *Lieutenant Evins praise shall now be told,*
> *Who in all actions was both brave and bold.*
> (*ibid.* 73–74)

A muster of 'two hundred gunners and matrosses' seems about right for an assemblage of twenty large calibre cannon, allowing a gunner and several assistants for each cannon, and with crews working in shifts. Even if the higher figure of thirty-four or thirty-five pieces is accepted, then a crew of five or six per gun does not seem unreasonable. The 'Watson' made Captain of the Gunners was Captain Alexander Watson, a gunner, and one of those slated for pardon by Lord Mountjoy should the rebellious citizenry return to obedience (Milligan 1951, 46), and possibly the gunner listed in the 1687 establishment (Table 6). Of James Murray, Robert Stevenson, and

Lieutenants Crookshanks, Dyell and Evins, we have no details, while of Captain Andrew Adams we know nothing other than he was a Strabane man. The 'Captain Gregory' mentioned was Capt. Robert Gregory, one of four Gregorys who were involved in the defence of the City. Along with his brother, Capt. George Gregory, he was responsible for the repair of gun carriages, and for the mounting of guns on the roof of the Cathedral.[37] Mackenzie wrote (*Mackenzie* 39) that

> *Capt. Gregory and some other Work-Men took care . . . to have Carriages made for the guns, some of which were so out of order, that sometimes we could not use them when we wanted them.*

The brothers also got guns onto the bell tower of the cathedral (Young. W.R. 1932, 150–151: Vere 1943, 19*ff*). Bennett (*True and Impartial Account* 27) described the mounting there of the guns, which he states were taken from Culmore:

> *And as the wise Governors and Officers considered what might disadvantageous to themselves, resolve upon something to be equally prejudicial to the Enemy, and knowing there were some guns to spare, which were brought up from the Fort of Kilmore [= Culmore], ordered two of them to be mounted on the top of the steeple of the church, being a great height commanding all Places about the Town within Cannon-shot:*

This can not have been an easy task for Captains Robert and George Gregory, not just in terms of the lifting of large and heavy lumps of metal onto the Cathedral (even if of smaller calibre), but also in mounting the guns so that they could be as effective as they obviously were.

A contemporary Dutch engraving shows the guns mounted on the roof of the Cathedral (Fig. 17a), and this was described by Walker (*Walker* 10)

> *Near the S.W. end of the Town, stands the Church; on the top whereof, being a flat roof, were placed two of our guns, which were of great Use in annoying the enemy.*

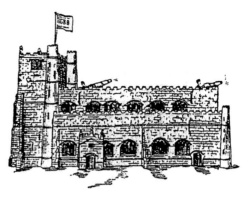

Fig. 17 (a) Detail from an engraving of the Siege of Londonderry, probably by Romeyn de Hooghe, showing cannon mounted on the Cathedral roof, (b) detail from the map by Joseph Bennett showing cannon mounted on the bell tower (*True and Impartial Account* frontspiece), (c) detail from the map by Captain Archibald Maculloch showing cannon mounted on the tower.

But, taken literally, this is quite improbable for a number of reasons. The Cathedral would have had a pitched roof (Fig. 18), making the preparation of any sort of stable platform difficult.[38] Further, even if this had been possible, the span of the roof would have made it not very secure when loaded with several tons of cannon plus their carriages, if the term 'great guns' is any guide at all.[39] Finally, as depicted

Fig. 18 Eastern elevation of the Cathedral in 1689 (after Simpson 1847).

in Fig. 17a, the field of fire would have been cut off in a fairly wide arc by the square bell tower. In fact, it is certain that the guns were mounted on the tower which, until the 1680s, supported a wooden steeple clad in lead. This had been dismantled and the lead put into store against its reconstruction, but the lead found service as a source of small-arms ammunition and later cannon shot. The much smaller cross-sectional area of the tower would have made reinforcing it to provide a good platform much easier and, of course, on the tower the gunners would have had a 360° field of fire through which to 'annoy' the enemy forces. It would seem obvious that when Walker and others referred to a 'flat roof', they intended the roof of the bell tower. Similarly, Bennett wrote (*True and Impartial Account* 27) that

> *The wise Governors and Officers . . . knowing that there were some guns to spare, which were brought up from the fort of Kilmore, ordered two of them to be mounted on the top of the Steeple of the Church, being a great heighth, commanding all places about the town within Cannon-shot:*

And in the frontspiece to his work, the guns are indeed shown on the tower, albeit with the incongruous addition of a steeple (Fig. 17b)! However, the fine detail of the Maculloch map shows two cannon on top of the square tower as one would imagine they were positioned (Fig. 17c).

The way in which the roofing lead was used provides another example of the expertise (not just ingenuity) of the defenders, who improvised when their stock of cast-iron balls ran out. For 24 June 1689, Walker (*Walker* 32) wrote

> *. . . Our Iron Ball is now all spent and instead of them we make Balls of Brick, cast over with Lead to the weight and size of our Iron-Ball.*

According to Mackenzie (*Mackenzie* 39), one '. . . Will. Brown, Adjutant to Governour Baker's Regiment, was industrious and dextrous in this piece of service.' The use of brick as a core for lead shot shows good practical

Plate 58 Used shot for a demi-culverin comprising a skin of lead cast over a brick core.

knowledge on the part of someone involved, and a spent example is preserved in the Chapter House of Londonderry Cathedral (Plate 58). The author of *Compleat Gunner* devoted a section on how to find the equivalent weight of lead and stone to replicate cast-iron shot (*Compleat Gunner* 40–41), while Norton (*Gunner* 87) cautioned that the gunner should know the 'proportions' (i.e. specific gravities) of different materials. He set down differences between substances, and calculated lead as approximately fifty percent denser than cast iron, stating that '. . . the proportion of Iron to Lead may be as 30 to 46.' In fact, the specific gravity of cast iron averages out in the region of 7.15, while that of lead is 11.34, showing the ratio offered by Norton to be very close indeed. Thus, if we consider a cast-iron ball of 4.5ins (11.43cm) diameter for a demi-culverin, on the basis of specific gravity alone we should expect it to weigh somewhere around 12.2lb (5.53kg), while the same ball cast in lead would weigh in the region of 19.6lb (8.87kg). Obviously, any attempt to use a ball of this weight in a demi-culverin would have required a proportional increase in the powder charge, thus greatly increasing the risk of catastrophic failure. So the use of a light core by the defenders was an eminently practical solution to the problem. The ball preserved in the Cathedral has been damaged in use and is no longer wholly spherical. It measures between 4ins and 4.25 ins in diameter (10.16–10.8cm) and now weighs 8lb 2oz (3.69kg), and was evidently intended to be fired from a demi-culverin. Although such a missile would not have been of much use in demolishing solid defences, against enemy troops and gun positions it would certainly have been as effective as its cast-iron counterpart.

In terms of shot, the defenders used not only solid ball, but also case or canister shot. Thus on 30 June, when the Earl of Clancarty attempted a rather rash assault (*Walker* 33), it was repulsed with heavy losses caused, at least in part by this fearsome munition.

> *At ten of the clock of the night my L. Clancarty at the Head of a Regiment, and with some Detachments, possesses himself of our Line, and enters some Miners in a low Cellar under the Half Bastion . . . Our men receive their Firing quietly, til they got to a right distance, and then thundred upon them. Our Case-Shot from the Bastion and small Shot off the walls second . . . his Lordship was forced to quit his post and to leave his Miners and an hundred of his best men dead upon the place . . .*

One of the very few specific references to actions involving ordnance in the pseudo-historical play by Mitchelburne is to this action, where the Governor calls to his forces to repel Clancarty, ordering that

> *. . . the Cannons from the Bastions fire, some with great shot, others to be charg'd with Bags of small-shot.*

Canister shot also appears to have been the form of charge that killed the French engineer de Massé, according to a report of 30 July from another engineer Lozieres d'Astier (Mulloy 1984, III, 37) that

> *Le sieur de Massé ayant esté tué hier . . . a 9 heures de matin . . . d'un coup de canon chargé de cartouche.*[40]

> *M. de Massé was killed yesterday . . . at 9 o'clock in the morning . . . by a shot from a cannon loaded with canister shot.*

And it would seem that canister shot was also used in the small guns of the 'Intelligence Barge'. Recounting an incident in which it was ambushed on a trip down the Foyle towards Dunalong, Aickin (*Londerias* 64) versified

> *As we return'd the enemy mann'd out*
> *Two large boats fill'd with some Dragoons on foot*
> *Th'one Star-board, the other us Lar-board hall'd:*
> *But Pilot Pogue with his wide Drake them maul'd;*
> *For as they thought to board our Barge, then he,*
> *Fir'd small shot among their company.*

The use of such an anti-personnel munition not only cut down on the use of evidently scarce resources of cast-iron shot, but also would have required no little skill, except at close quarters. When fired, the container would have started to disintegrate shortly after leaving the barrel, its contents expanding in flight like shot from a shotgun. Thus, to keep sufficient of the contents on target would have meant having a knowledge of how the balls would spread over distance, rather like in clay-pigeon shooting.

Another form of projectile consisted of two iron balls joined together by a length of chain, hence the name 'chain shot'. Particularly deployed by seaborne gunners both to destroy the rigging of an enemy vessel, as well as an anti-personnel munition,[41] chain shot was fired by Jacobite gunners at the Butcher Gate defences (Murtagh 2003, 394). Additionally, at other times they used heated shot, the value of which the defenders were also aware. Captain Ash referred to two incidents during the siege of Londonderry in 1689 in which heated shot fired into the City caused injuries in Pump Street, but no damage (*Ash Journal* 68). In Mackenzie's report of the activities of troops raised by Lord Kingston near Moneymore, County Tyrone we find an entry for 6 April 1689 referring to the use of heated shot (*Mackenzie* 27)

> *We killed nearly twenty of the enemy, and with hot iron bullets fired the town where they lay, and drove them all out of it.*

One of the many perils that the defenders had to face as a result of inadequate protective parapets was significant exposure to anti-personnel fire from the besieging forces, and against this they raised 'blinds' or 'gabions' – wicker or other containers (sometimes also called 'cannon baskets') filled with earth to absorb shot and splinters. Bennett (*True and Impartial Account* 23) described

> ... *the Governors ordering Blinds to be built on the Walls, to prevent the Enemy's shot against the men who were posted on the Works.*

A defender at the time, Captain George Holmes,[42] wrote that there were times when 'cannon bullets flew as fast as you could count them' (*Holmes* 264), and such protection was necessary for the gunners. Walker describes how Baker protected his men from enemy cannon fire using 'blinds' (*Walker* 30), and Mackenzie described their placement in Shipquay Street when fire was directed into the area from cannon in Strong's Orchard (*Mackenzie Narrative* 32). Similarly, Ash described how '... hogsheads were placed in the double bastion, filled with earth and gravel to secure the breast-work from the enemy's battering guns.' (*Ash Journal* 72: *True and Impartial Account* 23). Although we have no illustration of gabions on the City Walls, the Jacobites evidently used them extensively also, and one depiction is shown in Plate 59.

Both sides appear to have had the unpleasant experience of guns 'bursting'. The defenders of Londonderry suffered at least one burst gun (*Ash Journal* 72)

> *May 31st ... Both cannon and muskets played almost the whole day with much execution. A cannon near the Magazine burst, and hurt the gunner.*

The Jacobite gunners defending Culmore in June of 1689 appear to have suffered a similar failure in an exchange of fire with the frigate *Greyhound* (*Fleet Diary* 10: Murtagh 2003, 386)

Plate 59 The use of gabions by Jacobite troops to protect their gunners and ordnance.

... weighed anchor about eight o'clock in the morning and came to an anchor within cannon-shot of Culmore ... We therefore charged them first with a broadside, and they discharged theirs and by what we could observe one of their guns split.

And their large bronze mortar became cracked and unserviceable soon after it was first employed (*Jacobite Narrative* 67)

... the mortars had good effect for the time they were in use ... But the grand mortar being soon cracked, the damage ceased.

If the Jacobite gunners achieved anything, it was the destruction and death wrought by mortar fire and its occasional direct hits on stocks of powder. Psychologically, as a weapon of terror, it was highly effective. In his manual of siegecraft composed *c.* 1667–1672 (Rothrock 1968, 59–60), Vauban wrote of mortars that they should

... always be emplaced between the fortress and the heavy siege batterie ... These batteries are made with a simple breastwork to withstand cannon fire...Otherwise, just remember that the bigger the bombs the more damage they do ... I approve of the use of the great mortars that throw stones, all the more as it is difficult, if not impossible, to be certain of their trajectory. (The random character of their hits is discouraging to the enemy.)

The indiscriminate scatter of mortar shells which landed in Londonderry during the siege of 1689 had a serious effect on morale, and they certainly caused more casualties than any other artillery fire. The defenders were forced to adopt defensive measures such as dispersing their stocks of powder (*Ash Journal* 71), and Colonel Richards recorded (*Fleet Diary* 17) that

... the Derry people [have] uncovered the tops of their houses and have taken up the pavements of their streets the one to hinder the blast of the bomb to fire their houses, and the other to let the bomb bury itself in the removed earth, which in the splitting of the bomb does not kill or wound them, as the stones formerly did or would have done.

The mortars hurled hollow spheres of cast iron filled with powder. Walker recorded that some five hundred and eighty-seven shells were lobbed into the City between 24 April and 22 July 1689. The larger type weighing around 272 lb (122.47kg) contained between 15lb and 17lb of powder (e.g. *Ash Journal* 73). A 16ins mortar shell fired in on 10 July 1689 landed in the graveyard of Saint Columb's Cathedral.[43] It contained not a powder charge but the terms of surrender on offer (Lacy 1990, 133), and can be seen preserved in the porch of the Cathedral. Fragments of other shells are preserved in the Chapter House. The shells from mortars were detonated by fuses lit as the piece fired, and one of the many problems besetting the Jacobites was that fuses supplied at the start of the siege were of the wrong size. Before his death in front of the Walls of Londonderry, de Massé complained that there was no-one capable of making fuses for the bombs (Mulloy 1984, III, 27).

Notes to Chapter 3

1 The role of Charles as an early promoter of overwhelming artillery fire has recently come into question (e.g. Black 2002, 37–38). It should be noted that against his evident success at Monte San Giovanni, his guns signally failed shortly after to impress at Castel Nuovo in Naples.

2 But even the weakest of targets were proof against ineffective gunnery!

3 It was not just earth that was effective. At Worcester, during the English Civil War, dung was used to pack behind the walls. As Hutton and Reeves note (1998, 203), here it was a case of 'where there's muck, there's safety'! Dung was also used to shore up the defences in Londonderry. Ash wrote (*Ash Journal* 64) that

The street was barricaded between Cunningham's and Boyd's corners, with timber, stones and dung. In order to secure the Market House from the enemy's cannon which were directed that way.

4 Sebastien Le Prestre, Seigneur de Vauban (1633–1707), was perhaps the foremost European military engineer and architect of the later seventeenth century (e.g. Rothrock 1968). A Marshall of France and a favourite of Louis XIV, it was said of him that 'whatever he invested, fell; whatever he defended, held.'

5 Dating to around 1799, Plate 46 is a later copy of the original plan published around 1705 (Milligan 1996, Plate XXV). The profile is through one of the new bastions proposed for the Windmill area.

6 The ditch was frequently filled up with rubbish in places (e.g. *True and Impartial Account* 28: '. . . in some places this Ditch is filled up, not being kept clean for a long time:').

7 It is interesting to compare the careful planning of the siegeworks and gun emplacements at this siege as shown in Gilbert (1882, IV, frontspiece), with the seemingly haphazard dispositions at Londonderry in 1689.

8 Regarding the defences established by Sidney, a new identification of the site of the magazine is offered in Appendix B.

9 A map of the fort by Nicholas Pynnar shows a stone wall with rampart, but empty bastions, and instead gun ports improbably sited half-way up the walls (*TCD* MS 1209/23: reproduced in Moody 1939, Plate VII facing p. 188).

10 Provision of a brewery for the troops might seem a bit of a luxury, especially in view of its siting. However, like the Sidney/Randolph garrison of 1566–1567, large numbers of Docwra's forces were quickly laid low by sickness in 1600, something which was blamed on the quality of the water, and urgent arrangements were made to ship beer from London (*Docwra*, 11 and 33 note 26). It is likely that the brewery shown here was an attempt to provide potable liquor to cut down on the wastage through illness (McGurk 2006a, 75*ff*, 2006b, 166). And in 1647, one John Long of Londonderry was licensed to export 'certain hops' from Liverpool to the City 'for use of the Derry garrison.' (*Cal. SPI 1633–1647*, 750, 16 December 1647).

11 Interestingly, it is marked on a map of 1642 entitled *A map of ye kingdome of Ireland with perticular notes distinguishing the townes revolted or taken or burnt since the late rebellion* (*BL* Map 669.f.4.78). It seems most likely that the publisher had the detail of the area copied from earlier maps purely as a commercial exercise, and without any understanding of the actual situation on the ground.

12 Strabane was without a garrison in April 1641. We know this because on 6 April 1641 the Mayor and citizens of Londonderry petitioned Ormond to have the garrison removed. They wrote (*Carte MSS* 1, ff 405r–406v)

. . . the burthen of those 500 souldiers . . . is too heavie for us to beare because this City is not built fitt for that purpose. Strabane hath no souldiers. It is a populous town and the best market in this country . . .

Given events later that year, we have a classic example of Kipling's observation that

It's Tommy this, an' Tommy that,
An' "Chuck him out, the brute!"
But it's "Saviour of 'is country"
When the guns begin to shoot.

Similar attitudes were to be found in Londonderry itself (e.g. Perceval-Maxwell 1994, 43).

13 The history of the building of the City has been well covered by Moody (1939), Milligan (1996), Lacy (1990) and Curl (1986, 2000). For an analysis and discussion of the town plan, see Hunter (1981).

14 The O'Doherty tower house has been reconstructed close to what would have been its original site, and now houses the Tower Museum.

15 Thus, for example, the church-like structure to the south-east of the Diamond is almost certain to depict the intended site of the cathedral which was, in fact, built elsewhere. Also, the heavily fortified Market House depicted in the Diamond (Plate 21) was never built.

16 Wapping Lane runs from close to the old line of the bank of the Foyle, to Fountain Street, the closest bastion being Church Bastion. Milligan (1996, 77) noted that modern Bridge Street, which runs up to Ferryquay Gate was known as 'Wappin'. Should the Vintners' Company entry refer to an unrelated 'Wabion', another vague possibility, not mentioned by Milligan (*ibid.* 75–77), is that the word is a mutilation of the name 'Babbington', someone

whose dwelling is shown on Griffin Cockett's map of 1600 (e.g. Curl 2000, 99, Plate 24), although as with Wapping Lane and Bridge Street, in a position that would have been some way away from the later Water Bastion.

17 However, in 1663, Ormond had to order the demolition of 'cabins' which had been built on the walls (*Carte MSS* 144, f. 43, sixteenth March, 1663).

18 A publication of 1680, being a collection of military advice given by Thomas Digges to the Earl of Leicester in 1588, collated by the Master Gunner Thomas Adamson and augmented by a listing of the forces and equipment required to repulse a foreign invasion (*Englands Defence* 13), suggested that the rates of daily pay for a master gunner, a master gunner's mate, a gunner and a matross should be 5s, 3s, 2s and 18d respectively. Outside Dublin, gunners in Ireland did not achieve these levels.

19 This differential existed also with Leinster and Munster and Connaught.

20 However, powder was stored there during the siege of 1689 until fear of a direct hit from mortar shells prompted its move to more secure locations (*Ash Journal* 71).

21 It would seem that any planned works within the Cathedral precinct or in the adjoining Court House should take account of the possibility of uncovering at least some traces of the citadel, since there evidently was some substantial evidence above ground when Phillips drew this map.

22 The sketch map *BL* Maps K Top 54.29 has a number of notations in French. In the bottom right-hand corner of *BL* Maps K Top 54.30 is a crude scale in 'pieds' 'feet'. Also, the hand which annotated this map seems distinctly different from that of *BL* Maps K Top 54.31and of a later map of 1689–1690 attributed to Phillips *BL* 54.25(3), the annotations of which could have been written by the same person. Thus, it is not certain that *BL* Maps K Top 54.30 was the sole work of Phillips whose signature is absent, but may have involved collaboration with Jean Thomas, the French engineer who served the army of William III and was awarded a pension in 1704 on the establishment of Ireland (Thomas 2005, 27).

It seems not unreasonable to suggest that *BL* Maps K Top 54.29 might be attributed to Ingenieur Thomas.

23 We are most grateful to Mark Lusby for drawing this to our attention, and to Annesley Malley for reference to its source.

24 We are most grateful to Paul Kerrigan for these references.

25 A not dissimilar situation seems to have arisen in Coleraine, since Col. William Legge noted in 1662 (*NA* WO 55/1752, f. 156; Appendix A15) that the town

> . . . was reasonably well fortified in the late Troubles, but the works since neglected and now decayed. In this Towne is a Fort of Stone work erected but not finished, it is raised some ten or twelve foot high in Some places and I conceive it ought to be Completed or what is Done Demolished.

It is reasonable to deduce that the 'fort of stone work' is the citadel referred to by Captain William Webb.

26 The convention of dotted lines used to depict the citadel on most of these maps is also used on *BL* K Top 54.31, perhaps indicating that, like that structure, this ravelin was a relic.

27 But obviously small – e.g. ' two or three small pieces of cannon on the windmill' (*A Light to the Blind* 106).

28 Following the lifting of the siege of 1649, and his defeat of Irish forces at Scarrifhollis on 21 June 1650, Coote went on to lay siege to the stronghold of Charlemont in County Armagh, but already was planning subsequent operations in Connaught. Regarding the movement of ordnance, he wrote to Henry Ireton (Gilbert 1879, III, 149) that

> . . .if shipping be not appointed to attend us both for the transporting ordnance, ammunition and bread, it will not be possible to do any effectual service there.

29 As W.P. Kelly puts it (2001a, 41), referring to the battle fought at Carrigans in County Donegal on 23 April 1649, 'Protestant killed protestant at Carrigans as enthusiastically as they had killed the Irish before and after.' See also McKenny (2005, 89*ff*).

30 The defenders of 1689 did this also, with Captain Holmes (*Holmes* 264) recording that

> *In the first place, we burned all our suburbs and hewed down all our brave orchards, making all about as as plain as a bouling green.*

31 The 'Crook of Ember' is shown on the versions of Neville's maps of the 1689 siege. In a letter of 15 August (*Transactions* 5) Coote referred to the placing of ordnance here, saying

> *... our Enemies began much to increase both in number and activity, insomuch as they presently blockt up the passage by Sea as well as by Land, intrenching themselves upon the Crook of Ember in a fort, wherein they planted thirteen pieces of Ordnance.*

32 It was not just ordnance that was ignored. In 1674, for example, Londonderry had one hundred and ninety-three muskets described as having 'ye Stock and Lock Decayed' and eighty-one musket barrels that were 'old & Rusty' (*NA* WO 55/1752 f. 245). Apart from the evident neglect of the contents of the magazine, and of the defences and ordnance, the garrison seems to have suffered also. Thus on 6 May 1683, one Lemuel Kingdon wrote to the Earl of Arran (*Ormond MSS* n.s. 7, 21–22), stating

> *My Lord this garrison is in extreme want of money. Three of the company, vizt. Capt. Brooks, Capt. Berkeleys, and Capt. Philips have not received June pay.*

And in regard to the strategically important Culmore fort, the governorship was up for sale. It was reported in 1672 (*Cal. SPD* 1672, 614, 14 September 1672) that the then governor, Col. Gorges (brother of the Gorges who requested the demolition of the Londonderry citadel), was in such dire straits that '. . . his company (is) disbanded, so he now has the government of this fort and no men to man it.' And following the end of the Williamite war, once again complacency ruled. England and the Netherlands and their allies declared war on France and Spain on 14 May 1702, in what became known as the War of the Spanish Succession. In May of 1702, the Corporation noted (Milligan 1999, 162) that

> *... there now being a war proclaimed against France and Spain, and the carriages of the guns of this city being utterly decayed and therebye the said guns rendered unserviceable for the defence of this important place.*

It is quite likely that Milligan (1996, 162*f*) was correct in attributing the appointment of the French engineer Jean Thomas to inspect the fortifications and draw up recommendations to the representations made at this time to the Duke of Ormond.

33 What is perhaps surprising is that Mitchelburne, the military man who mirrored the events of 1689 in his play *Ireland preserv'd*, gave only the briefest of off-stage mentions to cannon, and provides no clue as to the complement.

34 The anonymous author is at odds also with the assessment by Walker of the stores available to the defenders at the start of the siege.

35 Thus, the engineer de Pointis (see below) 'a esté blessé d'un coup de mousquet' ('was wounded by a musket shot': *Négociations* 161, 14 May 1689) shortly after his arrival at Londonderry. Later, just as Comte d'Avaux was rejoicing in his recuperation, he was forced to report (*Négociations* 399, 19 August 1689) that

> *Je suis bien faché, Monsieur, de vous dire que le pauvre St. Martin a esté tué comme il faisoit tirer le canon, le jour de la deffaite de Mylord Monkassel; il a eu un coup de mousquet dans le ventre;*
>
> I am most vexed, Monsieur, to tell you that the poor St. Martin has been killed as he was preparing to fire the cannon, the day of the defeat of My Lord Mount Castle; he took a musket shot in the abdomen;

36 We are most grateful to Dr. Suzanne Funnell for the translations from *Négociations*.

37 The family was reduced to poverty in the aftermath of the siege, and Robert petitioned Lords Justices on 22 August 1716 (Vere 1943, 19–20), stipulating that

> *... your petitioner and his brother did mount the great guns on the steeple of Derry and repaired several of the carriages on the walls thereof.*

He was supported by both a certificate dated 10 December 1689, from Walker and Mitchelburne (Young 1932, 151: Vere 1943, 20–21) who wrote

> *Capt. Robert Gregory of Col. Lance's Regiment and Capt. George Gregory of Col. Crofton's Regiment did mount the great*

gunes on the Steeple of Londonderry and repaired severall of the Carriages on the walls, and p^rformed the office of Guners during the siege.

38 In his edition of Walker's account of the siege, Dwyer (1893, 132–133) followed what Walker appeared to say and stated that the roof was flat. The depiction of the Cathedral in the centre of the pen-and-ink illustration by Thomas Phillips in 1685 indicates a pitched roof (Thomas 2005, Plate I). Aickin (*Londerias* 23) wrote

> *There's a great Church* [i.e. the Cathedral]
> *from whose high Steeple*
> *Thunder and lightening goes to annoy the*
> *Foes.*

And Richards (*Fleet Diary* 21) noted how
> *. . . we saw flying upon the Derry steeple a much larger flag than was wont . . . which they lowered and hoisted four times, and fired two guns.*

Thomas Ash (*Ash Diary* 77) also refers to shooting 'from the steeple'.

39 See Appendix A14.3 for the weights of the ordnance identified as having been in the City and at Culmore in 1685.

40 In the earlier part of the seventeenth century, 'cartouche' (or 'cartridge') seems to have referred to measured charges of powder contained in paper or textile bags, but by the end of the century to case shot (e.g. Blackmore 1976, 223).

41 Smith (*Sea Grammar* 86) gave a brief definition of different types, including chain shot, concluding with the statement that
> *All these are used when you are neere a ship, to shoot down Masts, Yards, teare the sailes, spoile the men, or anything that is above the decks.*

42 Holmes was one of those who signed the declaration of 11 July authorising surrender negotiations.

43 Large fragments of a cast-iron mortar shell of probably 16ins calibre were recovered from seventeenth-century levels during the excavations at Irish Quarter, Carrickfergus, County Antrim (M.L. Simpson *pers. comm.* 2006).

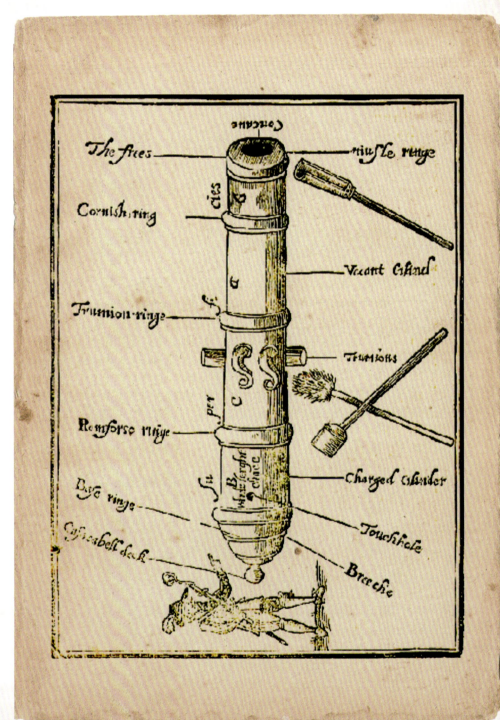

CHAPTER 4

The Origins of the Ordnance of the Sixteenth and Seventeenth Centuries

As with elsewhere in Europe, cannon had become an established part of the English prosecution of warfare in Ireland by the time Sir Henry Docwra landed with his expeditionary force at Culmore in May of 1600. The Irish too could use cannon, although not as a constant in their tactics, but primarily opportunistically. There had been ordnance in the general area of Lough Foyle for some time (for example, at Burt Castle in Co. Donegal (Plate 37), but the regular deployment of artillery both for offence and defence here began with Docwra. Between 1600 and 1689, the numbers of cannon recorded in the City and at Culmore fluctuated. Add to this the short-lived presence of ordnance at Dunalong, and its longer-term – if sporadic – presence at Lifford and Strabane, and we can perhaps (as a very crude estimate) suggest that somewhere in the region of sixty-five guns were brought to the area centred on Londonderry over the period, although obviously not all at the same time. And at the start of the eighteenth century, the City would appear to have acted as a repository for ordnance brought in from surrounding areas (as did, for example, Carrickfergus, Co. Antrim), with an inventory dated 28 January 1706, showing a total of seven hundred and six barrels of powder and forty-one iron guns, of which four are listed as 'unserviceable' (*NLI* MS 2274, f. 20).

The information which can be found in the extensive historic documentation provided by the archives of the Great Companies and other sources is augmented and largely confirmed by the stylistic evidence presented in Chapters 5-7. And in summary, it shows that there are three primary horizons of deployment of ordnance in the seventeenth century. The first is that initiated by Docwra in 1600 and represented by two Tudor cannon (possibly a third, now lost: p.9). The next comes between approximately 1615 and 1625, the time when the defences of Londonderry had been completed and, along with Culmore, supposedly were being provided with cannon by the City of London. To the third belongs a group of guns sent over in early 1642 in response to the Irish Rebellion which broke out in October 1641. Also we should consider cases such as the capture of the small Charles Fort built by besieging forces in 1649, which yielded fifteen pieces, including four small drakes (*True Relation* 13–14) that may for a time have been held in the Londonderry artillery park. But cannon which arrived in the area did not necessarily stay there. Obviously some were redeployed elsewhere, never to return, while others have disappeared through the attrition of history – for example, the cannon that travelled to Derry in 1566–1567 and was last heard of in Caernarvon in Wales (p. 81). And unserviceable guns were disposed of on a regular basis,[1] with bronze guns being melted down, and iron cannon frequently used as ballast for ships (e.g. by the East India Company – Brown 1990c, 19). Thus, for example, the culling of 'all such broken or other unserviceable ordnance' ordered by Ormond in July 1662 (*Carte MSS* 42, f. 646, 7 July 1662) is but one of a series of such commands. And the placing of old cannon as street furniture was another use for them (Plates 10–11).

One thing that is clear is that the City guns of the late sixteenth and seventeenth centuries were English guns brought over to protect English interests. The bulk date to the earlier part of the seventeenth century, and how they came to the City is inextricably tied to the Plantation of Ulster.

Background – the Plantation of Ulster

The 'Flight of the Earls' in September 1607 came as a total surprise to the Crown. This sudden departure of the scions of Gaelic Ulster left a power vacuum amongst the Ulster Irish, and large tracts of escheated land to dispose of.

Initially, it would seem that the redistribution of this might have been comparatively modest. But in 1608, goaded to breaking point by the heavy-handed and incompetent governor of Derry, Sir George Paulet,[2] Sir Cahir O'Doherty mounted a short-lived rebellion. Although easily suppressed and, in comparison with the recent Nine Years War, of little military import or impact, the consequences were a further hardening of anti-Irish attitudes and widening of the scope of the settlement of land by the English and consequent displacement of the native Irish.[3] Thus, for example, many English military servitors were rewarded with grants of lands around their garrisons, frequently in lieu of significant arrears of pay.

By 1608, the territory was being surveyed with a view to planting it with English settlers, and in 1609, optimistic reports were issued concerning the great potential of such an exercise (Curl 2000, 30*f*). Filling lands previously belonging to the native Irish with loyal subjects was perceived as having the benefits both of hastening the pacification of a region that had long been a source of problems for the Crown, and of generating new sources of revenue. But what soon became evident was that the Crown simply lacked the resources to meet the costs of such an undertaking.

A prime exponent of the potential of plantation was Sir Thomas Phillips, who lobbied tirelessly on behalf of the idea and was taken into the patronage of Sir Robert Cecil. By 1609, Cecil was involved in discussion with the City of London regarding the financing of what had been described in a pamphlet of 1608 as 'A Project for the Division and Plantation of the Escheated Lands in Ulster'. The basic scheme involved the establishment of a company (later to be known as 'The Irish Society': Moody 1939; Curl 2000), the shareholders of which would be the twelve Great Companies of the City of London, each in partnership with one or more of the minor Companies (Curl 2000). When the likely scale of investment became known, the canny businessmen of the City were largely less than impressed and, despite promise of great return, many had to be threatened – even gaoled – to wrest money from them. The history of the development of the Ulster Plantation was charted in detail by Moody (1939), and has been revisited more recently in major studies by Curl (1986 and 2000), who describes it (1986, 1) as

a tale of coercion, of heroism, of disaster, of failure, of noble aspirations, of ineptitude, of perfidy, of perjury, of cupidity, and of remarkable achievements against considerable odds.

A joint stock company, ultimately named 'The Irish Society',[4] was established with one side comprising the twelve Great Companies of the City of London and their affiliates, the other being the Crown (Curl 1986, 69–70). In return for a significant investment of funds, each of the Companies and their affiliates would receive a parcel of land for settlement, and the Irish Society as a whole would develop Corporations at Derry and Coleraine with due liberties, with Crown and City sharing the profits. The City was already familiar with this form of deal from a similar joint enterprise, the Virginia Company. Indeed, as we shall see below, one of the minor signatories to the original petitions to James I for its establishment, was a Liveryman of the Worshipful Company of Skinners, William Felgate (later a Warden of the Company), who also played a major role in the provision of munitions to Londonderry in 1620, 1642 and 1643 (pp 128-130).

The Articles of Agreement between Crown and City, signed on 28 January 1610, are of interest to us, not so much for that which they specify, as for that which they do not. In terms of provision for the defence of the Plantation as a whole, the only references in the twenty-seven clauses – and highly vague at that[5] – are (*Phillips MSS* 13–16):

20. ... *City shall have the Castle of Culmore ... maintaining a sufficient Ward and officer therein.*
24. ... *sufficient forces shall be maintained at the King's charges for safety of the Undertakers for a certain time ...*
27. ... *there be 60 houses built in Derry ... with convenient fortifications ...*

Hunter (1975, 82) drew attention to the recommendation made in 1611 by Carew that

Chapter 4 – The Origins of the Ordnance of the Sixteenth and Seventeenth Centuries

The fforte at Culmore delivered up to the Londoners where they are to keep a warde, but as yet it remains in the hands of Liuetent Baker w'thout anie other warde then his owne familie . . .

By the time of the Pynnar survey of March 1619 (*Cal. SPI* 1615–1625, 379, dated 28 March 1619), Culmore was described thus:

This fort or blockhouse is now in the hands of Captain John Baker; the walls are now finished and the castle built, all which is strong and neatly wrought, with platforms for their artillery; and this is the only key and strength of the river that goeth to the Derry.

And in 1620 (*infra*) a consignment of ordnance and munitions was sent for the specific use of the forces at Culmore.

While both sides were keen to make provision for the division of the spoils of the Plantation, requirements for the security of the sources of those spoils were more than somewhat understated. In fact, this lack of clarity regarding the nature of, and the division of responsibilities for, the provision of arms and defences was to be one of the many points of contention between the City and Crown for at least its first twenty-five years. It soon became clear to the City that the whole exercise was fraught with difficulty and uncertainties, and in 1611 the Haberdashers pulled out by selling their interest to two Company members (Curl 2000, 51*ff*).

The fortified Foyle estuary 1600–1639

As we have seen in Chapter 3, Culmore Fort was an integral part of the development of Derry and its security, and it was to here that some of the first substantial ordnance in the area was brought by Sir Henry Docwra, who recorded the pieces which he brought with him there in 1600 as being a 'brass' demi-cannon and two iron culverins (*Docwra* 43: Table 3). Between 1600 and 1603, Docwra pursued a vigorous military campaign against the allies of the Earl of Tyrone, including assaults involving artillery on Newtownstewart and Enagh Lough.

Thereafter, Derry, Culmore, Dunalong, as well as Strabane and Lifford were garrisoned, with troops supplied with ordnance. When in 1608, Sir Cahir O'Doherty rebelled and took Culmore and sacked Derry, one of his lieutenants, supposedly removed cannon from Culmore, with some pieces being thrown into the Foyle[6] as the rebels could not transport them (*OS Londonderry* 237).

Sir Oliver St John, Master of the Ordnance, produced an inventory dated 10 September 1611 (*Carew MSS* II, 95), that lists the armament of Culmore as comprising one 'brass' robinet and one saker and one falcon, both of iron, and that at Derry as one demi-cannon, two sakers, two falcons and one fowler, all of 'brass', plus one iron falconet (Tables 3–4). Further, we should note the presence of an iron saker at Dunalong, a decrease from the two 'pieces of iron artillery' noted and depicted on the map of 'Dounalong' of 1600 (Fig. 14c: McGurk 2006, 72–73, and 72, Fig. 5), also on the map (*TCD* MS 1209.14) of 1601–1602 in Trinity College, Dublin (Kerrigan 1995, 50–52, and 51, Fig. 25). The latter map, as with the depiction in Fig. 14d, also shows Lifford equipped with two cannon. As we shall see in Chapter 5, it seems reasonably certain that at least one, if not both, of the sakers bearing the rose-and-crown emblem were originally earmarked to be sent to Ireland in 1598.

An entry in the archives of the Goldsmiths for 22 August 1616, records the report on the developments in the Plantation by Alderman Peter Proby and 'Chief Commoner' Mathias Springham. In their comments on Culmore (*Carter MS* f. 621), they stated that

wee have viewd the Castle of Culmore . . . and where that fort had before but 3 pieces of ordenance, it will now require eight, for the defence thereof and to that end we have moved the Lords Justices . . . for fyve peices of ordenance out of his M^{ties} store at Derry for that ffort which they yielded unto, but resisted the ordering thereof, Because Sir Toby Calfeilde [Caulfield] *the Master of the ordenance there was then in England.*

There is something of a contradiction here between the implication that Derry had a sufficient arsenal to be able to spare five cannon,

Table 3 Examples of ordnance, munitions and gunners recorded at or ordered to be sent to Culmore, Lifford and Dunalong c. 1600–1639.

Date	Inventory	Munitions	Gunners	Notes	Source
16 Apr 1600	'one piece of demy canon of brass, two culverins of iron'			Culmore. Landed as part of Docwra's forces.	Docwra p. 43
1600	'twoo yron peeces of artillery'			Dunalong. Key to sketch map of 'Dounalong'	NA SP63/207 Part VI, 84.ii McGurk 2006, 72–73
1600	'ii yron peeces'			Lifford. Key to sketch map of 'the Lyfford'	NA SP63/207 Part VI, 84.iii McGurk 2006, 86–87
1 Jan 1611			A gunner	Noted to be moved along with a constable and 10 warders to Greencastle.	Cal. SPI 1611–1614, 8
30 Sept 1611	'brass' – 1 robinet, 'iron' – 1 saker, 1 falcon			Culmore	Carew MSS 1603–1623, 95
30 Sept 1611	1 iron saker			Dunalong	Carew MSS 1603–1623, 95
22 Aug 1616	'3 pieces of ordnance'			Culmore	Carter MSS, f. 621
19 Jul 1620	'iron ordnance … two demy culverins, fower sakers, two mynions, and two falcons'			Culmore. 'Ordinance sent for Ireland the 5th August Anno 1620'	Warrant for export of guns given to the City of London – NA SP 39/12: Appendix A1.1, account listing costs NAS RH15/91/61: Appendix A1.2
21 Mar 1627	'14 pieces of ordnance'			Culmore	Phillips MSS 84
16 Aug 1627	'2 demi culverins, 4 sakers, 2 minions, 2 falcons, all of iron and none of them mounted upon good Carriages …'	'19 barrels of corn powder … 600 iron shot … 29 worms ladles and sponges … 600 iron shot … gynne … 2 ropes 1 blockhead, 1 gynne pole, 18 lifters'		'… not so much as one gunner … As for ordnance … none of them mounted on good carriages;'	Phillips MSS 105–106

Chapter 4 – The Origins of the Ordnance of the Sixteenth and Seventeenth Centuries

Table 4 Examples of ordnance, munitions and gunners recorded at or ordered to be sent to Londonderry pre-1641

Date	Inventory	Munitions	Gunners	Notes	Source
Oct 1566–Apr 1567	culverin			Described by Carew as '…lost at the Dyrrey [=Derry], when it was burned, was afterwards recovered by George Thornton.'	Carew MSS 1589–1600, 2,18 March 1589
10 Nov 1566		7 lasts of corn powder		'A proporcion of Powder and other munition to be conveyed to Mr. Randolph … to Dyrie upon Loch ffoyle …'	NA SP 63/18, f. 82
27 Dec 1600	'six pieces, five of metall, one yron'			Listed in the key to Humphrey Covert's sketch of Derry.	NA SP 63/207 Part VI.84.i, McGurk 2006, 64–65
7 Jun 1601		3 lasts of 'corne powder', 1 last of 'cannon powder'		Sent to 'Lough Foile'. By this stage, Docwra was firmly established in Derry. His record of 20 June 1601 gives '60 barrels'	APC 1600–1601, 409, 446 f Docwra 58
30 Sept 1611	'brass ordnance' – 1 demi-cannon, 2 sakers, 2 falcons, 1 fowler 'iron' – 1 falconet				Carew MSS 1603–1623, 95
10 Jul 1615		6 barrels of gunpowder at £8 0s 0d		Entry in the Londonderry Port Book for 1615	Hunter 1975b
22 Aug 1615	'fyve peices of ordenance out of his Maties store at Derry'			Not a direct listing, but implies that at least five pieces were known to be there.	Carter MS, f. 621
21 Nov 1621		'a fourth part of the proporcon of armes … 16 lastes of powder …'		Part of a consignment destined either for Londonderry or Carrickfergus	APC 1621–1623, 90
1 Apr 1623			2 gunners at Derry at 18d per diem		NA WO 55/1752, f. 49

Continued over

103

Table 4 Continued.

Date	Inventory	Munitions	Gunners	Notes	Source
24 May 1625		'Cornpowder 37 barrels, Lead 5618 pounds'			Cal. SPI 1625–1632, 28
Dec 1625	'… the Ordnance lie on the ground saving one demy cannon I gott mounted.'				Milligan 1996, 53–54 (Letter from Lord Blaney to Lord Deputy Falkland)
10 Jan 1626	'only one demy-cannon is mounted'			Sir Thomas Phillips letter to the Lord Deputy	Cal. SPD 1625–1632, 84–85
16 Aug 1627	7 'of all sorts'			'… it is meet there be 20 pieces of ordnance and all accoutrements fitting them, as carriages, munition, gunners, etc., besides those 7 of all sorts that are already;'	Phillips MSS 899
26 May 1628	'10 guns at Londonderry'		'only one gunner'	Included in a report on artillery in Ireland by Sir Toby Caulfield, Master of the Ordnance.	Cal. SPI 1625–1632, 341, 26 May 1628.
9 Nov 1628	'the ordnance for Londonderry and Coleraine should be despatched'			Sir Thomas Phillips' remembrances for Ireland, incuding 'The master of the Ordnance to be asked what is required'	Cal. SPI 1625–1632, 400, 9 November 1628.
15 Mar 1632		Corne powder 100 barrels		Included in 'A neare estimate of the Powder, Armes and other habiliments of war …'	Strafford Str P1, ff 36–37

Chapter 4 – The Origins of the Ordnance of the Sixteenth and Seventeenth Centuries

and the facts that not only had construction of the stone walls just started, but also that on 6 October of the previous year, and again in November 1616, Bodley had reported unfavourably on the overall state of the defences (Curl 2000, 118–119).

The most obvious change at Culmore between 1600 and 1611 is the downsizing of the ordnance, with the loss of the large-calibre demi-cannon and culverins. It seems not unreasonable to suggest that the 'brass' demi-cannon which appears in the 1611 Inventory for Derry was that originally at Culmore (and one of those pieces subsequently removed by Sir Charles Coote Jnr. after 1649 – *infra*). After the success of Docwra's campaigns and the decisions to develop Derry as the major stronghold in the Lough Foyle area, such redeployment would have been logical. In any case, all of the implications are that from the time when Docwra first constructed his fortifications at Derry, there was a complement of cannon there, although we have no proper record.

The 1611 Inventory for Derry lists only seven pieces, of which four are small calibre. The implication is thus that between 1611 and 1616, new ordnance arrived at the City, but from where? The brass demi-cannon may well have come from Culmore, but records of the period make no mention of such redeployment. Similarly, a potential source would be the relocation of the sakers originally at Dunalong, which appears to have fallen into disuse by at least 1615.

Ordnance for Culmore

In 1619, Pynnar reported on Culmore that

This fort or blockhouse of Culmoore is now in the hands of Captain John Baker; the walls are now finished and the castle built, all of which is strong and neatly wrought, with platforms for the artillery;

It seems clear that the issuing of a Royal warrant on 19 July 1620, permitting the City of London, in the person of one Roger Rose to purchase and export ten pieces of iron ordnance 'into the Relme of Ireland for the defense of Culmore Castle' (Appendix A1.1 and 2), was the implementation of the next stage in the planning for a position of strength at the mouth of the Foyle. This provides the first direct evidence for the City of London supplying heavy weaponry to the Plantation. It is clear from the account set out in Appendix A1.2 that funding for these pieces came ultimately from the twelve Great Companies[7] and their subsidiaries, each of the twelve being billed for £29 04s 01d. It is tempting to see the five cannon which survive in the City and which bear the shield of the City of London as a part of this consignment. The list of types in the inventory of 1627 (Table 3) and those specified in the warrant match precisely (two demi-culverins, four sakers, two minions and two falcons). Indeed, two of the items in the accounting for this consignment comprise 'engraving' and 'cutting a mould for London arms'. As we shall see in Chapter 6, the London shield was cast as an integral part of the mould used for each cannon, and it is possible that these references are to the making up of a pattern of the arms to be applied to the moulds.

Roger Rose proved elusive, not the least hindrance being the fact that the word in the licence that follows directly after his name has proved virtually illegible. Although one possible reading is 'mariner', the more likely is 'merchant'. The surname seems not to be particularly common in England at this time, although occurring regularly in Scotland. However, how and why a Scotsman would be in a position to export ordnance to Ireland at this time is unclear, although James I did have a fondness for furthering the causes of his fellow countrymen. In fact, the extensive research on English port books by the late R.J. Hunter allowed him to offer clear indication that Rose was a merchant of Strangford, Co. Down, most likely English, and recently established there.[8] Entries in the Chester Port Book show that on 18 September 1620, Roger Rose imported to Strangford from Chester one tun of beer and five tons of coal 'for his use' (*NA* E190/1332/1 f. 31) in the *Grace* of Greenock, James Wilson Master. On 12 October of the same year he exported twenty-five cows from Strangford to Chester on the *Gennett* of Fairley, Humphrey Johnson, Master (*ibid.* 10v). Most important, though, is the fact that we can place Roger Rose or Roose[9] in the Port of London on 24 July

105

1620 with the *William and Joan* of London, corresponding to the accounts for the cannon consignment. An entry in the Port Book for 1619–1620 (*NA* E190/23/3 unpaginated) for this day refers to the 'W^m & Jone of London Roger Roose m^{tr}'. However, the reference to *John* Roose in the accounting suggests the possibility that Roger had a relation who was, in fact, the Master/owner or co-owner of the *William and Joan*. But of course, it could be that this is simple scribal error.

In any case, it seems very likely that we may identify Roger with the Roger Rose who was admitted as Freeman to the Merchant Taylors on 10 August 1601, having served his apprenticeship to one Robert Longrowe (*Merchant Taylors Freemen* 3, f. 125), and possibly with the Roger Rose, again a Merchant Taylor, who in May of 1633 leased from the Worshipful Company of Grocers a small tenement in Lambe Alley in London at a rent of 13s 4d *per annum* (*Grocers CM* 3, ff 504 and 509, 6 May and 29 June 1633). This Roger was one of a bunch of Roses admitted to the livery in the period 1594–1628, and there is ample precedent for members of a Great Company being involved in the arms trade.

Rose must have received the consignment from Edmond Turvill,[10] who also provided ordnance to the East India Company at least in the early 1620s (Brown 1990c, 20), and almost certainly was an independent trader who purchased ordnance from a variety of sources. His name does not occur in any listing of early seventeenth-century gunfounders, and it seems most likely that he was a supplier of preference rather than having any direct involvement in gunfounding. Turvill and John Browne I are mentioned in both of the sets of minutes below, and in each Browne is referred to as a gunfounder, Turvill not. Evidently in 1618 and 1619 he had been able to supply ordnance at the competitive prices of 10s 6d and 11s per cwt respectively, as noted at a Court of 31 March 1620 (*BL* IOR B/6, ff 553–554). The discussion, however, now was of a price of 12s per cwt (the same as paid for the Culmore consignment), something which was giving rise to complaint! The officers of the Company were prepared to offer 11s 6d per cwt, because 'he hath dealt honestlie and rightlie with the Companie', but he was holding out for 12s.

Thus, there was a suggestion that the Company should go to John Browne because of the quality of his products. Also, it was mooted that Turvill actually got many of his guns from Browne[11] 'and so maketh a second gaine and profit'. However, the decision went against Browne in no uncertain terms.

> . . . there being no trust in Mr. Browne's promises, and the Companie so often deceived by him, Mr. Deputie would not have to do with him any more.

It seems that Turvill was quickly back in favour again. In the record of a Court of Committees of the Company held on 21 July 1621, he was described (*BL* IOR B/7 f. 11) as

> . . .the man they best liked to deal withall both because his peeces are held to be of the best mine [= 'iron' or 'metal'] and likewise because he hath been observed to perform well at what he undertaketh

And in 1624, Court minutes noted 'Mr. Turvill to be dealt with privately for good ordnance which is rated higher than formerly.' (*Cal. SP Colonial* 1622–1624, 462, 8–10 December 1624). In effect, given his connections to both the East India Company and the Brownes, it seems quite likely that Turvill purchased the Culmore consignment from John I.[12]

This consignment has a further strong link to the East India Company in the form of Richard Mountney, the 'husband' of the Company, whose managerial duties included organising the loading, arming and provisioning of its ships (Chaudhuri 1965, 100–101). Here, he organised the transport of the Culmore pieces and took care of the administrative side of the proofing.

The John Evelin (Evelyn) who supplied the twelve barrels of powder was Sir John Evelyn, whose family was heavily involved in the gunpowder industry (Crocker and Crocker 2000, 8*f*; Edwards, P. 2000, 109). As we shall see later in this chapter, William Felgate was a merchant who at this time was on his way to becoming a very important player, not just in the arms and munitions trade, but also in the development of trade to the New World. Another name that is of interest here is that of

Thomas Covell, since Felgate was apprenticed to one Francis Covell, a Skinner, who rose to be a Warden of the Company. In fact, Thomas was the son of Francis, and was admitted to the freedom of the Skinners Company (*Skinners Apprentices* 2, f. 35) by virtue of patrimony in May 1608.[13] It seems reasonable to infer both that it was under Francis Covell that William Felgate got his introduction to the world of arms dealing and that this led (amongst other things) to his collaboration with Thomas on the Culmore ordnance consignment. That this was not a one-off arrangement is indicated by an offer to the Privy Council of 30 March 1622, made jointly with Thomas,[14] to sell 'round shott of Iron' of calibres ranging from culverin to falcon at £11 per ton (*NA* SP 14/128 f. 133).

The carriage maker John Horton can be identified with the John Horton who was an Ordnance Office craftsman, described in 1619 as 'Deputy unto Wm Wheatley his Mat^{es} Mr Carpenter for ye Office of ye Ordnance' and responsible for the construction of field carriages for Irish service (*NA* WO 49/48, f. 137, dated 1 December 1619). By October 1621, it appears that he had assumed the role of Master Carpenter (*NA* WO 49/50, f. 130r). However, he was dead by the end of March 1622, his last debenture being dated 1 March 1622 (*NA* WO 49/51, f. 48r), and on 31 March 1622, payment of this was recorded to his widow Alice (*ibid.* f. 54v). He is certainly the John Horton 'carpenter of London' whose will was registered 13 May 1622 (*NA* PROB 11/40, f. 74r), and in which he consigned his immortal soul to God and his goods and chattels to his 'deere and loving wife Alice' and to his children.

Disputes with the Crown

Following a series of reports on the state of the progress of the Plantation – by George Smithes and Mathias Springham in 1613, subsequently by Bodley in 1614 and 1616, Peter Proby and Springham in 1616, Nicholas Pynnar in 1619, Thomas Phillips and Richard Hadsor in 1622 – to say nothing of the ongoing, vitriolic outpourings of Sir Thomas Phillips, particularly between 1623 and 1629 (e.g. *Cal. SPI* 1615–1625, 514 no. 1246, dated 6 July 1624; *Phillips MSS 65ff*), there was much frigid correspondence between the Companies and the Crown. In May 1624, The Lords presented demands (*Cal. SPI* 1615–1625, 499), amongst which were:

Londonderry. – The eight bulwarks about the city of Londonderry are to be furnished with platforms of oaken timber, and with 20 pieces of ordnance as specified.

Four gunners to attend and use the artillery, and to have ready at all times the quantity of corn powder,[15] and iron shot and other materials enumerated.

7. Culmoore. – The three bulwarks in the fort of Cullmoore [Culmore] must be furnished with nine pieces of ordnance and two gunners to attend them, the necessary ammunition, and 18 warders always established for the guard of the fort, besides the two gunners, the said gunners and warders to be well paid from time to time.

The reference to Culmore suggests that the cannon delivered in 1620 had been redeployed, probably to Londonderry. However, to the charges that (amongst other things) they had failed to provide sufficient cannon for the protection of Londonderry and Culmore, the Common Council replied suggesting that, in their view, the Companies had fulfilled their obligations and that the King should take responsibility for some of the defence of the City. Their *Answer of the Common Council of the City of London to the forgoing Propositions of the Lords of the Privy Council concerning the alleged defects in their Ulster Plantation* included the following (*Cal. SPI* 1615–1625, 500–501, 2 June 1624)

1. Notwithstanding that they have fully performed their agreement of building and walling the City of Londonderry, will make bulwarks, sentinel houses, guard houses, and stairs for His Majesty's service; and as for ordnance, carriages, powder, shot, gunners, and other furniture thereto appertaining; they conceived that they were not tied to any such matter by any agreement and desire that His Majesty will furnish the same.

7. They conceived that Culmore was sufficiently furnished with ordnance, ammunition and warders.

Certainly Item 7 refers to the ordnance that had been sent to Culmore. Further, the pieces referred to in the Inventory of 1611 for Derry (Table 4) – almost certainly those brought over by Docwra in 1600 – were considered by the Companies to be Crown property and, as such, to be augmented in number by the Crown. It was not that the Companies felt that they had no obligations to provide arms for the defence both of the City and of their proportions. Indeed in 1619, for example, the Vintners set up a committee for the furnishing of 'warlicke furniture' to their tenants (*Vintners CM* 2, f. 243), while in 1620 the Merchant Taylors (*Merchant Taylors CM* 6, f. 28 dated 22 November 1620) when queried were able to list the small arms and munitions that they had sent.

Essentially, by the early 1620s, the Companies were feeling that they had ploughed in more than sufficient funds to meet their obligations under the Charter and, as many had feared from the outset, were seeing precious little profit, and little likelihood of other than a permanent drain on their coffers. That they had cut corners was not in doubt after the various surveys, and the Crown was not impressed by prevarication and pleadings of financial difficulty, but was intent on ensuring what it viewed as an acceptable level of performance. In September 1624, a committee of the Lords, which had been set up to investigate charges laid by Phillips against the Companies, presented their findings and recommendations to the King. What purportedly was seen by the Crown as underinvestment, neglect and rank bad management of the Plantation led to the King putting Phillips in charge of overseeing implementation of required improvements, which were set out in twenty-three clauses (*Cal. SPI* 1615–1625, 527–529, 24 September 1624; *Phillips MSS* 66*ff*). Those relating to defence, far more specific than those of the original Articles of Agreement, read as follows:

2. They are to provide platforms for their guns and carriage sheds, and all other necessities for their ordnance, which is to consist of 20 pieces, viz.: 6 culverins, 6 demi-culverins, 8 sakers,[16] with 2 gunners, the defence of the city being committed by H.M. to them.

3. To erect guard-houses and centinel-houses, and stairs to the bulwarks.

11. The fort of Culmore to be properly armed and garrisoned.

21. Londonderry to be victualled for four months for 400 men . . . Culmore for 20.

A different version is to be found in the records of the Privy Council (*APC* March 1625–May 1626, 158–159, September 1625). The relevant points in common read

2. That they make strong and sufficient platforms for their ordnance with carriages, sheds or coverings to keep the carriages from rotting,[17] guns and all other necessities for the use of the artillery, as powder, iron shot etc. The ordnance to be 20 pieces, (viz.) 6 culverins, 6 demi-culverins and 8 sakers, and two gunners to be provided at their charge. The guard and defence of the City being by His Majesty committed unto them, but what is requisite for the field we conceive it to be no part of their charge.

3. They are to build and erect guardhouses, sentinel houses, stairs and passages to the bulwarks and ramparts where they are deficient or defective.

11. That the Fort of Culmore be sufficiently cared for and furnished with ordnance, munitions and gunners according to the contract.

21. That the City of Londonderry be victualled for 4 months ever beforehand for 200 men . . . the Fort of Culmore for 20.

That they make strong and sufficient platforms of good oaken timber for their ordnance with carriages, sheades and coveringes to keep the carriage from rotting, gynnes and all other necessities for the use

Chapter 4 – The Origins of the Ordnance of the Sixteenth and Seventeenth Centuries

of the artillerie, as powder, ironshott etc., the ordnance and all other necessaries to be provided at their charge viz. :- six culverins, sixe demi-culverins and eight sacres with two gunners to attend them.

The death of James I in 1625 and the accession of Charles I only suspended for a while the escalation in the level of hostility between City and Crown. In 1625 the Crown ordered the sequestration of all income from the Plantation, although the Companies managed to circumvent this (Curl 2000, 136). A commission established in 1627 to report on the current state of the Plantation and on the performance of the City in fulfilling its obligations under the Articles was more than somewhat critical of a number of areas (e.g. Moody 1939, 242*ff*). Its report was sufficiently damning for the Crown to order again the sequestration of all rents from the Plantation. And, in terms of ordnance, Sir Tobias Caulfield's note (Table 4) of only ten cannon in Londonderry in August 1628, when provision of twenty had been stipulated, can hardly have helped the cause of the City of London.

The Phillips 'Collection' of 1629, in which he gave detailed figures for investment and profit, was the final straw as far as Charles I was concerned, and in 1630 proceedings against the City began in the Court of Star Chamber. After being found guilty in 1635 on all counts laid against it, the City was to be fined £70,000 and have its patent revoked. Following much haggling, it was agreed that in return for a full pardon the fine should be reduced to £12,000 and that all property in Ulster, and the income from it, was to revert to the Crown. As Curl notes (2000, 141), the whole proceedings constituted 'an arbitrary action concerned more with raising revenue than with matters of justice.' This outcome, along with the subsequent manoeuvrings of Lord Deputy Wentworth between 1635 and 1640 (Ohlmeyer 1996b), served only to heighten the hostility of the City to the Crown, influencing significantly attitudes at the outbreak of the English Civil War.

One point of note in the Phillips 'Collection' is his 'estimate' (*Phillips MSS* 129–131) of a total expenditure by the City between 1609 and 1629, including that of £558 on 'ordnance and munition' and £40 for 'mounts for guns' (i.e. carriages). Curl (1986, 86) points out that overall, his figures are clearly too low, an obvious result of Phillips' hostility towards the City. Just how inaccurate they could be is evident from the cost of the consignment of ordnance delivered to Culmore in 1620, some £64 more than his total of £236. The guns were priced at 12s per cwt and, even if there had been no price increase,[18] a similar weight of ordnance represented by the ten pieces recorded in the city in 1628, plus carriages would double that, really showing up the degree to which Phillips deliberately underestimated expenditure in his attempts to blackguard the Londoners. So, if we take the average cost of a carriage as between approximately £6 (as represented by the figure in the Culmore account: Appendix A1.2) and the £8 average charged in 1619 to the Ordnance Office by John Horton and Lewis Tate for a consignment of carriages for culverins and demi-culverins (*NA* WO 49/48, f. 137v dated 1 December 1619), Phillips' allowance of £40 for carriages would only have mounted six or seven guns. Thus, unfortunately, we cannot rely on him as any guide to numbers of cannon in the City in the early decades of the 1600s.

The surviving information for Londonderry shows that the number of pieces did not remain static. As with Culmore, redeployment seems to explain changes in at least two instances, since cannon were removed from the City, quite possibly as part of the mustering by the Lord Deputy Wentworth and Sir Christopher Wandesford of an Irish army to fight in Scotland, although it may have been due also to the broader policy of Wentworth of disarming the potentially troublesome Presbyterian population of Ulster.

An increase in inventory came when the small fortification of Charles Fort surrendered to Sir Charles Coote in 1649 following the collapse of the siege. According to Finch (*Finch* 13) it contained '11 peeces of ordnance and 4 small drakes' and these seem to have ended up in the Londonderry magazine, the drakes probably being those listed from 1660 (Appendix A14.1) onwards.[20] In addition, he noted – but without specifying materials or calibres – that two pieces were taken at New Buildings, some three miles to the south of the City.

109

Table 5 Examples of ordnance, munitions and gunners recorded at or ordered to be sent to Culmore and Strabane c.1640–1690.

Date	Inventory	Munitions	Gunners	Notes	Source
Nov 1641		'Thirty-nine Barrels of Powder ... besides Match and Bullets both for great Ordnance and Muskets, to Colmore Castle, for the Defence of that and Londonderry, and the Country about'		Culmore. Duke of Richmond's reply to charges brought against him by members of the House of Commons	*Lords J. 4*, 31 January 1642, 551
				A consignment of matériel sent to Sir Robert Stewart, Governor of Culmore Castle, by the Duke of Richmond at the behest of Charles I.	*A True and Breife Account* 298
3 Aug 1641			12d per day for a gunner	Sir Robert Stewart's petition to the King to be restored to the post of Governor of Culmore, dated 3 August 1661	*Cal. SPI* 1660–1682, 296
15 Feb 1642	'one great piece of ordnance'			Strabane	*Griffin* 3
25 Mar 1660	2 demi-culverins 5 iron sakers 2 iron minions 2 falcons	'half a barrel of powder seaven hundred great shot'		Culmore	NA WO 55/1752 f. 103 Appendix A 14.1
Sept 1660	'5 brass ffalcon drakes'			Culmore	*Carte MSS* 54, f519
Aug 1662	2 iron demi-culverins unmounted 5 iron sakers 1 mounted 2 iron minions unmounted 2 iron falcons unmounted			Culmore	*NLI MS* 2274, f. 11
1662			Gunner's mate at 10d per diem, Matross at 8d per diem	Culmore	NA WO 55/1752, f. 162
1662			a gunner	Culmore	NA WO 55/1752, f. 156
18 Aug 1663			a gunner at 10d per diem	Culmore	*Carte MSS* 165, f. 235r

Continued over ▶

Chapter 4 – The Origins of the Ordnance of the Sixteenth and Seventeenth Centuries

Table 5 Continued.

Date	Inventory	Munitions	Gunners	Notes	Source
27 Feb 1665			Gunner and matross	Culmore. Petition by the City of London who claim to have maintained a Captain, 10 warders, a gunner and matross there and now wished to be relieved of the responsibility.	*Cal. SPI 1663–1665*, 547
10 Jul 1674	2 demi-culverin, 3 saker, 3 minion – one broken at the muzzle, 2 falcons	Round shot for Demi cannon 2, Demi culverin 136, Saker 220		Culmore	NA WO 55/1752, f. 247 Appendix A14.2b
1 Apr 1666			a gunner	Culmore	*Cal. SPI 1666–1669*, 68–79
25 Mar 1676			a gunner's mate at £14:00:00	Culmore	*Carte MSS* 54, f. 448
5 Jun 1678		Powder 12 barrels 7lb, 1 barrel unserviceable		The same inventory for Londonderry lists no powder.	*Carte MSS* 54, f. 608
28 Feb 1681	Iron ordnance 11	Round shot 358 Powder 11 barrels 5 lb		The same inventory for Londonderry lists no powder.	*Carte MSS* 66, ff 401–402
25 Mar 1682	Iron ordnance, 10 mounted, 4 to be mounted		A gunner's mate at 14l 0s 0d	Culmore	*Carte MSS* 53, f. 704
25 Mar 1684	'brass ordnance' – 4 3-pdrs (cut), 2 falconett (cut) 'iron ordnance' – 2 demi-culvering, 4 sakers, 3 minion (1 broken at the muzzle), 2 falcon.	'36 barrels of powder 4 shot for demy cannon 172 shot for demy culvering 180 for saker'		Culmore. 'standing carriages serviceable'	*Ormond MSS* I, 394
1685	'brass ordnance' – 4 3-pdrs, 4 falconet, 'iron ordnance covered with brass ' – 2 demi-culverin, 'iron ordnance' – 4 saker, 3 minion, 2 falcon			Culmore	*Ormond MSS* II, 334–335

Continued over ▲

Table 5 Continued.

Date	Inventory	Munitions	Gunners	Notes	Source
22 Mar 1687			1 gunner's mate at 14l. per annum	Culmore	*Cal. SPD* Jan. 1686–May 1687, 397
23 Apr 1689	'4 falcon and 4 rabonette of brass, and 3 minion, 2 demiculverine, 4 sacker-minion and 2 falcon of iron'.			Culmore	*OS Londonderry* 239
1689	'Eleven, some 24, some 8 some 3 pounders'			Culmore	*Fleet Diary* 11

Table 6 Examples of ordnance, munitions and gunners recorded at Londonderry c.1640–1690.

Date	Inventory	Munitions	Gunners	Notes	Source
Nov 1641		'thirty barrels of Powder, with other Armes and Munition . . .'		Brought to Londonderry from Dublin by Captain Boulton.	*Lawson* 8.
Nov 1641		'Thirty-nine Barrels of Powder . . . besides Match and Bullets both for great Ordnance and Muskets, to Colmore Castle, for the Defence of that and Londonderry, and the Country about . . .'		Despatched by the Duke of Richmond on the order of Charles I	*Lords J.* 4, 31 January 1642. *True and briefe account . . .* 297
Oct 1641–Feb 1642	'. . . four pieces of Ordnance great and small'			This figure is recorded in a number of sources.	e.g. *Griffin* 4
4 Apr 1642		Fourteen barrels of powder			*Ormond MSS* new series II, 110
15 Jun 1642			'Allowance shall be given to One Gunner and his Mate . . . for Londonderry'		*Commons J.* 2, 1640–1643 624–626
1642	'. . . fifteene pieces of Ordnance . . . and foure we had before.'			'. . . sent thither by these worshipful and worthy companies . . .'	*Winter* 1643, 4 Doe Castle 5
18 May 1643		'two barrels of gunpowder wth a proporcon of match'		Sent by the Vintners	*Vintners* CR 4, f. 112
5 Jul 1643		'two barrels of gunpowder and 1 cwt of match'		Sent by the Clothworkers, with 12 spades, 12 shovels and 12 pickaxes	*Clothworkers* CM f. 81v
15 Aug 1643		'. . . two barrels of gunpowder and one hundredweight of match'		Sent by the Skinners. 'Mr ffelgate is intreated to provide, and furnish the same, and to bee paid by Mr Renter Warden.'	*Skinners* CR 3, f. 205v

Continued over ▶

Table 6 Continued.

Date	Inventory	Munitions	Gunners	Notes	Source
23 Sept 1643		Draft orders for payment to Henry Finch for supplies, swords and ammunition received in Londonderry			House of Lords, Journal Office HL/PO/JO/10/1/157. 9–30 September 1643
23 Mar 1660	'Iron: 12 demi-culverins, 2 sakers, 4 minions, 2 falcons brass: 4 drakes, 1 small peece of brass, 4 small field peeces'			'in the Citidell'	NA WO 55/1752, f. 102r Appendix A14.1
Sept 1660	'Brasse ordnance Mynions nil Ffalcon drakes 5'				Carte MSS 54, f. 519
16 Oct 1661		'The clerk of the store shall attend between 9am and 11am and shall be ready to issue powder to such as shall be licensed to buy it at 20d per pound. The following persons are also empowered to give licences . . . Co. Londonderry from Londonderry, Earl of Mount Alexander, and in his absence, John George (Gorge).'		Instructions by the Lords Justices and Council declaring how the King's subjects may be furnished with gunpowder.	Cal. SPI 1660–1662, 440–442
6 Aug 1662	'Demi-culverins 9 iron whereof 2 mounted, Saker 3 iron unmounted, Minion 4 iron unmounted, Falcon 2 iron unmounted'				Carte MSS 54, f. 517
Aug 1662	10 iron demi-culverin unmounted, 4 iron sakers unmounted, 4 iron minions unmounted, 4 brass minions, 2 iron falcons unmounted, 1 iron robinett unmounted	Powder 6 barrels, Culverin shot 64, Demi-culverin shot 440, Saker shot 100, Stone shot 64			NLI MS 2274, ff 10–12 Carte MSS 54, f. 519

Continued over ▲

Table 6 Continued.

Date	Inventory	Munitions	Gunners	Notes	Source
Aug 1662	Demi-culverin, 10 iron unmounted, Saker, 4 iron unmounted				NA WO 55/1752, ff 146r–147v Appendix A14.1
Aug 1662	'Brasse ordnance, Mynions 4, ffalcon drakes 0'				Carte MSS 54, f. 519
1662		6 barrels of powder, Shot – Demi-culverin 440, Saker 100	Gunner at 12d per diem		Carte MSS 54, ff 514–515 NA WO 55/1752, f. 162
1662	'some Twenty and odd Iron gunnes'			'... serviceable in themselves, but all dismounted.'	NA WO 55/1752, f. 155 Appendix A15
18 Aug 1663			A clerk of the stores at 20d per diem, a gunner at 12d per diem, a Matross at 8d per diem		Carte MSS 165, f. 235r
12 Jan 1665		'50 barrels of powder'			Ormond MSS I, 321
1 Aug 1665		36 barrels of powder			Carte MSS 54, f. 487
1 Jul 1667		19 barrels of powder			Carte MSS 54, f. 553
1 Aug 1667		36 barrels of powder			Carte MSS 54, f. 487
3 Apr 1668		15 barrels of powder			Carte MSS 54, f. 572
8 Mar 1668		Shot for saker 440, Shot for minion 100, Stone shot 64			NLI MS 2274 ff 10–11 Appendix A14.3
14 Dec 1669				'That your Grace will be pleased to order that the store there [Londonderry] be allowed so much munition of powder, match and ball . . . their [sic] being a very small quantity . . . That your Grace will vouchsafe the guns of the City of Londonderry to be speedily mounted upon carriages.'	Ormond MSS n.s III, 300 ('The humble proposals of Colonel John Gorges')

Continued over ▶

Table 6 Continued.

Date	Inventory	Munitions	Gunners	Notes	Source
9 Jul 1674	'Brass ordnance, 4 3-pdrs, 4 Faulconett Drakes, Iron ordnance, 10 demi culverin, 4 saker, 2 minion, 4 faulcon'	3½ barrels of powder, 1 'decayed'		Unmounted, 2 demi-culverins blown, 2 saker honeycombed, one cut at the muzzle, 1 falcon blown and unserviceable	NA WO 55/1752 f. 245
25 Mar 1676		No powder			Carte MSS 54, f. 448
5 Jun 1678		Powder 13 barrels 37lb			Carte MSS 54, f. 608
31 Jan 1679		Powder 3 barrels 50lb			Carte MSS 54, f. 609
28 Oct 1679		Round shot 508, Powder 0			Carte MSS 54, f. 622
28 Feb 1681	Brass ordnance 8, Iron ordnance 20		a gunner at 16 li 16s 0 d, a Matross at 11 li 4 s 0d		Carte MSS 66, ff 401–402
25 Dec 1682			a gunner at 16 li 16s 0 d, a Matross at 11 li 4 s 0d	In this listing, gunners at Dublin castle were being paid 19 li 12s 0d	Carte MSS 54, f. 458v NA WO 55/1752, ff 303–304
23 Jan 1683		Powder 36 barrels			Carte MSS 53, f. 694
25 Mar 1683	Iron ordnance. 20 mounted, 5 to be mounted		A clerk of the stores at 20d per diem, a gunner at 16 li 16s 0 d, a Matross at 11l 4 s 0d		Carte MSS 55, ff 704–706
17 Jul 1683		Barrels of powder 27 and 31lb			Carte MSS 53, f. 642
3 Feb 1684		26 barrels 81 lb			Carte MSS 54, f. 644
22 Feb 1684		Charge for carriage of 20 barrels of powder to Londonderry			Ormond MSS n.s. 7, 197
25 Mar 1684	'iron ordnance – 10 demy culvering, 4 sakers, 2 mynion, 3 falcon, 1 falconet'	31 barrels of powder, 431 iron shot for demy culvering, 77 iron shot for saker, 62 stone shot for culvering		1 saker 'honeycombed and clogged', 1 saker 'cut off at the muzzle', falconet 'blowne and unserviceable', 8 of the 'standing carriages' defective	Ormond MSS I, 393–394 Carte MSS 66, f. 441

Continued over ▶

Chapter 4 – The Origins of the Ordnance of the Sixteenth and Seventeenth Centuries

Table 6 Continued.

Date	Inventory	Munitions	Gunners	Notes	Source
1685	'Iron ordnance covered with brass – 10 demi-culverin, iron ordnance – 4 sakers, 2 minion, 3 falcon, 1 falconet'				*Ormond MSS* II, 334–335
22 Mar 1687			1 gunner at Londonderry at 16 li 16s. per annum		*Cal. SPD* Jan. 1686–May 1687, 397
25 Mar 1689		2 Barrels of Powder			*Inniskilling-men* 19
29 May 1689		107 barrels of powder		'We were greatly threatened with the enemy's bombs . . . took one hundred and seven barrels of powder out of the church and buried them.'	*Ash Journal* 71
5 Jun 1689	'. . . Great Guns of which they have 24 mounted upon the Bastions of the Walls, upon the Tower of the Church 2 . . . and 8 within the City . . .'	'near 500 barrels of powder . . . also bullets for their Great Guns . . .'			*Good News* 1 *Remarkable Occurrences* 1
1689	'8 sakers and 12 demi culverins'				*Walker* 10
1689	'. . . some guns brought up from Culmore . . . nine bastions about the town and three or four guns on each bastion . . .'				*True and Impartial Account* 27–28

Continued over ▶

A definite change in inventory is suggested by entries in the Derry Corporation Minutes between 1675 and 1682, concerning a demi-cannon, culverin and falcon, all of 'brass', supposedly taken from the City by Sir Charles Coote Jnr. (Appendix A17). According to these, the demi-cannon ended up in Kinsale, via Galway, while the other two pieces were sent to Galway and Sligo. The inventory of 1684 (from which has been abstracted Appendix A14.3) records a brass demi-cannon from Galway and installed at Charles Fort, County Cork, just outside Kinsale (*Ormond MSS* II, 377). The same inventory lists a brass falcon at Sligo and an iron culverin, unfortunately without giving the weight of the culverin (*ibid.* 391). While a brass falcon poses no problems, at no point since 1626 (Tables 3–4) was a demi-cannon recorded either in the city or at Culmore, although it is just possible that this is the piece recorded as having been lost at Strabane in 1642, and which could have been later recovered. Further, below demi-cannon, the heaviest calibre recorded in 'brass' at any time is minion. One possible explanation is that the demi-cannon and culverin were captured from the Royalist forces when Charles Fort and New Buildings surrendered to Coote in 1649. However, had such heavy calibre weapons been at the disposal of the besieging forces, one would have expected them to have been used against the defences with some effect. When referring to their ordnance, Finch only refers to balls of 4lb weight, certainly not to demi-cannon (*Finch* 9).

A further possibility is that the Corporation were mistaken in identifying a brass culverin for an iron one. Of the guns sent to the City in 1642 (Table 7), one was an iron culverin from the Skinners Company (Appendix A8), the arrival of which was confirmed by the Reverend Richard Winter. Significantly, it is missing from all inventories from 1660 (Appendix A14.1a) onwards, and is the only one of the Company guns not to be listed as being in the City then.

Allowing for the fact that the records are very sparse for the period *c.* 1630–1660, there seems no record of when Coote might have removed guns from the city, although it seems very likely that it would have been when he took his forces to invest Charlemont in County Armagh. In August 1650, in response to his reports (Gilbert 1879, 3, 149), the Irish Committee noted that Coote was short of great shot for demi- and whole cannon and for demi-culverin, having used up the entire supplies for the north of Ireland at the siege of Charlemont, and ordered despatch of fresh stocks (*Cal. SPD* 1649–1650, 295–296, 20 August 1650). This indicates that Coote had and had used ordnance of these three calibres against Charlemont, with the Londonderry magazine being one of the two possible sources.[21] It may be also that he took these or other guns from the City for his campaigning in Connaught in 1651.

What is abundantly clear is that from the arrival of the first guns destined specifically for the defence of the city, through to 1689, the complement was not static, but rather depended on deployment – local or further afield – as and when military commanders saw fit.

The Irish Rebellion and the Guns of 1642

On 22 October 1641, the Irish Rebellion broke in Ulster like a storm. It had not been foreseen by any, and one contemporary writer, Sir Audley Mervyn, noted that it was 'conceived among us, and never yet felt to kick in the wombe, nor struggle in the birth' (*Mervyn* 1). Led by Sir Phelim O'Neill, the insurgents quickly gained control of the major Ulster strongholds, with the exceptions of Carrickfergus and Lisburn in County Antrim, Londonderry, Culmore and Coleraine in County Londonderry and Enniskillen in County Fermanagh. And out of Ulster, the action 'diffused through the veines of the whole kingdome', although signally, Dublin was not captured.

While reports soon circulated in England to the effect that the rebellion had claimed the lives of tens of thousands of Protestants (e.g. Barnard 1993, 175*f*; Simms 1997), the estimates of most objective modern historians put the figure of those murdered at around four thousand (e.g. Ohlmeyer 1996a, 163). Nevertheless, the sheer ferocity of some events (which resonate down to the present in Unionist martyrology, as in the massacre at the bridge at Portadown) created an atmosphere of the deepest fear in England, both for the safety of the 'poore distressed protestants' and for very the survival of English authority in Ireland. The desperation felt by the administration in Ireland is clear from the correspondence of the Lords Justices from November 1641 onwards (*Ormond MSS* II, 7*ff*). Some thirty barrels of powder arrived by ship in Londonderry from Dublin in early November (*Lawson* 8), described as

> ... *the first reliefe and supply which came thither for the supplies of the Regiments and Souldiers there, without which they had been utterly lost and perished, as being destitute before of any Powder or Armes.*

Sir Robert Stewart, Governor of Culmore was commissioned on 'November 19 or thereabouts' (*True and breife account* 297) to raise a regiment[22] in the defence of Ulster, later reporting (*ibid.*; cf. *Lords J.* 4, 31 January 1642) that

> *His Majestie was also graciously pleased some few daies after the said commissions to send over a proporcion of muskatts, pikes, powder, match ... which were delivered to him att Colimore, within three miles of London Derry, by a servant of my Lord Duke of Richmond,*[23] *with a letter from his Lordship to the said Sir Robert Stewart, desiring him that if they stood in need of Ordinance to send to Sir William Coachran, his lordship's steward in Scotland, who would deliver us what ordinance we desired out of his Majesties Castle of Dumbartone.*

It is not clear just what ordnance could have been sent from Dumbarton, since it had only recently come back into English hands under the provisions of the Treaty of Berwick, having been taken by Covenanter forces on 26 March 1639. Although Covenanter sympathies may also have played a part, the garrison does not seem to have put up too much resistance, possibly due to a lack of supplies, which suggests that it was not particularly well stocked (e.g. Stevenson 1973, 140; Fissell 1994, 15). However, Stevenson (1981, 51) notes that Charles II agreed with the Scottish Parliament that he should *buy* from their owners arms and munitions stored at Dumbarton. But in any case, this offer clearly did not bear fruit, since on 8 January 1642, and again on 10 January, the Mayor and Aldermen of Londonderry wrote to the Lords Justices, describing the plight of the City (Hogan 1936, 1*ff*). Their letter of 10 January (*ibid.* 4) informed their Lordships that the City was seriously lacking in ordnance, stating that

> *The late Lord Deputy very unfortunately caused our best and most usefull ordnance to be carryed away from us; we beseech your Lordships to send them or some others to us with carriages ready made and some materialls for other carriages, for heere there is nothing to make them of;*

This was confirmed in the pamphlet *Newes from London-Derry in Ireland* dated 15 February 1642, in which we find one William Griffin writing of the rebels (*Griffin* 3–4) that they

> ... *burnt the town of Strabam* [Strabane]*, where they destroyed many in the fire, and took from us there one great piece of Ordnance; and they have another, which they got further in the Country with which and their force they beat downe all the houses in this town; for wee have in strength of men and arms to oppose them now, but foure pieces of ordnance great and small; this Towne doth need at least twenty pieces of Ordnance and a thousand men ...*

A letter of 27 April 1642 from the Mayor and Aldermen of Londonderry to the Scots Major-General Robert Munro[24] in Carrickfergus (*Extracts* 7), began

> *We of this city of Londonderry and other parts; have either bin forgotten, or given over for loste, as we conceive;*

and went on to explain that

> ... *want of powder and arms here hath bin our ruine. It is with great providence and goodnesse of God that we are hitherto preserved, having bin so ill armed and provided for; all the arms within his Majesties store here were shipt to Dublin the last summer,*[25] *and nothing left here but ony decaid calivers*[26]...

concluding with a plea for

> ... a good and large proportion of powder, match and lead, muskets, swords, pikes, some spades and shovels, whereof we have not any; and of these or what else may be had, as much as ye can possibly spare us, for we want all things fit to defend a distressed country and to offend a despirate enemy.

There are two possibilities as to who could have ordered the removal of ordnance from the City. The first, obviously, is Lord Deputy Thomas Wentworth, elevated to Lord Lieutenant and to the earldom of Strafford in January 1640, the second his successor Sir Christopher Wandesford whose short time in the post[27] coincided with the final stages of organising the 'new army' to be used in Scotland against the Covenanters. To where either Strafford or Wandesford might have sent the Londonderry guns remains a mystery, although since the army mustered at Carrickfergus, it is not impossible that they were taken there in the first instance, sometime in the earlier part of 1640. Planning had been ongoing since 1639, and Strafford informed Lord Cottington on 10 February 1640 stating that he would have '... 3,000 horse and foote... I shall have by Whitsuntide eight thousand spare armes, twelve field pieces and eight great ordnance...' (Firth 1895, 8). On 24 March, he told Wandesford that he was planning to have '30 pieces of ordnance' (Knowler 1739, II, 399). The use here of the term 'great ordnance' is a little ambiguous, as normally one would expect it to be reserved for pieces of at least culverin calibre, more likely demi-cannon and above. There was one demi-cannon recorded in the Lough Foyle area, but it was lost at Strabane in February 1642. It is possible therefore that the City was stripped of its smaller calibre ordnance while 'great ordnance' was obtained from elsewhere. In either case, however, it seems clear that the purchasing of arms via Strafford's agent William Railton did not include ordnance (e.g. Wedgwood 1961, 277).

It is noticeable, however, that Sir William St Leger who had charge of the training of the troops at Carrickfergus seems to have made no mention of this (e.g. *Carte MSS* 1, ff 231–232, 17 August 1640) in his reports. Similarly, in correspondence between Wandesford and Strafford over the various delays in mustering, provision of artillery apparently finds no place (e.g. *ibid.* ff 210r–211v, dated 30 June 1640 and ff 239v–241r, dated August 1640). Finally, in a fairly comprehensive summary report from the Lords Justices (*ibid.* ff 405v–406r) concerning the disbanding of the army – which includes detail of army pay and notes on the transportation of troops abroad – ordnance is not mentioned. Indeed, it is noticeable that the only reference to the disposition of matériel is where their Lordships decreed that

> *If there shall bee any powder or other munitions issued to any of the companies that they shall deliver the same...*

Alternatively, as suggested by the letter of 27 April 1642, the Londonderry pieces might have been sent to Dublin (but not in 1641) either as a part of the policy of Strafford to ensure that northern Presbyterians had as little access to weaponry as possible, or in general preparation for the forthcoming hostilities in Scotland, or both. However, it is not clear whether 'arms' in the later letter would have included ordnance. In any case, the disbanding of the new army, coupled with the outbreak of the Irish Rebellion, probably saw them dispersed beyond record or trace, wherever the road from the city had taken them.

On 19 January 1642, the Court of Common Council of the City of London considered the Irish situation, hearing a report from Sir Thomas Barrington. It was decided that measures – including a significant cash loan[28] – were to be taken in support of the people of the Ulster Plantation. On 24 January, the Mayor, Sir Richard Gurney, duly issued a precept to the Companies, copies of which are preserved in the records of most of the companies. Referring to

> ... *the miserable calamity and distress of the poor protestants in Ireland at this presente through the inhuman and bloody cruelty of the rebells there who spare not the protestants whomsoever they come taking away there lives in a most diabolicall and barbarous manner utterly exterpating whole families and townes...*

Gurney called for 'timely aid and succour to bee sent thither [to Ireland] for suppressing those blood thirsty rebells', in the form of 'bread corne or otherwise as to them shallbee thought most meete'. A 'Poll Office' was established at the Guildhall, and sums ranging from £10 from the Pewterers (*Pewterers CM* 4, f. 343v), £20 from the Blacksmiths (*Blacksmiths WA* 4, f. 236), £50 from the Brewers (*Brewers CM* 16, record dated 10 February 1642) and £80 from the Clothworkers (*Clothworkers AC* f. 11v), through to £160 from the Grocers (*Grocers WA* 12, f. 446) and £200 from the Merchant Taylors (*Merchant Taylors WA* 18, f18), were paid over to the administrator, Robert Bateman, Chamberlain of the City of London. In addition, a number of the companies decided to send wheat and other foodstuffs.[29] The Clothworkers are the only Company who admitted in their minutes to any debate in Court over whether or not the relief funds were 'for London Derry or for his Maties subjects in generall', discussion seemingly having been particularly frank and comradely (*Clothworkers CM* ff 54r–55v, dated 5 March 1642). The decision came down on the side of the 'subjects in generall'.

When, presumably, more news had come in of the progress of the first months of the rebellion – and the appeals from Londonderry had reached the London – the defensive needs became clearer. Gurney issued a further precept on 18 March 1642, calling specifically for ordnance for the defence of the City (Appendix A2). Most the companies responded rapidly and sympathetically, prompted by lurid reports of atrocities against Protestant settlers by the ' bloody papisticall rebells'. Although the accounts show clearly that a cannon was purchased by the Skinners, their Court Minutes have no record of the decision, unlike those of the other ten Companies who contributed. Of the twelve Great Companies, a notable exception were the Haberdashers who, apart from a donation of fifty quarters of wheat following the January precept, made no discernible contribution either in terms of money or guns. While they had disengaged early from the whole Plantation project, a further reason for this may be found in the minutes of a Court of 9 March 1642, in which the Company noted (*Haberdashers CM*, f. 310r)

that it was 'destitute of moneys by reason of the great loane of October 1640 which they were putt unto.'

The Vintners faced a revolt from their affiliates who refused to make any contribution whatsoever (Appendix A12). Nevertheless, by mid-May, some fifteen cannon of various calibres, along with carriages, powder and shot and 'other appurtenances' had been promised, with the last Company, the Vintners, committing on 18 May. The purchases (Tables 7–8) are confirmed in the accounts[30] of nine of the eleven contributing Companies (those of the Salters and Goldsmiths not having survived).

We have an important source of confirmation that these cannon actually arrived in Londonderry sometime probably between May and July of 1642. This comes from an account of affairs in the City up to November 1642, and written in early 1643 by the Reverend Richard Winter (*Newes from the North of Ireland*), who is identified by Milligan (1996, 70) as Rector of Ardstraw (near Strabane, County Tyrone). Winter was quite specific in his description of the aid sent by the Companies to the City, although he did not give a date-range for its arrival. His listing of the ordnance sent is included in Table 7 below for purposes of comparison with the information provided by the records of the individual Companies. As can be seen, his figure of fifteen cannon accords with the total from the archives. In seven of the Company accounts the type is given, with Winter's identifications corresponding exactly in five cases. Winter also noted that each piece was accompanied by 'an Oaken carriage, 30 shot, Ladle, Sponge and every other utensil thereunto belonging.' Again, the accounts of five of the Companies list specific gunners' accessories as being supplied, and two others note the purchase of 'appurtenances' (Table 8), while seven sets of accounts list payments for carriages. And in the 1660 inventory of ordnance at Londonderry (Appendix A14.1), all but the Skinners' gun are included in a total of twenty-nine pieces of both iron and 'brass'.

It is most difficult to determine when precisely the guns purchased by the companies were sent over and when actually they arrived.[31] The minutes of the Committee for Irish Affairs for 20 April 1642 (Snow and Young 1987, 421) record that

> *Whereas the present state and condition of the city of Londonderry in Ulster and some propositions in the behalf of the inhabitants thereof were this day presented unto the lords and others his majesty's commissioners for the affairs of Ireland, it is now thought fit and ordered by the said commissioners that the lord admiral be desired that the ship called the* Charity *may receive directions from his lordship to carry thither the ordnance and arms yet here and the ammunition at Carrickfergus which are designed for that place, and after the delivery thereof to ride in the river of Lough Foyle for the guard of the parts thereabouts till further directions.*

This raises the strong possibility that at least some of the Company guns were ready for transport by this time. Vaughan's letter of 27 April confirms that the guns had not left England then. Certainly, the carriage and 'appurtenances' for the Fishmongers' gun, if not the gun itself, might not have been ready to travel before 9 May, since it was at a Court on that date[32] that the decision was taken to add these to the gift from the Company (Appendix A6). Further, the situation regarding the *Charity*[33] is less clear from a further entry in the minutes for 6 May (*ibid.* 441), which states that

> *Whereas the lords and others his majesty's commissioners for the affairs of Ireland were this day informed that a ship called the* Charity *of London, formerly designed and appointed for the carriage of some pieces of ordnance, arms, and ammunition to Londonderry (in Ireland) for supply and relief thereof, was not sufficient burden to carry the same, it is now ordered that the lord high admiral of England be desired that directions may be given for carrying in that ship as much as she can well bear and that another ship of convenient burden may be hired for carrying the residue, which shall be paid for at the end of the service.*

However, it is clear from the record in the accounts of the Clothworkers (*Clothworkers AC* f. 11v: Appendix A13) that their saker at least was '. . . shipt in the Charity of London William Younge Master to be delivered at London Derry.' If a second vessel was hired, we do not seem to have a record of its name or that of its master.

The weight of the cannon in total was certainly significantly augmented by that of their carriages, and the likely burden for all fifteen guns, with their carriages and 'appurtenances' would have been in excess of sixty tons. It is worth noting that one of the charges paid by the Vintners and the Clothworkers was to William Felgate for shipping (Table 8). Given that William and his brother Tobias are known to have had interests in several ships, it is tempting to suggest that at least part of the consignment was sent using his maritime contacts, which included the owner and/or Master of the *Charity* or possibly a second but unnamed, vessel.

The tenor of a letter from Sir William Stewart to Ormond, dated 20 July 1642 (*Carte MSS* 3, f. 333), suggests that the company guns may have arrived by then. He wrote

> *And although we have made some shifte to gett some Musquets out of Scotland and other ways; yet wee are marvellous destitute of Pykes, Swords and Ammunition, wee bought some powder at some 8^l and some 10^d per barrell . . .*

From this it would seem that it was a lack of hand weapons and powder that was the problem, and that the requirement for ordnance had been met. Thus, we may conclude with reasonable certainty that all fifteen guns gifted from London had arrived at the latest by the start of July 1642.

It is clear that the various Companies took note of what the others were doing and in some cases adjusted their contributions. Thus, the Grocers waited to see what the others would do before deciding to send their two demi-culverins (Appendix A4), while the Fishmongers on realising that some were sending more than just ordnance, increased their gift by including powder, shot, carriages 'and other things' (Appendix A6).

Despite the obvious concern for their members in Ulster, it is not unfair to say that well before the 1640s, the Companies had wearied of the burden of the Plantation. It is clear also that their response to the plea for finance and ordnance for the 'reliefe of the poor protestants' was based more on sympathy than on any considerations of business, despite the stress

Chapter 4 – The Origins of the Ordnance of the Sixteenth and Seventeenth Centuries

Table 7 The cannon recorded as purchased by the Great Companies and the Londonderry ordnance listing of the Reverend Richard Winter and the 1660 Inventory (Appendix A14.1a).

Company	Type	Recorded 1642 weight	1660 inv. weight†‡	Actual weight	Cost	Cost per cwt	Bought from	Purchased by	Richard Winter	1660 inventory
Mercers**	2 'peeces of iron ordnance'		35cwt 2qtr 14lb 36cwt 0qtr 0lb	35cwt 2qtr 1lb	£61 09s 07d		Samuel Ferrers	'Wardens'	2 demi-culverins	2 demi-culverins
Grocers	2 demi-culverins	36cwt 1qtr 14lb 35cwt 2qtr 0lb	36cwt 1qtr 14lb 35 cwt 1qtr 0lb	35cwt 1qtr 3lb	£48 00s 00d	13s 6d	Samuel Ferrers		2 demi-culverins	2 demi-culverins
Drapers†	2 minions		16 cwt 0qtr 0lb 16 cwt 1qtr 0lb		£10 16s 00d £10 19s 4½d	13s 6d			2 minions	2 minions
Fishmongers*	1 demy culverin		35 cwt 3qtr 0lb	35cwt 1qtr 7lb	£38 13s 00d		Samuel Ferrers	Warden Greene	1 demi-culverin	1 demi-culverin
Goldsmiths††	'an iron peece of ordnance'		30cwt 0qtr 0lb						1 saker	1 demi-culverin
Skinners	'a peece of ordnance . . .'	43cwt 0qtr 0lb			£25 16s 00d	12s 0d	East India Company		1 full culverin	missing
Merchant Taylors*	2 demi culverins		36cwt 0qtr 14lb 34cwt 0qtr 14lb	36cwt 0qtr 2lb 33cwt 1qtr 26lb	£67 08s 00d		Samuel Ferrers	Capt. Langham Mr. Stone	2 demi-culverins	2 demi-culverins
Salters††	'a piece of ordnance'		26cwt 0qtr 0lb	24cwt 3qtr 23lb					1 saker	1 demi-culverin
Iron-mongers**	1 'peece of iron ordnance' = 1 saker in accounts	25cwt ½qtr 0lb	35cwt 0qtr 0lb		£26 16s 00d		Samuel Ferrers		1 demi culverin	1 saker
Vintners	1 'demy culvering'	30cwt 1qtr 0lb	30cwt 1qtr 0lb	29cwt 3qtr 1lb	£20 09s 04d	13s 6d	Samuel Ferrers	Warden Gardiner Robert Child	1 saker	1 demi-culverin
Clothworkers*	1 'sacar' [saker]	22cwt ½qtr 0lb	22cwt 0qtr 0lb		£15 03s 09d	13s 6d or 14s 3d	Samuel Ferrers	Captain Edmund Foster	1 saker	1 saker

* the cost listed in the accounts includes all 'appurtenances' ** includes cost of carriage † MS damaged – space left where weights should have been recorded, price estimated †† accounts for the period have not survived

123

Table 8 Payments for munitions, accessories and services for the Londonderry cannon in the accounts of the Great Companies for 1642–1643.

Company	Powder	Shot	Other	Supplied by	Cost	Total spent
Mercers	Unspecified	Unspecified	divers materials to be sent with them	William Felgate	£06 18s 0d	£07 19s 6d
			'charges about trying them [the demi-culverins]'	William Franklin	21s 6d	£61 09s 7d
						£69 09s 1d
Grocers			Carriages	John Pitt	£06 0s 0d	
			Wheels and axle trees	Thomas Bateman 'wheelwright'	£05 5s 0d	
			Ironwork for carriages		£06 10s 0d	
			'preparing stopping and culloring' and 'other charges'		£04 19s 0d	
			'searching and proving'		£00 15s 6d	
			engraving of company name	Abraham Preston	£00 10s 0d	£29 2s 10d
	Unspecified	Unspecified	ladles, staves, sponges, wadhooks and 'other things'	William Felgate	£05 03s 4d	£48 0s 0d
						£77 2s 10d
Drapers*	Unspecified quantity	Unspecified	Engraving		£00 10s 0d	£21 15s 4½d
			'watching and looking to' – i.e. searching		£00 3s 6d	£0 13s 6d
						£22 08s 10½d
Fishmongers	3 barrels‡	1½ cwt‡	'Carriage rammers & spuinge'	Samuel Ferrers		
Goldsmiths†						
Skinners			the carriage and appurtenances			
			Services by 'smith, painter and other workmen'	Mr. Felgate	£11 8s 6d	£25 16s 0d
	2 barrels‡‡	1 cwt‡‡	Unspecified	Mr Felgate	£06 7s 2d	£17 15s 8d
					no record	£43 11s 8d
Merchant Taylors			'trying the ordinance	Mr. Felgate	£06 9s 0d	£8 0s 6d
			loading and carriadge	Mr. Franklin	£00 21s 6d	£67 8s 0d
			ingraving of the culverines'	Abraham Preston	£00 10s 0d	£75 8s 6d
Salters†			engraving			

Continued over ▶

* manuscript damaged † accounts for the period have not survived ‡ possibly sent after July 1643 ‡‡ sent in May 1643

Chapter 4 – The Origins of the Ordnance of the Sixteenth and Seventeenth Centuries

Table 8 (Continued.)

Company	Powder	Shot	Other	Supplied by	Cost	Total spent
Ironmongers			'Trying of the peece			
			30 Iron shott, ladles Spring wadhooks linstock pinning iron and horse	William Franklin	£00 8s 6d	
				William Felgate	£01 17s 4d	£3 01s 8d
			proofe powder		£00 15s 10d	£26 16s 0d
						£29 17s 8d
Vintners			Carriage	'carriage maker'	£3 0s 0d	
			Carriage wheels and 'other materials'	Bateman the wheelwright	£2 12s 0d	
			'graveing' the wheels	'smith'	£0 3s 6d	
			Iron wheel rims and other materials		£3 3s 6d	
			'colouring' carriage and wheels	Mr. Franklin	£0 17s 0d	
			proving the piece	Mr. Preston	£0 11s 0d	
			engraving of company name	Mr. Felgate	£0 5s 0d	£14 3s 0d
	Unspecified	Unspecified 'proportion of match'	spunge, ladle and shipping		£3 11s 0d	£20 9s 4d
	2 barrels‡				no record	£34 12s 4d
Clothworkers			'carriadge for a sacer together with payntinge the said carriadge powder to trie the Sacar and for shott sponges ladles etc and charges in shippinge of it'	Mr Stilgoe	£8 17s 6d	£11 10s 0d
				Mr W[illia]m Felgate	£2 12s 6d	£15 3s 9d
						£26 13s 9d
					TOTAL	£412 17s 8½d

* manuscript damaged † accounts for the period have not survived ‡ possibly sent after July 1643 ‡‡ sent in May 1643

125

on the fact that they had paid for the building of Londonderry.[34] Also, August 1642 saw the outbreak of the English Civil War, and thereafter the minds of the merchants of the City of London were focussed on the struggle between the King – whom they felt had treated them exceedingly badly – and Parliament which, in the main, they supported. An appeal was made on 17 March 1643 by the Mayor and Council of Londonderry for food and powder (*Cal. SPD 1625–1649*, 647, 17 March 1643). Apart from warning of the closeness of famine, they wrote

Also, pray move the Londoners to give us some powder to their guns, for want thereof we dare not try them.

A further appeal was made in May of 1643 by Robert Goodwin, a Draper and Town Clerk of Londonderry, to at least four of the Companies – the Fishmongers, Skinners, Vintners and Clothworkers – for powder and other provisions. The Skinners, Vintners and Clothworkers all agreed to send supplies, while the Fishmongers deliberated twice on the subject and decided to wait on the other Companies to see what they did. There is no record of the outcome of their deliberations.

Thereafter, apart from occasional references to relief for members affected by the Irish Rebellion, Londonderry and its defensive needs play little part in Company records.

Pricing the ordnance

It was standard practice in the sixteenth and seventeenth centuries for ordnance to be purchased by the hundredweight, and the accounts of the Grocers (Appendix A4), Drapers (Appendix A5), Skinners (Appendix A8), Vintners (Appendix A12) and Clothworkers (Appendix A13) all record costing by weight.[35] The accounts of the Ironmongers (Appendix A11) give a weight for their saker, but do not tell us what the price per hundredweight was. The Grocers, Drapers, Vintners and Clothworkers paid 13s 6d per cwt for their pieces to Samuel Ferrers,[36] while the Skinners who purchased from the East India Company paid 12s 0d per cwt, possibly because they were purchasing 'second-hand'. This is all the more likely, given that William Felgate was a Warden of the Company and best placed to get a suitable discount!

The going rate for civilian cast-iron ordnance in the 1640s appears to have been in the region of 13s 6d per cwt. We can make a crude estimate of the price paid by the Ironmongers by subtracting the likely costs of the carriage, by comparison with those charged to the Grocers, Vintners and Clothworkers. The Grocers paid a total of £17 15s 0d for two carriages with all of their ironwork and iron-shod wheels, making £8 17s 6d each, the same price paid by the Clothworkers, while that of the Vintners totalled £9 16s 6d. However, the Vintners in addition paid a 'paynter' 17s 0d, so that for roughly the same work as the Grocers, the price would have been £8 19s 6d. However, the Clothworkers costs included 'paynting', suggesting that 'Mr. Stilgoe' was more competitive in price than Bateman and Pitt unless, of course, this carriage remained unpainted. Taking a simplistic average, therefore, as £8 17s 6d, we are left with an estimate for the Ironmongers cannon of around £17 18s 6d, giving a price of just under 14s 3d per cwt, which is on the high side. However, there is a significant discrepancy between the weight cited in the accounts (25cwt ½qtr 0lb: 1276kg) and that recorded in the 1660 inventory (35 cwt: 1778kg), although the most likely explanation[37] is that this is a simple error of transcription (Appendix A14.1).

With regard to painting, in March 1639, Anthony Hancock charged the Office of Ordnance for the 'twice pryming, stopping and laying fayne Lead Cullo^{re} in Oyle' of field carriages at '11d per yard' (*NA* WO 49/75, f.101v). These carriages averaged some '18 yards', giving a cost for the work of around 16s 6d each. Each 'coyne' [quoin] was charged at 2¾d, so that a pair for a carriage cost 5½d. Thus, the charge to the Vintners of 17s 0d for the 'paynting' of their carriage was virtually identical to that paid by the Office of Ordnance (16s 11½d) for this particular consignment.

Part of the cost of a field carriage depended on the weight of the piece which it was to carry,[38] yet the Grocers who bought heavier guns paid less for the overall assemblies than the Vintners. The difference here seems to have been in the degree of decoration applied. If we

Chapter 4 – The Origins of the Ordnance of the Sixteenth and Seventeenth Centuries

assume that the Ironmongers also went for ostentation, and increase the cost of the carriage to that of the Vintners' saker, the theoretical cost of the Ironmongers' saker is reduced to £16 19s 6d, giving a price per cwt of 13s 6½d. We may note that Thomas Bateman the wheelwright was paid between £2 12s 0d and £2 12s 6d for pairs of wheels,[39] irrespective of the fact that the one set was for carriages for demi-culverins, the other for minions. We should note in passing, however, that the price apparently charged in 1646 by one William Roberts for providing the mounting for a 12½ins diameter mortar cast by John Browne[40] was recorded as £40 3s 7d!

The damage to the accounts of the Drapers means that we can read only a part of the cost of the two minions which they purchased. However, the 1660 inventory (Appendix A14.1) lists them as weighing 16 cwt and 16cwt 1qtr (a detail inexplicably missing from the otherwise very full accounts of the company – the accountant actually included the word 'weighing' but left a blank space after), while the accounts do give a cost of 13s 6d per cwt. This would give a price of £10 16s 0d for one and £10 19s 4½d, for the other, suggesting thus that the original sum paid for both was £21 15s 4½d. Since we can read the first figure in the accounts as being £20+, coupled with the decision that the pieces should not cost 'more than 40 marks' (1 mark = 13s 4d), or £26 13s 4d, it is clear that their purchaser stayed within this limit.

Suppliers and craftsmen

Tables 7–8 show just how good the surviving records are, and we know of no other group of earlier seventeenth century cannon anywhere which can be linked specifically with so many of those involved in their production and furbishment. In fact, we know the names of six who sold the guns to the Companies and provided all accoutrements and organised their proofing, and have a quite remarkably detailed record for several. This is especially significant when we consider that we have also a direct living descendent – Don Felgate – of one of the two main suppliers, William Felgate. And the link between Felgate and the other key player, Samuel Ferrers (*infra*), is interesting in that both were liverymen of companies quite unrelated in their primary callings to the trade in weapons and munitions, Felgate being a Skinner and Ferrers a Grocer.[41]

It is unfortunate that Abraham Preston, whose elegant engraving we know marks out the surviving Company guns, seems to have left no record, and that the smith who made what would have been a substantial quantity of ironwork for the carriages is unnamed, although quite likely to have been one Thomas Hodgkins.[42] The carriage maker 'Mr. Stilgoe' seems to have left no identifiable trace, while the craftsman who 'colored' the carriages has remained wholly anonymous, although it could possibly have been the Anthony Hancock, described in one Ordnance Office debenture of 18 March 1639 as 'of London, Paynter' (*NA* WO 49/75, f.100r).[43]

Thomas Bateman who lived in Whitechapel, near to the Tower, became the Ordnance wheelwright in 1625, a position he held until 1658 when his son Matthew was appointed. He died shortly after, his will being proved on 8 April 1659 (*NA* PROB 11/289). Thomas possibly was one of the earliest members of the fledgling Company of Wheelwrights that petitioned the City of London for incorporation in 1630. The Wheelwrights were subject to much scrutiny, as were their co-applicants the Coachmakers, on the grounds that some members of both had been involved in the supply of shoddy goods. As a result, there were long delays and then the English Civil Wars supervened. Nevertheless, he supplied wheels and axles for the Ordnance for field and standing carriages and limbers, trucks for naval carriages and general wheelwright services, from earliest days of King Charles, through the Civil War and First Dutch War.

In fact, it was not until 1670 that the Wheelwrights finally achieved Guild status in their own right, the first Master being Matthew Bateman, who took the office again in 1697 (Bennett 1970, 159). Matthew Bateman survived the Restoration and continued as ordnance wheelwright. He also appears to have been in place through the reign of James II and up to and including that of William and Mary. Thus, he would have been in position at the time of the 1689 siege.

In 1700, Thomas and John Bateman billed the Board of Ordnance for four pairs of wheels and other accoutrements (*NA* WO 51/60, f. 721), and Thomas and John are described as 'captains' in Ordnance records of 1715 (*NA* WO 51/95, f. 76r). John Bateman was Master of the Guild in 1704 (Bennett 1970, 159). Such a concentration of surnames in the affairs of the first years of the Company can hardly be coincidence, and it seems probable that the Thomas Bateman of the 1642 guns was the sire of a line of Bateman wheelwrights. In fact, a Matthew Bateman was still the Ordnance wheelwright in 1760 (*NA* WO 51/212, f. 28r), indicating that the family held the position for well over a century – at least four generations.

Thomas is listed (often in association with the carpenter John Pitt (*q.v.* below) in the early 1650s (*Cal. SPD passim*) as having received payments both for wheels and whole vehicles, not to mention such items as wheelbarrows (e.g. *NA* WO 49/75, f. 47r). This, in itself is interesting, since John Pitt is on one occasion described as a wheelwright, and there was obviously a great deal of overlap in the work of wheelwrights and coachmakers. In addition to wheels, Bateman was evidently involved in the production of everything from pickaxe handles and wheelbarrows (e.g. *NA* WO 49/72, f. 43v) to whole vehicles, as references to payment for 'waggons' and tumbrils (two-wheeled carts which accompanied the troops and carried tools and supplies: e.g. *Cal. SPD* 1650, 572, 3 April 1650) suggest. Equally, Pitt produced wheels on occasion. However, unlike Pitt, Matthew Bateman survived the Restoration in post.

William Felgate is a most interesting character of whom we have quite detailed knowledge, thanks in no small part to the research of one of his direct descendants, Don Felgate.[44] The eldest of four sons[45] of Erasmus Felgate[46] 'yeoman' and Anne Hedge – the others being Robert, John and Tobias[47] – William was born at Stonham Aspal in Suffolk, some 15km to the north of Ipswich, and baptised there on 13 March 1572. He served his apprenticeship as a Skinner to one Francis Covell from 1589–1597 (*Skinners Apprentices* 1, f. 408), entering his service on the Feast of Saint Michael the Archangel.[48] It may well be that his apprenticeship was not served solely to the trade of Skinner, but rather was an introduction to the arms trade. As we have seen, an early transaction in which he was involved was that of the consignment of cannon to Culmore (p. 105), and one of his collaborators was Francis' son, Thomas, who provided muskets and gunners' accessories, something in which William also specialised later.

He became a freeman[49] on 3 October 1597 (*ibid* f. 466), and subsequently was admitted to the livery on 10 May 1603 (*Skinners CM 1577–1617*, ff 343v and 345v). He was one of the signatories to the 1609 and 1629 Charters of the Virginia Company of London, owning five shares which he purchased for £12 10s 9d each. William also purchased one share of around twenty-four acres in Bermuda, and 'William Felgate' appears as one of 'Warwick's Tribe' ('tribe' was used for 'parish') on a map of the island prepared in a survey of *c.* 1615–1617 by Richard Norwood for the Somers Island company, and published in 1627 by John Speed. His evident knowledge of the colonies led in 1633 to his becoming one of the Commissioners for Virginia to the Privy Council.

William went into business as – amongst other things – a ship's chandler and, with his youngest brother Tobias and others, was part owner of the *James*, a vessel of 120–140 tons (*APC Colonial* 1613–1680, 96, 14 November 1625). In April of 1618, he sold the Venetian Ambassador to England supplies worth £946 18s 0d as part of the fitting out of seven ships and 500 infantry (*Cal. SP Venetian* 1617–1619, 209 and 377), in 1620 was involved in the Culmore consignment, and in 1637 was listed as a supplier of 'gun powder and munition for shipping' (*Cal. SPD* 1637, 456, September 1637). One of his earlier ventures seems to have been into the London property market. He is listed in the Middlesex Session Roll for 1611 as being in prison awaiting trial at 'Le Olde Baylie', following complaints over the disturbance caused by workmen converting a large house in Petticoat Lane into tenements.

In 1629, a complaint was made against William and Tobias to Thomas, Lord Coventry, Lord Keeper of the Great Seal by the other five owners of the *James* concerning voyages to Virginia in 1626, 1627 and 1628 (*NA* C3/416/88, dated 1629). The burden was that

Chapter 4 – The Origins of the Ordnance of the Sixteenth and Seventeenth Centuries

William Felgate was victualler of pease butter cheese oatmeale candles powder shot match and all manner of other provisions at his owne rates and prices and the said Tobyas Felgate went always as Master in the said ship and so had the sole managinge and orderinge of all business concerninge the same and to sett downe what reckonings accompts hee pleased in all of the several voyages resumminge to himselfe all offices and places in the said ship.

in short, that they would appear to have been guilty of creative accountancy to the detriment of their partners. In the same year, William was involved in another dispute, this time with one Terrick Reinerson or Reynardson, Master of the *Fortune* of Shoreham, over the loss of over two thousand hogshead staves, the case finally being settled by the Admiralty Court judge, Sir Henry Martyn (Harris 1983, 97).

Retaining his involvement with the Skinners, William became Renter Warden on 20 June 1622 (*Skinners CB* 3, 1617–1651, f. 60r), and successively was Third Warden in 1632 (*ibid.* f. 136v), Second Warden in 1633 (*ibid.* f. 141v), First Warden in 1634 (*ibid.* f. 147v) and Master Warden in 1637 (*ibid.* f. 163r). It was in his role as a Warden of the Skinners that, at a session of their Court of Assistants on 15 August 1643, he was charged with organising their gift of powder and match to Londonderry, which he duly did (Appendix A8). Felgate married twice and sired a number of children, none of whom made names for themselves. However, his daughter Anne, born in 1614, seems to have married his apprentice Thomas Frere, and died (possibly in childbirth) at Fersfield in Norfolk in 1643. He died[50] in November 1648 and was buried at All Hallows, Barking, apparently having left a will which, although registered, cannot now be found.

William spent some time in Virginia in the 1620s, and was married – probably for the second time – to a sister of the highly influential merchant William Tucker (Brenner 1993, 120). He became deeply involved in the tobacco trade, something which shows also in the activities of his brother Robert who got into trouble in Bermuda over evasion of the tax on tobacco, at one point being sentenced (Kennedy 1971, 167), along with one Robert Jenour, to stand in the public pillory for four hours with a 20lb bale of the weed strapped to his back! In 1640 he was a partner in a venture with Maurice Thomson – a partner of his brother-in-law William Tucker – and one Samuel Vassall in trading ventures to Virginia and the West Indies (Brenner 1993, 137 and 190).

In 1628, it was noted that a large quantity of powder had been brought to a storehouse 'belonging to Mr. Felgate at the sign of the Still in Homesditch [Houndsditch] in a vinagre yard . . .' (*APC* 1628–1629, 60–61 dated 30 July 1628). Officers of the Ordnance were ordered to sieze all that they could find there and to hold it until Felgate could prove that he had come about it lawfully, and to pay him off if the powder was fit for the King's service. In 1629, a Captain John Heydon and Sir Paul Harris (Master and Surveyor of the Ordnance) deposed that they had found forty barrels of powder 'in the stoarhouse of Mr. Felgate of Houndsditch', twenty of which were marked with a broad arrow. While there were perfectly legitimate ways for powder belonging to the Crown to get into private hands (as, for example, when 'spoiled' powder was sold on), the presence of official markings on the stock found with Felgate indicates the possibility of some shady dealings!

William was listed in 1638 as a resident of the parish of All Hallows Barking, which is nearest to the Tower of London, his house attracting an annual tithe of £21 (Dale 1931, 3). Indeed, he served there as a churchwarden 1612 and 1613. In *c.* 1642 he was living in Tower Street in the parish, still with a storehouse in Houndsditch. The Tower was the principal depot for the storage of provisions of war and, as a result, the residents of the surrounding area included a high proportion of weapons makers and suppliers.[51] Between 1642 and 1643, there were complaints that Felgate was building a house in the moat of the Tower, overlooking the inner areas to the point where those inside could be fired upon.[52] It is quite possible that the house was not for William, but for his brother Robert who attended his last meeting as Burgess in Virginia in April 1642, returning to England probably in that year. In the accounts of the Vintners and Clothworkers for the cannon sent in 1642, part of the payment to William Felgate was for 'shipping' (Appendix A12 and A13) – in the case of the Clothworkers citing the *Charity* as the carrier – and it is most tempting to see a link between this and his maritime interests and those of this brothers.

On 24 November 1642, the House of Commons Journal (*Commons J.* 2, 863) recorded that it was

> *Ordered, That Mr. Vassall and Mr. Ashe do examine what is become of the Ninety Barrels of Powder of Mr. Frere's and Mr. Felgate's, stayed by the Committee for the Militia, and delivered by the Orders of this House.*

Interestingly, but probably wholly coincidental, is the fact that William Felgate (along with a number of other merchants) was a signatory to a peace petition dated 22 December 1642, while Thomas Frere, his former apprentice,[53] had been a moving force in raising a similar petition dated 14 December 1642 (Lindley 1997, 341–342).

Samuel Ferrers was an agent for the royal gunfounder, John Browne (see pp201 *ff*) along with one Richard Pierson.[54] Ferrers, like William Felgate, lived in the parish of All Hallows Barking in a house attracting an annual tithe of £20 (Dale 1931, 4), and had his premises at the Half Moon in Thames Street in the parish of Saint Botolph, Bishopsgate (*Cal. SPD 1644–1645*, 607, 24 June 1645), which he leased from the Mercers Company (*Mercers CM 1641–1645*, ff 21v, 31r–32v, 33v).[55] Like Felgate, Ferrers became a liveryman of one of the Great Companies, in this case the Grocers. He was apprenticed in February of 1610 for eight years to one Giles Fleming (*Grocers WA* 9, f. 385r), becoming a freeman on 26 June 1619 (*Grocers WA* 10, 1611–1622, f. 332), and was admitted to the livery on 5 November 1627 (*Grocers CM* 3, f. 356). He became a member of the Court of Assistants on 20 November 1645 and subsequently attended Courts in 1646 and 1647. On 1 September 1647, he was chosen Corn Renter for the year.[56]

Ferrers was the agent for 'commercial' weaponry, while Richard Pierson dealt primarily with the state (*Cal. SPD 1644–1645*, 607, 24 June 1645), both working with Browne's factors Henry Quintyne (or Quintine) and Thomas Hawkins (*ibid.*). Browne was detained by Parliament on suspicion of assisting the Royalist cause, and in August 1645, Ferrers and Browne's son-in-law Thomas Foley[57] were put in charge of the works by Parliament. They were required to relinquish control back to Browne at the end of December 1645, in return for compensation of £1000 (*Commons J.* 4, 30 December 1645).

William Franklin was the prover of cast-iron ordnance for the Ordnance Office by January 1627, and was responsible for proof-testing State ordnance at the Tower of London from 1627 to 1658. By the 1650s he had become Proof Master, a title which he held to the end his career in 1658 (Barter Bailey 2003, 66–67). His duties included preparing the field close to the Tower, making up the temporary butts there where the merchant guns were normally proofed, arranging their transport to the field and back, proofing the guns and then weighing them. As Proof Master, he travelled down to Kent to proof the guns close to Browne's foundries. In addition to his official duties, he also carried out private work such as that for the Merchant Taylors and Vintners, and for the English East India Company, carrying out a survey of all their guns in 1634. He died probably in 1659.

In the 1660s his son, Dr Richard Franklin, continued as Ordnance Proof Master. His wife was described as 'a pretty lady' by Samuel Pepys, who met her on the day of the coronation of Charles II in 1661, appropriately watching the fireworks (Lathom and Matthews 1970, 2, 86).

John Pitt had become Ordnance carpenter by June 1642, after the death of his predecessor Matthew Banks (who succeeded John Horton in 1622). He supplied the basic bodies and the quoins of the different sorts of carriages required by the Ordnance, working in different woods. For example standing carriages were made from oak and ships carriages from elm. He also carried out general carpentry for the Ordnance, making chests for transporting arms, repairing the crane on the Tower Wharf, as well as supplying carpentry tools. He worked at the buildings at the Tower, the Artillery Garden, and in the Minories where he had his own workshops.

In a warrant for payment issued on 1 August 1649, he is referred to as a 'wheelwright' and slated for payment for 'necessaries for carriages for Ireland' (*Cal. SPD* 1649, 583). In 1650 he was paid for 'carpentering for the train of artillery' (9 May) and 'for filed (sic!) carriages, carpenters' tools, & c. for the artillery train' (9 July), in association with Thomas Bateman (*Cal. SPD* 1650, 576 and 581). Pitt was also paid for providing tools in 1651 (*Cal. SPD* 1651, 574, 1 July 1651). It seems not unlikely that Pitt was another Ordnance Office craftsman who could have been a company liveryman. The records of the Worshipful Company of Coachmakers and Coach Harness Makers, founded in 1677, were destroyed in the Blitz, but it is unlikely that Pitt was a member of the Livery, and the name is not mentioned in the Company history.[58]

In 1643, he was compensated for being made a prisoner by royalists at Guilford when returning to London from working at Portsmouth, the Cavaliers stealing his sword, instruments, coat, horse and bible, This rather suggests where his sympathies lay! Nevertheless, Pitt continued until at least July of 1661 (*NA* WO 49/80 f. 21, WO 49/97 f. 88), when he was still described as the Master Carpenter for the Ordnance.

Notes to Chapter 4

1 In fact, ordnance could be a positive impediment to military manoeuvres so that, for example, in December 1643 Hamilton sent six heavy pieces plus other guns back to Scotland on the grounds that they were useless to him (Furgol 2003, 83). Regarding obsolete ordnance, a cull in England of cast-iron 'turned and nailed guns' (e.g. Barter Bailey 2000) in 1684, yielded a total of seven hundred and eighteen pieces for disposal (*Carte MSS* 40, f. 349).

2 However, Hunter (2004) suggested that perhaps Paulet got a worse press than he actually deserved.

3 It could be argued that such displacement has been overstated, since there was much speculation and selling of leases, so that many Irish became tenants on their ancestral lands, thus losing status rather than territory. We are grateful to Dr. John McGurk for this.

4 One of the original titles of the company was the 'Society of the Governor and Assistants, London, of the New Plantation in Ulster, within the Realm of Ireland'. After 1660, it was called 'The Honourable The Irish Society', normally contracted to 'The Irish Society'.

5 Indeed, as Curl (2000, 44) notes, the degree of imprecision throughout is 'miasmic'.

6 Colby wrote – without citing his source – that

Felimy Mac Devitt who had been placed in charge of the garrison [Culmore] *by O'Doherty . . . when the fort was besieged . . . Mac Devitt . . . took flight himself with his followers in two vessels, conveying with him a part of the cannon, and casting the remainder into the sea.*

7 However, such payments do not appear in the individual accounts of the Companies.

8 Another vague possibility is that this person was in some way related to Levan de Rose, a Dutch military engineer who was employed in work on fortifications in Ulster in the first years of the seventeenth century (Loeber 1979, 233). Rose became a naturalised Englishman on 19 January 1618, but returned to The Hague in his native Holland in 1620 to attend to a lawsuit (*ibid*.). However, a search of Dutch archives revealed nothing of his family (information kindly supplied by Mrs Yvonne Prins, Centraal Bureau voor Genealogie, The Hague). A 'Loies de Rosse', described as 'engineer' was being paid 15s *per diem* in 1599, according to records (*Cal. SPI* April 1599–February 1600, 97, 18 July 1599), while 'Lennan de Rose' was paid £122 0s 0d for one year of work in 1608 (*Cal. SPI* 1608–1610, 80). And although Holland was at that time a significant marketplace for English iron guns (e.g. van Wakeren 1996), there is nothing in the warrant of 1620 to indicate that the ordnance was either manufactured in or exported from other than England, and so this identification seems most unlikely.

9 Spelled 'Roose' in the London Port Book but Rose in the Chester Port Book.

10 Also spelled Turvyll and Turvile. It is possible that he is the Edmond Turvill (Turvile), Ironmonger of Saint Dunstan's East who, in a

marriage licence granted by the Bishop of London on 18 October 1636, is named as giving permission – *in loco parentis* – for the marriage of his niece Mary Heath of Saint Leonard's, Shoreditch, to one Ephraim Pagitt of Deptford.

11 Coupled with the fact that the guns sent to Culmore were brought to London overland, this lends support to the suggestion that Turvill drew on more than one source. In 1620, Turville is noted as having brought guns this way 'at greate inconvenience' (*BL* IOR B/6, f. 553, 31 March 1620), indicating a source or sources sufficiently removed from the River Medway and the water transport routes often used by the Brownes and other founders.

12 In December 1619, John Browne cast six cast-iron pieces – three culverins and three demi-culverins – for the Board of Ordnance to send to Ireland (*NA* WO 49/48, f. 139r), but there is no seeming concordance between the recorded weights of these and any of the pieces destined for Culmore.

13 *Thomas Covell son of Mr Warden Covell was this daie p^{re}ferred and admitted to his freedom by patrimony iij^s iiij^d*

14 The other petitioners were Robert Papworth and William Dyer.

15 The Calendar puts a comma between 'corn' and 'powder', but there is no doubt that what is actually being referred to is 'corn powder'.

16 At the start of his account of the siege of 1689, Walker records the ordnance as eight sakers and twelve demi-culverins, but since fifteen of these pieces must date from 1642, no concordance is to be sought between the two lists.

17 Either this was not done, or at least such storehouses were not maintained, since in the 1660 inventory (Appendix A14.1), carriages which had accompanied guns sent over in 1642 are described as 'rotten'.

18 Interestingly, in 1644 John Browne charged £35 per ton for drakes of 'special metal' and £18 for cutts, and prices certainly had gone up since the 1620s. (*NA* WO 49/81, f. 44v) However, the Ordnance always paid a premium for their guns, and possibly there was an element of profiteering, too. Browne, however, would probably have claimed that Ordnance cannon were usually of a larger calibre and greater length than those required by merchants, so that they were difficult to dispose of if the Ordnance did not want them. Further, he would have pointed out that they were expected to go through a more severe proof than a merchant gun (which need not actually be proofed at all), and that his drakes and 'special metal' guns had been through more processing than ordinary guns. We may further note figures in the report of 1685 by Thomas Phillips and Lord Dartmouth on fortifications in Ireland, of an estimated cost of £8725 for providing new fortifications at Belfast with '. . . 250 iron guns mounted on standing carriages, with furniture all complete to each gun, excepting ammunition' (*Ormond MSS* II, 322). Even if the calibres are unspecified, and allowing for inflation, this figure of £34 18s 0d per gun fully fitted out compares remarkably well with the 1642 figures of approximately £35 (see Table 7).

19 Guns made by combining non-ferrous metals with wrought iron seem to have been part of an attempt to produce both cheaper and lighter ordnance. They have their origins in the Netherlands between *c*. 1620–1630 (Gilmour 2000), and have been found in locations from England to Australia. The example from the *Batavia*, lost off Australia in 1629, shows a remarkable complex of wrought iron, copper and lead, exposed when a section was cut longitudinally (Green 1980, 49, Figs. 5 and 6: *cf.* Guilmartin 1982). None of the demi-culverins in the Derry assemblage showed any trace of non-ferrous components. It is not unlikely that – as with any true bronze guns – such might have been lost to posterity in an attempt to melt them down as valuable scrap. Although, by and large rare in Ireland in this inventory, Charles Fort, Kinsale, County Cork is listed as having a total of sixty such guns of different calibres.

20 Finch (*Finch* 13–14) described these as 'four small drakes upon one carriage', while the inventory of 1660 (Appendix A14.1a) lists 'small Field peeces of Brass in a frame decayed', suggesting that this might have been an example of a multiple gun.

21 The other magazine potentially capable of supplying ordnance was Carrickfergus, County

Chapter 4 – The Origins of the Ordnance of the Sixteenth and Seventeenth Centuries

Antrim, almost the same distance from Charlemont as Londonderry.

22 Along with his brother Sir William Stewart, Sir Ralph Gore and Sir William Cole.

23 James Stuart, fourth Duke of Lennox and first Duke of Richmond.

24 Virtually the same letter was sent to the Lords Justices (Hogan 1936, 3–5).

25 If the 'last summer' in this letter were to refer to 1641, then responsibility for this would have rested with the Lords Justices, since Strafford had been in prison since 11 November 1640 and was executed on 12 May 1641, while his successor, Wandesford, was dead also.

26 *pace* Hazlett (1938, I, 47) and McKenny (2005, 37) who quote 'culverins', the readings of 'calivers' by Hogan and Gilbert are certainly correct.

27 Wandesford took over from Strafford as Lord Deputy on 1 April 1640, was seriously ill by late November and died on 3 December 1640.

28 The sum to be raised was £100,000, but this target was not reached. By December 1642, various companies were receiving stern correspondence from the House of Commons regarding their failure to stump up. In reply, the Clothworkers replied that they had already paid £2120, having been saddled with a bill for £5,500 to which they had never agreed, and were too poor to pay more. Others amongst the minor companies pleaded simply that they could pay nothing (*Cal. SPI* 1633–1647, 372–373, 8 December 1642).

29 In addition, later in 1642 Parliament ordered special collections to be made in churches (e.g. *Commons J.* 2, 1640–1643, 12 December 1641). The contributions of the various Companies were acknowledged in various parliamentary motions (e.g. those of the Drapers, Fishmongers and Merchant Taylors being recorded on 31 January 1642 – Coates *et al.* 1982, 233).

30 The accountant for the Skinners employed a device well-known to his modern counterparts, namely splitting costs across two financial years. Thus, the provision of carriages and the purchase of powder was entered for the year 1641–1642, while cost of the cannon – purchased from the East India Company – was pushed back into the accounts for the year 1642–1643.

31 A number of writers (e.g. Thomas 1999, 276, n. 17) follow the mistaken account in the Irish Society publication of 1822 of each of the twelve Great Companies sending two cannon each in a flotilla of four ships.

32 Unless, of course, this was retrospective ratification of a decision taken earlier by persons with that authority.

33 It is possible that this is the *Charity* listed as a 6-gun merchant pinnace and part of the 'Winter Guard' of 1642 (Powell 1962, 198), and which took part in action with the *Eighth Whelp* on 4 June 1643 (*ibid.* 39). A vessel of the same name was being used as a troop carrier in 1646, this time by Parliament, as witnessed by an order for the feeding of troops on board it and another called the *Bennet*, which in December were standing off Carrickfergus (*Cal. SPI* 1633–1647, 552, and 556, 3 and 4 December 1646).

34 To put the scale of donations – perhaps thus of the real level of concern – into some sort of perspective, the Vintners, who spent a total of £67 13s 4d on ordnance and accessories, and donated a further £100 in cash as well for 'reliefe', spent some £220 8s 11d on 'dinners' in the year 1641–1642 (*Vintners WA* 1636–1658). And this pattern is repeated across the Great Companies.

35 Between 1547 and 1553, the Ordnance Office purchased iron guns at a price of 10s per hundredweight, one hundredweight being defined as 'five score and twelve pounds' (Barter Bailey 1991, 11–12).

36 The accountant for the Clothworkers wrongly entered 16s 6d per cwt, but the price paid for a saker of that weight shows clearly that the actual price was 13s 6d (Appendix A13).

37 At 35cwt costing 13s 6d per cwt, there would have been only £3 3s 6d left for the carriage, less than half of what was paid by other companies. One possible explanation is that this piece was cast as a demi-culverin but with the bore of a saker, the intention being to circumvent restrictions on the sale of demi culverins to some third party, who could then

overbore it to the higher calibre. This would then imply that the gun came on a ship's carriage, but Occam's Razor requires explanation by scribal error.

38 An inventory of 4 March 1635, gives costs of ships' carriages for culverins, demi-culverins and sakers as £3 15s 0d, £3 15s 0d and £3 5s 0d respectively (*Strafford* StrP 24–25, no. 217).

39 Against this, in 1647 the Irish smith Turlough Duff was paid £1 5s 0d each for two pairs of wheels for culverins (*Cal. SPI 1633–1647*, 663, 18 May 1647), around half of the price paid to his English counterparts.

40 This was recorded (*Cal. SPI 1647*, 500, 5 August 1646) as

> *The Lord Lieutenant to order £40 3s 7d to William Roberts for mounting the mortar-piece newly made for Ireland.*

41 Another liveryman of the Worshipful Company of Grocers involved in the trade in cast iron ordnance was Thomas Westerne (Brown 2001), who was 'admitted into the Livery and Clothing of this Company' on 20 May 20 1658 (*Grocers* CM 4, f. 430).

42 Thomas Hodgkins replaced Lewis Tayte as Ordnance blacksmith in 1638, and produced ironwork such as lynch pins, cap-squares and bindings for the gun carriages, limbers and wagons, as well as smiths' tools. Between 1648–1651, he occurs as a creditor in warrants for payment issued by the Council of State, in conjunction with Thomas Bateman and John Pitt (e.g. *Cal. SPD* 1650, 576, 2 May 1650). In fact, throughout the 1640s and 1650s, Hodgkins worked with Bateman and Pitt to put together the artillery trains, including those sent to Scotland and Ireland. He kept his position after the Restoration and was still working up to the early 1670s. For 14 July 1646, it is noted by the Committee for Irish Affairs (*Cal. SPI 1633–1647*, 475) that

> *Mr. Pierson and William Browne the gun-founder are to deliver to Mr. Hodgkins of the Tower the mortar-piece lately made for the Irish service, in order that it may have a carriage fitted to it.*

43 He would appear to be the only artisan listed as providing the service of 'stopping and coloring' carriagework to the Office of Ordnance, and was paid for his services until at least 1651 (*Cal. SPD* 1651, 579). He was not, as far as one can tell, a resident of East Cheam.

44 We are most grateful to Don Felgate for generously sharing with us his research on his forbears and allowing us to use it here.

45 There was also an elder sister, Katherine, about whom we know nothing other than that she was baptised in Stonham, Apsal in 1569, and a younger sister Elizabeth about whom, again, we know nothing other than her year of baptism, 1577. One of the two evidently was dead before 1622 when Erasmus dictated his nuncupative (deathbed) will, as he refers to four sons and a daughter. Also, Anne appears to have died before this as well, as his executrix is named as 'his wife Margerie' (*IRO* 1C/AA1/11/10). There appears to have been a further son, called Erasmus after his father and born in 1580 and who died in infancy.

46 In the parish register of Stonham Apsal is an entry – no day or month – reading *Baptizatus est Erasmus ffelgate 1546*. Erasmus wrote his will in March 1622, and was listed as living at that time in the parish of Saint Botolph, Aldersgate.

47 **John Felgate** was baptised at Stonham Aspal on 20 March 1574. We know virtually nothing about him, other than that he owned some 1200 acres at Chequers Neck on the Chickahominy River in Virginia. He was already dead when his son Thomas was apprenticed as a Skinner for nine years to his uncle William from February 1621 (*Skinners Apprentices* 2, f. 73r: the exact date has been obliterated by water damage). The entry reads

> *Thomas ffelgate, son of John ffelgate, late of Aspoole Stanham* [Stonham Aspal], *in the Countie of Suffk yeoman Dec* [deceased] *hath putt himself App^r to William ffelgate Cittizen and Skinner of London, from Christmas last past, for nyne yeares.*

Unlike his contemporary as apprentice to William, Thomas Frere (see note 53 below), he does not appear to have served out his time.

Captain Robert Felgate was baptised on 2 March 1578 at Stonham Aspal. He joined the army, but no record of his early service has been found. Robert arrived in Bermuda in March 1614 as Captain to look after William's interests there. By this time he had developed skills as an engineer and repaired forts and built new ones, including the building of a 'musket profe (gun)powder store' of cedar. He lived in Bermuda, apart from a couple of trips back to London, until he returned in 1627 following a power struggle on the island over the payment of tax on tobacco, having been on the losing side (Kennedy 1971, 166–167). Along with several others, Robert was also accused of embezzlement, overcharging for supplies, and for using soldiers as his private servants (*ibid.* 172). In August of the following year he was appointed Muster Master for the colony of Virginia (no doubt with some help from William) and sailed there in 1628 (*APC Colonial* 1613–1680, 128, 6 August 1628). Settling on 350 acres on the York River between King's Creek and Felgate's Creek which bears his name, he became a Burgess, attending meetings on the running of the colony. Robert married twice, siring one son, seemingly called 'Erasmus' after his grandfather, and one daughter. Returning to England for good, probably in 1642, he wrote his will in London on 30 September 1644, and died shortly after, being buried at All Hallows on 4 October 1644.

Tobias Felgate was born probably in 1587 at Pettaugh in Suffolk, some 3.5km to the east of Stonham Aspal, but no record of his baptism has been found. He was apprenticed to his elder brother William as Skinner between 1601 and 1611 (*Skinners Apprentices* 1, f. 489) but evidently did not take to the trade.

Tobias ffelgate the sonne of Erasmus ffelgate of the towne Petto [Pettaugh] *in the county of Suffolce* [Suffolk] *yeoman hath put him selfe apprentice to William ffelgate citizen and Skinner of London from the feaste of the annunciation of the blessed virgin Mary* [25 March] *Anno dni 1601 for tenne years.*

He next appears as Mate aboard the *Edwin* bound for Virginia in 1617, returning home the following year. In 1619 he was again Mate on the *Margaret* of 45 tons taking thirty-five settlers to found a new colony at Berkeley in Virginia, and in the same year was Master aboard the *Supply* taking out another fifty-six. In a reference to accounts relating to a voyage to Virginia in 1619, he is described as 'pilot' (*HMC* Fifth Report 341). For several years, up to at least 1626, he sailed in the *James* of 120–140 tons of which he was Master and part owner with William and several others (*APC Colonial* 1613–1680, 96, 14 November 1625). In 1623, in a written statement, he claimed to have sailed as Mate or Master five times to Virginia. In 1627, 'Toby Fellgate' was described as a 'chandler of London' in a deposition regarding goods which he had sent some time before to Londonderry on the *Isaac* of Shoreham. Part of the consignment was a cask of tobacco for Captain Baker of Culmore (Appleby 1992, 161, deposition of John Tranckmore dated 26 February 1627). He had a 150-acre plantation adjacent to that of brother Robert in Virginia. Tobias was married three times and survived by his son William (b. 1612) who lived in the Colony. He dictated his nuncupative (deathbed) will at Christmas 1634, mentioning a son 'William', and died shortly after at Westover in Virginia.

48 The entry in the Apprenticeship Registry of the Worshipful Company of Skinners reads

William ffelgate sonn of Erasmus ffelgate of Staniamaspole [Stonham Aspal] *in the county of Suffolke yeoman hath put himself apprentize to ffranncis Covell ffrom the ffeast of S*^{t} *mighell* [Michael] *Tharch angell in anno dm* [domini] *1589 ffor Eight yeares.*

The Feast of Saint Michael the Archangel is celebrated on 29 September, and originally was a holy day of obligation.

49 The clerk who recorded this initially recorded his first name as 'Erasmus' – his father's Christian name, before crossing that out and inserting 'Willm' above. The entry reads

Willm

~~*Erasmus*~~ *Felget late appticed with ffrancis Covell was sworne and admitted and paid iiis iiiid* [3s 4d]

50 A William Felgate died in 1660 and his estate was immediately embroiled in a major legal wrangle (*NA* C10/109/1). But this William was a son of Tobias, hence a nephew of William the Skinner, and in 1659 was living on King's Creek in York County, Virginia (Tyler, L.G. 1892, 83).

135

51 It was this parish that suffered 'fire and devastacon by Gunpowder' in 1649.

52 The erection of buildings on the Tower ditch was a not uncommon, if illegal, occurrence. Thus, for example, on 4 July 1620, the Privy Council ordered immediate demolition of a number of offending structures (*APC* 1619–1621, 237*f*). Entries in the House of Lords Journal for July 1642 onwards document the dispute between William Felgate and Sir John Conyers, Lieutenant of the Tower of London, over a house which Felgate had built (*HMC* Fifth Report 38). The opening shot was from Conyers on 16 July 1642, who petitioned the Lords:

> *William Felgate has recently erected a house upon a piece of ground between the ditch of the Tower and the Inner Tower Hill where the scaffold stands. The house is of such a height that the battlements of the Tower have lost the view of a great part of Tower Hill and the scaffold, and are made unserviceable in case any opposition should arise on that hill against the Tower, and the Tower itself is exposed to great danger both of fire and shot from the new building. Prays that an order may be issued for demolishing the house.*

To which Felgate responded with a petition, asserting that

> *King James granted a lease of certain waste lands about the Tower with liberty to build. Petitioner, having a lease of a portion of the said lands, commenced to build a small tenement thereon. Complains of the oppressions he has suffered in consequence at the hands of Sir John Conyers, who has pulled down a portion of his tenement, and kept petitioner a prisoner in the Tower.*

The King's Surveyor, the famous Inigo Jones, was ordered to inspect the building and duly reported back on 19 July (*ibid.*) stating that

> *The house hinders the prospect of the most part of the hill from the Tower, and may be a prejudice to the safety thereof, and an evil precedent for the raising higher of many mean houses in the neighbourhood . . .*

But the matter evidently was not resolved, since on 2 January 1643, Conyers once again raised complaints. *See also Lords J. V, 532 from Conyers, dated 6 January 1643 (ibid. 67).*

53 Thomas Frere, born in 1607, was apprenticed for nine years to William Felgate as a skinner on 10 October 1620 (*Skinners Apprentices* 2, f. 72r), becoming a freeman on 20 January 1630 (*ibid.* f. 102v). He later set up in business in his own right, and served as a Common Councilman for Wapping in 1660 and for Clapham in 1674 (Woodhead 1966, 74).

54 It was Pierson who supplied new weights to the furnace installation built at Brenchley for John Browne in 1638 (p. 33).

55 In April 1642, the Common Council of the Mercers (*Mercers CM* 1641–1645, f. 33r) agreed to extend Ferrers' lease by twelve years on account of the work that he had put into their property.

> *Upon the peticon of Samuel fferrers grocer, it was now granted that in regard of the cost he hath bestowed upon his Tenem^t on Towerhill since the Company passed[?] him a grant of the lease of the same he shall have[?] twelve yeares added to his present terme.*

There is no record of any renewal in or around 1654, suggesting that Ferrers had retired or died by then. We are most grateful to Gary Haines, Archivist of the Worshipful Company of Mercers for this information.

56 The Companies had been encouraged by successive Lord Mayors to keep stocks of corn from which the poor could be supplied when bread was dear, and some companies kept their own granaries. Corn was purchased when it was cheap, sold from time to time to prevent spoiling, and then replaced. In the Grocers Company, the Corn Renter was responsible for inspecting corn in store and was concerned with its buying and selling. As there seem also to have been loans from Company Members for the purchase of corn, necessitating receipts and acquittances, it may have been that he also oversaw these and the books detailing the movements of the corn, even if he did not keep the books himself. The Grocers Company, having lost its assets in the Great Fire of London in 1666, discontinued the practice of storing corn. We are most grateful to Pauline Siddall of the Grocers Company for this information.

57 Thomas Foley, who married Anne Browne in 1622, is the Thomas Foley of the important west Midlands dynasty of ironmasters (Schafer 1997; Johnson, B.L.C. 1997), and of the Foley-Browne partnership.

58 Information kindly supplied by David Burgess-Wise, Archivist of The Worshipful Company of Coachmakers and Coach Harness Makers. A John Pitt is listed as a churchwarden of Saint Botolph Aldgate in 1658–1659, but with no other information (Woodhead 1965, 130).

CHAPTER 5
The Elizabethan Guns

Table 9 Summary of the main features of the Elizabethan guns (dimensions in inches, weights in pounds. metric equivalents (cm and kg) in square brackets)

Number	Type	Length	Weight	SG	Bore	Mark
C7	Saker	102 [259]	2183 [990]	6.69	3.94 [10.0]	Tudor rose-and-crown
C12	Demi–culverin	128 [300]	3417 [1550]	6.86	4.50 [11.6]	Tudor rose-and-crown, initials 'TI' [=TJ] weight stamp [3]3 3 0

Both guns have a pair of mouldings in front of the trunnions and one behind, and a rose-and-crown cast centrally onto the first reinforce. Such guns have two possible origins – either they are broadly Tudor, dating from *c.* 1550–1610, or they belong to the class known as 'Borgard Pattern' which date to 1716–1726 (McConnell 1988, 89), usually the more likely of the two. There are three main criteria which can be used to distinguish between them:

- Tudor guns usually have a comparatively elongated and elaborate cascable (e.g. Smith 1991, 35, Fig. 17), while the Borgard has a simple, round cascable with a single fillet;
- The Tudor gun usually has a very straight muzzle, while that of the Borgard has a pronounced flare as, for example, with the guns displayed at Carrickfergus Castle;[1]
- On Tudor guns, both of the double mouldings are on the second reinforce, while on the Borgard, one moulding is in the reinforce and the second on the chase.

A further distinguishing feature is the positioning and form of the rose-and-crown emblem itself. On Tudor guns, it is to be found on the first reinforce, while on the Borgards it will be on the second, usually squarely in line with the trunnions. There seem also to be stylistic differences between the earlier and later depictions of both rose-and-crown. Thus, the cross surmounting the crown is much more elongated on the Borgard pattern than in those of the Tudor period. From all of this, we can deduce that both cannon in Londonderry belong firmly in the Tudor period. As noted in Chapter 1 (p. 10), a number of sources refer to a gun with the letters 'ER' on either side of the Elizabethan emblem. Close examinations of the surfaces of both C7 and C12 show that neither of these guns ever bore such lettering, indicating that there was possibly at least one other gun of this period, now lost.[2]

C7 – *Saker of 8ft 6ins* (Fig. 19)

This cannon has a single moulding behind the trunnions and a pair of mouldings before. It has a long cascable and a rose-and-crown on the first reinforce. The muzzle is short and quite straight and apart from the royal emblem, there are no other surviving marks.

C12 – *Demi–culverin of 10ft* (Fig. 20)

The cannon has a single moulding behind the trunnions and a pair of mouldings before. The cascable is long and ornate, while the muzzle is short and quite straight. There is a rose-and-crown on the first reinforce, and below this the letters 'TI' and the date '1590' engraved in, along with a weight mark reading '[–]3 3 0'. The 'TI' mark can be identified as that of Thomas Johnson (see pp199 *f*), the Queen's founder of iron ordnance. Along with the engraved date of 1590, we can place this this piece squarely into the last decade of the sixteenth century and perhaps attribute its arrival in Derry along with C7 to none other than Sir Henry Docwra. The weight mark is almost certainly to be fully expanded as 33cwt 3qtr 0lb, which gives a weight of 3780lb (1715 kg). However, the weight of C12 as measured today is, in fact, some 363lb heavier.

It was thought that this might be the gun on which the letters 'ER' were present on either side of the rose-and-crown but, after stripping off of the overburden of old paint, it was evident that there had never been any such lettering. Nevertheless, reports going back to *OS Londonderry* in 1835 refer consistently to such a gun. A cannon illustrated by Milligan (1996, Plates XV and XVI) in his work on the City is described being the 'ER' gun, but the images are indistinct and it seems much more likely that this is one of the guns bearing the shield of the City of London. It would appear that the form of the mouldings of the first reinforce ring in Milligan's illustration and that of C12 are different.

A number of guns survive with marks associated with the Johnson family. There is a demi–culverin dated 1576 in the Naval Museum, Lisbon, marked with the letters 'II', which has been identified as the mark of John Johnson, and with a remarkably similar cascable to this gun (Trollope 2002, 54). Cannon 13 from The *Mauritius*, a Dutch VOC ship lost in 1609 includes a cast-iron falcon inscribed with the letters 'TI' and a merchant's mark (L'Hour *et al.* 1989, 118). Another (unpublished) gun in Fort Nelson, Portsmouth also bears this mark. Both of these guns have only a single series of mouldings on either side of the trunnions. Recently, a gun dating to *c.* 1594, very likely by Thomas Johnson, has been discovered in the fortifications of Karatsu Castle in Japan (Verhoeven and Brown forthcoming). Finally, at Sluis, in the Netherlands there is a minion of totally different form, but also signed 'TI' (Willeboordse 2008).

The rose-and-crown

Unhappily, although recognisable as such, the rose-and-crown emblems are badly eroded and have lost much of their detail (Fig. 21). In particular, neither has retained the cross

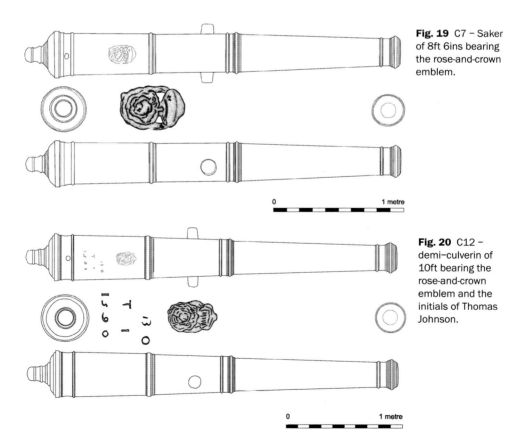

Fig. 19 C7 – Saker of 8ft 6ins bearing the rose-and-crown emblem.

Fig. 20 C12 – demi–culverin of 10ft bearing the rose-and-crown emblem and the initials of Thomas Johnson.

Chapter 5 – The Elizabethan Guns

that surmounts the crown on better-preserved examples (Fig. 22).

The emblem was used as a symbol for government or royal ownership from at least 1529, when it appears on a saker cast by Francisco Arcana for Henry VIII (Blackmore 1976, 58), and is then recorded on other guns up to the reign of Elizabeth I. Two very fine examples are found on a matching pair of bronze falcons recovered from the wreck of an unknown vessel in Larne Lough, County Antrim, and in the collections of the Ulster Museum, Belfast.[3] On the first reinforce of each of these is a gartered rose-and-crown, the inscription *Elysabetha Regina*, the names of the makers, Thomas and John Owen, and a date of 1559.[4] The morphology of these guns compares with that of other known examples of the work of the Owens (e.g. Blackmore 1976, 60–63).

There is no record of what James I had on his cannon, and it is not until the reign of Charles I that we have both records and surviving cannon which allow us to see that he had a rose-and-crown, usually with his monogram *CR*. By 1650, this had been replaced with the arms of the Commonwealth, the flag of St George and the Irish harp. With the Restoration, the rose-and-crown and the initials *CR* came back into use, and a campaign began to remove the offending Commonwealth arms. One such gun with the arms removed and a *CR* engraved over the top has recently been found in Fort York in Toronto, Canada (Trollope 2007, 49). Thereafter the rose-and-crown with the 'Royal' monogram was used until *c.* 1700, after which, and until *c.* 1727, the rose-and-crown alone was cast on iron guns. After *c.* 1727, it was finally replaced with the monogram of the reigning monarch.

The rose-and-crown emblems indicate that the guns were made for the government and their dating puts them firmly before the handing over of this part of Ulster to the London Companies. Its appearance on surviving iron ordnance before 1650 is quite rare, as few iron guns were bought by the government before the Civil War. The earliest are on a pair of iron

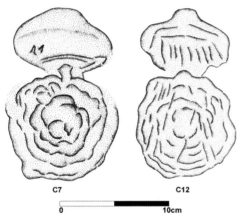

Fig. 21 The surviving rose-and-crown emblems.

Fig. 22 Tudor rose-and-crown emblems on English brass cannon: (a) Henry VIII dated 1529, (b) Henry VIII dated 1546, (c) Edward VI *c.* 1550 (after Blackmore 1976, 44).

demi-culverins from Pevensey Castle which are accompanied by the letters 'ER' (Blackmore 1976, 62). These have been redated from the reign of Elizabeth back to that of her brother, Edward VI (Barter Bailey 1991, 15).

Other early examples are to be seen on a pair of iron cannon (nos 25 and 26) recovered from the *Vereenigde Oostindische Compagnie* (Dutch East India Company, VOC) ship *Mauritius*, which was wrecked in 1609 off the Gulf of Guinea in Africa (Roth 1995, 121–122). They are both dated 1587, and probably were made by John Philips, who cast both bronze guns at Houndsditch (with his brother Richard), and cast-iron guns in Sussex with Thomas Johnson (L'Hour *et al.* 1989, 120). The *Mauritius* guns also have the same double band before the trunnions and single after, but have a much shorter, plainer cascable. A new cannon to add to the list of comparative guns without cypher is a short saker or demi-culverin of 7½ft at Mehrangarh Fort, Jodhpur, India (catalogue 1741: Balasubramaniam and Brown forthcoming).

In fact, the closest parallel to each of the Londonderry rose-and-crown guns is the other! There are a number which are broadly similar, and which date to the latter years of the sixteenth century and early years of the seventeenth century, although most do not bear the rose-and-crown. Other iron guns which have a short, straight muzzle, similarly arranged mouldings and a long cascable (but no rose-and-crown) include numbers 12, 15, 19, 23 and 24 from the *Mauritius* (L'Hour *et al.* 1989, 115–121, Fig. 5.5), an unpublished iron saker from Enkhuizen in the Netherlands, and an iron minion from the *Sea Venture*, which was lost off Bermuda in 1609 (Wingood 1982, 335). This last is engraved 'F-R P' which has been identified as standing for *fecit Richard Phillips*, John Phillips' brother. However there are some doubts about this identification, since there is no evidence that Richard ever cast iron guns, nor is there another example of the use of 'F' to stand for *fecit* on an iron cannon. Another possible candidate might be Richard Polhill, who rented Horsmonden furnace after Thomas Johnson and before Thomas Browne. However it is possible also that the letters refer to the owner of the gun, rather than the manufacturer.

The Elizabethan expedition to Lough Foyle and the identification of the cannon

The Ordnance debenture books have a number of references to the expedition to Lough Foyle. The military stores for it were originally assembled in August 1598, and the books show several references to artillery and artillery-related material. These include a cast-iron falcon, one of the smallest and lightest guns available and weighing 10cwt 2qtr 0lb (1176lb: 533kg) from Thomas Browne, newly-appointed gunfounder to the Queen, and father of John Browne (*NA* WO 49/22, f. 66v). This gun appears to be the only one to have been bought specifically for the expedition, but it was not the only one. The records show further expenditure on ladles, sponges and rammers for a demi-culverin, saker and another falcon. William Smeaton the wheelwright, John Hedland the carpenter and Martin Hopkins the blacksmith built three field carriages, for one each of these pieces (*NA* WO 49/22, f. 67r, f. 68r, f. 69r).

Three cannon were delivered out of Her Majesty's stores on the 22 August 1598. They were all of cast-iron, and consisted of a demi-culverin of 33cwt 3qtr 0lb (3780lb: 1715kg), a saker weighing 21cwt 0qtr 0lb (2352lb: 1067kg) and a falcon weighing 10cwt 3qtr 0lb (1204lb: 546kg). This falcon does not appear to be the same as the gun purchased earlier from Thomas Browne. The two heavier guns taken out of Her Majesty's stores were not replaced until June 1600 (*NA* WO 49/26, f. 52r). Accompanying the artillery were the field carriages, round shot (120 for demi-culverin, 200 for saker and 400 for falcon) and powder, as well as the usual spare parts for carriages – tools for loading guns and making up cartridges, tampions, a 'gin' for moving the guns and other sundries (*NA* WO 49/22, f. 133). The items were despatched at the request of the Earl of Essex in a letter of 12 August (*NA* WO 49/22, f. 132), and were to be sent to Lough Foyle via Sir Henry Bagenal in Dublin. The stores were transferred from the Tower to the two hired merchant ships – the *Mary Rose* and the *Guyance* – lying on the Thames at Ratcliffe, to the east of the City of London, which were to transport them to Ireland (*NA* WO 49/22, f. 67v). The speed with which they were assembled (in a mere ten days between 12 and 22 August) may provide the reason why a substitute had to be found for the falcon ordered from Thomas Browne.

However it is likely that these guns did not make it to Lough Foyle at this time, as the expedition was delayed. In the same month, Bagenal was defeated and killed at the battle of the Yellow Ford, and the troops destined for Lough Foyle were sent instead to Cork, Kinsale and Waterford where they were absorbed into forces in Munster under Sir Thomas Norris (McGurk 1997, 70). What happened to the artillery in the meantime is unknown. In February 1599, further supplies were delivered to Essex, including fourteen field carriages and block carriages, four field carriages for demi–cannons, four field carriages for culverins, three spare carriages for a cannon, demi–cannon and culverin and three unspecified block carriages, (*NA* WO 49/24, f. 25v). Bronze guns shipped at this time to Ireland included a demi-culverin perrier and two fowlers with their chambers (*NA* WO 49/24, f. 81v).

The presence of a demi-culverin with the same weight and which also appears to have been in Londonderry in 1660–1661, is strong evidence that the original three cast-iron guns did reach their destination. However, it should be borne in mind that it was the custom to only weigh iron guns at this period to the nearest quarter rather than pound, so that for each hundredweight there are only four possible weights, whereas if they had weighed to the nearest pound, there could have been 112. This means that in practical terms, the same weights occur over and over again, so that is more difficult it give a positive identification, although clearly it is most tempting to identify C12 as that originally earmarked for Lough Foyle. It is possible also that the saker is the piece which survived at least through to the nineteenth century and bore the initials 'ER'.

Notes to Chapter 5

1 These guns, clearly Borgard pattern, have display panels wrongly attributing them to the Tudor period.

2 Given the practice in recent years of painting letters onto the cannon – for example, having 'Roaring Meg' in white lettering on the breech of C6 – it is not wholly impossible that the letters 'ER' were painted onto one of the two rose-and-crown pieces as early as the 1830s and that the references stem from that.

3 Ulster Museum acquisition nos A12.1987 and A13.1987. We are most grateful to Winifred Glover for this information.

4 John Owen and his brother Robert became the royal gunfounders in 1546.

CHAPTER 6
The Guns of the Seventeenth Century

The seventeenth-century guns can be divided into two main groups – first, those dating to the period between *c.* 1610 and 1635, five of which bear the shield of the City of London, and those which can be fixed definitely to just before the earlier part of 1642. The dating evidence for the earlier group rests on a combination of archaeological comparison and historical documentation, while that for the latter rests primarily on historic documentation, backed up by the inscribed names of a number of the London Companies along with the date 1642. Of particular interest and significance amongst the earlier group are the identifications of two cannon from the works of the Royal Gunfounder, John Browne, while for the later group, it is, of course, the matching of inscriptions on and historical records of seven out of the fifteen pieces provided by the London Companies in 1642. In addition, there is one gun of falcon calibre, now badly disfigured by corrosion and with no distinguishing markings which, on broadly typological grounds could be assigned to the seventeenth century. It shares some features with guns in Youghal, County Cork, reputedly cast for the defence of the town in 1642 by Richard Boyle, but the condition is such as to make attribution uncertain.

A further point of note is that, almost certainly, none in either group displays any surviving weight marks. However, in most cases, corrosion has damaged the relevant surface areas where these might have been expected, so that it is impossible to say whether or not they might have been present originally. Nevertheless, those which have surfaces preserved reasonably well show so no sign of any weight marks, and this indicates strongly that these weapons were not produced for government service. Not only was it necessary to know the weight when building a carriage, but the Board of Ordnance required that pieces for government service were so marked. In fact, it is only in the case of C21 that there is the faintest hint of Roman numerals on the base ring, but corrosion makes this identification very tentative.

The guns of c. 1610–1630

A total of nine cannon can be ascribed to this period (Table 10), and these divide into three groups – two bearing a 'club-and-arrow' motif, five with the shield of the City of London and two showing no markings.

C8 and C20 – Demi-culverins of 9ft 6ins bearing the 'club-and-arrow' mark

Cannon C8 and C20 can be treated together, since they are very close in size, weight and mouldings, and bear similar markings. They are both demi-culverins and, at 3117lb (27cwt 3qtr 9lb) and 3047lb (27cwt 0cwt 23lb) respectively, accord with the shorter, lighter demi-culverins in the 27cwt league supplied by John Browne to the Office of Ordnance in 1625. These were intended to arm ships hired to protect the fishing and Newcastle coal fleets during the wars with Spain and France (e.g. *NA* WO 49/54, f. 44r). For most of this period, a demi-culverin intended for service in the King's Navy tended to have been heavier and longer (up to 11ft 6ins and weighing over 4000lb), reinforcing that idea that C8 and C20 were intended in the first instance for the merchant and civilian market, rather than government service, something further reinforced by the lack of weight marks.

The faces of the cascables are each marked by a pair of rings below the base ring, separated from a group of four by a broad and slightly protuberant band (Figs 23 and 24). This is matched also on many of the other cannons,

145

The Great Guns Like Thunder

Table 10 The main characteristics of the cannon of c. 1610–1635.

Number	Type	Length	Weight	SG	Bore	Mark
C2	Demi-culverin	120.1 [305]	3333 [1512]	6.750	5.20 [13.2]	London shield
C8	Demi-culverin	102.8 [261]	3117 [1414]	6.954	4.80 [12.2]	'club-and-arrow' [both cast in] IB [at touch hole – chiselled] H [on breech face – chiselled]
C13	Demi-culverin	120 [305]	2826 [1282]	6.890	4.06 [10.3]	London shield
C16	Saker or demi-culverin	108 [274]	2676 [1214]	6.937	4.33 [11.0]	Letter 'C' in punched dots on the second reinforce (note 2 below)
C17	Saker	97 [247]	2004 [909]	6.784	3.74 [9.5]	London shield
C18	Demi-culverin	120 [305]	2875 [1304]	6.863	4.05 [10.3]	London shield
C20	Demi-culverin	102 [259]	3047 [1382]	6.876	4.45 [11.3]	'club-and-arrow' [arrow chiselled?]
C21	Demi-culverin	120 [305]	3342 [1516]	6.954	4.53 [11.5]	none
C25	Saker or minion	79* [201]	1667 [875]	6.892	3.50 [8.88]	London shield

* muzzle missing to behind where the muzzle astragal would have been

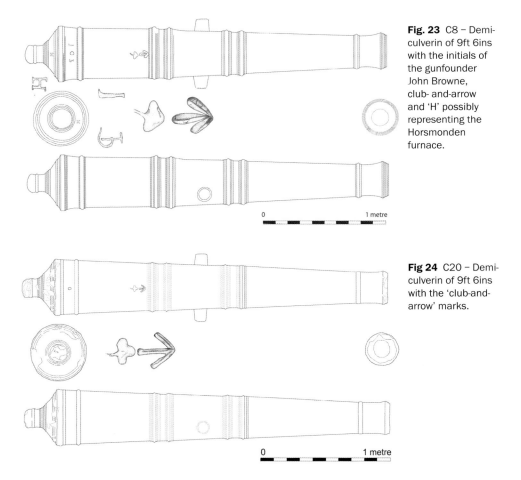

Fig. 23 C8 – Demi-culverin of 9ft 6ins with the initials of the gunfounder John Browne, club- and-arrow and 'H' possibly representing the Horsmonden furnace.

Fig 24 C20 – Demi-culverin of 9ft 6ins with the 'club-and-arrow' marks.

including C1, C3, C4, C6, C9, C10, and C11. The button itself is a fairly simple baluster moulding, with a single plain fillet on an almost parallel-sided neck below a dome-shaped end. The forms of the muzzles are similar, although unfortunately, corrosion has so damaged the mouth of C20 that no trace of any original moulding survives.

Their general shape, and the very broad but even double set of double rings – a feature that one of us (Brown 1995, 115) has defined as characteristic of a 'proto-finbanker' – can be paralleled with a number of other surviving cannons. These include a gun from the *Trial*, an English East Indiaman lost off Australia in 1622 (Green 1986, 203, Fig. 7), an unidentified saker from a wreck of about 1630 in the Erme Estuary (Oldham *et al.* 1993, 326, Fig. 4), some guns from the *Batavia,* a Dutch East Indiaman lost off Australia in 1629 (Green 1980 and 1989, 47–59; although these are in too poor a state to make more than general comparisons), and a group of guns recovered from a wreck off Terschelling, northern Holland (Brinck 1996, 9).

The marks on C8 and C20

1 'IB' AND 'H'

C8 has the letters 'I' and 'B' engraved on either side of the touchhole (Fig. 23); unfortunately, the equivalent area on C20 has been too badly damaged by corrosion for any trace of a similar engraving to have survived. The initials represent the name 'John[2] Browne', otherwise 'John Browne' the gunfounder and second of the Browne dynasty of Royal gunfounders which dominated cannon production during most of the seventeenth century.

At the time of writing, four, possibly five, other broadly contemporary guns marked 'IB', and attributable to John Browne, are known. One comes from the Terschelling group, and has 'IB' either side of the vent, a 'clover leaf', the date 1623, and crossed anchors engraved indicating that it was owned by one of the Dutch Admiralties (Brinck 1996). The second is a minion drake dating to the 1640s and with IB on either side of the vent, from the vessel *Swan* which was lost off Mull in 1653 (Martin 2004, 85 and Figs 6–7). A third cannon has been identified as a demi-culverin used by the Dutch West Indies Company[3] (Brinck 2005, 43–45), while the fourth is a saker or demi-culverin of 8ft, also with a double set of double bands in Mehrangarh Fort, Jodhpur, India (catalogue no. 1780: Balasubramaniam and Brown forthcoming). There is also a possible fifth gun at Mehrangarh Fort (catalogue no. 1732), but the marks are quite faint.

C8 has the letter 'H' engraved at the breech. There are two possible interpretations for this. First, it may represent which of the Browne furnaces it was cast in – Horsmonden in Kent, as opposed to Barden or Brenchley. In support of this is a seventeenth-century iron gun in the Rotunda at Woolwich[4] which has a 'B' in the same place. The second interpretation is that this is a mark of the Board of Ordnance put there in the late seventeenth century. The Board of Ordnance had a campaign to engrave cannon with different marks, including 'H' for 'home-bored'. The impetus for this was the increasing popularity and use of the so-called 'drake', a gun with a tapering powder chamber as opposed to the older type, the 'home-bored' where the chamber was of the same diameter as the bore. The drake obviously required a smaller charge of powder and, since there were not significant exterior differences to distinguish between the two types, it was very necessary that gunners knew which they were handling in order that they did not use the wrong size of charge. Thus, in 1683 (*NA* WO 47/12, 75v), 'brass' and iron guns were examined and engraved with an 'H' if they were home-bored, or a 'D' if a drake (i.e. the type found on the Mull wreck). Such an 'H' is visible on a cannon recovered from the *Winchester Castle*, which was lost off Florida in the 1690s (Brookfield 1941).

2 THE 'CLUB'

This raised (and thus cast-in) mark is found on both guns, some 6cm behind the first reinforce ring. Precise parallels are found on two guns of the second quarter of the seventeenth century. The first is from the *Trial,* an English East Indiaman lost off Australia in 1622 (Green 1986, 203, Fig. 7). More important is the second, recovered from the wreck off Terschelling, northern Holland and dated 1623, which displays also the initials 'IB' of John Browne (see above). This second piece quite neatly ties together both cannon to John Browne and, if interpretation of the incised 'H' on C8 as representing the Horsmonden foundry is correct, then to the same production centre also.

3 THE BROAD ARROW

This presents a potential problem. It is normally the mark of ownership of the British government, although the arrows on these two pieces seem sharper than is usually found. The regular practice of putting it on guns may have been introduced as late as November 1682, when the Board of Ordnance issued an order detailing marks that were to be put on brass and iron guns (*NA* WO 47/12, f. 75v). All guns from culverin down were to be marked with a cold chisel between the first reinforce ring and the vent with a broad arrow 'fair and deep' to prevent confusion with 'hired' guns. Payments show that this campaign took place over the next few years, and it is clear that the opportunity was taken to differentiate smaller calibre guns which could be easily confused with each other (e.g. *NA* WO 51/28, f. 214; WO 51/29, f. 195v). The absence of this mark on the other Londonderry cannon may possibly indicate that C8 and C20 were obtained from different sources, possibly a government depot, to enhance the defences of Londonderry before or after the Williamite siege, but this seems quite unlikely. We should note also that the two Borgard-pattern guns, now preserved in Carrickfergus Castle, Carrickfergus, Co Antrim (p. 139) have obviously chiselled arrows just behind the second reinforce.

A problem with the 'proof mark' interpretation is that the arrow on C8 is of different form to that on C20 (Fig. 24). Whilst it is impossible to be dogmatic, the arrow on C8 gives the strong impression that it was cast in like the raised 'club' just behind it. The lines are distinctly rounded as opposed to those of C20, which have the comparatively crude and angular lines that certainly can be associated with the use of a cold chisel. Should this be the case, it means that C8 represents the association of club-and-arrow as a distinct mark, while the arrow on C20 would easily have been added at some date after November 1682. It is possible also that the pairing of both represents a previously unknown composite mark.

C2, C13, C17, C18 and C25, all bearing variants of the shield of the City of London

These guns are all linked by exhibiting quartered shields which in three cases (C2, C18 and C25) are certainly of the style which forms a part of the arms of the of the City of London. Erosion of the devices on C13 and C17 makes this a tentative ascription only. However, we know that the London Companies provided ordnance for the defence of the City and for Culmore in the years following completion of the City Walls. Since the shields are all cast in, it seems very likely that these guns were produced specifically for Londonderry, as opposed to having been bought 'off-the-peg' as was the case of the guns of 1642. Indeed, it is not impossible that some, if not all, are pieces referred to in the warrant issued to Roger Rose in 1620 (pp 105*ff*).

C2 Demi-culverin of 10ft

This gun is in better condition than the others in the group. In particular, the detail of the coat of arms is crisp, and the profiles of the double set of double bands are still quite clear. The calibre is quite large, a little below that of a culverin, which suggests that it is a demi-culverin widened with use or age rather than a rusted-up culverin.

The shape of the cascable and the assemblage of rings on the breech are similar to those of C13, C16, C17 and C25. The cascable is distinctive, in particular the 'lip' at the neck. This form can be found on a number of cannon outside this assemblage, including on a badly damaged saker that was set unhappily in concrete on the town walls overlooking Saint Mary's Church of Ireland graveyard in Youghal, County Cork, but now removed for conservation, and on a demi-culverin recorded by the late St John Hennessy at Ballymullan Barracks, Tralee, County Kerry. A sixteenth-century example, very similar in

Chapter 6 – The Guns of the Seventeenth Century

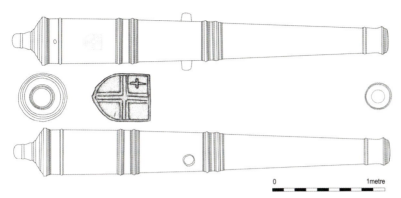

Fig. 25 C2 – Demi-culverin of 10ft.

Plate 60 Cast-iron saker on the town wall of Youghal, County Cork.

Plate 61 Cascable of a cast-iron demi-culverin in Ballymullan Barracks, Tralee, County Kerry (*Hennessy Archive*).

form, is found on a cast-iron cannon from the wreck of the Spanish Armada vessel *La Duquesa Santa Anna* (p. 52).

Other parallels include a demi-culverin, A90, in the Tojhusmuseum, Copenhagen, thought to have been purchased in the time of Christian IV (1588–1648) for the Danish navy (Mortensen, 1999, 207; The Tojhusmuseum, 1971, 17); and four demi-culverins recovered from an unknown, but almost certainly, Dutch wreck off Terschelling, two of which are illustrated, one in Trollope (2002, 60) and the second in Brinck (2004, 52–53). Two of the group have the crossed anchors of the Dutch Admiralties, Roman numerals and some sort of inventory number, and one has a weight, inventory number and what appears to be a monogram of 'H' and 'N' on the trunnion face, which is a little damaged.

The Terschelling guns have not been properly published yet, although one of them is discussed in Trollope (2002, 60), who suggests that the cascable represents a short span of time in gun production. However, Trollope is over-reliant on Ordnance papers for identifying cannon, so that he is less dependable when dealing with years in which the Brownes were not supplying iron guns to the government, and also for the other gunfounders who supplied the merchant and export market. Recent additions to the group include a gun in the Cloisters Museum, Riga, and at least one, and possibly two, in the Military Museum in the Forbidden City, Beijing (S. A. Walton *pers. comm.*). Guns whose resemblance is not so close as these include a cannon from Fort Derby, Isle of Man, an unpublished culverin at Fort Nelson, Portsmouth, Hampshire, marked 'IA' and with a horseshoe-shaped mark, and a gun (catalogue no. 1780) on the walls of Mehrangarh Fort in Jodhpur, India (Smith 1991; Chatterji 2001, 79).

There are a number of guns which have a similar profile of the double set of thick double rings symmetrically arranged. In both proto-finbankers and finbankers proper, it is more common for the front ring of each pair to be wider than the back ring and for the rings themselves to have an asymmetrical profile. C8, C17 and C20 have the same arrangement as this gun, and other cannons with a similar profile of double set of thick double rings include the cannon in the Cloisters Museum, Riga, the two cannons in the Military Museum, Forbidden City Beijing (*supra*), and a broken gun in Deal castle. Other possible comparanda include pieces from a number of shipwrecks, although their condition is not good enough to be absolutely reliable. These are cannon 10 from the *Mauritius*, a VOC ship lost in 1609, the saker from the East India Company ship the *Trial*, lost in 1622 off Australia and possibly guns 4 and 5 from the VOC ship *Batavia*, lost in 1629 (Green 1986, 1989; L'Hour *et al.* 1989).

The very straight muzzle differs from the muzzles of C8 and C20, and is closer to C13. A parallel is provided by the Terschelling gun with the 'IB' mark and the date 1623 (Brinck 1996). Other examples, none of which are from dated contexts unfortunately, include a gun on the wall of Bridlington Harbour, North Yorkshire, a broken fragment of cannon in Deal Castle, Kent, and a gun in store at the Manx Museum in the Isle of Man.

C13 – Demi-culverin of 8ft

Superficially, this cannon resembles the proto-finbankers C2, C8 and C20 already discussed, but it exhibits a number of significant differences from the others, most obviously in the shape of the cascable and the profiles of its sets of rings. It is also much shorter than the others, at 8ft.

The cascable has the same 'lip' at the neck as C2, C17 and C25. Similar features occur on a few other surviving cannons, including the Tojhusmuseum demi-culverin A90, and the Terschelling demi-culverins, one of which is a demi-culverin of 8ft, remarkably similar to this example, but with a weight and a number and letter engraved on the breech. These guns also resemble the Londonderry example in the profiles of the rings, which do not have a symmetrical arrangement. The highest band is not in the middle but towards one end, unlike the symmetrical arrangement of bands in C8, C20 and C21.

There are somewhat similar cannons in the Manx Museum, Isle of Man (Smith 1991, 33-34), as well as the unpublished culverin marked 'IA' at Fort Nelson, Portsmouth, Hampshire.

Chapter 6 – The Guns of the Seventeenth Century

C17 – Saker of 8ft

For general comments made on this type of cannon, see under C2. Like the other guns with the London arms, it is divided into three by a two sets of two bands of multiples rings. The two in front of the trunnions seem a little more widely spaced than the other examples. The breech and cascable are similar to those of C2, C13, C16 and C25, the main difference here being the wide flared muzzle, while the other guns have straighter and more elaborately ribbed muzzles.

C18 – Demi-culverin of 10ft

This cannon is in poorer condition than its fellows which makes the drawing of comparisons more difficult. The cascable seems shorter and stubbier than those of the other London guns, but this may be in part due to damage. It has a short, straight and highly ribbed muzzle, similar to those of C2 and C13.

C25 – Saker or minion

This piece, a saker or possibly a minion, probably of 8ft, has lost its muzzle and has been broken off behind where the muzzle astragal would have been. It is not a cutt, as the break is ragged. Of this group, it has the simplest of mouldings, arranged in two pairs and seemingly closest in form to C9, although corrosion has taken its toll of the detail of the astragals. The form of the cascable is very similar to that of C17 in particular, as well as to those of C2, C13 and C16. Although badly damaged, the quartering of the shield can just be made out, along with traces of the quartering of the cross and the groove around the outline, both seemingly close to these features on C2.

The City of London Shield

The shield that forms the central element of the arms of the City of London combines the Cross of Saint George along with the red

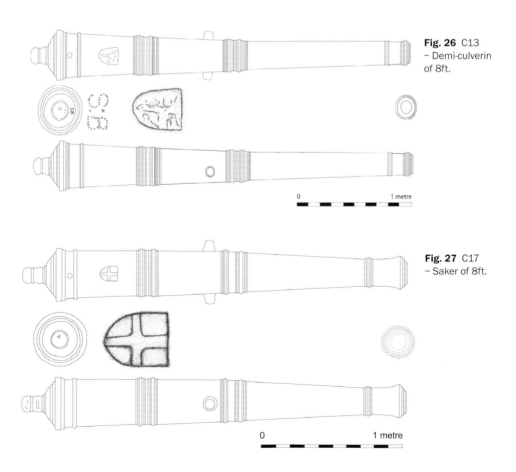

Fig. 26 C13 – Demi-culverin of 8ft.

Fig. 27 C17 – Saker of 8ft.

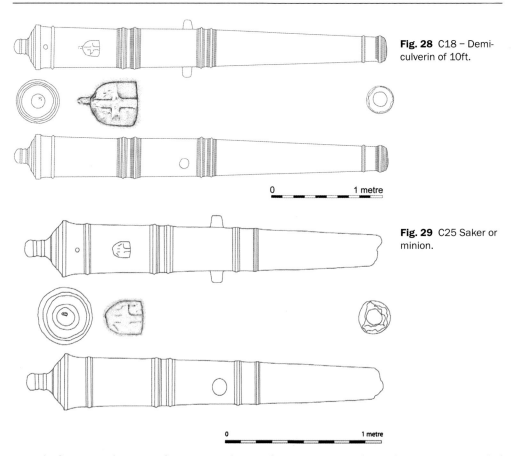

Fig. 28 C18 – Demi-culverin of 10ft.

Fig. 29 C25 Saker or minion.

Sword of Saint Paul. We are fortunate in that C2 preserves all of the essential details – the '... cross gules, in the first quarter a sword in pale point upwards of the last'. One point to note is that on C2, possibly also C25, the cross appears as a 'cross quarterly quartered', a feature which suggests a two-colour scheme for the printed version.

Although the shields on C13, C17, C18 and C25 are severely eroded, it seems nevertheless that C13, C17 and C18 have a more rounded lower margin than those of C2 and C25. Further, the distinct groove which bounds the shield of C2 is absent from the other examples, although it is possible that C25 once had one before corrosion damaged the surface.

While it is clear that this group of guns was cast specifically for the City of London, the questions are by whom, and when. Had this been a job lot cast as one order, it might have been expected that there would be more homogeneity in terms of the organisation of mouldings and form of cascable at least. Obviously, the input of John Browne to this part of the assemblage, along with the documentary evidence, makes him the most likely candidate, but in the period *c.* 1615–1625, Maresfield furnace in Sussex was being operated by the Crowe family. Sir Sackville Crowe, a young friend of James I, managed to get the monopoly of merchant export of cannon in 1621, despite howls of protest from the Brownes, who did eventually manage to come to a working arrangement with him (Brown 2005, 60-61). Certainly, Maresfield is a potential contender

Fig. 30 City of London Shield on C2.

Chapter 6 – The Guns of the Seventeenth Century

for supply of a cannon being exported legally to the north of Ireland in the early seventeenth century.

Another candidate for gunfounder is Stephen Aynscombe, whose long-term career can best be described as colourful, being that of an illegal gun-runner who occasionally lapsed into legitimacy. In the early seventeenth century, the government was concerned that English ordnance was finding its way into the hands of potential enemies, and was increasing control of its export (Barter Bailey 2003, 58). At the same time, the Brownes were steadily extending their influence and attempting – with success – to gain a complete monopoly in English gunfounding. This pincer movement might explain why Aynscombe embarked on his illegal activities. He was involved in gunfounding in the 1610s and 1620s, at the Mayfield and Pounsley furnaces, Sussex. His cannons were frequently seized by government agents (as, for example, in February 1621: *APC* 1619–1621, 340–341, 2 February 1621), and he often had to lodge bonds for good behaviour with the local magistrates. However the records show that he also had legitimate exports and that he had strong contacts with the Netherlands, both with agents in Britain and directly with merchants in Amsterdam (*APC* 1613–1614, 428, 7 May 1614).

The furnace at Ashburnham in Kent was also in operation in this period, run by the Relf family. The Brownes objected to their operations and they seem to have ceased operations by the late 1630s. In any case, this furnace seems to have been less active during this period than those at Maresfield and Mayfield.

C16 and C21 – unmarked demi-culverins

C16 – Demi-Culverin of 9ft

This gun – either a saker or a demi-culverin – has double sets of double bands similar to those on C2, C8, C9, C13, C17, C20, C21 and C25, while the cascable is of the same shape as C2, C13, and C17. However there are a number of significant differences in the details of its elements. In particular these can be seen in the profiles of the bands, which have an uneven distribution of the rings making up each. In C16, the bands themselves are uneven, with the rear band in both sets being narrower than the front one. In addition, the front ring in both sets is asymmetrical, with the highest ring being towards the rear of the band. On most of the cannons with double sets of double bands, all are of equal width, with the highest ring set in the middle. However this example is closest to C2, one of those guns with the Arms of London, to C20 with the 'club' mark and to C21. The muzzle has a straight flare, similar to those on C17 and C20 (of the guns with double bands) and most of the London Company guns.

C21 – Demi-culverin of 10ft

This cannon does not appear to have any marks, although there may be traces of a weight engraving on the base ring. It is possible with the eye of faith to make out an 'IX' which may represent the Roman numeral for '9', but this

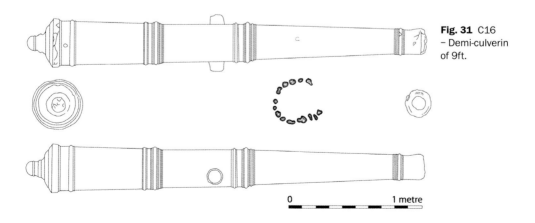

Fig. 31 C16 – Demi-culverin of 9ft.

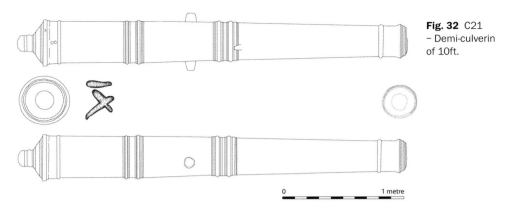

Fig. 32 C21 – Demi-culverin of 10ft.

is very speculative. Were this piece to have had its weight marked on it, it would be the only one of the Londonderry guns of this period to show this feature, although it would be unusual for an English piece to have a weight in Roman numerals. The chase astragal shows a distinct flaw in the mould, and it is also noticeable that there seems to have been a problem with one vent, as a second one appears to have been drilled out beside a partial attempt.

This gun bears a strong resemblance to the 10ft demi-culverin from the Terschelling wreck, and to C8. Like the Terschelling piece, this cannon has the double set of double rings and a very short, straight-sided muzzle rather than the more usual long, bell-shaped mouth. The cascables also appear similar and can be compared also to C20. The very straight muzzle indicates a date in the period *c.* 1610–1625, and its similarities to C8 and C20 in particular, as well as to the Terschelling demi-culverin, suggests strongly that this gun was cast by the Brownes.

The guns of 1641–1642 and beyond

Of the fifteen guns recorded in contemporary documents as having been sent by the London Companies specifically for the defence of Londonderry in response to the outbreak of the Irish Rebellion on 23 October 1641, seven certainly survive.

The demi-culverins all show a great degree of uniformity in dimension and style and, although purchased by the individual Companies through their agents (see the various records in Appendix A), give the strong impression that they could be the products of a single foundry, with the names of the Companies having been engraved by the same hand, that of Abraham Preston (see p.127). However, when we look at the overall listing for the ordnance supplied by them, at least one (the culverin sent by the Skinners), came second-hand through

Table 11 The main characteristics of the cannon of 1641–1642.

Number	Type	Length	Weight	SG	Bore	Mark
1	Demi-culverin	120 [304]	3333 [1512]	6.750	4.50 [11.43]	Vintners London 1642
3	Demi-culverin	120 [304]	3750 [1701]	6.830	4.25 [10.80]	Marchant Taylers London 1642
4	Demi-culverin	90 [226]	2795 [1268]	6.890	4.92 [12.50]	Salters London 1642
5	Falcon	66 [168]	549 [249]	6.225	2.95 [7.5]	
6	Demi-culverin	120 [304]	3955 [1794]	6.900	4.71 [12.00]	Fishmongers London 1642
9	Demi-culverin	120 [304]	3977 [1804]	6.990	4.80 [12.19]	Mercers London 1642
10	Demi-culverin	120 [304]	3951 [1792]	6.950	4.92 [12.50]	Grocers London 1642
11	Demi-culverin	120 [304]	4034 [1830]	7.067	4.60 [11.68]	Marchant Taylers London 1642

Chapter 6 – The Guns of the Seventeenth Century

John Browne's agent, Samuel Ferrers. However, since Browne also sold to the East India Company from which the Skinners bought and, given that they paid 12s per cwt as opposed to the 13s 6d paid by other Companies, it is quite likely that this too was a Browne gun, albeit perhaps second-hand.

C1 – Demi-culverin of 10ft

The cannon is divided into three fields by two broad, single mouldings. The divisions are marked with distinct steps, in comparison to the more gradual, uninterrupted taper which can be seen on those guns with double sets of rings. In contemporary documents this is type of cannon is called 'fortified' (e.g. *NA* WO 49/75, f. 220*ff*; WO 49/87, f. 156; WO 47/2, f. 68; WO f. 47/3, 82). It is engraved VINTERS LONDON 1642 (Fig. 33), but the weight markings do not appear to have survived. However, the inventory of 1660 (Appendix A14.1a) gives the weight of the piece as 30cwt 1qtr 0lb (3388lb, 1537kg), and in this study it weighed in at 29cwt 3qtr 1lb (3333lb, 1512kg). This is on the light side for a demi-culverin of this length, although in 1640 the English government did buy at least two iron demi-culverins with weights close to this (e.g. *NA* WO 49/71, f. 33).

In terms of detailed comparison, the closest in form to this piece is C4, in particular in terms of the mouldings on the barrel. There is also a small but growing number of surviving English cast-iron guns which have been dated to the 1640s or 1650s and can act as comparanda. One is the 3-pdr or minion drake from the *Swan,* lost in the 1650s but probably dating from the 1640s, which was cast by John Browne; this has the same general pattern and the initials 'JB' (Martin 2004). There are two culverin drakes of comparable design from the Commonwealth period. The first, thought to have been lost at the Battle of Schveningen and dating from *c.* 1653, is at the Royal Armouries (Wilson 1988). The second has been recently been identified in Fort York, Toronto and has had its commonwealth arms removed and replaced with an engraved CR (Trollope 2007). All of these have similar general patterns with a pair of single mouldings dividing the gun into three parts.

A fourth gun has recently been identified from a wreck identified as the *Great Lewis,* flagship of the Parliamentarian navy, which was lost off Duncannon Fort, County Waterford in 1645 (Kelleher 2004). A fifth possible parallel is a badly damaged iron cannon raised from the wreck of the *Avondster*, which was lost through an accident in Galle harbour in 1659, and which survived the recent tsunami (Parthesius *et al.* 2005). It comes from a ship, the *Blessing*, which was purchased by the English East India Company in 1641. Some years later she was captured by the Dutch, renamed and absorbed into the VOC fleet until her subsequent loss. The gun in question is in a poor state, but the cascable and breech are identical to those just mentioned, so that it is possible it formed part of her original East India Company armament While the mouldings of the breech and cascable of the Vintners' cannon resemble the guns discussed above, there are also significant differences. The Commonwealth guns have flared muzzles, as would

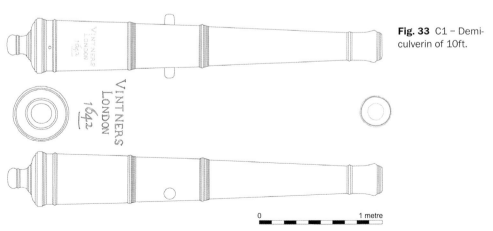

Fig. 33 C1 – Demi-culverin of 10ft.

155

be expected from naval ordnance, while the mouldings of the Vintners' cannon appear to be of a more simple form.

C3 – Demi-culverin of 10ft

This piece is divided into three fields by two single mouldings, with a semi-circular dip in the moulding in front of the trunnions, and thus can be described as 'fortified'. It is engraved MARCHANT TAYLERS LONDON 1642, and at present the Merchant Taylors appear to be the only one of the Great Companies both of whose guns have survived (along with C11) which makes for an interesting comparison. There are no weight markings but the inventory of 1660 (Appendix A14.1a) gives the weights of their demi-culverins as 34cwt 0qtr 14lb (3822lb, 1734kg) and 36cwt 0qtr 14lb (4046lb, 1835kg). These weights are in line with the weights of iron demi-culverins bought by the government in the 1630s and 1640s. The weights recorded in this study are 33cwt 1qtr 26lb (C3: 3750lb, 1701kg) and 36cwt 0qtr 2lb (C11: 4034lb, 1830kg), once again showing a remarkably close agreement, allowing for the ravages of time and differences in weighing techniques.

For comparative guns, see those discussed under C1. The main difference here is that the muzzle is more flared, similar to Commonwealth naval guns.

C4 – Demi-culverin of 7ft 6ins

The gun, which is engraved SALTERS LONDON 1642, is divided into three fields by two broad mouldings, however, unlike the other Company guns, it has a gradual taper rather than the 'fortified' profile. 1642. No weight markings are evident, but the 1660 Londonderry inventory (Appendix A14.1a) lists the Salters' cannon as a demi-culverin weighing 26cwt. In this study it was found to weigh 24cwt 3qtr 23lb (2795lb, 1268kg), a discrepancy greater than in the other cannon in the group. It was identified in the Richard Winter list as a saker (Table 7), probably because of its short length, but its present calibre confirms that it is a demi-culverin.

Most of the guns sent in by the Companies in 1642 are very similar, in that they have the same general pattern. However the Salters' cannon has a number of pronounced differences. First it is shorter than the other guns, at 7½ft rather than 10ft. Second, this piece does not have such pronounced reinforces as the others, so that the profile is between the more tapered shape of the earlier guns and the fortified cannons such as C3. Third, it has a different pattern of mouldings that are wider and more elaborate than C3, without the usual indent in the first band in front of the trunnions. However the general shape and distribution of the rings and mouldings at the cascable and breech are similar to the other pieces, particularly C1.

Unfortunately C4 is not in particularly good condition so that comparisons are imprecise. There are few parallels, one being a cannon of unknown bore, also 7½ft long, presently at Churchill House Museum, Hereford (currently uncatalogued and on display on Castle Green in Hereford[5]). The distribution of the rings of this piece bears some resemblance to that of the Salters' cannon.

C6 – Demi-culverin of 10ft

The most famous of the City cannon, engraved: FISHMONGERS LONDON 1642 but known best as 'Roaring Meg', it is divided into three fields by two broad single mouldings. The divisions are marked with distinct steps, as compared to the more gradual, uninterrupted taper that can be seen on those guns with double sets of rings. In addition to the small corpus of similar cannons mentioned under the other entries, C6 shares a number of characteristics with other cannons from the 1642 consignment. Like C1, C3, C9 and C10, it is a demi-culverin of 10ft, and in general pattern resembles C1, C3, C4, C10 and C11. However, it does have a very pronounced dip on the band in front of the trunnions, a feature that is visible also on C3, C10 and C11. The muzzle is flared out with rings at the front, a form shared C3 and C4

In general, the shape of the breech with three bands at the neck, two at the rim and the cupped ball cascable resembles those of C1, C3, C4, C9, C10 and C11. On the other hand, its cascable with a slight nipple

Chapter 6 – The Guns of the Seventeenth Century

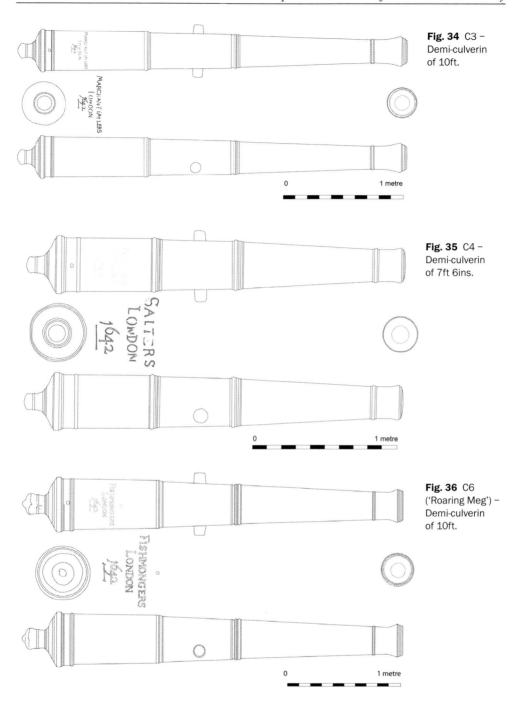

Fig. 34 C3 – Demi-culverin of 10ft.

Fig. 35 C4 – Demi-culverin of 7ft 6ins.

Fig. 36 C6 ('Roaring Meg') – Demi-culverin of 10ft.

is unique in the collection, although there is similar feature on a seventeenth-century saker in the Round Tower at Windsor Castle.

C9 – Demi-culverin of 10ft

The cannon is divided into three fields by two sets of double mouldings, and is engraved with MERCERS LONDON 1642 (Fig. 37). The general shape is a gradual, uninterrupted taper, unlike the stepped and fortified guns such as Gun 3 and 4. The muzzle is very straight with rings rather than a swell, indicating it was for land rather than sea service (Smith 2001, 34, Fig. 13). Any weight markings that might originally have been present have not survived. However, the 1660 Inventory (Appendix

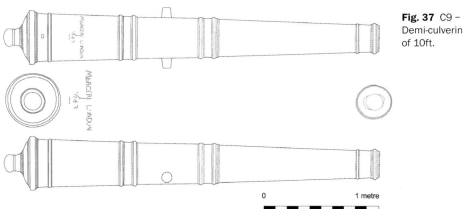

Fig. 37 C9 – Demi-culverin of 10ft.

A14.1a) indicates that the Mercers gave two demi-culverins with weights of 35cwt 2qtr 14lb (3990lb, 1810kg) and 36cwt 0qtr 0lb (4032lb, 1829kg), which are within the range usual for this type of cannon. This piece weighs in at 35cwt 2qtr 1lb (3977lb, 1804kg) making it most likely to be the second of the two pieces listed.

This is an unusual gun in the Londonderry collection in that although one of the Company guns, it does not resemble the others, which are of a generally different type with single mouldings and a stepped appearance. It is much closer to C8, C13, C20 and C21, all of which have a tapered shape and double mouldings. Of these, the cascable and breech rings of C8 are closest in form. In fact, the closest parallel to C9 is Cannon 1732 at Mehrangarh Fort, Jodhpur. The two guns are identical in pattern and length, as well as in the shapes of the cascable and breech, and muzzle, although the weight on this gun suggests that it is a saker rather than a demi-culverin. The Indian gun appears to have the initials 'IB' on either side of the touchhole but they are quite faint (Balasubramaniam and Brown, forthcoming). Also similar are the John Browne demi-culverin from the Terschelling wreck, a demi-culverin in Windsor Castle (Smith 2001, 34 and Fig. 13) and a 7ft iron gun at Churchill House Museum, Hereford (currently uncatalogued). These latter have very similar cascables, but in general both are in a poor state and some of the original features have gone under layers of paint and rust (Smith 2001, 34).

C10 – Demi-culverin of 10ft

It is divided into three fields by two single mouldings, with a semi-circular dip in the moulding in front of the trunnions, in other words, a 'fortified' gun. Like C1 in particular, the divisions are very marked with distinct steps, in comparison to the more gradual, uninterrupted taper of those pieces with the double sets of rings.

The gun is engraved GROCERS LONDON 1642 (Fig. 38). There are no weight markings, but the 1660 inventory (Appendix A14.1a) attributes to the Grocers two demi-culverins with weights of 35cwt 1qtr 0lb (3948lb, 1791kg) and 36cwt 1qtr 14lb (4074lb, 1848kg) which are within the usual range for this type of cannon. The modern result of 35cwt 1qtr 3lb (3951lb, 1792kg) falls between the two, but again with close agreement.

In general the rings and mouldings of the cascable and breech, with its two groups of triple rings as well as the mouldings of the barrel, bear a strong resemblance to these guns discussed above. However the muzzles of this gun and C11 are without the flared, bell shape, having instead a short, straight muzzle with rings, suggesting that they were intended for land service rather than for use onboard ship.

C11 – Demi-culverin of 10ft

The piece is divided into three fields by two single mouldings, with a semi-circular dip in the moulding in front of the trunnions, again

Chapter 6 – The Guns of the Seventeenth Century

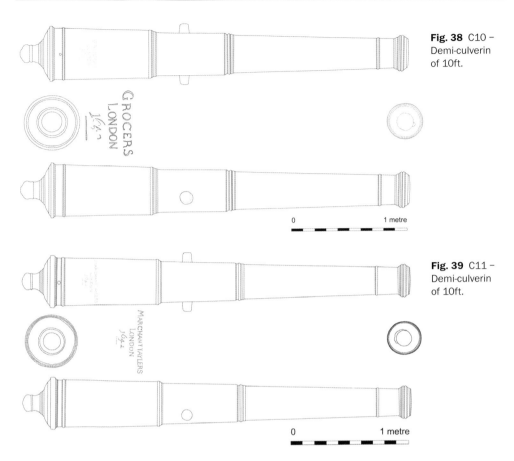

Fig. 38 C10 – Demi-culverin of 10ft.

Fig. 39 C11 – Demi-culverin of 10ft.

a 'fortified' gun, where the divisions are very marked with distinct steps. It is engraved MARCHANT TAYLORS LONDON 1642, and is the sibling of C3 (Fig. 39). There are no weight markings but the 1660 inventory indicates that the demi-culverins weighed 34cwt 0qtr 14lb (3822lb, 1734kg) and 36cwt 0qtr 14lb (4046lb, 1835kg). The weights recorded in this study are 33cwt 1qtr 26lb (C3: 3750lb, 1701kg) and 36cwt 0qtr 2lb (C11: 4034lb, 1830kg), showing close agreement.

In general the rings and mouldings of the cascable and breech, with its two groups of triples rings as well as the mouldings of the barrel compare well with C1, C3, C9 and C10. However, as with C10, the muzzle lacks the flared bell. In this it differs from the other Merchant Taylors' piece, C3, which definitely appears to have a muzzle swell.

In summary, it can be suggested that the London Company guns show a degree of stylistic diversity that supports the documentary record that they were purchased piecemeal and not as a homogeneous batch. The Company records (Appendix A) show that six, possibly seven, at least were purchased from Samuel Ferrers, the commercial agent for John Browne I (Table 7).

C5 Falcon of 5ft 6ins

This piece (Fig. 40) has been badly damaged by corrosion, and the surfaces bear no distinguishing marks. A botched mounting of the gun for museum display involved drilling into the faces of the trunnions and inserting bolts to increase their length. Thus, any markings that might have been present there have been lost. The form of the muzzle is unusual in that it displays a marked chamfer, while the outer surfaces have hints of a spiral pattern that is only really detectable under raking light and by touch. The flattened button is not dissimilar to that on guns from Youghal, County Cork, reputedly cast in 1642 by Richard Boyle for the defence of the town, and the overall form of the cascable might

159

The Great Guns Like Thunder

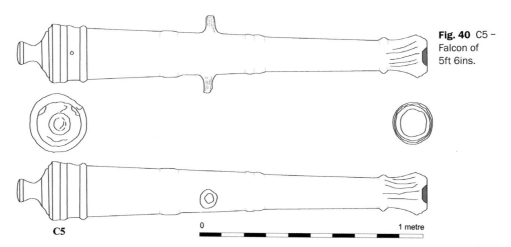

Fig. 40 C5 – Falcon of 5ft 6ins.

be compared to that of one of the guns from Hereford Museum (currently uncatalogued and on display on Castle Green, Hereford). The suggestion of some form of deliberate relief on the surface, along with the flared and chamfered muzzle is reminiscent also of a woodcut of a small field-piece in a pamphlet of early 1642 (*True Newes* 5).

The bore has been somewhat enlarged by corrosion, suggesting that it was originally around that for a falcon, namely 2.75ins (e.g. Blackmore 1976, 229). The inventory of 1660 lists two falcons, one at 1000lb weight, another with no weight recorded. Apart from the minions attributed to the Drapers, there are two others listed (Appendix A14.1a) with weights given as 479lb (217kg) and 492lb (223kg).

Iron falcons and minions are listed virtually from the first establishment of an artillery park at Londonderry and while this piece cannot be attributed with any certainty to a particular period, it is not unlikely to be roughly contemporary with the other guns discussed here, in other words seventeenth century.

Notes to Chapter 6

1 The initials 'SB' are punched into the breech of this cannon as a series of unconnected dots. This is unlikely to be contemporary with the manufacture or early use and is more likely to be much later graffito. Guns often have marks, letters, numbers etc. engraved on them

Plate 62 Woodcut published in early 1642 showing a gunner with a small field piece.

in the course of their working lives, but marks of this nature being punched in are, to date, unknown.

2 The letter 'I' was regularly used in place of 'J' at this time.

3 Currently in private hands in Zoutkamp, Holland.

4 This gun currently has no accession number and has not been published.

5 Information kindly supplied by David Stevens, Hereford Museum and Art Gallery.

CHAPTER 7
The Guns of the Eighteenth and Nineteenth Centuries

Plate 63 John Wilkinson cannon (C19) restored and mounted on its new carriage, on display in the Memorial Garden, Londonderry.

C19, C22 and C26 – 6-pdr cannon by John Wilkinson

C19 and C22 were placed in the past on the lawn of the house of the Bishop of Derry, while C26 has recently been located at Brook Hall, both on the Culmore Road on the outskirts of the City. The most recent provenance of C19 and C22 prior to Pennyburn Depot was See House on the Culmore Road, while before it was taken to Brook Hall, C27 had been at George's Quay between the Foyle Bridge and Culmore.[1] These three pieces are, for all practical purposes, identical in weight, dimensions and form (Table 12), the only significant difference between them being in the survival of detail of the marks on the trunnions, and in the fact that C26 lacks a chase astragal. They are 6-pdr cannon of 4½ft and were civilian pieces, intended for the merchant market, which fired a ball weighing 6lb (2.72kg), hence the nomenclature. Each has a quite plain cascable with a circumferential moulding on the button, a rectangular vent patch with characteristic teardrop-shaped depression, simple astragals, and the letter 'B' clearly visible as cast into the face of the right-hand trunnion (Plate 64a). Before corrosion took its toll, these letters were obviously large and well-formed. The word 'SOLID', written in a half circle, is partially visible on the face of the left trunnion of C19 (Plate 64b). Corrosion damage to C22 has removed any trace of such a mark, while traces are visible on C26 when viewed with the eye of faith.

The 'B' stands for Bersham, near Wrexham in north Wales, showing that they were cast

Plate 64a Bersham mark on C19.

Plate 64b Traces of SOLID mark on C19.

163

The Great Guns Like Thunder

Table 12 The eighteenth- and nineteenth-century guns

Number	Type	Length	Weight	SG	Bore	Mark
14	3- or 4-pdr	53 [135]	1010 [458]	6.890	3.125 [7.9]	Letter 'P' on first reinforce.
19	6-pdr	53 [135]	913 [414]	6.933	3.78 [9.6]	Letter 'B' on right trunnion face SOLID left trunnion face.
22	6-pdr	53 [135]	922 [418]	6.950	3.78 [9.6]	Letter 'B' on right trunnion face.
23	24-pdr	96 [243.8]	4306 [1954]	7.120	5.76 [14.6]	АЛКСНД-ЗВД (Alexandrovski works – Petrozavodsk) 24-℔ (24-pdr) 120-П (120 pud = 4333lb 182_ (date last digit obliterated).
24	3- or 4-pdr	66 [167.5]	503 [228]	6.710	2.60 [6.6]	
26	6-pdr	52 [132]	838 [380]	6.786	3.50 [8.9]	Letter 'B' on right trunnion face, indications of 'SOLID' on left trunnion face.
27	6-pdr	51 [130]	820 [317]	6.763	3.50 [8.9]	Crowned 'P' and fleur-de-lys on first reinforce.

by John Wilkinson (pp 204*ff*) at his foundry there (Brown 1988, 325). The legend 'SOLID' on C19 shows that this is a gun bored out of the solid,[2] therefore at the time, both up-to-date and expensive. In fact, both of these are 'B-SOLID' products of Bersham.

They are based on what became known as the 'Armstrong pattern' which was introduced into British military service in 1729 and was current up until 1787. We can date these pieces with a high degree of confidence to the period *c.* 1773 (when the 'B-SOLID' trunnion mark makes its first appearance – *ibid.* 1988, 106) to 1796. The last known reference[3] to Wilkinson supplying guns dates to 1796, when the final guns definitely marked with 'B-SOLID' were proofed on 9–10 May for Wiggins and Graham (*WPB* 5).

These were not guns for government service, as they have no royal badge or any other markings on the barrel, and also they are shorter than the normal government pattern 6-pdr. Information from the Ordnance Bill Books for the period 1773–1796 indicates that standard lengths for government service were 6, 6½ and 7ft, although a few were made in non-standard sizes of 4½ and 8½ft (*NA* WO 51/259–313 *passim*; *NA* WO 52/6 f. 102). Thus, at around 4ft 5ins, these three guns could fall into this latter category. Cannon of this type were cast by gunfounders for the civilian market, usually for smaller merchant ships, coastal communities or landowners who wanted some defence but also wanted something lighter and cheaper than a normal cannon.

Thus, for example, in 1799, The Butterley Company of Derbyshire wrote (Riden 1990, 133) to a prospective customer about cannon casting:

With respect to Cannon much depends upon the manner in which they are executed, and something on their dimensions. Those used by Government are bored out of solid & turned on the outside. Those for Merchant Service are seldom finished in that Stile, generally not turned, and often cast with Cores to reduce the expence of boring. We wish to know what are the sorts you want, whether you expect us to prove them, and whether you would provide Models, or we must make them to drawings . . . (we) are now casting some cannon (4, 6 & 9 Pounders) for the Liverpool Market bored out of the solid but not turned.

A piece for all practical purposes identical is to be found (on a rather inappropriate carriage on a mound – supposedly a famine burial) in front of Christ Church in Limavady, County

Chapter 7 – The Guns of the Eighteenth and Nineteenth Centuries

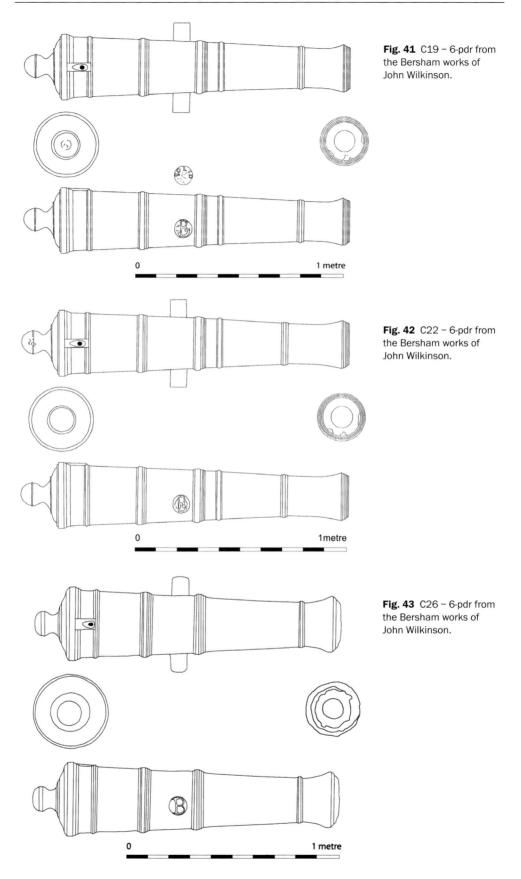

Fig. 41 C19 – 6-pdr from the Bersham works of John Wilkinson.

Fig. 42 C22 – 6-pdr from the Bersham works of John Wilkinson.

Fig. 43 C26 – 6-pdr from the Bersham works of John Wilkinson.

Londonderry (Plate 65). This gun is supposed to have been presented in the nineteenth century by a rector of Christ Church to Captain Hanna of Drumachose House, County Londonderry.[4] Another product of Bersham has been located in the grounds of Glendarragh House, just outside the City (Plate 66)[5] along with a rather odd piece probably dating to the 1820s.[6]

Another Wilkinson gun with strong Londonderry associations is to be found in the collections of Fermanagh County Museum (Plate 67). It came from the house of a Miss. P. Abernethy of Ballygawley, County Tyrone who donated the piece to the museum.[7] It originated from the vicinity of Culmore, according to museum records 'opposite Culmore'. Unlike the Limavady and Glendarragh House guns, but like C26, it lacks a chase astragal. Nevertheless, like the other examples, it belongs to the same period as the City cannon, i.e. c. 1773–1796.

Somewhat removed from Londonderry, but neverless of certain original provenance on the City Walls in the earlier nineteenth century[8] is a 6-pdr now displayed outside Saint Andrew's Presbyterian Church in Kingston, Ontario (Plate 68). Like all of the cannon in Northern Ireland, it has a circumferential moulding around the button, and like four of them has a chase astragal. A plaque on the wooden stand[9] states

Plate 65a John Wilkinson 6-pdr outside Christ Church, Limavady, County Londonderry.

Plate 65b 'B' Bersham mark.

Plate 65c 'Solid' mark.

Chapter 7 – The Guns of the Eighteenth and Nineteenth Centuries

Plate 66 Two guns from the grounds of Glendarragh House, Termonbacca, County Londonderry. The piece in the foreground is the Wilkinson 6-pdr. (*Courtesy of Mr. S. McKean*)

Plate 67a John Wilkinson 6-pdr at Fermanagh County Museum, Enniskillen, County Fermanagh. (*Courtesy of Fermanagh County Museum*)

Right: **Plate 67b** Bersham mark,

Far right: **Plate 67c** SOLID mark.

SHANNON'S CANNON

Came from the ramparts of Londonderry, Ireland

Where it defended Protestantism from 1649 to 1688

Presented to William Shannon of Kingston in 1865

In 1909 to St. Andrew's Presbyterian Church

By Apprentice Boys Derry Lodge #1

Restored in 1990 by

The St. Andrew's Church Veteran's Association

The gun was taken from Londonderry in 1865, and presented to one William Shannon, Grand Secretary of the Orange Order in Ontario East (Plate 69), who was convinced, albeit quite wrongly, of the role of the cannon in beating off the 'bloody papistical' hordes from the Walls of the City in the seventeenth century. Born in Londonderry, probably in 1834, Shannon emigrated to Canada where he was listed as a schoolteacher in 1857.[10] He appears to have received the gun from the Murray Club of the Apprentice Boys of Derry, of which he

167

Plate 68 Wilkinson gun taken from the Walls of Londonderry in 1865, and now displayed outside Saint Andrew's Presbyterian Church in Kingston, Ontario in Canada. (*Photo courtesy of Will McConnell*)

Plate 69 William Shannon.

was elected an honorary member in 1862,[11] as a token of their esteem for the way in which, in 1860, he resisted calls for the removal of Orange regalia from a welcoming party for the Prince of Wales who was visiting Kingston.[12] Regarding its arrival in the city, the *British Whig* of 18 July 1865, recorded that

> *The cannon 'Queen Bess' so called by her owner, Mr. William Shannon of this city, in honour of that great Protestant Sovereign in whose reign the Plantation of Ulster was undertaken, arrived yesterday morning in this city from Londonderry. She is a field piece about six feet in length, 1080 pounds in weight, and a six pounder. She laid in the depot of the Grand Trunk Railway during the day, where she was visited by hundreds of anxious and thoughtful spectators. The gun was used during the three several sieges of the Maiden City in 1641, 1649 and 1688. In commercial language she is worth so much old iron, but as an historical relic, no price could be named as adequate to express her value. It is believed that this is the only piece of ordnance used during that momentous period and in that doomed city, that was ever permitted to leave it, and the man must have strong claims upon his fellow countrymen, to whom this veritable relic has been forwarded*

Shannon was obviously inordinately proud of his cannon and had it fired[13] every Twelfth of July and Twelfth of August. Although badly damaged by corrosion, and covered in the inevitable thick layers of paint, it is possible to make out the letter 'W' on one trunnion, suggesting that this is yet another product of the Wilkinson foundry.

The Wilkinson works often sold guns of this type in pairs or batteries of six or eight and, given the great similarities between the examples from Londonderry, Limavady and Enniskillen – and their respective histories – it is perfectly possible that they were originally brought to the City in one batch. The fact that another probably Wilkinson gun seems to have been taken to Canada from the City Walls in the earlier nineteenth century indicates that perhaps there were originally six.

These guns were very popular in the disturbed times surrounding both the Wars of American Independence and the early years of the French Revolutionary Wars. In her novel *Ennui,* published in 1809 but set at the time of the 1798 uprising in Ireland, Maria Edgeworth (1809, 266) described the fishing lodge on the estate of Lord Glenthorn in the west of Ireland:

> *At the lodge there was a small four-pounder, which had been frequently used in times of public rejoicing; a naval victory, announced in the papers of the day, afforded a plausible pretence for bringing it out.*

Although the City cannon are 6-pdrs, they could have fulfilled a similar role. C19 and C22 were displayed for many years on the lawn of the See House of the Bishop of Derry

Chapter 7 – The Guns of the Eighteenth and Nineteenth Centuries

and Raphoe at Culmore Road, Londonderry until being removed to the stores of Derry Museum in 1990. It is also worth bearing in mind that in the days before the telegraph and telephone, cannon such as this were used to alert local communities to important news, or to warn of danger.

Another unprovenanced 6-pdr of very similar form, recently acquired by the Ulster Museum in Belfast, has the letter 'F' on its left-hand trunnion and 'SOLID' on the right, but no other markings.[14] This is probably from the Phoenix Foundry of William Fawcett in Liverpool, and also dates to the period immediately after 1800 (Brown 1990b). Other 6-pdrs but probably slightly later in date, can be found at Ardglass Golf Club, County Down, where one carronade and one 6-pdr bear the 'solid' legend on one trunnion face and the 'F' of Fawcett on the other.

Wilkinson exported his bored cannon widely, both within the British Isles and internationally, and guns with the B-SOLID mark can be found at the Museum of Artillery at Woolwich, Bamborough Castle, Northumberland, Fort Amherst, Kent, Gosport Council, Heeresgeschichtliches Museum, Vienna, Museo del Ejercito Espanol, Madrid, Bay View, Digby County, Nova Scotia, Canada, Brimstone Fort, Saint Kitts, in an abandoned fortification on Ascension Island and, as can be seen in Plate 70, in Mozambique.[15]

C14 – 3- or 4-pdr c. 1727–1787

This is one of the guns (along with C15) that Colby (*OS Londonderry* 100) noted as having been set in a pavement as street furniture, in this case Shipquay Street.[16] With its bore of 3.125ins and length of 53ins, this is a 3- or 4-pdr, the style of which is based on the Armstrong pattern current from 1727 to 1787. The vent patch indicates a date post-1730. The presence of the engraved 'P' rather than the royal cipher indicates it was intended for the civilian market.

This pattern was also used without the cipher for civilian cannons, for merchant ships, as well as for vulnerable communities and landowners. There are no surviving marks on the trunnion faces, which are badly corroded, and any weight marks that might have been placed close to the breech have been totally obliterated by corrosion resulting from the embedding of the gun in the ground. However, after

Plate 70 Wilkinson 6-pdr in Mozambique.

169

cleaning, traces of a solitary letter 'P' became visible between the first and second reinforces (Fig. 44). Whether or not this might have been surmounted by a crown is not possible to tell due to the state of the surface. This shows the gun was proofed commercially, which was a much less rigorous procedure than the government proof at Woolwich. An unmarked cannon at Mullennan,[17] County Londonderry, would seem to belong to the same type and date-range (Plate 71).

C24 3- or 4-pdr

When viewed initially, it was thought that this piece could be an early falcon on account of its slender shape and bore of 2.6ins. There are no distinguishing marks surviving, and thus a close identification is not possible. However, further examination revealed the badly corroded remains of a vent patch, a feature that indicates a date after *c.* 1730 (e.g. Blackmore 1976, 248).

C27 English 6-pdr with French marking

Like C25 and C26, this piece has its earliest known provenance as George's Quay on the Foyle. From its calibre, it is a 6-pdr, and it is very close in form to the Wilkinson 6-pdrs described above. Without the fleur-de-lys element, which appears superficially to be surmounted by a crown (Fig. 46), its general form with simple rings and astragals and the plain cascable with a button with plain circumferential moulding, it would invite close comparison with these guns. However, close examination shows that the crown is actually associated with a letter 'P' that has been almost obliterated by the engraving over it of the fleur-de-lys. On the basis of form, this is an English gun, and the 'crowned P' denotes a gun that has been proofed officially. Thus, it would seem that we have an example of an English piece that fell into French hands by one route or another, and then ended back up in British hands again, but there are no remains of any trunnion markings that might have identified the foundry.

George's Quay was called after Sir George Hill[18] who was MP for Londonderry City from 1795–1801 and 1802–1830. Hill was also Captain-Commandant of the Londonderry Yeoman Legion from 1796, and was Major and later Lieutenant-Colonel of the County Londonderry Militia from 1797–1822. He is perhaps best known as the person who arrested Wolfe Tone in October 1798. Hill had been a contemporary of Tone at Trinity College in Dublin and, after Tone was captured following a naval battle between English ships and the French warship *Hoche*, recognised him and had him arrested and sent to Dublin for trial. The *Hoche* was the flagship for a fleet of vessels, sent along with troops as a military expedition in support of the 1798 rising. Following her surrender, the badly damaged

Plate 71 Cannon at Mullenan, County Londonderry. (*Photo courtesy of Mr. Robert Moore*)

Chapter 7 – The Guns of the Eighteenth and Nineteenth Centuries

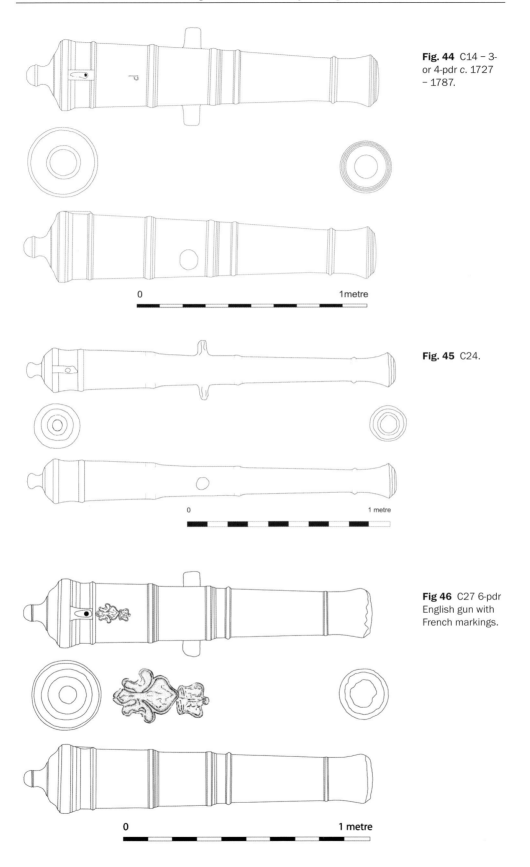

Fig. 44 C14 – 3- or 4-pdr c. 1727 – 1787.

Fig. 45 C24.

Fig 46 C27 6-pdr English gun with French markings.

171

Hoche was towed into Lough Swilly, and other French ships were captured and brought into the Lough as well (e.g. James 1837, II, 124 *ff*). Thus, it is not impossible that this piece came into Hill's possession from the *Hoche* or one of the other vessels.

C23 Russian 24-pdr captured at the fall of Sevastopol in the Crimea in 1855

This Russian 24-pdr is one of about four thousand pieces of artillery captured at the fall of Sevastopol in 1855, and one of some eight hundred scattered throughout the former British Empire – from Australia to Canada – as propaganda to demonstrate the weaponry with which the British and their allies had been confronted during the Crimean War (Hennessy 1996, 27). Hennessy (*ibid.*) identified some twenty-two such guns which were distributed in the 1860s throughout what became the Irish Republic, and in the course of this study, in addition to the Londonderry specimen, a further three have been identified in modern Northern Ireland.

The Crimean war was a dreadful affair, with heavy casualties in battle, not to mention the staggering losses from disease and infection in the wards of Scutari where Florence Nightingale gained her heroic reputation. This was really the first campaign in which the horrors of war and the incompetence of commanders were subject to intense media scrutiny, and the despatches to the *Times* of London by William Russell made grim reading. The losses sustained both from combat and disease raised serious questions in the public mind, and it was perhaps in no small part due to this that the decision was taken to distribute a large portion of the captured arsenal throughout the Empire, to plant the idea of the ferocity of the firepower with which the expeditionary forces had been faced.[19] The City piece, one of four placed in towns and cities in modern Northern Ireland, arrived in 1860 amidst much fanfare, mounted on its original cast iron carriage for the formal presentation by a Lieutenant-Colonel Hobbs. The cannon itself was in good condition, but the carriage was

Plate 72 C23 – Russian 24-pdr from the Crimea, before conservation and in its original location at Clooney Terrace in the Waterside.

of very poor quality, with many casting flaws evident (Plate 73).

As with all Russian cannon of this period, there are details of calibre and weight[20] engraved into the trunnion faces (Plate 74a and b), while on the barrel – between the first and second reinforces – is cast the Imperial double-headed eagle (Plate 74c). Unfortunately, each trunnion has suffered damage towards the bottom of its face such that details of the factory director on trunnion 1 are indecipherable, while of the date on trunnion 2, we can make out only three of the four digits. The readings that can be taken from the faces with certainty are:

Plate 73 Casting flaws in one of the carriage wheels highlighted during treatment.

Chapter 7 – The Guns of the Eighteenth and Nineteenth Centuries

face 1: inventory number 18547 (this is also stamped into the top of the trunnion)
factory of manufacture АЛКСНД-ЗВД = Alexandrovski works, Petrozavodsk near Kronstadt in Karelia

Director's name – illegible, but most likely consisting of 7 or 8 letters, thus either ФУЛЛОНЪ (Foullon) or ГАСКОИНЪ (Gascoigne)

face 2: calibre – 24–Њ=24-pdr
weight 120–П=120 *pud*=4333lb (1966kg)
date 182_

According to Bara (1985, 48), the director of the Alexandrovski works between 1818 and 1833 was Alexander Foullon (ФУЛЛОНЪ) and, since we can reconstruct with confidence a date in the 1820s, the missing information on trunnion face 1 is the name of Alexander Foullon.

The remaining guns from the Crimean war in Northern Ireland are:

The Mall, Armagh City, County Armagh (Plate 75c)

face 1: factory of manufacture ЛУГАНСКАГО ЗАВОДА = Lugansk works, in Soviet times Voroshilovgrad, in the lower Ukraine. The rest of the legend has been obliterated by corrosion (Plate 75a).

face 2: calibre – 36 . ФУ : = 36-pdr
weight 179 : 30 = 179 *pud* 30 *funt* = 6495lb or 2.9 tons (2946kg)
date 1808 (Plate 75b)

The Director's name has been obliterated, but is most likely to be Neilus (Hennessy 1996, 29). Local tradition maintains that the piece was captured by the Armagh militia at Sevastopol.

Newry, County Down, outside the Town Hall (Plate 76)

face 1: inventory number 6524
face 2: calibre – 24–Њ = 24-pdr
weight 126–П = 126 *pud* = 4550lb or 2.03 tons (2064kg)

Plate 74a C23 Trunnion face 1.

Plate 74b C23 Trunnion face 2.

Plate 74c C23 Imperial Russian eagle.

Plate 75a Armagh – trunnion face 1.

Plate 75b Armagh – trunnion face 2.

The Great Guns Like Thunder

Trunnion face 1 has been badly disfigured by corrosion, and any detail that was there below the inventory number has been lost when the surface spalled off. Trunnion face 2 is also badly damaged, although the calibre and weight are reasonably clear.

Castle Gardens, Lisburn, County Antrim (Plate 77)
Due to corrosion damage, all that can be read on either trunnion of this 24-pdr is the calibre – 24℔.

Plate 75c Russian 36-pdr on the Mall, Armagh City, County Armagh. (*Photo courtesy of Dr. Greer Ramsay, Armagh County Museum*)

Plate 76 Russian 24-pdr outside Newry Town Hall, Newry, County Down.

Chapter 7 – The Guns of the Eighteenth and Nineteenth Centuries

Plate 77 Russian 24-pdr in the Castle Gardens, Lisburn, County Antrim.

Notes to Chapter 7

1 C19 and C22 were donated to the Council by Bishop James Mehaffy. George's Quay on the Foyle was the most recent known provenance for the Brook Hall cannon. We are most grateful to Annesley Malley for information regarding C19 and C22, and to Phillip and David Gilliland regarding the cannon now at Brook Hall.

2 Wilkinson was the first to bore out cannon from solid, an innovation with wide-reaching consequences.

3 Most of the year 1797 is missing from the relevant Proof Book.

4 We are grateful to the Reverend Canon Samuel McVeigh, rector of Christ Church for this information, and for permission to include it and these photographs here, and to Paul Thompson of Conservations Solutions Ltd. for drawing it to our attention.

5 We are grateful to the owner, Mr. Samuel McKean, for kindly permitting inspection of these pieces and reproduction of this photograph.

6 This is to be the subject of a separate publication (Brown *forthcoming*).

7 We are most grateful to Sinead Reilly, Fermanagh County Museum for providing this information and the photographs.

8 We are most grateful to Ross McKenzie, Curator of the Museum of the Royal Military College of Canada, Kingston, Ontario in Canada for this information.

9 We are most grateful to Frank Carey, Institute of Scots-Irish Studies, University of Ulster, Magee Campus and Eilish Quigley for providing this transcription.

10 The information on William Shannon is taken from the splendid website set up by Alex Rough to document the Orange Order in Canada – www.members.tripod.com/~Roughian. We are most grateful to him for assistance and information.

11 The *Kingston News* of June 20th, 1862 carried the following information

> *At the May meeting of the Murray Club of 'Prentice Boys, Londonderry, on motion of William Madden, the honour of honorary membership was unanimously accorded to Mr. William Shannon of Kingston, Canada . . . This tribute was a recognition of Shannon's part in making Kingston 'the Derry of Canada'.*

12 When the Prince's ship docked, there were Orangemen there to greet him. However, the Duke of Newcastle refused to allow the Prince to come ashore unless they dispersed and their insignias and banners were removed. But Shannon, who was the organiser, stood firm

and the Orangemen refused to budge. As a result, the Prince's ship sailed off without the Prince having set foot on land and, as it sailed away, Shannon declared that Kingston was 'the Derry of Canada'.

13 Historic guns in Londonderry were often fired, and were not just kept in the city. Thus, for example, a report in the *Tyrone Constitution*, reproduced in the *Londonderry Guardian* of 9 September 1869, recorded

> *THE APPRENTICE BOYS' CANNON.– On Friday last, Mr. Nelson, photographer, of this town (Omagh) attended at Strathroy, for the purpose of taking a photograph of the cannon at present in charge of Commander Scott R.N. A number of ladies and gentlemen from the town and neighbourhood were present to witness the proceedings. The guns were efficiently manned under the discretion of Commander Scott, Messrs Hillyard and Scarlett. A salute was fired after the photograph was taken.*

The Mr. Nelson referred to may have been either Robert or Alexander Nelson who were photographers in Omagh at this time, although nothing more is known about them (Maguire 2000, 39). We are most grateful to David Maconaghy for supplying this information.

14 We are most grateful to Tom Wylie and Trevor Parkhill, Dept. of Local History, The Ulster Museum Belfast, for this information. F-Solids are also found at Caher Castle, County Tipperary.

15 We have been unable to trace the precise location where this photograph was taken, and would be most grateful to anyone who can provide this information.

16 Now missing after being removed from its location in Pump Street to the council depot at Pennyburn.

17 We are most grateful to Mr. Robert Moore for permission to view and photograph this piece.

18 Interestingly, Hill was related to one Hugh Rowley who was Storekeeper of the Ordnance for Culmore from 1690 to 1692.

19 In fact Sevastopol, the centre for the Russian Black Sea fleet, had some one hundred and seventy-two cannon of various calibres mounted for action. But although the artillery park contained some four thousand pieces which could in theory have been deployed during the nearly one year of siege, a significant number were obsolete and/or unserviceable (Hennessy 1996, 27).

20 The weight is given in *pud*, a Russian unit of measurement equal to 36.1lb or 16.38kg, and divided into 35 *funt* equivalent to 1.03lb or 468gm.

21 For a discussion of Russian artillery production in the eighteenth and nineteenth centuries and the roles of foreigners therein, see Bara (1985).

Chapter 7 – The Guns of the Eighteenth and Nineteenth Centuries

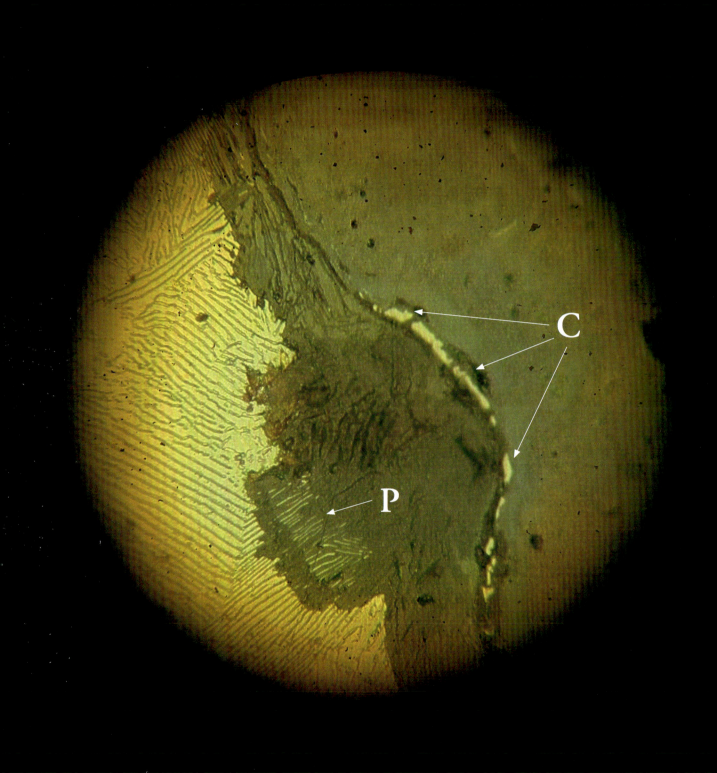

CHAPTER 8
Some Observations on the Technology of the English Cannon

Introduction

Much of what we know about gunfounding in the sixteenth to eighteenth centuries derives from contemporary descriptions and depictions of casting in bronze, not in iron. In fact, there has been very little work published on the technology of cast irons of the early industry in England, apart from brief studies such as those of Schubert (1957, 398-399), Tylecote (1972, 1975) and Hartley (1992), and the theoretical considerations of Rostoker (1986), Barter Bailey (2000, 80*ff*) and Murphy (2001). Other studies have in the main looked at material produced accidently during the bloomery smelting of iron from the Romano-British period onward (e.g. Craddock and Lang 2005). It is inferred that from the late-sixteenth century at least, as with the casting of bronze cannon, it was the practice to cast iron guns vertically,[1] breech down, to allow the impurities to rise to the muzzle area and into an extra space called the gun head, which was later removed (Figs 5 and 6). Important evidence for this comes from excavations at four Wealden sites – Pippingford, Scarlets, Maynards Gate and Batsford (Cleere and Crossley 1995, 255*ff*), in particular at Pippingford, where a small gun was uncovered complete with gun head (Crossley 1975, 28 and Fig. facing p. 28). Some small-scale excavations at the Wilkinson works at Bersham have uncovered evidence for casting pits (Grenter 1992). However, we do not have anything like the breadth and depth of documentary and pictorial evidence that survives for bronze gunfounding as, for example, in the series of detailed later-eighteenth century depictions of the whole process at the Royal Brass Foundry (Jackson and de Beer 1973; Brown 2000).

In this study, we were able to take samples[2] from what, in the main, is a well-defined group of guns with some distinctive outliers, to examine their metal structures, hardness values and chemical compositions and to take measurements of the specific gravities both of the samples and of the actual cannon themselves.[3] In addition, it has been possible to look in some detail at the compositions and genesis of inclusions in the metals, and to draw some conclusions as to cooling regime. The purpose of this segment of the project has not been to attempt to provide definitive answers to questions of casting technology, the quality of the ordnance or ore exploitation, but rather to provide an assemblage of basic data and to derive what general conclusions can be drawn reasonably from it, thus hopefully providing some signposts for further lines of study. Constraints on resources and time have precluded the inclusion of a fully detailed technical report at this time. Thus, we shall not be presenting here detailed metallographic examinations of each gun, but rather some representatives of the structures observed.

Cast Iron

For much of its history, iron was smelted in the solid state by the so-called 'direct' or 'bloomery' process (e.g. Scott 1991, 9*ff*), but by the mid-sixteenth century the evolution of the blast furnace had reached the stage where it was possible to produce the large volumes of molten 'cast iron' required by gunfounding. Cast iron is an alloy of iron (Fe) and carbon (C) with more than *c.* 2% C, usually around 3.5%C (Fig. 48) and with other elements, in particular silicon (Si), phosphorous (P), sulphur (S) and manganese (Mn). In the late sixteenth to eighteenth centuries, iron cannon appear to have been cast in the main directly from the output of the blast furnace, as opposed to remelted pig iron, and as a result there is reason to believe that there was good separation from the silicate slag resulting from the smelting process because of the great difference in densities between that and the molten iron. Thus, as the results of this study confirm, we can expect only a very few slag inclusions, particularly in comparison with the levels observed regularly in early bloomery wrought iron. Nevertheless, if the foundrymen were not careful, liquid slag could have been drawn in to the pour, thus increasing the possibility of inclusions in the metal.

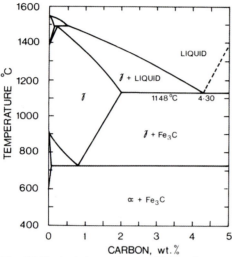

Fig. 47 The basic iron-carbon equilibrium diagram.

Depending on the composition and cooling rate (Fig. 47), cast iron can solidify according to the thermodynamically stable Fe-graphite system or the metastable Fe-Fe$_3$C system. The classic historic classification, based on the colour of the fracture surface, recognises two broad types – 'white' which has a silvery, crystalline fracture surface, and 'grey' with a dull-grey fracture surface, the difference resulting from the formation of an Fe$_3$C eutectic in white irons, and a graphite eutectic in grey irons. As a general rule, a low rate of cooling promotes the formation of graphite over Fe$_3$C, so that the final structure of a grey cast iron consists of graphite flakes in a matrix of the eutectoid structure pearlite (made up of lamellae of α-iron, or ferrite, and cementite or Fe$_3$C), often with pure ferrite associated with the graphite flakes.

As a hypoeutectic iron (less than 4.3%C) cools, the first solid phase to appear is austenite, a solid solution of C in γ-Fe, which crystallises in the form of dendrites. As the temperature falls, these continue to grow thus enriching the remaining liquid in carbon until the eutectic temperature of 1148°C and composition of 4.3% C is reached (Plate 78). At this point, solidification begins from numerous points within the melt, and graphite and austenite are deposited giving a structure with flakes of graphite dispersed in an austenitic matrix. When the temperature reaches 723°C, the austenite undergoes transformation to pearlite (Plate 79a). The cooling of a hypereutectic iron (greater than 4.3% C) begins with the formation of coarse flakes of kish graphite and, as with a hypoeutectic iron, when the eutectic concentration is arrived at, finer flake graphite and pearlite crystallise out.

(a)
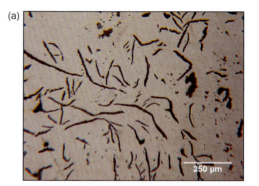

(b)
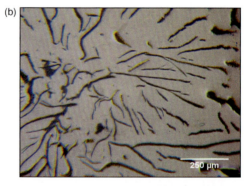

(c)
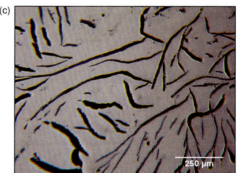

Plate 78 Graphite types observed in polished but un-etched specimens (a) C3 trunnion area, Type A, (b) C5 muzzle area, Type B, (c) C8 muzzle area, Type C.

Chapter 8 – Some Observations on the Technology of the English Cannon

Table 13 Summary of element compositions, SG and Micro-SG, inclusion levels and hardness values[4]. (Those values marked with an asterisk refer to averages from several samples.)

	%C	CE	%Mg	%Al	%Si	%P	%S	Ti ppm	V ppm	%Cr	%Mn	Average burden	TiN-TiC	MnS-MnFeS	%MnS-MnFeS	macro SG	micro SG	Average HRE
C1	3.03	3.40	400ppm	0.119	0.718	1.741	0.082	118	913	0.389	0.566	3.535	1	519	0.272	6.750	6.846	82.167
C2	3.12	3.59	0.075	600ppm	1.085	1.649	0.083	37	239	0.255	0.843	3.909	12	1105	0.278	6.985	7.004	96.600
C3	3.83	4.22	0.658	1.139	0.996	0.969	0.102	1444	4867	0.335	0.823	5.033	30	1370	0.481	6.830	7.025	79.650
C4	3.48	3.85	0.273	1.028	0.892	1.134	0.225	83	262	0.312	1.003	4.867	11	841	0.261	6.890	7.346	93.567
C5	3.59	3.92	0.442	1.440	0.817	0.992	0.135	99	233	0.296	0.995	5.117	0	1269	0.229	6.225	6.847	88.600
C6	2.87	3.27	0.098	1.097	0.981	1.144	0.262	128	194	0.198	0.823	4.603	69*	805*	0.403*	6.900	7.003	85.900
C7	3.63	4.19	0.295	1.051	1.507	1.196	0.157	114	262	0.316	0.898	5.421	17	1034	0.346	6.690	7.245	87.100
C8	4.16	4.87	0.04	0.937	2.035	1.090	0.181	226	215	0.266	1.139	5.689	66	1074	0.262	6.954	6.983	99.167
C9	3.65	4.04	0.083	1.076	0.994	1.034	0.122	111	268	0.386	0.688	4.383	15*	991*	0.324*	6.990	7.063	91.833
C10	3.52	4.13	0.376	1.133	1.745	0.982	0.247	171	228	0.355	0.651	5.490	1	814	0.301	6.950	6.577	93.450
C11	3.96	4.35	0.189	1.187	0.9634	1.076	0.408	152	265	0.333	0.640	4.797	11	377	0.472	7.076	6.731	101.567
C12	3.27	3.65	0.266	1.428	0.944	1.060	0.111	102	251	0.323	0.803	4.937	10	905	0.238	6.860	6.987	86.500
C13	4.08	4.70	0.304	1.505	1.784	0.897	0.090	80	262	0.318	0.966	5.865	24*	2285*	0.816*	6.890	6.908	98.300
C14	3.26	3.80	300ppm	0.148	0.970	2.773	0.000	64	272	0.230	0.505	4.738	32	874	0.323	6.886	7.170	95.467
C16	3.16	3.53	0.374	1.564	0.952	0.989	0.239	28	226	0.308	0.580	5.007	54	1251	0.433	6.937	6.869	65.267
C17	3.26	3.85	600ppm	1.416	1.659	1.044	0.234	86	232	0.323	0.746	5.424	14	746	0.356	6.784	7.133	93.067
C18	3.16	3.49	0.000	500ppm	0.741	1.203	0.067	27	187	0.211	0.506	2.662	9	1751	0.389	6.863	7.159	101.600
C19	2.98	3.53	100ppm	0.043	1.334	1.701	0.102	100	315	0.390	0.340	3.809	78	1147	0.320	6.933	6.823	99.167
C20	3.25	3.86	0.345	1.401	1.758	0.873	0.05	156	260	0.287	0.935	5.649	59	1907	0.428	6.876	6.930	73.100
C21	3.32	3.82	500ppm	1.358	1.360	1.006	400ppm	84	270	0.307	0.730	4.762	27	1483	0.308	6.954	7.113	88.567
C22	3.07	3.63	400ppm	0.111	1.437	1.435	0.109	116	292	0.408	0.298	3.692	111	1614	0.543	6.950	7.166	83.000
C24	3.61	4.01	0.000	0.036	0.833	1.642	0.033	62	268	0.386	0.905	3.802	19	2740	0.300	6.706	7.013	83.367

181

The presence of both Si and P influences the eutectic and thus the final solidified structure. Increasing levels of Si combined with P tend to create a hypereutectic grey cast iron with pearlite in a phosphide eutectic matrix, which becomes almost continuous for levels above 0.4–0.7%P (Bailey and Samuels 1976, 129). The size of the phosphide eutectic cells in this matrix reduces with increasing levels of P. A very slow rate of cooling can promote the decomposition of pearlite into ferrite and graphite flakes (Plate 79b).

All of the Londonderry guns have solidified with the formation of graphite and show classic grey cast iron structures. Twenty-one out of the twenty-four included in this part of the study have CE values below 4.3% and thus can be classed as hypoeutectic, with the remaining three having values between 4.35% and 4.87% making them hypereutectic. All show elevated values of P and accordingly, the phosphide eutectic is prominent in nearly all of the microstructures (Plate 79c). The structure of C14 is of note in that it had a P content averaging 2.77%, and at such a high level, the structure shows compacted or vermicular graphite in a phosphide matrix (Plate 79d). Such a structure is also common in cast irons with less than 0.002%S, and analysis of C14 showed no traces of this element.

Murphy (2001, 92–93) noted that while shrinkage porosity should not have been a problem with cast-iron guns, as temperature falls one should look for that resulting from the release of gases absorbed by the molten metal before pouring. Indeed, one of the features of many of the guns studied here was the occurrence of significant numbers of voids within the body of the metal. This feature was well-known and evidently regarded as commonplace by seventeenth-century gunners, and in extreme form was knows as 'honeycombing' (p. 34*ff*). During solidification, there are regions of solid material surrounded by a liquid, and the voids which appear as dark patches are caused by gas escaping up through the mould (Plate 79e–f, 80 and 81). Obviously, porosity will effect the physical properties of the metal, with the greater the degree meaning the poorer the quality.

The reason for positioning a cannon mould vertically, breech-down, is usually taken to be to allow impurities such as entrapped slag, gas and any low-melting point constituents, to rise to the top of the casting and be concentrated in a gun head which was removed later (Fig. 6d). It seems logical, if perhaps somewhat simplistic, to suggest that vertical casting should have produced cannon in which there are discernible gradients in the element burden, graphite form and distribution and specific gravity from breech to muzzle. In addition, given their much lower density, numbers of inclusions should increase from breech to muzzle, although there was not time within the scope of this study to do any quantitative assessment.

Element Burden

Chemical analysis (Table 13) showed that in addition to Si, P and S, there are frequent and significant amounts of magnesium (Mg), aluminium (Al), chromium (Cr), and manganese (Mn), all obviously deriving from the ores from which the metals were smelted.[9] This non-ferrous burden comes from one of two sources – solid solution and the occasional physical inclusions deriving from the smelting and casting processes. Thus, for example, Si as silicates will have some contribution from inclusions as well as from its presence in solid solution. The content of P, on the other hand, is most likely to derive from its presence in combination with iron. The levels of Mn and S derive from MnS or mixed manganese and iron sulphides, since the levels of Mn are more than sufficient to account for the low S. Titanium (Ti) occurred at trace levels, but contributed to small and distinctive carbo-nitride (CN) inclusions, some of which showed also vanadium (V) and/or niobium (Nb). Also, the relative mobilities of the different impurities must be taken into account, since in a vertical casting it is likely to be the case that rates of upward movement will be affected by cooling rate. A further factor to be considered is the effect of corrosion in some samples where voids resulting from gas evolution had been exploited.

As a rough guideline, with vertical casting we might expect to find that the 'cleanest' metal is in the breech area, the 'dirtiest' at the muzzle face, the area representing the junction

Chapter 8 – Some Observations on the Technology of the English Cannon

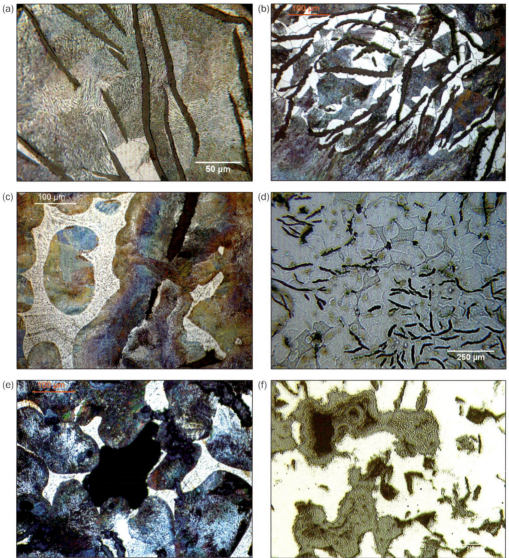

Plate 79 Structures observed in the assemblage: (a) C20 Kish graphite and pearlite, (b) C9 Kish graphite plus ferrite and pearlite, (c) phosphide eutectic with ferrite and graphite, (d) C14 compacted graphite, (e) C7 gas void (black, centre) with phospide eutectic, graphite and pearlite, (f) C3 voids (dark-grey) partially filled with corrosion products (grey).

between the muzzle and the gun head. One very obvious factor that would affect the state of the metal at the muzzle face would be the size of the gun head, in other words its capacity to take up impurities rising from the body of the casting. If, on the other hand, a piece was cast horizontally – thus without any reservoir to receive a significant proportion of undesirables – we might expect these to pool along the upper surface. Whereas one may expect occasionally to find traces of the removal of the gun head, horizontal casting would not have lent itself to any form of feeder of significant diameter to leave its mark on the finished surface. Although not really clear in photographs, the unevenness that can be detected on the face of the muzzle of C10 could be the traces of where the gun head was sawn off less cleanly than in all of the other guns in the assemblage with undamaged muzzles.

However, as may be seen from Figs 48-49, the situation is by no means clear cut. From Fig. 49, only C5, C16 and C19 show a distinct gradient from breech to muzzle, while C6, C7, C10 and C11 indicate a clear decrease in burden between breech and muzzle. Against

183

this, C4, C8, C9 and C20 appear to show that the burden is greater at the breech than at the muzzle, while the remaining results are ambiguous. Because of the wide variation, the average values shown in Fig. 49 only offer a vague indication.

C10 is of particular interest since the muzzle sample showed significant voids, partly exploited by corrosion, but also filled with debris that comprises primarily fragments of material with the appearance of ceramic detritus, almost certainly deriving from the mould (Plate 80) and contributing to the results.

On a slightly tangential issue, the muzzle region of C10 also offers us an interesting insight in to the progress of corrosion in a cast iron of this period. Plate 81 shows the interface between the surviving pearlitic structure and the void and its contents. The original edge of the void can be seen as a dark line running roughly down the centre of the image (marked 'E'). To the left is the void, while immediately to the right is a transitional zone in which can be seen clearly small white flecks of remanent cementite (marked 'C') and the traces of the pearlitic structure in the form of relict carbides (marked

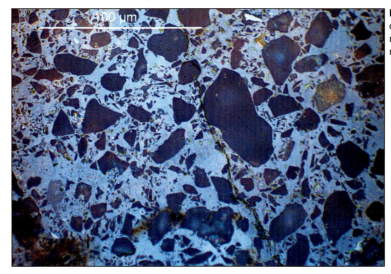

Plate 80 Fragments deriving from the mould material in a void at the muzzle of C10.

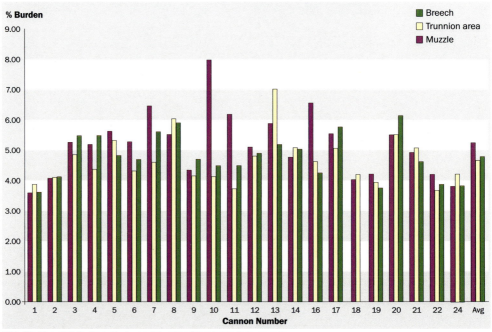

Fig. 48 The distribution of element burden from breech to muzzle.

Chapter 8 – Some Observations on the Technology of the English Cannon

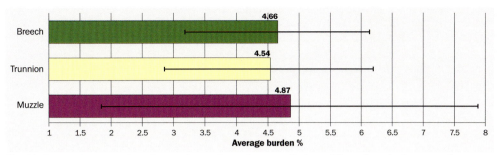

Fig. 49 Average burden at breech, trunnion and muzzle areas. Horizontal lines show the 2-σ spread.

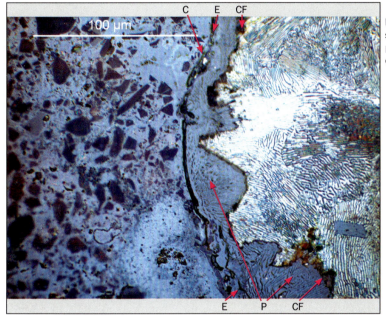

Plate 81 Remanent structures in corrosion products in the muzzle of C10.

'P'). In the frontspiece to this chapter, remanent cementite and pearlite are also marked 'C' and 'P' respectively. Separating this transition zone from the surviving pearlitic structure is a dark corrosion front (marked 'CF'), and what we observe here is very similar to that which has been observed in mediaeval artefacts made from bloomery wrought irons and steels (Scott 1976 and 1991, 18, Plate 1.4.2e).

If we consider the ambiguous results for C3, C8, C13, C21 and C24, where the greatest burden appears to be in the region of the trunnions, it is a purely subjective view, but during their treatment, it seemed that the number of flaws appearing at the surface was greatest in the underside of these pieces in a roughly eliptical pattern extending on either side of the trunnions and over the first reinforce and beyond. The pattern on C8 was roughly as depicted in Fig. 50, although unfortunately this gun was not included in group sampled round the circumference at the trunnions, since the possible significance of these traces had not at that time been grasped!

For those cannon where three samples were taken from the trunnion area (from the underside, from the approximate middle and from the top), then there would appear to be a trend for the undersides to have the highest burden of impurities (Fig. 51). However, of these, although the histograms for C6, C7 and C9 in particular suggest the migration of impurities towards an upper, horizontal surface, any concordance is less than clear, although like C8 the underside of C6 most certainly exhibits a roughly elliptical region of major flaws partly exploited by corrosion (Plate 82). It should be borne in mind, however, that surface flaws could very likely also be caused by gas generated by reactions between the molten metal and the mould irrespective of the orientation of the mould, or by bubbles clinging to mould surfaces if the pouring of the metal was not without turbulence.

185

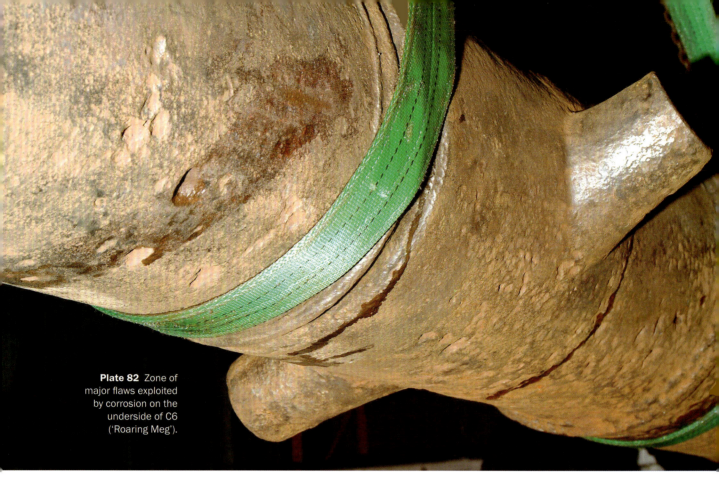

Plate 82 Zone of major flaws exploited by corrosion on the underside of C6 ('Roaring Meg').

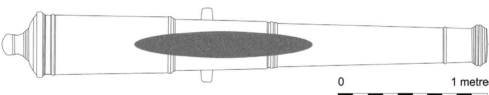

Fig. 50 Approximate distribution of concentration of the most distinctive surface flaws on the underside of C8.

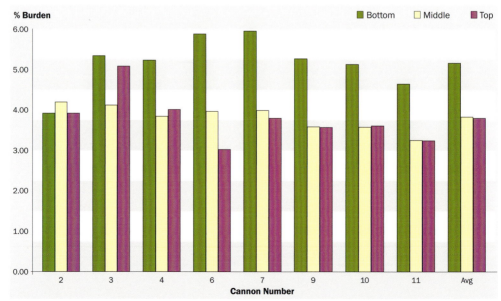

Fig. 51 Variation in percentage burden around the circumference of cannon at the trunnions.

Specific Gravity

The specific gravity (SG) of modern cast irons falls within the range 6.8–7.8g/cm³ (e.g. Angus 1976, 112–113; Calister 2007, A4). And in his monumental study on metallurgy, Percy (1864, II.3, 863*ff*) gave the same range of values for pig irons produced using hot and cold blast from a variety of ores. It can be seen from Table 13 that the macro-SGs of the cannon (the results derived from measuring the specific gravity of the whole cannon) in the assemblage fall into the lower end of the range, although as might be expected, there is a wider spread of micro-SG values (measurements made on individual specimens). The nineteenth-century Irish scientist, Robert Mallet, noted in 1856 not only that the density of cast-iron cylinders cast vertically increased with depth, but also that there was a decrease in density as the size of the casting increased (Mallet 1856, 24–25). Thus, if cannon were uniformly cast vertically, breech down, it would seem only logical to expect that there would be a discernible gradient in density or specific gravity from breech to muzzle. The overall plot of micro-SG values from breech to muzzle (Fig. 52) indicates a trend to decrease, although the variation is wide. However, the distributions of specific gravities from breech to muzzle in individual cannon (Fig. 53) present a picture equally unclear as that for the element burden. While there are distinct decreases from breech to muzzle in C1, C2, C10 and C11, the situation is reversed somewhat in C3, C7 and C19, while once again the remainder indicate no clear differentiation.

Further, although it might seem possible that levels of burden would have at least some detectable effect on the densities of the

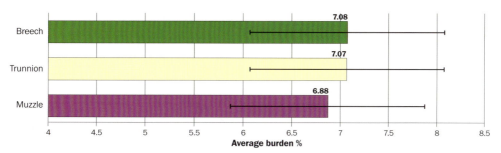

Fig. 52 Distribution of micro-SG values from breech to muzzle. Horizontal lines show the 2-σ spread.

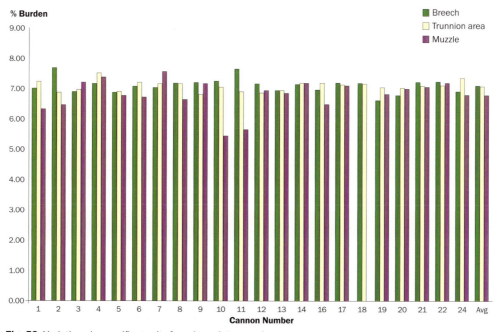

Fig. 53 Variations in specific gravity from breech to muzzle.

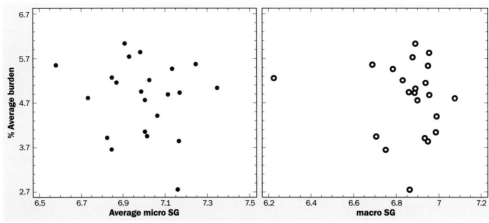

Fig. 54 Scatter plots of average burden vs average micro-SG and SG.

metals, calculations show that for the guns in this study at least, there is no global statistical correlation, something reflected in the scatter plots in Fig. 54.

Table 14 Predicted density vs observed

Cannon	macro SG	Average micro SG	Predicted
1	6.75	6.85	7.25
2	6.99	7.00	7.20
3	6.83	7.03	7.10
4	6.89	7.35	7.17
5	6.23	6.85	7.16
6	6.90	7.00	7.30
7	6.69	7.25	7.08
8	6.95	6.98	6.92
9	6.99	7.06	7.13
10	6.95	6.58	7.10
11	7.08	6.73	7.06
12	6.86	6.99	7.22
13	6.89	6.91	6.97
14	6.89	7.17	7.10
16	6.94	6.87	7.25
17	6.78	7.13	7.16
18	6.86	7.16	7.25
19	6.93	6.82	7.20
20	6.88	6.93	7.16
21	6.95	7.11	7.17
22	6.95	7.17	7.19
24	6.71	7.01	7.11

A further complication when considering the density of the metal overall is introduced by the voids resulting from gas evolution during cooling (Plate 79e and f). It is noticeable, particularly in the case of the macro-SG values, that the density of the metal of all of the cannon falls into the lower end of the range. Angus (1976, 112f) cites a calculation for the theoretical density based on the total C, Si and P values

$$\text{Density in gm/cm}^3 = 8.11 - (0.223 * \text{total C\%}) - (0.91 * \text{Si\%}) - (0.071 * \text{P\%})$$

However, when we look at the predicted values against the actual for both macro-SG and averaged micro-SG (Table 14), we find that the real values are in most cases lower than expected, up to 7% for micro-SG, while for the macro-SG values it goes as high as 13%. Simple statistical analysis indicates no significant correlation between the predicted and actual values.

As Angus noted, however, bulk density of large castings is usually lower than that observed for small samples, due to gas porosity (*ibid*). Further, a decrease in the amount of pearlite in a grey cast iron will further reduce density due to an increase in the graphite fraction. The fact that there are many more voids in our samples than would be expected in modern cast irons, coupled with the effects of slow cooling, offers at least a partial explanation for these results.

Graphite Form and Distribution

The polished specimens were examined as per BS-ISO 945 to determine the quality of the metal with reference to the form and distribution of the graphite present and the sizes of the flakes.[10] Image analysis software, was used to locate the graphite particles in an image and measure the peripheral lengths (Plate 83). In the majority of cases, flakes were elongated and thus the size of the graphite could be estimated by simply halving the peripheral length.

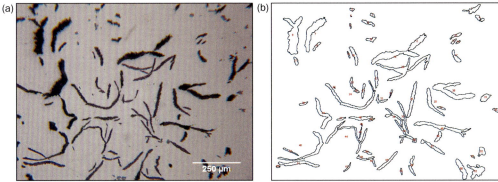

Plate 83 (a) Graphite flakes in C1, (b) the output of the image analysis software.

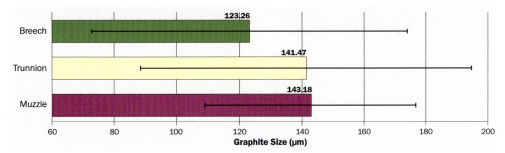

Fig. 55 Distribution of graphite sizes from breech to muzzle. Horizontal lines show the 2-σ spread.

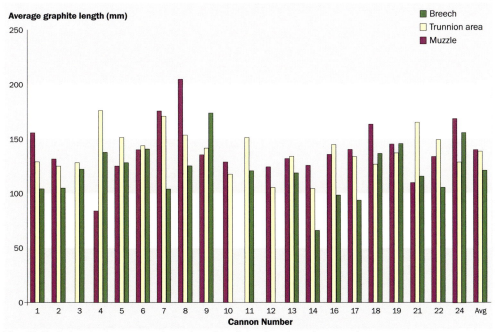

Fig. 56 Variations in the average sizes of graphite flakes from breech to muzzle.

The ranges of particle sizes are shown in Figs 55–56, where it may be seen that there is evidence of a trend in increasing size from breech to muzzle, although the variances are wide.

Hardness

Taking the average values from the trunnion regions together as 87.89, the Rockwell hardness values (HRE) show a basic trend from highest hardness in the breech region, lowest at the muzzle (Fig. 57). As can be seen, however, there are wide variations within each region and lower values are due, in part at least, to voids occurring within the sample.[11] Nevertheless, taking the hardness evidence into consideration, such a trend might be expected with larger graphite flakes having a tendency to float upwards, thus potentially causing an improvement in the physical properties of the metal in the lower reaches of the mould. Set against this, however, would be the slow cooling that would allow more pearlite to decompose to graphite and ferrite, thus reducing strength and softening the metal.

To gain some idea of the possible course of cooling in a cast-iron cannon, a core was taken from the breech face, through to the powder chamber of C6 ('Roaring Meg') and examined both for its microstructure and its hardness profile. Hardness measurements were taken every 5mm along the length of the specimen to determine variations in mechanical properties through the wall of the cannon. In addition, the measurements were repeated every 120° around the specimen axis.

Apart from the two values at the very tip of the core, which represent the interior of the bore that had suffered heavy corrosion damage, it can be seen that there is for all practical purposes no gradient in terms of hardness. And

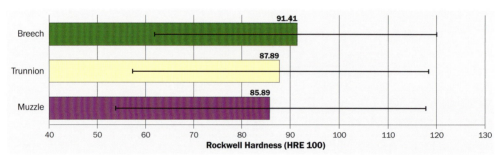

Fig. 57 Distribution of hardness values from breech to muzzle. Horizontal lines show the 2-σ spread.

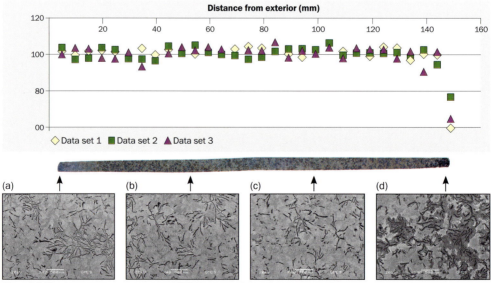

Plate 84 Hardness measurements and SEM images of the microstructure from the outer surface to the interior of the powder chamber of C6. The dark patches in image (d) are corrosion.

examination of the microstructure shows no trace of any coarsening of pearlite or increase in the size of graphite flakes from outer to inner surfaces (Plate 84a–d), suggesting that in this region at least, the metal cooled at a more or less uniform rate across the section.

Physical Inclusions

The initial optical microscope study showed that there were few if any silicate slag inclusions other than material in the corroded surface zones. The principal type of non-metallic inclusion present was dove-grey, usually of rounded form, but occasionally showing some facetting, identified as manganese sulphide (MnS) or manganese-iron sulphide (MnFe)S. In addition to these was another type, which is smaller and generally facetted, ranging in colour from red-pink to pink-gold (Plate 85).

Initial analysis in the SEM using Energy Dispersive Spectroscopy (EDS) confirmed that the dove-grey inclusions were of manganese sulphide or manganese-iron sulphide (Fig. 58).

The identification of the smaller, facetted inclusions proved to be much more difficult. Energy-dispersive X-ray analysis showed them to contain Ti, and usually also Fe (*cf.* Barraclough and Kerr 1976, 72). The presence of iron in the spectra raised the possibility that these inclusions could be the iron-titanium intermetallic compound $TiFe_2$. However, the measured bulk Ti contents (Table 13) are below the point at which the metal should remain in solid solution in the iron at elevated temperature, and thus should not form a compound. In addition, as it proved problematic to find inclusions large enough to prevent the possibility of the X-ray signal being generated by the surrounding matrix, it was difficult to be sure that there was iron present in the inclusions. In fact, after examining the Ti:Fe peak ratios for inclusions of different sizes, it was concluded that there was little iron present and that there must be other elements

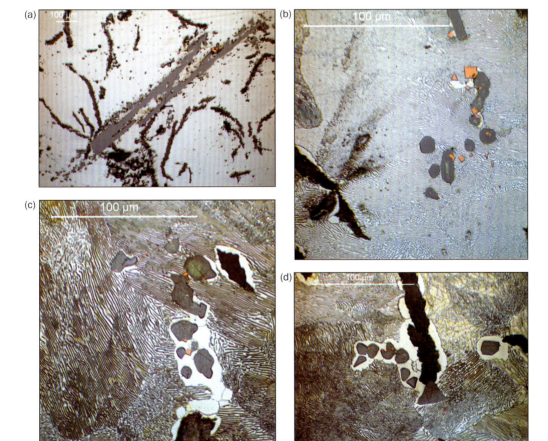

Plate 85 (a) C6, (b) C8, (c) C9, (d) C9 showing dove-grey MnS inclusions (dove grey) and pink-gold carbo-nitrides.

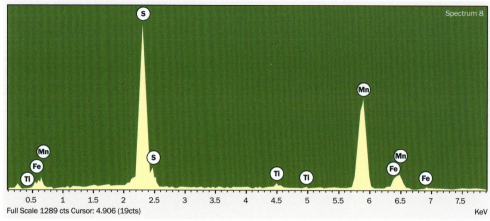

Fig. 58 EDS spectrum from (MnFe)S inclusions.

present, although the identification of these was difficult.

Unfortunately, the samples were carbon coated for the SEM analysis making the detection of this element impossible during standard analysis. In addition, the levels of oxygen detected were similar to those found on the polished iron, thus suggesting that they were not titanium oxide inclusions. Further analysis using uncoated samples in the electron probe microanalyser indicated the presence of both carbon and nitrogen. But the interference between the Ti L-α and N K-α X-ray peaks and the larger than expected C peak – when compared with a TiN standard – still left some uncertainty as to the identification of these inclusions. However, the Raman spectrum from one of the larger, more golden-coloured inclusions offered a good match with that of a polished titanium nitride standard, thus confirming their identification as titanium nitrides. Those inclusions of a redder hue are more likely to be carbo-nitrides – Ti(CN) – but due to the X-ray interferences involved there was insufficient time to determine the likely range of C:N ratios involved (cf. Morrogh 1941, 207-253, where the term 'cyano-nitrides' is used).

Optical imaging showed that that the Ti-rich particles were often on the edges of the MnS inclusions or surrounded by them, although occasionally they did occur as isolated crystals. Plate 86, comprising energy-dispersive X-ray maps, shows these relations. It is possible that one of the phases acts as a nucleation site for the growth of the other, but as yet the exact order of growth is not clear.

The number of the MnS/(MnFe)S and Ti-rich inclusions, and the percentage of the area of the surface areas of the samples taken up by MnS/(MnFe)S was determined using JEOL 6480LV SEM with an Oxford Instruments INCA energy dispersive X-ray spectrometer.[12]

(a)
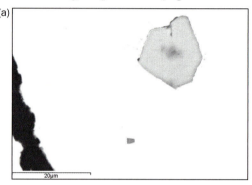

(b)
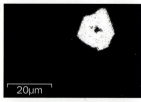

(c)

(d)
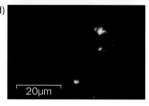

Plate 86 MnS and Ti-rich inclusions (a) SEM image of MnS inclusion (top right) and Ti-rich inclusion (lower middle – the grey mass on the left is a graphite flake), and energy-dispersive maps of the distributions of (b) Mn, (c) S, (d) Ti.

Chapter 8 – Some Observations on the Technology of the English Cannon

The choice of conditions for these experiments was a compromise between the ability to detect small particles, the need to cover a large enough region for the results to be represented, and the time constraints on machine time. That used detected most MnS/MnFeS inclusions, but there were distinct problems with the detection of the Ti-rich particles. First, it was clear that very small particles were being missed – but to halve the size of the pixel (minimum detectable particle size) results in the analysis taking four times as long. Additionally, close association with the manganese sulphides resulted in a Ti-rich particle being analysed together with the MnS particle. Where the proportion of Ti-rich area to MnS was high, the presence of the carbo-nitrides could be inferred safely. But where there was only a very small particle associated with a large MnS inclusion, such a presence was missed. Thus, it can be safely assumed that there was an under-reporting of the numbers. This was true in the case of samples such as C5 where no inclusions of this type were detected by the automatic analysis, but were found by optical examination.

The percentage of the area that the MnS inclusions occupy (Table 13) is very similar for all the samples (between 0.2% and 0.5%, with a mean of 0.37% ± 0.26 at 2-σ), with the exception of C13 which had much higher MnS cross-sectional area (0.82%). Most of the samples had a ratio of around 60 ± 0.96 at 2-σ MnS-type inclusions to every Ti-rich inclusion detected. There were three exceptions – C1, C5 and C10 – where the relative number of Ti-rich inclusions detected was low (zero in the case of C5). Given that there has not been a quantitative study of Ti(CN) inclusions in early grey cast-iron objects in Britain before, it is difficult to determine whether these differences are important.

There have been a few studies, such as those by Wayman *et al.* (2004, 16-17), and Craddock and Lang (2005) looking at Chinese cast-iron statuary, that have identified Ti-rich particles. Craddock and Lang (*ibid.* 38) noticed such inclusions when studying Charles Dawson's Beauport Park fake Roman cast-iron statue. In commenting on their analyses, they made reference to the presence of vanadium (V) and niobium (Nb) in some of the inclusions, suggesting that the ore smelted contained ulvöspinel, which in turn indicated exploitation of a magnetite type ore associated with an igneous intrusion. They argued that if this was the case, it would exclude iron ore sources in the south-east and Midlands of England for the iron of these statues.

Some of the Ti(CN) particles from the cannon also showed the presence of V and/or Nb, although the levels of these elements were below the detection level for most of the spectra. It was only in the case of those inclusions with a higher C content than normal that the proportion of these elements became detectable in the spectra gathered during the automated runs. Samples which included several Nb-containing inclusions were C8 and C20 – guns produced by John Browne in the Weald, C12 produced by Thomas Johnson and C7 possibly also attributable to him, as well as C19 and C22 guns produced by Wilkinson at Bersham in Wales. On the basis of these results, it would seem that the presence of V and/or Nb in the Ti-rich inclusions is not necessarily an indication of the use of magnetite ores (which are not common in Britain). The source of these elements could be the mineral rutile, a titanium oxide. This is a common detrital mineral found ubiquitously in low concentrations in sedimentary rocks. Rutile is largely composed of titanium and oxygen, although the mineral may also contain both V and Nb (Deer *et al.* 1966, 416). Thus it is not possible to dismiss the Weald as a significant source of iron ores containing these elements.

Examination by one of us (Salter) of a number of fragments of early, Victorian and modern grey cast irons and experimental material produced accidentally during bloomery iron smelting all show the presence of titanium intermetallic inclusions no matter what the source of the ore. Not all have yet been examined intensively enough to determine if they contain V and/or Nb, but current evidence would suggest that the presence of these minor elements is not characteristic of a particular type of ore in itself.

A very basic multivariate cluster analysis using the major elements does indicate the possibility of groupings among the analyses (Fig. 59). We find that a number of the cannon fall together as one might expect were they to have been produced under similar conditions

193

of ore source and furnace regime. Thus, C19 and C22 form one cluster, while C8 and C20 fall together in another, and C7 and C20 are put into a wider grouping. Similarly, C2 and C18, two of the London shield guns that could be a part of the Culmore consignment are also paired, but C13 and C17, also showing the London shield, are much further apart. However, as is widely accepted, simplistic provenance analysis of this type is fraught with uncertainty, and so these observations should be taken as mildly interesting rather than offering any firm indications.

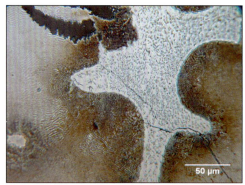

Plate 87 Micro-crack running from bottom right to top left across pearlite (dark) and phosphide eutectic (light).

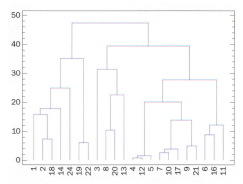

Fig. 59 Clustering of analytical data.

Evidence for Firing

One of the questions posed at the beginning of this project concerned the possibility of telling which of the cannon had actually been fired during its operational lifetime. Working guns were subjected both to physical and thermal shock and, it would seem not unreasonable to suppose that such would have left some mark upon the microstructure. Since the physical force exerted by firing is primarily pressure, percussive effects (such as the distortion of ferrite on cold percussion and the formation of Neumann bands) may be ruled out. However, as Rostoker noted (1986, 84), firing involves an impulse stress that can create and exaggerate small cracks. C16 exhibited such a micro-crack (Plate 87), although its origins have not yet been determined.

Gunpowder deflagrates at over 2000°C (e.g. Kelly, J. 2004, 115) and the heating of guns during action was a common source of problems. Thus, one might expect that if the temperature was raised sufficiently over a period of hours, some alteration of microstructure would occur. However, given the sort of slow rates of cooling that are suggested by the structures observed here, it would be difficult to distinguish any alteration in structure that might arise from what we might term a 'firing anneal' from that resulting from the original slow cooling in the mould. One possible indication is provided by the regular appearance of spiny irregularities on the surfaces of many of the graphite flakes, the result of a secondary deposition of graphite on cooling through the γ–α critical range (e.g. Angus 1976, 9).

The irregular forms of the flakes observed in Plate 88 (also Plates 78, 79b, 85a and 87) contrast with the smooth outlines of those in Plates 79a and 85b suggesting possible annealing. And if metal reached sub-critical temperatures in the region of 500–600°C, we might expect to see more in the way of the breakdown of pearlite to graphite and ferrite (e.g. Plate 79b: Murphy 2001, 80–81). However, our structures are being observed on samples taken from the outer surfaces, with the maximum depth being around 1.5cm. It would really only be the first few millimetres into the surface of the interior of the powder chamber where metal might reach such heats and thus be the zone where the effects of heating from firing might be found. But in the case of the core taken into the powder chamber of C6, the graphite all exhibits the same morphology along its length.

Currently there is no real data on the temperatures that cast-iron guns would have reached during the course of a prolonged action in the late sixteenth and seventeenth centuries, although their bronze counterparts

Chapter 8 – Some Observations on the Technology of the English Cannon

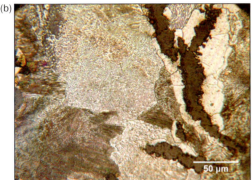

Plate 88 Secondary deposition on graphite flakes (a) C12, (b) C6.

were known to suffer plastic deformation, suggesting temperatures of a minimum of 600°C. And bronze guns were known to split and tear in intensive use, indicating that the heat generated by continuous firing could lead to local temperatures as high as 800-900°C for short periods. However, given the different thermal properties of cast irons and bronzes, this provides us with a rough guide only to the sorts of temperatures that could be generated. Mallet (1856, 44–48 and plate opposite p. 45) suggested that droop in bronze guns was caused by a temperature differential of perhaps only 300°F (149°C).

In addition to the heat generated by the deflagration of the powder, the effects of thermal stress would have been increased by the practice of damping down after each shot to ensure that no burning particles from the previous discharge could ignite the next charge. Clearly, until we can obtain cores that reach the interior of the bore, we can only speculate. But here again, it should be remembered that the sort of levels of corrosion encountered in C6 are likely to be commonplace, thus rendering interpretation difficult.

Conclusions

Much more work remains to be done on this assemblage, including the mechanical testing which restrictions on time and resources prevented us from addressing. Further, without a sufficiently large body of comparative data, these results exist in isolation and it would be imprudent to extrapolate out from them too widely. Nevertheless, we may draw some preliminary conclusions.

1. The evidence supports the view that cast-iron cannon were cast in the vertical. Although by no means clear-cut, it would appear that the various trends for changes in compositions and properties from breech to muzzle are best explained by this. There is pooling of impurities along the lengths of some of the guns, and indications that the highest burden lies in the region of the trunnions. This might be suggestive of horizontal casting but overall, this seems unlikely in view of the other data.

2. There is nothing in the analytical data to suggest that the majority of the guns identified as coming from the output of the Browne dynasty (or their Wealden contemporaries) need not have been produced from iron smelted from Wealden ores, such as the clay ironstones analysed and discussed by Worssam and Gibson-Hill (1976) and Tylecote (1972, 66–67; 1986 124*ff*). While the presence of V and/or Nb in Ti(CN) inclusions in general might indicate magnetites as one possible source, the results presented here offer the liklihood that when sufficient data has been gathered, such analyses will prove quite ubiquitous and not really offer a marker for one type of ore over another.

3. It would appear also that overall, the quality of metal and castings does not vary much from the work of Thomas Johnson to that of John Wilkinson some two hundred years later. This suggests that while the blast furnace and its operation evolved significantly (e.g. Schubert 1957, 195*ff*; Cleere and Crossley 1995), foundry practice in general did not necessarily keep pace. There were, however, claims by John Browne in the 1620s to have developed a 'refined' cast iron (p. 201), and by Prince Rupert in the 1670s to have produced cast iron that could be 'fyled and forged as

195

wrought iron is' (Barter Bailey 2000, 1). John Browne's refined iron was also supposed to have been one third lighter than 'conventional' cast iron, but none of the guns with which we can associate him here show anything like this kind of weight:size ratio when compared with other contemporary cast-iron pieces. It is noticeable that the specific gravities of the cannon are all at the lower end of the range of 6.8–7.8g/cm³, with C8 and C20 which can be identified with certainty with Browne, and most likely with dates in the early 1620s, coming out at 6.954g/cm³ and 6.876g/cm³ respectively. Even if we take a median value of 7.3g/cm³ for the specific gravity of cast iron, the Browne guns are only some 5–6% lighter than might be expected, and this can certainly be accounted for by the porosity observed (*cf.* Angus 1976, 114). On this evidence at least, it seems not unlikely that the weight reductions that he achieved were not through any metallurgical innovation, but more likely through thinner castings. Annealing of guns could have achieved further decomposition of pearlite to ferrite and graphite (*cf.* Plate 79b), thus making the metal easier to machine, but at a loss of strength.

4. At this point in time, it is not really productive to do other than speculate on the possibility that features such as secondary deposition of graphite, decomposition of pearlite to ferrite and graphite and microcracks provide evidence that the guns were actually fired.

Notes to Chapter 8

1 In 1856, Robert Mallet noted that 'Guns have long been cast in a vertical position.' (1856, 23*f*).

2 Samples were core-drilled from at least three locations on each cannon – the breech face, the underside midway between the trunnions and at the muzzle face. This was done using a diamond coring-bit held rigidly on a floor mount and kept under a constant stream of coolant. In the cases of eight of the guns, additional samples were taken in the region of the trunnions from the top surface and from the level of the trunnions.

3 Specific gravities were determined according to the formula

$$\text{Specific Gravity (SG)} = \frac{\text{weight in air}}{\text{weight in air} - \text{weight in water}}$$

4 Multiple samples were taken from each gun and the values here represent the averages determined. C25, C26 and C27 were identified too late for them to be included in this study. C23 was not included since Russian ordnance was considered to be too far removed from the focus of this study. The full analytical data is held as part of the project archive by Derry City Museum.

5 The carbon equivalent values (CE) were calculated using the formula

$$CE = \text{Total \%Carbon} + 0.3*(\%\text{Silicon} + 0.3\%\text{Phosphorous}).$$

6 The 'burden' is defined as the total percentage of all non-ferrous elements, excluding C. Ti and V values are given as parts per million.

7 The values for TiN–TiC and MnS–MnFeS refer to the number of inclusions per unit area of section.

8 These values refer to the percentage of surface area occupied by MnS–MnFeS inclusions.

9 Analyses were carried out in the State Laboratory of the Irish Republic at Celbridge, Co. Kildare, and we are most grateful to Drs Connor Murphy and Joe Foley for for carrying out this work and for their enthusiastic and generous support throughout the project.

The samples in disk form were filed to remove sharp edges and the surfaces cleaned with acetone to remove dirt and oil deposits. They were then analysed by Energy Dispersive X-Ray Fluorescence (EDXRF), on an ED2000 (Oxford Instruments), using semi-quantitative fundamental parameters (FP) for quantification. The EDXRF instrument used for analysis is factory pre-programmed with a FP method for determining major and minor elements in metals and alloys. A certified reference material in disk form of Gray Iron (B.S. 20E) was purchased from MBH Ltd. (U.K.). It was prepared for analysis in a similar manner as the samples. This contains 3.24% carbon and is of comparable chemical composition as the samples, and was assigned as a similar standard to the FP method in order to quantify more accurately the composition of the samples. Results were calibrated against a standard sample supplied by the Brammar Standard Company (14603 Benfer Road, Houston TX 77069, USA) Standard B.S. 20E grey cast iron. These data form part of the archive held by Derry City Council Heritage and Museum Service.

C	3.24000	Mn	0.80000
Mg	0.00018	Co	0.00600
Al	0.00600	Ni	0.15600
Si	2.29000	Cu	0.23000
P	0.04200	Zn	0.00018
S	0.04400	Mo	0.04200
Ti	0.01700	W	0.00000
V	0.00700	Sn	0.00093
Cr	0.08800	As	0.00300
Total burden 6.9723			

Cast iron standard values.

A multi-element set-up monitor (MES) standard was used to check the drift of the EDXRF system. A sample spinner was used to compensate for inhomogeneity effects and optimise the elemental results. Samples were placed in a sample cup and analysed as per the pre-programmed method for determining major and minor elements. Ni, Cu, Zn, Mo, W and As were all detected at trace level in parts per million, and are not listed here.

10 These data form part of the archive held by Derry City Council Heritage and Museum Service.

11 The tests were conducted using an Indentec Rockwell testing machine, 100kg load and a 0.32mm (1/8in) indenter, with the scale being referred to as HRE 100. All specimens were tested in a 'V-block' mount, with the necessary adjustment to accommodate the specimen curvature. In fact, two muzzle samples, from C6 and C18, were so poor as to have been excluded from consideration.

12 The 'Feature' facility of the INCA system was used to identify the inclusions based on the combination of measured intensity of the back-scattered electron (BSE) signal to locate and analyse the inclusions. The technique works by locating all of the possible inclusion locations on the image of each field from the back-scattered electron image, taking into account that this will include regions where corrosion and the interaction of the Fe and graphite signals give a similar back-scattered electron signal. The next step is to obtain an energy-dispersive spectrum for each of those possible inclusion sites using a short count time and to determine whether the spectrum contains S and/or Ti above a certain concentration. If those criteria are met then a more accurate spectrum is obtained using a longer count time, and the data – morphological and spectral – from the analysis of each inclusion is added to the database for that sample. This process was repeated automatically for a number of fields, so that for each sample a region roughly 3mm by 5mm – or as close to an equivalent area as the shape of the polished area would allow – was scanned, without including areas of excess corrosion.

CHAPTER 9
The Cannon Founders

Throughout this study, the name of Browne has dominated discussion of the seventeenth-century guns. As we have seen, many of the cannon can be attributed to the Browne dynasty of royal gunfounders, specifically the first John Browne, and one (C8) quite possibly to their foundry at Horsmonden in Kent. As we can connect the Stuart period cannon with the Brownes, so we know that one of the two Tudor pieces was cast by their predecessor as royal gunfounder, Thomas Johnson. Three of the four late eighteenth century 6-pdrs were cast by John Wilkinson, a founder who not only left his mark on cannon technology, but also on the evolution of the steam engine and hence on the whole of the Industrial Revolution. His work is also represented by at least five other pieces around the City or known in the past to have had a Londonderry provenance. Finally, since the Frenchman Alexander Foullon – the director of the factory where the Russian 24-pdr was cast – is discussed in detail by Bara (1985) and his products by Hennessy (1995, 1996), we shall not consider his work here.

Thomas Johnson

The predecessors as royal gunfounders of the more famous Brownes, the Johnsons, were another dynasty of gunfounders (see Teesdale 1991 for the careers of the whole family). John Johnson, Thomas' father, had helped Peter Baude, a gunfounder in bronze to Henry VIII, to cast the first successful cast-iron cannons in the Weald. John Johnson is said – on no particular evidence – to have been the son of Cornelius Johnson, maker of wrought iron artillery to Henry VIII,[1] and the nephew of Henry Johnson, Surveyor of the Ordnance under the same monarch. These two Johnson brothers had come from the Low Countries to work for the Tudors in the early years of the sixteenth century.

Between 1567 and 1577, Thomas Johnson was living at Maresfield in Sussex, the same parish as Ralph Hogge, the Queen's gunfounder for whom he worked and by whom he was probably trained. Thomas succeeded to the position of Queen's Gunstone Maker and gunfounder following the death of Hogge in 1585. In his career he worked with other founders and at a number of furnaces. He may have worked at Maynard's Gate, Sussex in 1574 (Cleere and Crossley 1995, 344) and in the 1580s probably at Scarlets furnace in Kent (*ibid*. 354) and possibly the Cowden furnace, also in Kent (*ibid*. 325). In August 1589, Thomas Johnson, described as 'of Hartfield', took over the lease of Horsmonden furnace (the same foundry that the Browne family would use in the next century) from William Ashburnham and was still there the following year (*ibid*. 340). His main colleagues were John Phillips, a London gunfounder, and Francis Johnson, presumably a relation. In 1587, Johnson and John Phillips were allowed special privileges to move cannons, which would be recognized by their being marked with the arms of the Queen.[2]

Thomas Johnson was casting guns as early as 1581, and for the Crown from 1584. Between then and March of 1593, he cast three hundred and forty-five pieces for the Crown (*Cal. SPD* 1591–1594, 336), at a total weight of 440 tons and averaging 25cwt per gun. As well as government guns, he exported cast-iron guns abroad. In 1595, he cast the iron guns for the Earl of Cumberland's famous ship, the *Mare Scourge*, which later formed part of the fleet of the East India Company (ffoulkes 1969, 47). Johnson was said to have used Horsmonden furnace for casting ordnance, the guns being sent up to Tower Wharf, in line with Government regulations introduced in 1574 (e.g. Barter Bailey 2003, 53). In 1574, the authorities were becoming concerned at the levels of sales of English ordnance abroad and required gunfounders to provide a bond of £2000 – an enormous sum for those days – as guarantee that they would not manufacture ordnance without a specific licence (ffoulkes 1937, 74–75). Johnson was one of those who seems to have followed regulations, and this led to some of the problems (including being pursued for debts) which arose for him in the early 1590s. The weavers of Cranbrook threatened him because they thought he was using all of the local timber resources for ironmaking.[3] And in 1595, he was unable to meet his commitments to the Ordnance Office because of lack of capacity and his inability to persuade the Sussex founders to help him. They claimed this would mean breaking the bonds given as part of controls on the supply of iron guns and their export. The Council were forced to ask Lord Buckhurst for help with the furnaces he controlled, Buckhurst having the monopoly in supplying the merchant market at this time (Barter Bailey 2003, 57).

A number of surviving Debenture Books for the Office of the Ordnance cover the last years of Thomas' life, and give details of his business with the government. Payments cover deliveries of shot, ranging from that for demi-cannon weighing 32lb each, down to falcon calibre weighing 2lb, and cross-bar shot from demi-culverin down to falcon (NA WO 49/17, ff 2, 79 and 135). In 1594 he was paid for cast-iron guns – four demi-culverins for Scilly, weighing just over 6 tons and worth £64, four long demi-culverins and a long saker with shot for Guernsey for which he was paid £91 10s 0d, four minions for the ship *Quittance,* worth only £29 and four culverins and two demi-culverins 'being faire longe yron ordnance', worth £118, as well as more shot (NA WO 49/18, ff 17r, 27v, 57r, 124r). Also in August of that year, stores had been issued to Johnson for double-proofing culverins, bastard culverins[4] and demi-culverins (NA WO 49/18, f. 158).

Deliveries continued through 1595, and on 24 March the Ordnance received nine demi-culverins, three heavier than the rest and more expensive, in total £153. The following month Johnson was paid £73 for two bastard culverins, weighing 39cwt (1981kg) each and two demi-culverins of 33cwt (1676kg) each. There were also four payments for ammunition in the year, (NA WO 49/19 *passim*), and most of these receipts bear his signature.

The last payment to Thomas Johnson was on 22 December 1595, and by 27 March 1596, his widow Mary was being paid by the Office. On that date she was paid £132 15s 0d for seven demi-culverins and four sakers (NA WO 49/20, f. 35). In April she was to be paid by the Privy Seal for four more demi-culverins and four sakers, as well as shot from demi-cannon down to falcon, the total coming to £547 17s 6d (NA WO 49/19, f. 46). An even larger payment of £727 16s 5d for shot was made to her on 20 August (NA WO 49/20, f. 118). A last payment to 'Marie Johnson widowe' for £196 10s 0d was recorded on 26 December 1596, for two culverins and nine demi-culverins (NA WO 49/19, f. 190). Mary also asked for financial assistance to move some of these last guns from Rochester.

The Browne dynasty

The first John Browne (John I) was the best known of the important family of gunfounders based in Kent, who for four generations, were the Gunfounders to Elizabeth I and the Stuarts, but who also supplied Parliament from the outbreak of the English Civil War in 1642 (Brown 2004b, 2005a) until the Restoration. It was certainly he who cast the guns sent to Londonderry in 1642, as well as most of those brought there probably in the 1620s. His father Thomas succeeded Thomas Johnstone as royal gunfounder, while John I (died 13 June 1651) took over from his father sometime around 1615. Thomas acquired his first licence in 1589 to cast iron ordnance at Ashurst in Kent (ffoulkes 1937, 75), and although he was obviously successful,[5] it was his son who really built up the business into almost a monopoly in a career that lasted four decades. Both he and his son had strong trading links with the Amsterdam merchants, in particular Elias Trip, and with the financier Philip Burlamachi, two of the most important customers for English cannon for Europe, particularly in the first two decades of the seventeenth century (e.g. van Wakeren 1996, 31).

It is not known when Thomas died. Traditionally it is said to have been in 1615, the year in which John Browne received the title of Gunstone Maker, but there are too

Chapter 9 – The Cannon Founders

many debentures post-dating 1615 to make this seem reasonable. No will that can be attributed to him seems to have survived, so that at present it is not possible to offer an exact date for his demise. From 1619, most of the payments are to his son John I, who would become the most famous and influential member of the family. The last debenture in Thomas' name is dated 4 February 1620 and is for round shot (*NA* WO 49/49, f. 13).

Although the Browne dynasty figures large in official records, very little documentation survives to shed light on the details of their operations. Edwards (undated) has drawn together a most useful account of the family in the seventeenth century but, as she noted, family information on business dealings is for all practices non-existent. But the situation is similar with other contemporary founders such as Sir Sackville Crowe and Steven Aynscombe in England, and Richard Boyle, Richard Blacknall and Charles Coote in Ireland. There are three main areas to be considered, probably overlapping to some degree. First, there were really no conduits for the survival of business or industrial documentation at that time, outside the records kept by officialdom. Thus, most of the surviving Browne records are where he touches against government. Second, much of the day-to day-work would have been carried out without the need for paper, especially since most of his workmen would have been illiterate. Later records do survive from the 1650s as a part of the archives of the Foley family ironworking operations[6] (e.g. Farrow 1984; Edwards 2000, 94), and this company survived in the ironworking business until much later than the Brownes, affording them a home to ensure their survival.

A third factor to be considered is that traders in the arms market may not infrequently have had reason to keep their activities secret. For example, a valued customer and ally of the country one day could be the national enemy of tomorrow – as, for example, with the Dutch who were major customers for English guns in the early seventeenth century and with whom the English subsequently went to war on three different occasions from the 1650s to the 1670s. It would seem evident that it was to the advantage of Browne and his contemporaries to keep certain dealings secret and to trust that, like today, the bureaucracy could be trusted to accept bribes, to turn a blind eye when deemed expedient, or simply to be too incompetent to notice what was going on. Thus, it is difficult to escape the conclusion that in terms of their business, major arms dealers in the seventeenth century often moved in a world as murky as that of their modern counterparts. John I, in particular, appears to have had more than a little disregard for any regulations that might restrict his opportunities for making money, and it seems not unlikely that the lack of internal documentation on his operations is not all to be put down to historical misfortune, with some element of a practice of secrecy. The fact that nothing of his instructions to his son has survived is probably down to this, at least in part. But at the same time, his surviving broadsides to officialdom suggest that in his mind at least, he was much more sinned against than sinning!

John I is known to have introduced a number of new developments, including a type of light gun called a 'drake' (Martin 2004). He claimed also to have invented a new form of 'refined' cast iron, lighter than that in normal use, which he was offering to the East India Company in 1621.[7] And on 28 April, it was recorded that his 'light-weight' cast-iron guns had survived double proof (*Cal. SPD* 1625–1626, 293). Since weight of ordnance was an important consideration in the arming of shipping, there was significant interest in this technology (e.g. Cipolla 1965, 64*f*). Both of these involved Browne charging the government a lot of extra money for his cannon, although in at least one instance the officer responsible for proofing such guns was dubious over their accuracy (*Cal. SPD* 1625–1626, 279–280, 13 March 1626).

John received his grant of arms on 12 December 1626 and famously, probably in 1637, cast a cannon in the presence of King Charles I (Blackmore 1976, 65–65). If rumour is to be believed, his one overt political act appears to have been his attendance on the King when he tried to arrest the five MPs in Parliament (*Cal. SPD* 1644–1645, 619). Otherwise, John I at least went with the money! By early 1640s, he was based in London, in Martin's Lane by the Old Swan in Thames Street, while his son, John II, remained at

Horsmonden, Kent where he received weekly letters from his father, instructing him on production requirements (*Cal. SPD* 1644–1645, 591, 607).

Always with an eye for opportunity, in the 1630s John I erected a bronze furnace at his ironworks in Kent at a time when the government needed bronze cannon to supply the navy. In the Civil War, the parliamentary forces quickly seized control of Kent and, once Parliament took control of the Ordnance and Navy in September 1642, Browne supplied them with guns and ammunition. However, he and his son were accused of having sent workmen to Oxford to the King's service and to be implicated in an attempted royalist rising in Kent. On 23 June 1645, the Committee of both kingdoms decided that it was '. . . to examine Mr [John] Browne [the gunfounder] and his son.' (*Cal. SPD* 1644–1645, 605–606). Parliamentary records (*Commons J.* 4, 182–183) note

> *That Mr. Browne the Gunfounder, and his Son, shall be forthwith sent for in safe Custody: And that all their Papers be seized on: And that no Person be suffered to speak with either of them, but in the Presence and Hearing of their Keepers.*

He, his son John II and their servants and workmen were closely questioned by officials of the Parliament and, although set free, they never had the full trust of the Roundheads (*ibid.* 20, 605), although they still provided ordnance to the government. With the Restoration of Charles II in 1660, the previous politics of the Brownes appear to have been quietly overlooked, and George Browne, grandson of John I, was appointed as gunfounder to the new King (Straker 1931, 164). This is a case where the 'Restoration' means literally that. The clocks were returned to 1642, with everything put back in place, including the Royal Gunfounders, whether or not they had helped Parliament, even whether they had given closet aid to the Royalist cause (which, in the case of Browne's workmen going to Oxford, they probably did).

John I had some direct involvement with supplying government ordnance for Ireland, and on 14 May 1642, the minutes of the recently-established Committee for Irish Affairs recorded (Snow and Young 1987, 449) that he billed £931 1s.08d for

> *. . . provisions made by him of certain ironwares and engines belonging to the fireworks and train of artillery for the present expedition into Ireland . . .*

This was confirmed for payment on May seventeenth (*ibid.* 453)

> *It is this day also ordered by the lords and others his majesty's commissioners for the affairs of Ireland that the lord lieutenant of Ireland he desired to give order to Mr. Nicholas Loftus, deputy treasurer at wars for that kingdom, to pay unto John Browne. Esquire, His majesty's gunfounder, the sum of 931li 1s.08d. which together with 500£ formerly paid unto him is in full of his demand for fifty-nine petards, four mortar pieces. One hundred fifty-two great grenadoes of 12 inches. Two hundred and sixteen grenadoes of 9 inches. Three-hundred and ninety-three hand grenadoes of dcmiculverin height, six hundred hand grenadoes of saker height. And four iron mortar pieces, which were provided for him by order of the said lord lieutenant of Ireland for the service of that kingdom and reviewed for their weight by Captain Greene. As appeareth by the particulars subscribed by the said John Browne and Captain Greene dated the 13th day of this instant May.*

In 1646, he was commissioned by the Committee for Irish Affairs to make 'a good mortar piece of 12½ins diameter[8] . . . for the Irish service' (*Cal. SPI* 1633–1647, 454, 4 June 1646; 475, 14 July 1646) at a price of £8 10s 0d per cwt. This 'brass' piece was to be delivered by his agent Richard Pierson[9] to 'Mr. Hodgskins' at the Tower to be proofed, and to have a carriage fitted by one William Roberts (*ibid.* 500). It evidently passed proof, as he was paid for this and for one hundred and twelve 'granadoes' (mortar shells) the sum of £307 14s 0d (*ibid.* 500).

However, he seems not always to have had happy dealings with Ireland, and on 7 October

1642, he petitioned the House of Commons (*Cal. SPD* Charles I, 1641–1643, 400–401), claiming that in 1640 he had been commissioned to produce a batch of twenty demi-culverin drakes for a customer there, but that

> ... he that bespoke them has since fled the country, being indebted to petitioner, not only for the said ordnance, but 442l. besides.

But is should be borne in mind that John I was a frequent petitioner to the Crown on real or imaginary wrongs, making large claims for losses (e.g. *Cal. SPD* 1635-1636, 18–19, dated 1635) which at this distance, we can neither verify nor contradict.

As well as supplying cannons for the Royal Navy, the Brownes cast cannons for both the English and Dutch East India Companies, also for export in general and for the civilian markets. John I subsequently fell out with the English Company, whose officers accused him of producing shoddy guns at exorbitant prices. He later tried to sue the blacksmith whom the Company used to mend guns.

The Brownes ran what was probably the largest iron-working operation in Britain, claiming at one time to employ two hundred men. Normally they used the furnaces at Brenchley, Barden and Horsemonden, although they could take on other furnaces with short leases and sub-contract to other founders if necessary. In the course of his career, John I seems to have pursued with vigour an attempt to gain a monopoly position in the supply of iron and bronze cannons in England, ruthlessly using his government contacts and the law to pursue those who opposed him. He was in dispute over the grant of 24 December 1620, to Sir Sackville Crowe for naval ordnance (*Cal. SPD* 1619–1623, 202)

> ... for the sole making of iron ordnance for shipping of the kingdom, except his Majesty's service ... keeping the market on Tower Hill supplied, and not raising the price above 13l per ton.

a patent renewed 31 August 1626 (*Cal. SPD* 1625–1626, 573). And in December of 1626, he petitioned the Crown against Crowe's patent[10] to supply the merchant market (*Cal. SPD* 1625–1649, 181 *ff*). However, Crowe had a powerful patron in the Duke of Buckingham, and it was not until his assassination that Crowe's position weakened sufficiently. Finally, in 1635, John Browne paid the enormous sum of £12,000 to the Crown to secure the sole right to produce iron shot and ordnance (Edwards 2000, 95). In 1639, by Order of Council he was granted 'letters of patent privelege for the sole making, new boring and selling of iron ordnance for 21 years in England, Ireland and Wales. (*Cal. SPD* 1639, 531, 29 September 1639). Although not always successful, by the outbreak of the Civil War, there do not appear to have been any major independent founders left, suggesting that his drive for monopoly had been largely successful.

The activities of the Brownes in their capacity as government gunfounders for more than eighty years has tended to overshadow the existence and careers of the other gunfounders, notably Sir Sackville Crowe, and also Steven Aynscombe (pp 152-153). Moreover, much of the available information about these and other founders is related to their law-breaking activities – i.e. smuggling guns out of the country, either to avoid paying duty or to sell to unauthorised customers (e,g, Cleere and Crossley 1995, 171–172) – or else to complaints by the Brownes that their patents and monopolies were being infringed. However, we know from other sources (e.g. Brown 2001, 19) that there were at least four furnaces capable of producing cannon in Sussex and a fifth near Cardiff in Wales. As furnaces were often taken on for short leases, it can be difficult to work out exactly which gunfounder was working at which furnaces.

John I died on 13 June 1651, and was laid to rest beside the body of his first wife Martha in the Chancel of Saint Margaret's Church, just outside the village of Horsmonden in Kent.[11] A visitor in 1795 remarked on the imposing monument of black marble in the church, with its long inscription. However, this no longer exists – possibly having been removed by the nineteenth-century vicar, the Rev. William Smith-Marriott (Edwards undated, 134–135). The resting place of Martha Browne is supposedly marked by a brass plaque set into a cast-iron plate in the chancel (*ibid.* 134), but is no longer visible due to the unsympathetic installation of decking. A slab that might commemorate John I is listed in the unpublished notebooks of Leland L. Duncan and dated 1922,[12] but could not be found on a visit in 2006, apparently concealed under other decking at the rear of the church. At the time of writing, the one visible funerary monument related to the Brownes was to be found in the nave, a commemorative slab to Anne, wife of George Browne, unhappily badly damaged, with one edge under wooden decking, and the whole carelessly covered with coarse carpet (Plate 89).

The text reads

HEERE [lies b]VRIED YE BOD[y] [of anne wife] OF GEORG[e] BROWN[e] ----- GENT AND [e]LDES[t] [daughte]R [o]F WALTER D[ob]ELL [of st]REATE IN SUSSE[x] --- WH[o] [depa]RTED THIS MORTALL L[ife] [14th] OF DECEMBER 1650 L[eaving] [o]NE ONELY SON GEORG[e]

According to Edwards (*ibid.* 138–139), Anne Dobell of Streat in Sussex married George Browne in 1647 and died in 1650.

John Wilkinson (1728 - 1808)

Then let each jolly fellow take hold of his glass
And drink to health of his friend and his lass,
May he also have plenty of stingo and pence
And Wilkinson's fame blaze a thousand years hence.
From a folksong in honour of John Wilkinson (Davies 2001, 21)

John Wilkinson, known in his time as 'Iron Mad Wilkinson', was a very tricky customer, a friend and partner (for a time!) of James Watt and Mathew Boulton and brother-in-law of one of the founding fathers of modern chemistry, Joseph Priestly. Often cantankerous and argumentative, he fell out with most of his family during his long life (Dawson 2004), while his probity was called into question not infrequently. In 1800, towards the end of his career, one contemporary described him as 'one of the most hard hearted, malevolent old scoundrels now existing in Britain', a sentiment

Plate 89 Memorial slab to Anne (née Dobell), wife of George Browne, son of John Browne I, in the nave of Saint Margaret's Church, Horsmonden, Kent.

echoed by his brother-in-law[13] (Clarke 1984, 4). He famously wrote his own epitaph (*ibid.*), telling the world that

Peace is a most desirable thing and the more so to one of my constitution who cannot be angry by halves. Resentment with me becomes a matter of business and stimulates to action beyond any profits.

Nevertheless, despite the often harsh criticisms he received, it is hardly understatement to suggest that he was one of the foremost innovators and drivers of the British iron industry in the latter half of the eighteenth century. And his fixation with iron led him, amongst other things to install iron pews, windows and an iron pulpit at the Wesleyan chapel at Bradley near Wolverhampton. However, his business interests were not wholly centred on iron, and he also had significant stakes in the banking, canal and land sectors.

John was born in Furness in Lancashire, the son of Isaac Wilkinson, himself a noted ironmaster, innovator and non-conformist. Isaac introduced improvements in moulding techniques, and amongst his inventions was a double-bellows system for providing a continuous blast to the smelting furnace, which he patented in 1757 (no. 713: e.g. Cranstone 1991). In 1747, he and John also attempted, unsuccessfully, to use peat as a fuel[14] at Lindale in the Lake District. To get peat to their works, they dug a canal through the bog and constructed the first ever iron canal boat to carry it. In 1787, John repeated the feat (Davies 2001, 10–11) with the construction of *The Trial*, modelled on the wooden narrow canal boats, some 70ft (21.34m) in length and with a beam of 6ft 8½ins (2.04m).

During his career, he operated a number of iron furnaces including Willey in Shropshire, and Bersham and Brymbo in North Wales. Like his father, he was a man of vision, and was a subscriber in 1779 to the construction by Abraham Darby of the first iron suspension bridge at Coalbrookdale in Shropshire. In gunfounding, his innovations comprised the perfection of machinery to bore out true barrels for cannon,[15] and his pioneering work to rifle barrels. After some problems, he received a patent (number 1063) for his boring apparatus in 1774 (Dickinson 1914, 22 and 58), while in 1789 he was granted a patent (number 1694) for the rifling of cannon barrels to improve both accuracy and range (*ibid.* 30 and 58; Lake 2003, 13–14). Interestingly, but not unusually for the time, neither patent application is accompanied by any form of drawing, probably a deliberate omission to deny competitors easy access to his technology. An innovator in iron production, he was one of the first to harness the power of the steam engine in his foundries, and introduced innovations in the puddling hearth (*ibid.* 15), coke-making (e.g. Beaver 1951, 135) and the cupola furnace, also anticipating by over forty years the introduction by Nielsen of the hot blast in furnace technology (Davies 2001, 22).

John began working for his father at the Bersham ironworks and they started to export small guns in June 1756. Later, he left Bersham and moved to Willey in Shropshire where he began to cast cannon for the government. In the 1760s, the Wilkinson businesses went through a 'restructuring' when, having married one of the main shareholders at Bersham, John was able to oust his father. In the late 1760s and early 1770s he leased more works, and set about rationalising and specialising the use of each furnace. Under this reorganization, Bersham was used for casting cannon, and it is probably there that he developed and perfected his cannon-boring technology.

John Wilkinson succeeded in producing iron guns with true bores out of solid castings by mechanical boring, something that previously had been done with limited success on the continent for bronze guns only. Before solid casting, iron guns were cast round a core which was then removed and the bore reamed out (Fig. 6). Because the core not infrequently shifted during the casting process, this often meant that bores could be off-true or even crooked. Further, the exaggeration of casting flaws (p. 34*f*) could have catastrophic consequences for the gunners who used such pieces. Although boring machinery had been constructed in the earlier eighteenth century by, amongst others, Jean Maritz in Switzerland (e.g. Kennard 1986, 108), Wilkinson was the first to make the technique a real commercial success. Casting solid and boring out had been done by fixing the cannon in place and using a rotating cutting head (Fig. 7). However, given that casting defects were reasonably commonplace, and because it was difficult to keep rigid the boring bar, the cutting head could follow the line of least resistance. As a result, while the section at any given point was circular, the

Plate 90 *Squire John Wilkinson* by Thomas Gainsborough,[16] c. 1776 (*Staatliche Museen zu Berlin*).

bore itself was not necessarily a true cylinder, nor indeed true with the outside surface. What Wilkinson did was to reverse this, with the cannon made to rotate while the drill-bit remained stationary, allowing production-line output of guns with true bores (Plate 91). In fact, boring out significantly improved the quality of British cannon and put them for a time ahead of any competitor in the field.

Anthony Bacon was a shipping magnate, ironmaster and MP who, like Wilkinson, had his origins in north-western England. In 1773, acting on behalf of Wilkinson, he offered the Board of Ordnance three guns cast in different irons – smelted from coke, from charcoal and a mixture of both – and, some months later, three guns bored out of the solid (*NA* WO 47/82 and 83 *passim*). The Board were so impressed by the solid-bored pieces that they decided in future they would only purchase such guns.

Having received his patent, Wilkinson threatened other founders for infringement, including Jones of Bristol, his father's new partner, and the Walkers of Rotherham who had taken his father's side in the dispute. However the Ordnance Board managed to have the patent set aside, claiming that it was neither in the public interest nor an original idea. Wilkinson next tried to get a monopoly by supplying all the guns needed by the government, offering them thousands of tons in the mid-1770s, but again the Ordnance Board had no intention of concentrating all the orders with one contractor (*NA* WO 47/88, f. 250). Most of the guns supplied at this period were marked SOLID, although occasionally some were not; the Harrisons had to supply affidavits from John Wilkinson that some unmarked guns had been cast solid.

In April 1783 the Board issued a general order for casting to cease and for founders to get affidavits for guns already cast before this date. New and harsher conditions were introduced which the Harrisons refused to accept and therefore the Board would not receive their guns, which were left at Woolwich until April 1787 when the Harrisons asked for them again to be taken. However in December 1788 the Board, growing impatient, reiterated their order to remove the guns which had been lying at Woolwich since the end of the last war and in January 1789 the Harrisons finally arranged for a boat from Chester to remove them (*NA* WO 47/112 and 113 *passim*).

A quite separate outcome of the development of the technique for boring iron guns was that it provided James Watt and Matthew Boulton with true-bored iron cylinders to the precision required for their steam engine (e.g. Dickinson 1958, 183), thus giving major impetus to the industrial revolution. The lack of precision-bored cylinders that could maintain pressure had held up the development of the steam engine. Wilkinson went into partnership with the two innovators, and for some twenty years they enjoyed a near-monopoly, with Boulton and Watt insisting that customers bought parts from the Wilkinson foundry. The relationship was terminated as a result of a Wilkinson family quarrel which erupted when the younger brother William returned from France. The two men fell out and, in retaliation for various provocations, in early 1796 William began to supply Boulton and Watt with the details of pirate engines built by his brother without their knowledge and in infringement of their patent (Soldon 1998,

Plate 91 Reconstruction of the Wilkinson cannon-boring machine (Science Museum, London).

241*ff*). The partners sued John successfully and broke off their relationship, establishing the Soho works in Stoke-on-Trent as an independent operation.

In August 1775, Marchant de la Houlière, a Frenchman, watched a 32-pdr being cast at Bersham. This visit was instrumental in John, and his younger brother William, being invited to France, first to advise and later to set up a new cannon foundry at Le Creusot (Lake 2003, 11). Although not a particularly successful operation,[17] this French connection also did not endear him to the British government, particularly when France backed the new American republic in its struggle with the British. Indeed, his technology was introduced to America in the 1790s by Henry Foxall (Braid 1991). This may be one of the reasons why, in later life, he always used at least one and sometimes two agents in dealing with the Ordnance Board, sometimes actively employing them to disguise his exact involvement in gunfounding. However, another fruit of the French adventure was the contract to supply all of the cast-iron pipework[18] for the Paris waterworks, some forty miles in total length (Davies 2001, 15).

With the outbreak of war in 1793, Bersham B SOLID guns were again being proofed for government service. This time Wilkinson used two agents – Gordon and Stanley, successors to Harrison and Co, and Wiggan and Graham. The guns, which the Ordnance Board had refused to accept in the 1780s, appear to have been offered again and this time, as they were in desperate need of guns, were accepted. However his guns were not held in such high regard as they had been in the previous war. As early as 1794, Wilkinson noted that the gun proofs were much stricter and the founders were not having such good results. Gilbert Gilpin, John's former manager, wrote to William Wilkinson that Bersham was having trouble keeping up the high standards now required. In 1795 Thomas Blomefield, the Inspector of Artillery at Woolwich, wrote to Wiggan and Graham asking if the 18-pdrs on their way from Wilkinson were to be subject to the usual proof and later he commented on the poor performance at proof of recent guns. The anonymous author of the folk song in his honour (*ibid*. 21) composed the verse

Our thundering cannon too frequently burst;
A mischief so great he prevented the first;
And now 'tis well known, they never miscarry,
But drive all our foes with a blast to Old Harry.

Blomefield suggested that Wilkinson should be used to fulfil a contract for guns for Portugal rather than continue casting for the Government, a clear sign that the Board now considered him in the second rank of founders. Certainly no more guns which can definitely be attributed to Wilkinson were received by the Ordnance Board after 1797, although contemporary naval lists suggest that there were Wilkinson guns aboard the *Victory* at Trafalgar.

The Bersham works, which have been excavated in recent years and are now a heritage centre (Williams 2001), went into decline in the 1790s after the quarrel between John and his brother William, and the 6-pdr B-SOLID cannon was largely replaced by the lighter and cheaper carronade, produced from *c*. 1790 at the Carron works in Falkirk in Stirlingshire, and its derivative, the gunnade.

John Wilkinson died on 14 July 1808. As with his life, his passing was a more than somewhat eccentric affair. He had arranged to be buried in a cast-iron coffin, and while his body was being transported in a wood and lead coffin across Morecambe Bay to what was to be his final resting place on his estate at Castlehead in Cumbria, the pall bearers were caught by a particularly swift incoming tide and fled (Davies 2001, 23). When they returned, the coffin had to be dug out of the sands. Then it was discovered that the wooden coffin was too large for its intended outer shell, and so he was interred temporarily until a new one could be cast. After he had been exhumed and placed in the new coffin, it was then found necessary to blast out a hole deep enough in which to bury him decently. He had also had cast a monumental iron column, a very early example of box casting. Some 40ft high (12.2m) and weighing over twenty tons (Plate 92), this was erected over his grave on the estate. However, when the house changed hands a few years later, the new owners were not enamoured of the sight outside their parlour window, and so there was a move to the churchyard of Saint Paul at Lindale-in-Cartmel, Cumbria. More recently, the obelisk

The Great Guns Like Thunder

was relocated yet again, this time to a small and obscure plot at a minor junction on the A590 from Grange-over-Sands, some 200m from the entrance to Lindale village. There is a raised plaque of Wilkinson in profile, and the inscription below, reads

> JOHN WILKINSON;
> IRONMASTER
> WHO DIED XIV JULY, MDCCCVIII
> AGED LXXX YEARS:
> HIS VARIOUS WORKS
> IN DIFFERENT PARTS OF THE
> KINGDOM
> ARE LASTING TESTIMONIES
> OF HIS UNCEASING
> LABOURS;
> HIS LIFE WAS SPENT IN
> ACTION
> FOR THE BENEFIT
> OF MAN,
> AND, AS HE PRESUMED
> HUMBLY TO HOPE,
> TO THE GLORY OF GOD.
>
> LABORE ET HONORE

Although at his death, his empire was quite extensive, the legal wars that broke out between his heirs, the Trustees of his estate and his illegitimate children by the mistress whom he took when in his 70s, over a few years consumed all. By 1828, most was sold off to meet debts, while several of the claimants were forced into bankruptcy. Standing by the obelisk, his last grandiose gesture to posterity, and remembering the collapse of his empire, one cannot help but be reminded of the lines penned in 1817 by Shelley of the monument to another proud ruler of an empire:

And on the pedestal these words appear:
"My name is Ozymandias, King of Kings:
Look on my works, ye mighty, and despair!"
Nothing beside remains. Round the decay
Of that colossal wreck, boundless and bare,
The lone and level sands stretch far away.

Notes to Chapter 9

1 Cornelius Johnston was almost certainly the craftsman responsible for the manufacture of the wrought iron guns found on the *Mary Rose*.

Plate 92 The Wilkinson obelisk at Lindale-in-Cartmel.

2 The guns on the *Mauritius* which have John Philips' initials (L'Hour *et al.* 1989, 119–121), also have 'ER', the rose-and-crown and the date 1587.

3 Fifty years later, they made similar accusations against the Brownes (*Cal. SPD* 1637, 290-291, 7 July 1637).

4 The normal culverin threw a ball of 18lb, while this particular bastard culverin was a smaller gun, throwing a shot of only 13lb. In general, the term 'bastard' refers to a gun of non-standard calibre.

5 In 1612, Thomas was granted a life pension of 18d per day in recognition of his gunfounding skills (ffoulkes 1969, 75).

6 Thomas Foley married Anne Browne, daughter of John I and, on whose death, acted as executor of his will, subsequently taking a significant financial interest in the Browne operations.

7 It was minuted (*BL* IOR B/7 f. 11) that at a Court of the East India Company held on 13 July 1621
> *The Court was acquainted with a project of Mr. Browne an iron founder to make Ordinance of Iron that shallbe as light as Brasse and of as good effect.*

Also *cf.* Cipolla (1965, 65*f*).

8 *Cal. SPI* 1633–1647, 500, gives the diameter as 12ins.

9 *Cal. SPI* 1633–1647, 475, refers to 'Mr. Pierson and William Browne the gunfounder'. The clerk appears to have confused John I with Captain William Browne, master of the *Elizabeth* of Liverpool (*ibid.* 557), who was probably charged with taking the mortar by water to the Tower.

10 It is not at all clear if he was aware of the dealings between Crowe and the Blacknall and Wright partnership that had, seemingly, Royal blessing for the production of iron ordnance in Ireland (p. 53, note 16).

11 The graves in the churchyard include the last resting place of John Austen, great-great-great-great grandfather of the famous novelist Jane Austen.

12 The entries for Saint Margaret's, Horsmonden, transcribed by Jeremy Stroud and checked by Frank and Zena Bamping, are currently listed on the website of the Kent Archaeological Society, with the URL http://www.kentarchaeology.org.uk/Research/Libr/MIs/MIsHorsmonden/01.htm.

13 Priestley, who wrote of a discussion on innovations in which Wilkinson had seemingly claimed for himself inventions of others, stated that '. . . this is not the only incidence in which the Invidiousness, the Malevolence and the Badness of John Wilkinson's Heart has been apparent to me.' (Clarke 1984, 7).

14 A number of attempts were made in the eighteenth and early nineteenth centuries to use peat, including at Creevelea, County Leitrim where probably the best-preserved remains of a blast furnace in Ireland still survive (e.g. Meehan 1906).

15 Wilkinson seems also to have employed talent, since one of his employees was Richard Roberts who in 1817 went on to make an important contribution to the development of the lathe (Bradley 1972, 13–14).

16 A much less flattering portrait, by Lemuel Francis Abbot, is to be found in the collections of the Ironbridge Gorge Museum Trust (Williams 2001, 56, Fig. 1), and further portraits (equally unflattering) are included in the collections of the Science and Society Picture Library.

Interestingly, but probably quite coincidentally, Humphrey Gainsborough the brother of Thomas Gainsborough (who painted the portrait shown in Plate 90) and a Non-conformist minister, invented a steam engine with separate condenser, seemingly independently of Boulton and Watt. At the time of his death, he was working on a design for a second type (Tyler, D. 2006). It is perhaps idle speculation to consider what conversations might have taken place at sittings between his brother and John Wilkinson!

17 Nevertheless, the works did produce iron guns for the French navy, a number of which survive.

18 Having been cast in section, these pipes later gave rise to the rumour that Wilkinson was exporting cannon to the French during a time of war (Clarke 1975).

A True and Perfect Inventary of Such Gunns and Other Artillery as are received by Mr Hugh Bareley the Younger Clerke of his Matis Stores this 29th March 1660.

In the Cittidell		C	qr	lb
	Imprimis one Demy Culverin of Iron mounted but the Carridg and Wheels Rotten, of the Mercers London qt	35	2	14
	Item one Demy Culvering of Iron unfitt of ye Mercers qt	36	–	–
	More one Demy Culverin of Iron mounted but ye Carridg and wheels rotten of the Marchat Taylors London contoyning	34	0	14
	More one Small Peece of Brass Mounted both Carridg Rotten contoyning	1	3	25
	More one Brass Drake unmounted contoyning	192		
	More one Brass Drake unmounted contoyning	188		
	More one Demy Culverin of Iron Mounted but the Carridg rotten of the Fishmongers contoyning	35	3	
	More one Demy Culverin Mounted but ye Carridg rotten of ye Vintners contoyning	30	1	
	More one Demy Culverin unmounted contoyning	33	3	
	More one Drake Brass unmounted contoyning	188		
	More one Demy Culverin unmounted of the Marchant Taylors contoyning	36		14
	More one Iron Saker unmounted weight	21	2	
	More one Minion Cutt unmounted of Iron Contoyning	479		
	Item foure Small foild peeces of Brass in a frame Decayed			
	More one Iron falcon Unmounted			
	More one Demy Culverin Salters qt	26	Unmounted	
	More one Minion Cutt of Iron qt	492	Unmounted	
	More one Demy Culverin Goldsmiths qt	30	Unmounted	
	More one Saker Clothworkers qt (ye Carridg Decayed)	22	Mounted	
	More one Minion of Iron Drapers qt	16	Unserviceable	
	More one Saker Iron Mongers qt	35	Unmounted	
	More one Demy Culvering Grocers qt	35	Mounted but not Serviceable	
	More one Minion Mounted but not Serviceable Drapers qt	16	1	–
	More one Demy Culverin mounted but not Serviceable Grocers qt	36	1	14
	More one Falcon of Iron unmounted qt	1000		
	More one Brass Drake mounted but ye Carridg rotten qt	190		
	Item three old Demy Culverin Ladles, one Saker Ladle foure Sponges & wormes one Minion Ladle			

APPENDIX A
Contemporary Documents Relating to the Londonderry Ordnance

A1.1 LICENCE OF 19 JULY 1620 TO THE CITIZENS OF LONDON TO TRANSPORT ORDNANCE TO CULMORE (NA SP 39/12)

James by the grace of God etc. To the Comissioners of and for our Treasury for the time being, and to our right trusty and wellbeloved Counsello^r the Lord Carew Baron of Clopton M^r of the Ordinance greeting. Whereas humble suite hath bene made unto us by the Citisens of our City of London that we wold be graciously pleased to grant them license to transport a certaine quantity of Iron ordnance into our Relme of Ireland for the defense of Culmore Castle there neere Londonderry, we graciously inclyning to their peticon, have given and granted, and by these we do give and grant them liberty and license to transport out of this Our Relme of England into our Kingdome of Ireland for the service aforesaid tenne peeces of Iron ordenance of these sev^{r}all kindes following, that is to say two demy culverins, fower sakers, two mynions, and two falcons, together with twelve musketts and twelve barrells of powder, cariages, shott and such other provisions as appertaine to the said tenne peeces of ordenance. Wherefore we do by these p^r[ese]nts will and authorize yo^u and every of yo^u respectively to give order to all and any our officers whome it doth or may concerne to suffer and permit Roger Rose [merchant[1]] or his assignes to buy and transport from time to time out of any our portes of this Relme of England towards our said Kindom of Ireland the said number of Iron ordenance and of the kinds aforesaid together with the said munition and provision belonging to them, wherfour he or they shall require the same without any lett or interruption of any our officers whatsoever, any Act, Statut, proclamacon or restraint to the contrary notwithstanding. Provided that yo^u likewise charge and require our officers to have a speciall care that under color hereof there be not transported a greater number or for any other place or of any other weight then is here expressed. And these our letters etc

This contayneth yo^{re} Maties warrant to pass the Privy Seale wherby yor Matie is pleased to give license to the Citisens of London to transport tenne peeces of iron ordnance together with such other munition as apertains to the same, into yo^{ur} Maties Relme of Ireland for the defense of Culmore Castle there, and is don by order of Mr Secretary Calvert.[2]

Windebank[3]

A1.2 DETAILS OF THE TRANSACTION UNDERLYING THE LICENCE OF 19 JULY 1620 (NAS RH 15/91/61[4])

The 5th August anno 1620

A noate of x. peeces of Iron Ordinance what they cost wth Charges etc. shipt for Culmore Castle in Ireland as appeareth at Large in Londons Jornall follio 131 and 132 viz:-

Imprimis paid to Edmond Turvill for 10 peeces of great Iron Ordinance Viz. 2 dennie [=demi] culverings 4 sackers [=sakers] 2 miniones and 2 faukens [=falcons] waing all 243^c 1^{qr} at xij^s the hundreth   £145 19 00

211

Paid to Mr. Turvill for cartage of them overland to London for expedition	£005 00 00
Paid to John Horton for making 10 Carrages for the ordenance one Gynn compleate, coynes, beds, wheeles, ironwork etc. as per his noate	£059 01 00
Paid to the East India Company for 1000 round Iron shott waing 35ᶜ 2ᵍʳ 25ˡⁱ at 8ˢ and 10ᶜ 3ᵍʳ 13ˡⁱ at 10ˢ per hundreth and portage Inwards 1ˢ 9ᵈ is in all	£009 16 02
Paid to John Evelin for 12 barrells of new gunpowder at iiijˡⁱ per Barrell comes to	£048 00 00
Paid to Thomas Covell for 12 muskets, ladles, spunges, and powder cases for the Ordinance	£014 03 00
Paid to William Felgate for 73ˡⁱ of stronge powder and 51ˡⁱ of shotte to prove the Ordenances	£003 18 00
Paid to Richard Mountney which he disbursed aboute proofe of these Ordinance in carringe and recarringe them to the fields, graving the Cittize armes uppon each peece and shippinge the shotte abourde	£005 03 00
Paid to Samuell Callvert which he disbursed at Signet and to Clerks for feese in processing his Majesties licence to shippe out the Ordinance	£007 13 00
Paid to the Tower Porters for removing these Ordinance to the Craine and shipping them	£001 05 06
Paid for cutting a mould for Londons armes taking out a Cocket for Searchers fees	£001 02 06

<u>*Jornall 131, 132*</u>

Jornall 139

Paid to John Roose [Rose?] for fraight and charges of Ordenance and other Provitions shipped in his shippe the William and Joane	£026 00 00
Paid by Captain John Baker for unladinge and mounting the said Ordenance	<u>£007 13 10</u>
Carried over to the next side	£344. 15. 00
Item more bought the 12ᵗʰ May 1621 and shipped in the May flower Mr John Betson to be dellivered at Cullmore to Captaine John Baker for service at that Forte viz. *Paid to George Petty for 3 piggs of leade waing 8ᶜ 3ᵍʳ 10ˡⁱ at 8ˢ 6ᵈ the hundreth waite*	£003 15 00
Paid to Thomas Covell for one hundreth waighte of match	£001 15 06
Paid for a bill of store searcher cartage wharfage and shipping	<u>£000 04 00</u>
Somma totalis is	<u>£350 09 06</u>
One twelvth parte whereof commeth unto	£029 04 01

*Besides the Customes here in London which with
Much a doe wee got remitted
Of which some of £29 04 01 the Companie of
Waxchandlers Founders and Turnors are
To pay one xvjth part which is*   £001 16 06
*Soe is the nett rest due by the right
Worshipfull Companie of Haberdashers*   £027 07 07

Indorsed: Ordinance sent for Ireland the 5th August Anno 1620.

The consignment of 1620 is discussed in Chapter 4 (pp 105-107). Regarding the supplies sent in 1621, the *Mayflower* was in London on 11 May 1621 with a cargo that included 'aquavite', sugar, soap, paper, tobacco pipes, pepper and cloves (*NA* E190/24/1 f. 57v). She is named as the '*May fflower* of London Derrie', with her Master recorded as being 'John Betson of Coleraine', in depositions of 27 April 1622 (Appleby 1992, 145). In these, Betson and other crew members (Patrick Ray of Londonderry and John Knocke of Culmore) described how the vessel was boarded by a man-of-war out of La Rochelle and had some of her cargo siezed before being let go. The *Mayflower* also took cargo to and from Chester in 1620 (e.g. *NA* E190/1332/1, f. 11v and *passim*), where the port books also refer to her as 'of Derrie' and 'of London Derry'. The Captain John Baker who received the ordnance is the same Baker referred to in the Carew and Pynnar surveys. He held Culmore from the City of London until his death at Christmas 1626 (*Phillips MSS* 97).

The Great Companies

A key source for the origins of at least some of the Londonderry cannon is to be found in the archives of eleven of the twelve Great London Companies who were involved in the early seventeenth-century Plantation. In these we find transcribed the original precepts from the City of London to the Companies which lay out what was being asked of them in the way of money and provisions, records of the discussions of these requests and, in some cases, detailed accounts of purchase. Some of the Company records are sparse (e.g. Salters), while others provide a wealth of detail (e.g. Clothworkers, Vintners and Grocers) on their involvement with the ordnance.

A2 PRECEPT FROM THE SIR RICHARD GURNEY FOR THE SUPPLY OF ORDNANCE TO LONDONDERRY, 18 MARCH 1642

Following the reports coming out of Ireland, the Lord Mayor of London issued an appeal for relief for 'the poor protestants in Ireland' on 24 January 1642. And in response to direct appeals from the citizens of Londonderry who reported on 10 January 1642, that they had only four cannon for their defence (p. 114), a further precept (Plate 93) was issued by the Lord Mayor on 18 March, specifying that the Companies should as a matter of urgency send ordnance. This transcript comes from the Court Minutes of the Worshipful Company of Merchant Taylors (*Merchant Taylors CM 7*, f.145).

To my loveing freinds the M^r and Wardens of the Company of Merchanttailo^{rs} London.

Whereas the Cittie of London Derry is built and fortified at the chardge of the Companies of this Cittie, and for the present in greate danger by the rebellion in Ireland (the preservation whereof as a peece of greate importance) is of much concernm^t to the generall State of that Kingdome, but much more for the interest of this Cittie there, whereof upon mocon the last Comon Councell due notice being taken, it was propounded that the Companies should inlardge their late voluntary contribution for releif of London Derry by addicon of some ordinance to bee provided for that Cittie, and that I the Lord Maio^r should recomend the same to the severall Companies wherefor I doe notifie the promissed unto you desireing that upon your consultation you will resolve of doeing something therein by provideinge one or more peeces of Artillory for the said Cittie of London

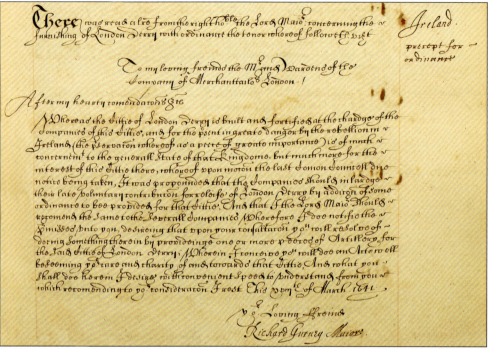

Plate 93 The Precept of 18 March 1642.

Derry, wherein I conceive you will doe an acte well beseeming yor care and charity of and towards that Cittie, and what you shall doe herein I desire with convenient speed to understand from you which recomending to yor consideracon I rest this xviiith of March 1641.

*Yo^r Loving Friend
Richard Gurney Maior*

Various versions can be found in the archives of most of the Great Companies.

A3 THE WORSHIPFUL COMPANY OF MERCERS

Mercers Acts of Court 1641–1645 ff 25v–25r

Ordnance for London Derry

At a Generall Court this 31st of March a⁰ 1642

Upon the reading of a letter from the r. hoble the Lord Mayor of this City of the 18th of this instant month, this Court in inlargement of their late & voluntary contribution of CC^{li} for the relief of that Citty London Derry in Ireland did now condiscend & agree that there shalle be provided & sent over to the said City for the safety and defenn^s thereof two peeces of Iron Ordnance at the charge of this Comp^a, the price of both not exceeding One Hundred markes, the same to be bought by Mr Wardens and such as they shall call unto them for their assistance in that behalfe.

Although no date for payment is given in these entries, they are bracketed by payments dated to the end of May. There are no separate entries related to carriages and, as with the accounts of the Ironmongers (see A11), the figure of £61 9s 7d would certainly cover both the cannon and their carriages.

Mercers AC f. 167v

	li	s	d
Paid Samuel fferers for two demy culverins to be sent to London Derry bt per bill	lxi	ix	vii
Paid William ffranklin for charges about trying of them bt per bill		xxi	vi
Paid William ffelgate for powder and bullets used in the trying of them and divers materials to be sent with them		vi	xviii

Appendix A – Contemporary Documents Relating to the Londonderry Ordnance

A4 THE WORSHIPFUL COMPANY OF GROCERS

Grocers CM 4, ff 43–44, dated 4 March 1642

f.43 *This day was read in Co^{rt} a lre from the right hono^{ble} the Lord Maio^r directed to this company herein desireing this companies care and provision for the furnishing of Londonderry in Ireland wth some peeces of Artillory being in great danger by reason of the rebellion wch may bee a helpfull means for the preservation thereof and thereupon due consideracon being had it is agreed and ordered that Mr Wardens shall* [f.44] *enquire what other comp– doe in this kinde and that they shall have power to doe the like or to joyne wth other companyes in the furnishing of the said citty (as is desired at the charge of this company.*

The Wardens seem to have followed their instructions to the letter and, although there are no further references in *Grocers CR* to ordnance, *Grocers WA* 12, f. 446 contains a wonderfully complete account of the purchase of two demi-culverins and accessories (Plate 94).

	l	ss	d
Item paid into the Pole Office towards the releife of London Derry in Ireland upon a l^{ttr} from the Lord Mayor by ord^r of Parliam^t requesting some contribucon thereunto according to an ord^r of Co^{rt} of Assistants the sume of	160	00	0
Item paid Mr Samm^{ell} fferrers for two demiculverings w^t 36-1-14 & 35-2-0 att xiij^s vj^d [13s 6d] per C[wt] for the guard of the Cittie of London Derry according to an order of the Co^{rt} upon a l^{tr} from the Lord Majo^r by order of Parliament the sume of	048	00	0
Item paid John Pitt Carpenter for carriages for the two demiculverings as appeareth by bill the sume of	006	00	0
Item paid Thomas Bateman wheelewright for wheeles and axle trees for the carriages per bill the sume of	005	05	0
Item paid for the ironwork for the carriages and wheeles w^t 3^{cwt}-3^{qt} -27^{lb} att 3_^{d} per lb the sume of	006	10	0
Item paid for engraving the carriages and wheeles the sume of	000	03	6
Item paid Abraham Preston for engraving the demi culverings with the Comp^a escutcheon and inscripcon	000	10	0
Item paid for charges of searching and proving the demi culverings	000	15	6
Item paid for drawing preparing stopping and culloring the demicull and other charges per severall billes	004	19	0
Item paid W^m ffelgate for powder and shott to prove them and for ladles staves spunges wadhooks & other implem^{ts} and shott to send into Ireland per bill	005	03	04
	237	10	04

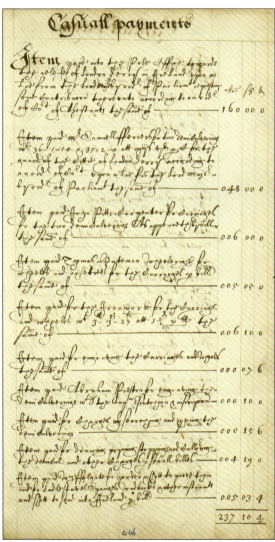

Plate 94 *Grocers WA* 12 f. 446, detailing the merchants who provided the guns and their equipment.

A5 THE WORSHIPFUL COMPANY OF DRAPERS

The Court of Wardens considered the two mayoral precepts together, deciding to send a significant quantity of wheat to Ireland, with a portion earmarked specifically for Londonderry. They also agreed that should it be more appropriate, the equivalent value in money be sent, and further resolved to send 'greate gunns' to the value of forty marks 'and not above' (1 mark = 13s 4d = ⅔ of one pound £) or £26 13s 4d. The calculation on p.127 shows that their purchaser did! Following a decision to provide wheat, it was ordered that

Drapers MR f. 15v

> There shal be bought and provided by the court of y^e wardens such and so manie greate gunns and ordinance to be sent & given to ye citty of Londonderry in Ireland (as of ye free guift of this company) for ye better safety and defence of that place and shall in value amount unto ye some of Forty Marks and not above.

It is unfortunate that the accounts are very badly damaged at the margins, so that information has been lost.

f. 54 [left-hand margin damaged]	
[–] paid for boat hier when ye irish committee were imployed [abo]ut ye companies corne that was sent for Ireland ye some of	v^s iiij^d [5s 4d]
[I]tem paid for ye watching & looking to of two peeces of ordinance [bo]ught by ye company to be sent to London Derry aforesaid for [–] better defence against ye rebells there ye some of	iij^s vj^d [3s 4d]
[–] for 4 white feathers[5] for iiij men of ye company to [–]t and appointed to train amongst ye trained band y^e [some of]	xxx^s [30s]
[–] for 4 white feathers[5] for iiij men of ye company to [–] given and sent to London Derry whereby to make it [–]t they are of ye companies guift to that place the [some of]	x^s [10s]
f. 55 [right-hand margin damaged]	
Item paid for two minions bought by ye company to be sent to London Derry for ye better defence of that place against ye rebels there ye same two peeces weighing [weight figures missing] a^t xiij^s vj^d [13s 6d] per C^t ye some of	xx[–] [20–]
Item paid for carriadges for ye same peeces and ye painting of them ye some of	xvj[–] [26–]
Item paid for shott powther and other things for & about ye triall of those peeces ye some of	[–] [–]

A6 THE WORSHIPFUL COMPANY OF FISHMONGERS

On 28 March 1642, The Court of Assistants decided to provide one demi-culverin to Derry (*Fishmongers CR* 3, f. 578), and the record of this is followed by a further resolution of the court to send wheat to Ireland. This followed the payment on 22 March of £75 into the general fund administered by Robert Bateman, Chancellor of the City of London (*Fishmongers AC* 1, f. 116).

Fishmongers CR 3, f. 578

> A Demy Culvering to be provided for London Derry
>
> This day uppon reading a ltr from the right ho^{ble} the Lord Maior of this Citty dated the eighteenth of March instant directed to this company for enlarging their voluntary contribution for reliefe of London Derry by providing one or more peeces of Artillary for the sayd City of London Derry uppon consultation had Itt was now thought fitt and agreed to provide a demy culvering for the defence of the sayd City of London Derry to bee in readines whensoever his Lo^r.pp shall bee pleased to require the same and send it away for the sayd City of London Derry and that Lo.pp shall be hereof certified by the wardens of this company.

Later, at the Court held on 9 May 1642, the Company decided to keep up with the Jones and to add a carriage and ammunition to their contribution.

Fishmongers CR 3, ff 589 – 590

> Demyculveryng &c for London Derry
>
> Item this court understanding that most companyes doe give a Carriage & Bullets

Appendix A – Contemporary Documents Relating to the Londonderry Ordnance

*Rammers & Spuinge w.*th *such appurte-n*^a*nces to bee sent w.*th *their ordinance into Ireland itt is therefore by this court that Mr Warden Greene do buy the like and send them away with this companyes demyculveringe for the defence of London Derry in Ireland.*

The following year, on 5 June 1643, the Town Clerk of Londonderry, Robert Goodwin, petitioned the Court of Assistants for powder, but a decision was deferred.

Fishmongers CR 3, f. 669

London Derry

Item this day Mr. Goodwin Townclerke of London Derry in Ireland moved this Courte to give two barrells of Gunpowder and cwt of Match to bee sent to London Derry towards the supply of their want thereof therewith to be considered of the next Court.

In fact, the request was not considered until the Court held on (*ibid.* 3, f. 684) 31 July and then the outcome was to wait to see what the other companies might do. Both the Skinners and Vintners responded positively with gifts of powder and so, although there are no further references to the subject and nothing in the accounts, it is not impossible that the Fishmongers drew from their stores to supply the City.

Fishmongers CR 3, f. 684

Powder and Match for London Derry

This day uppon the humble petition of the Maior and Commonality and Citizens of the City of London Derry in Ireland for some Gunpowder and Match Pickaxes Shovells and Spades for the defence of the said Citty itt is thought fitt and ordered by this Court that when other Companyes of this Citty shall contribute in this kind Mr Wardens of this Company or any two of them doe cause three barrells of Gunpowder and one hundred weight and a halfe of Match parcell of this Companyes and therefore to bee delivered for the defence of the said Citty of London Derry to such person as shall be authorized to convey the same thither.

Sadly, the company accounts for the relevant period have been badly water damaged, so that the entry relating to the cannon is barely legible.

Fishmongers AC 1, f.136

> Paid then to Warden [–] Allen for money by him paid to Mr Samuell fferrers therupon a bill signed for a Demy culverynge with the appurtenances sent by this Company to London Derry in Ireland by order of Courte   xxxviii^{li} xiiij
> [£38 14s 0d]

A7 WORSHIPFUL COMPANY OF GOLDSMITHS

The Goldsmiths debated the precept of 18 January at a Court held on 30 January (*Goldsmiths CM 1639–1642*, ff 169v–r), deciding like the other Companies to provide money and corn to Ireland in general, but with specific mention of relief for Londonderry. They replied to Gurney on 4 March (*ibid.* f. 174r), confirming their readiness to send wheat on demand. The precept of 18 March was discussed at a Court on 24 March 1642.

Goldsmiths CM 1639–1642, ff 181v–181r

f. 181v *Ireland*

At this Court was read a letter from his Lor^p *dated the 18*th *of this instant & directed as before the contente thereof intimateing that whereas the City of London Derry is built and fortified at the charge of the Companyes of this Cittye for the present in great danger by the Rebellion in Ireland for p*^{re}*vencon whereof upon mocon att the last Comon Counsell itt was agreed that the Companyes should enlarge their late voluntarye contribucon for releefe of London Derry by addicon of some ordinance to bee provided for that Cittye and that his Lor*^p *should recomend the same to the severall Companyes whereof his Lor*^p *notifieinge the same to this Companye by the aforesaid letter doth desire that upon consultacon they would resolve of doeinge somethinge therein by proveidinge one or more peeces of Artillery for the said Cittye of London Derry and his Lor*^p *to understand thereof with convenient speed w*th *letter beeinge taken into consideracon by this Courte itt is agreed & soe ordered that this Companye will freely give one iron peece of Artillery fitt for service beseeminge the gift of this Companye (all things considered) w*th [f. 181r] *the carriage and appurtenaunces thereof belongeinge and to bee provided so soone as possible may bee wherein the Wardens care & expedition is desired callinge unto them such of the Assistants as they thinke fitt to be assistinge unto them in provision thereof And to let his Lor[p] understand the Companyes resolution therein as occasion shalbee offered.*

Unfortunately, the accounts for the period have not survived.

A8 WORSHIPFUL COMPANY OF SKINNERS

The Court Records of the Company show no specific mention of provision of ordnance for Derry although, as with the other Companies, there is the standard reference in a resolution of 25 January 1641 to offer relief (*Skinners CR 3*, f. 193r) for the 'woefull and miserable estate of the protestants in Ireland'. The Company recorded its intention to involve their affiliates in the Companies of Girdlers, Stationers and Bakers. The Court Minutes, however, make no mention of the precept of 18 March and, unlike those of the other participating companies, they contain no reference to the purchase of ordnance. Nevertheless, the accounts for 1641–1642 (*Skinners AC 6*, f. 783) show expenditure on a 'peece of ordinance sent to London Derry' in their financial year which (like those of all of the Companies) ran from Lady Day (25 March) to Lady Day of the following year.[6]

There is no reference to ordnance anywhere in the accounts for 1641–1642, but in those of the following financial year, 1642–1643, we find the purchase of a cannon from the East India Company (*Skinners AC 6*, f. 814), the weight of which indicates strongly that it is the full culverin listed by the Reverend Winter in his account of the events of 1641–1642 (see p.123). It seems that as with modern accounting practice, expenses from one financial year were held back to the next.

The Skinners, along with the Vintners (possibly also the Fishmongers – see A6 above), were one of three companies which, on 15 August 1643, considered a request from Derry for powder and match (*Skinners CR 3*, f. 205v).

two barrells of powder for Ireland

> *At this Courte upon the humble request of Mr Goodwin and Mr Barrington Agents for London Derry Itt is ordered and agreed that two barrells of gun powder and one hundredweight of match shalbee att the Companyes charge sent over to Ireland, and Mr ffelgate is intreated to provide, and furnish the same, and to bee paid by Mr Renter Warden.*

Their accounts for year 1643–1644 show this payment on f. 853.

	l	s	d
f. 783			
Paid to the smyth; painter and other workmen for worke done about the peece of ordinance sent to London Derrye	011	08	06
Paid M[r] ffelgate upon two bills about the same ordinance	006	07	02
f. 814			
Paid the East India Companye for a peece of ordinance cont. 43[c] weight att 12[s] per cent	025	16	00
f.853			
Paid Mr. ffelgate for 2 barrells of powder and a hundred of match sent by order of Court to London Derry	010	18	00

A9 WORSHIPFUL COMPANY OF MERCHANT TAYLORS

This resolution of the Court of Wardens of 1 April 1642, follows on directly from the precept sent to the Companies by Sir Richard Gurney.

Merchant Taylors CM 5, f. 145

> *2 demy culvering to be provided*
>
> *Whereupon it is ordered that the Wardens and Captaine Langham and M[r] Stone shall take care to provide two demy culverings with the furniture thereunto or such other ordinance as they shall think be fitter*

for that purpose soe that the charge thereof doth not exceed one hundred marks which our Master is to pay and this order to bee his dischardge.

The Company accounts for 1642 show payment for the two demi-culverins. Unlike the records of the Grocers, Drapers and Vintners, however, the accountant has scattered the various items throughout the accounts, and so the ordering shown below is that of other Company accounts headings.

Merchant Taylors AC 18, ff 19v–r, 20r and 40r

	li	s
f. 19r		
Item paid to Mr fferers for two demy culverings which the Company did send towards ye furnishing London Derry for defence against the rebells and for other things thereto ye bill	67	8
f. 19v		
Item paid to Mr. Ffelgate for tryinge ye ordinance per bill	6	9
f. 20r	s	d
Item paid to William ffranklin for loading and carriadge of the ᵈⁱ culverings wᶜʰ were sent for Ireland and things thereabouts per bill	21	6
f. 40r		
Item paid Abraham Preston for ingravinge the culverines	s 10	

It would appear that the accounts clerk mixed up the payments for Felgate and Franklin, given their respective roles in this business. In answer to the earlier precept, the Company (*ibid.* f. 18v) also paid over £200 to the general relief fund.

A10 WORSHIPFUL COMPANY OF SALTERS

The Salters' Accounts for the period have not survived. However, there is a brief entry in the Court Minutes for 22 March 1642.

Salters CM 1627–1684, f. 237

Ireland & Ordnance

Upon the motion of Mr. Jacob Garrad that this Court will be pleased to furnish and bestow a piece of Ordnance to be sent for the first service, This Court perceiving it to be a fit and good gift are willing that there shall be a piece brought of such worth and goodness as the Master and Wardens shall think fit and the Company's name to be engraven thereon to be delivered for that service.

A11 WORSHIPFUL COMPANY OF IRONMONGERS

The Court held on 23 March decided to send one piece of ordnance with accessories (*Ironmongers CR* 4, f. 367), while the accounts list their donation as being a saker.

A peece of Iron to be provided for the fortifying of London Derry

Also a ltr from his Loᴾᴾ: of the 18ᵗʰ of this month was read. The assosiate Comppˢ being present wherein his Loᴾᴾ doth recomend from the Comon Counsell that this Compᵃ would provide one or more pcs of Artillery for the fortifying of the Citty of London Derry in Ireland wᶜʰ is in great danger there Whereunto answere is returned wᵗʰ Consent of the Assotiate Comppˢ that they will provide for that service one good saker peece of Iron ordnance wᵗʰ carriage ladles spunges ramers and appurtenances thereunto belonging.

The associates referred to were the Brewers, Pewterers, Carpenters, Barber-Surgeons, Coopers and Scriveners, and the Barber-Surgeons and Cutlers at least gave specifically towards relief of the distress of Londondcrry, although with no mention of ordnance. At a Court on 7 March (*Barbers CM* 5, f. 293) the Barber-Surgeons decided[7] that

. . . xxˡⁱ shalbe presently payd over towards the reliefe of London Derry and not more at the present . . .

On the same day (*Cutlers CR* 1, unpaginated, dated 7 March) the Cutlers gave 40 marks (1 mark = 13s 4d = ⅔ of a pound £) or £26 13s 4d to alleviate 'the miserable distresse of London Derry in Ireland '.

The Ironmongers' Accounts for 1641–1642 are reasonably detailed and show that, as with other companies, they bought their saker from Samuel Ferrers.

Ironmongers WA 5, ff 251–252

The cost and charges of an Iron Saker w^t 25^C ½^{qtr} sent for the citty of London derry viz	
Paid to Samuell fferrers for the peece carriadges Iron work wheeles etc	26. 16. -
Paid William ffranklin for trying of the peece	. 8. 6
Paid William ffelgate for 30 Iron Shott ladles Spring wadhooks linstock priming iron and horse	01. 17. 4
ffor proofe powder at the tryall of the peece etc	. 15. 10

There appears to be an error of recording in the 1660 inventory (A14.1 below), since the weight of the saker is given here as 25cwt ½qtr 0lb (see A.11 above), and 35cwt in the inventory, far too high for a normal saker. To illustrate, if we take the cost per cwt as 13s 6d, then at 35cwt, this piece would have cost in the region of £23 12s 6d, leaving only some £3 3s 6d for the carriage and all of its fittings, something only possible if it had been mounted only on a ship's carriage (p. 133, note 37). And if this was not the case, then with the average cost of the carriages which came in 1642 is in the region of £8 18s 6d, thus indicating that the Ironmongers may have paid somewhat over the odds for their gun at 14s 3d per cwt. But the much more likely explanation is simple scribal error in 1660, since in the inventories of 1674 and 1684 there is one saker referred to as weighing 25cwt.

A12 WORSHIPFUL COMPANY OF VINTNERS

In response to the precept of 18 January, the Vintners (*Vintners CR* 4, f. 71) decided at a Court held on 15 January 1642 to offer assistance, but waited until they saw what the contributions of the other Companies would be. However, at the next Court held 3 February (*ibid.* f. 71), the decision was reached to contribute to the 'reliefe of the distressed Protestants in Ireland, who are grievously oppressed by the papistical rebels there'. When Gurney issued his second precept for the provision of cannon, the affiliates of the Vintners – all but the Tylers and Bricklayers[8] – declined to contribute when summoned to a Court held on 24 March (*ibid.* ff 75–76)

f. 75 ye companies interested in Ireland do deny to contribute towards ye peece of artillery.
At this Co^{rt} of all the companies who are interested with this company in London derry were comanded to appear here this day & there appeared some members of the severall companies hereafter mentioned viz Woodmongers, Weavers Plombers, Poulterers, Blacksmiths, Fruiterers & Curriers^1 to whom ye ltr of ye Mayor dated ye 19th of this instant March [f. 76] was openly read concerning ye providing of one or more peeces of artillery to be sent to London derry for reliefe of ye same and said companies returned answer for ye present they are not willing to contribute towards ye providing of ye said artillery; it is now therefore ordered and thought fitt ye further consideracon shalbee taken of this busines.

Nevertheless, at their next Court on 14 April, the Vintners resolved to send a demi-culverin with accessories (*ibid.* f. 76).

f. 76 One demiculvering of iron & carriage & other necessaries to bee sent to Ireland
This day ye Master wardens and assistants here assembled taking into consideracon ye great troubles now in Ireland and particularly the desires of the common councell of this City signified by a ltr from Sir Richard Gurney Lo: Mayor of this Citty for ye furnishing the city of London Derry in Ireland with great ordynance whereof there is greate need, has now agreed and thought fitt one demiculvering of iron shall bee forthwth provided with a carriage and all other instruments thereonto belonging at the charge of this company and sent with all convenient speed, and that our Master and Mr Ashwell Mr Gardiner wardens and Mr Rbt Child shall provide the same and Mr Warden Gardiner to pay for it and the charges thereonto belonging.

The Company responded to the request from Londonderry for further assistance in 1643, deciding on 18 May 1643, to send gunpowder and match (*ibid.* f. 112). There is no corresponding entry in the Company accounts, although as the entry suggests, it would most likely have been drawn from their store of arms and ammunition.

It is ordered that two barrells of gunpowder wth a proporcon of match answerable thereunto shalbee delivered to Mr Robt Goodwin, to bee by him sent to London Derry in Ireland from this company for ye better provision, furniture & defence of that citty against ye rebells in Ireland.

The company accounts show both the financial contribution towards the general fund for the 'distressed subjects in Ireland' and the costs of providing the demi-culverin (*Vintners WA 4*, July 1641–July 1642).

According to the same accounts, the company spent on entertainment ('dinners') in 1641–1642 the sum of £220 8s 11d!

April 1	To the pole office towards the reliefe of the most distressed subjects in Ireland as by an aquittance may appeare	100 00 00
May 26	To Mr fferrers for a demy culveryng w^t 30^c 1^{qr} at 13^s 6^d per cwt	20 09 04
	ffor graveing the wheeles and carriages	00 03 06
	To Bateman the wheelwright for wheeles & other materialls as by bill	02 12 06
	To the smith for shooing the wheeles with iron	03 03 06
	To the paynter for colouring the carriage and wheeles	00 17 00
	To the carriage maker	03 00 00
	To M^r ffranklin for prooving the peece and other disbursem^{ts} as by bill	00 11 00
	To M^r ffelgate for powder shot ladle spunge for shipping the peece and carriage & for other particulars as by his bill	03 11 00
	To Mr Preston for graveing the demiculvering	00 05 00

A13 THE WORSHIPFUL COMPANY OF CLOTHWORKERS

The company subscribed to the general relief fund (*Clothworkers AC* 1639–1649 f. 11v) controlled by Sir Robert Bateman. This entry has beside it a marginal date of 'March 25th 1642' and thus, presumably, is part of a group forming the end-of-year accounting.

Item paid to Sir George Whitmore and Sir Robert Bateman, Chamberlaine of this Cittie fowerscore poundes which was given by a Court of Assistants towards the releife of the distressed Protestants in Ireland as appears by their acquitance of the seaventeenth of March 1641.

A meeting of the Court of Assistants of the Clothworkers on 23 March (*Clothworkers CO* 1639–1649, ff 146r–147v) instructed its Quarter Warden, Captain Edmund Forster, to buy a saker, with carriage and all accessories.

ff 146r–147v

Court of Assistants 23rd March 1641: A Sacar provided for Londonderry

Whereas the right hono^{ble} the Lord Maior of this City by his letter of the 18th of this instant month, did signify unto this Board that the City of Londonderry being built and fortified at the charge of the Companies of this City is now in greate danger by the Rebellion in Ireland, and that the preservation thereof is of much concernement, especially for this City there, and that at the last Common Council it was propounded that the Companies of this City should enlarge their contribution for the reliefe of Londonderry, by the addition of some ordinance to be provided for that City, and that his Lordship should recommend the same to the severall Companies as by the said letter may more at large appeare. This daie upon reading of the said letter in open Court and upon due consideration had of the premisses, It is ordered & agreed that this Company with all convenient speede shall out of the money belonginge to the stock of this house provide and furnish one piece of Artillary called a Sacar, with the carriage and other the appurtenances, for *the better defence of the said Citty, And that these wordes shall be thereupon engraven vizt The Clothworkers of London 1642 as well to distinguish it from others as to be knowne to be the proper goods and chattells of this Company. And Cap^n Edmund Forster the present QuarterWarden is hereby requested (assisted with any two or more Assistants of this Company whome he shall think fitt to make the choice of) to buy and provide the same, and of the tenor of this present order, the Clerke of this Company is hereby appointed to signify the Lord Mayor, in answer to his said letter.*

A brief note in the Irish Accounts (*Clothworkers IA* 1620–1671, f. 8v) records

1641 Item paid for warlike provision for London Derry £26 13s 09d forster

However, the full record of expenditure is to be found in *Clothworkers AC* 1639–1649, f. 11v, which belongs to the same grouping as the report of payment to the relief fund. This totals to £26 13s 09d, corresponding to the figure recorded in the Irish accounts. The accountant has made an error in recording the price per cwt of the saker, but the figure given as paid for the saker is correct for 13s 6d per cwt.

Item paid to Mr Stilgoe for a carriadge for a Sacar which was provided by this Company and shipt in the Charity of London William Younge Master to be delivered at London Derry to the said Cittie by this Companie for the better defence thereof together with payntinge the said carriadge as per bill appears	£ 8 17s 6d
Item paid Mr W[illia]m Felgate for powder to trie the Sacar and for shott sponges ladles etc and charges in shippinge of it as per bill appears	£ 2 12s 6d
Item paid Mr Samuell Ferres [Ferrers] for an iron Sacar which was sent to London Derry as above said it weighed 22 C[wt] ½ which at 16s 6d pro C[wt] comes to as per bill appears	£15 3s 9d

The Clothworkers were also receptive to the further appeal made to them in 1643 for munitions and supplies. At a Court held on 7 March (*Clothworkers CM* f. 81v), is it recorded that

This day upon the humble petition of the Maior and Comonalitie and Citizens of the City of Londonderry, to bestowe upon them somme powder and match spades shovells and pickaxes, as this Company shall think fitt. It is ordered and agreed that they shall have two barrells of gunpowder and 100 weight [1cwt] of match out of the store of this company, and likewise one dozen of spades and dozen of shovells and one dozen of pickaxes, to be provided by the Quarter Wardens of this Company out of the moneys belonging to the stock of this house.

And in the corresponding accounts (*Clothworkers AC* 12 August 1643), we find

Item pd for 12 spades, 12 shovells and 12 pickaxes which were given by this Company to London Derry, and for 6 pickaxes more for this Companyes use	£004 01s 00d

A14 THREE INVENTORIES OF THE LONDONDERRY STORES 1660–1684

Surviving records of the Irish Ordnance Office are sparse for the first half of the seventeenth century, and it is not really until after the Restoration that regular and detailed reports start to be available for the City. This section makes no pretence to offer a detailed or comprehensive survey, but is rather included as illustrative, giving three of the more detailed examples, copies of which can be found in the Carte MSS, the Carew MSS, the various War Office series and in manuscripts in the National Library of Ireland. Each of these lists is part of an overall inventory of stores in the various principal fortifications in Ireland, and they provide snapshots of the contents of the City magazine and that of Culmore at different points in time. Noticeably, Londonderry and Culmore are usually grouped together, although not infrequently Culmore is absent. And from time to time, even substantial inventories covering a number of fortifications in Ireland (e.g. *Carte MSS* 30, ff 119r–123v, dated 26 July 1622 and *Carte MSS* 54, f. 608, dated 5 June 1678) have no reference to Londonderry and/or Culmore.

Appendix A – Contemporary Documents Relating to the Londonderry Ordnance

A14.1a A True and Perfect Inventory of Such Gunns and Other Artillery as are received by Mr Hugh Barclay the Younger Clerk of his Mat's Stores this 23rd March 1660[9] (*NA* WO 55/1752, f. 102).

Londonderry In the Cittidell	C	qr	li
Imprimis one Demy Culverin of Iron mounted but the Carridg and Wheeles Rotten, of the Mercers London, qt	35	2	14
Item one Demy Culvering of iron unfixt of ye said Mercers qt	36	–	–
More one Demy Culverin of Iron mounted but ye Carridge and wheels rotten of the Marchant Taylors London conteyning	34	0	14
More one small Peece of Brass Mounted but the carridg rotten contayning	1	3	15*
More one Brass Drake unmounted Conteyning	190li		
More one Brass Drake unmounted Conteyning	188li		
More one Demy Culverin of Iron Mounted but ye Carridge rotten of the Fishmongers conteyning	35	3	–
More one Demy Culverin of Iron Mounted but ye carridge rotten of ye Vintners conteyning	30	1	–
More one Demy Culverin unmounted Conteyning	33	3	–
More one Drake Brass unmounted Conteyning	188li		
More one Demy Culverin unmounted of the Marchant Taylors contayning	36	–	14
More one Iron Saker unmounted weight	21	2	–
More one Minion Cut unmounted of Iron Conteyning	479li		
Item foure Small Field peeces of Brass in a frame decayed	–	–	–
More one Iron falcon Unmounted	–		
More one Demy Culverin Salters qt	26C	Unmounted	Unmounted
More one Minion cutt of Iron qt	492li	Unmounted	Unmounted
More one Demy Culverin Goldsmiths qt	30C	Unmounted	Unmounted
More one Saker Clothworkers qt (ye Carridg Decayed)	22C	2qr	mounted
More one Minion of Iron Drapers qt	16C	Unserviceable	Unserviceable
More one Saker Iron Mongers[10] qt	35C	Unmounted	Unmounted
More one Demy Culvering Grocers qt	35C	1qr	Mounted but not Serviceable
More one Minion Mounted but not Servicable Drapers qt	16C	1qr	–
More one Dimy Culvering Mounted but not Servicable Grocers qt	36	1	14
More one Falcon of Iron unmounted qt	1000 li wt		
More one Brass Drake mounted but carridg rotten qt	190li		
Item Three old Demy Culverin Ladles, one saker Ladle foure Spunges & 1 worme One minion Ladle			
* the scribe corrected this value from 25.			

223

Imprimis five Iron Sakers	1 weighing	2700	
	1 weighing	2700	
	1 weighing	2700	
	1 weighing	2700	
	1 weighing	2100	
Item two Minions of Iron	1 weighing	1900	
	1 wth a broken Mussle wt	1700	
Item two Demy Culverins	1 weighing	3700	
	1 weighing	3700	
Item two ffaucons	1 weighing	1300	
	1 weighing	1300	

A14.1b A True Inventory of What Artillery and Amunicon I received in the Fort and Castle of Culmore upon the 25th of March 1660 (*NA WO 55/1752, f. 103*)

Nine Spunges and Ladles Half a Barrell of Powder Forty Skains of Match Seaven Barrells of Muskett bullits Seaventy two Serviceable Muskett Barrells & Seaven hundred great shott after fifty percent

A14.2a Ordnance Amunicon and other Stores & Habiliam^{ts} of Warr Remaineing in his Ma:^{ts} Citty & Store of Londonderry taken ye 9th day of July 1674 (*NA WO 55/1752 ff 245–246*).

		Length of ye Peece feet inches		Weight	Number	
Brass Ordnance	Three pounders	02	03	—	4	} unmounted
	Faulconett Drakes	02	00	—	04	
Iron Ordnance	Di Culvering blowne	10	00	33: 3: 00	—	1
	Di Culvering	09	00	30: 1: 00	—	1
	Di Culvering blowne	10	00	35: 3: 00	—	1
	Di Culvering	10	00	36: 0: 00	—	1
	Di Culvering	10	00	35: 2: 00	—	1
	Di Culvering	10	00	34: 0: 14	—	1
	Di Culvering	10	00	36: 0: 14	—	1
	Di Culvering	08	00	26: 0: 00	—	1
	Di Culvering	10	00	36: 0: 14	—	1
	Di Culvering	10	00	35: 2: 14	—	1
	Saker	09	00	25: 0: 00	—	1
	Saker hony Comb'd & Seal'd	10	00	—	—	1
	Saker	09	00	23: 0: 00	—	1
	Saker Cutt of at the Muzle & hony Comb'd	07	03	21: 2: 00	—	1
	Mynion	07	06	16: 1: 00	—	1
	Mynion	07	06	16: 0: 14	—	1
	Faulcon	07	06	10: 0: 00	—	1
	Faulcon	03	10	— 482^l —	—	1
	Faulcon	03	10	— 472 —	—	1
	Faulcon blowne & unserviceable	05	03	—		01

		Serv^{bl}	Unserv^{bl}
Round Shott for	{ Culvering stone	62	
	Di Culvering	431	
	Saker	077	
Ladles for	{ Di Culvering	–	02
	Saker	–	01
Rammers		–	02
Powder		3 barr^{lls} –	1 barr^{ll} Decayed
Standing Carridges Broake		00	02
Gin and Block with 2 brass Sheevs		00	01

The aforesaid particulars were viewed and remaineth in charge wth Capt Hugh Barclay clerke of the Stores in the said Citty of London^{derry} the Day and yeare above written. (*Jonas Moore / W. Robinson*)

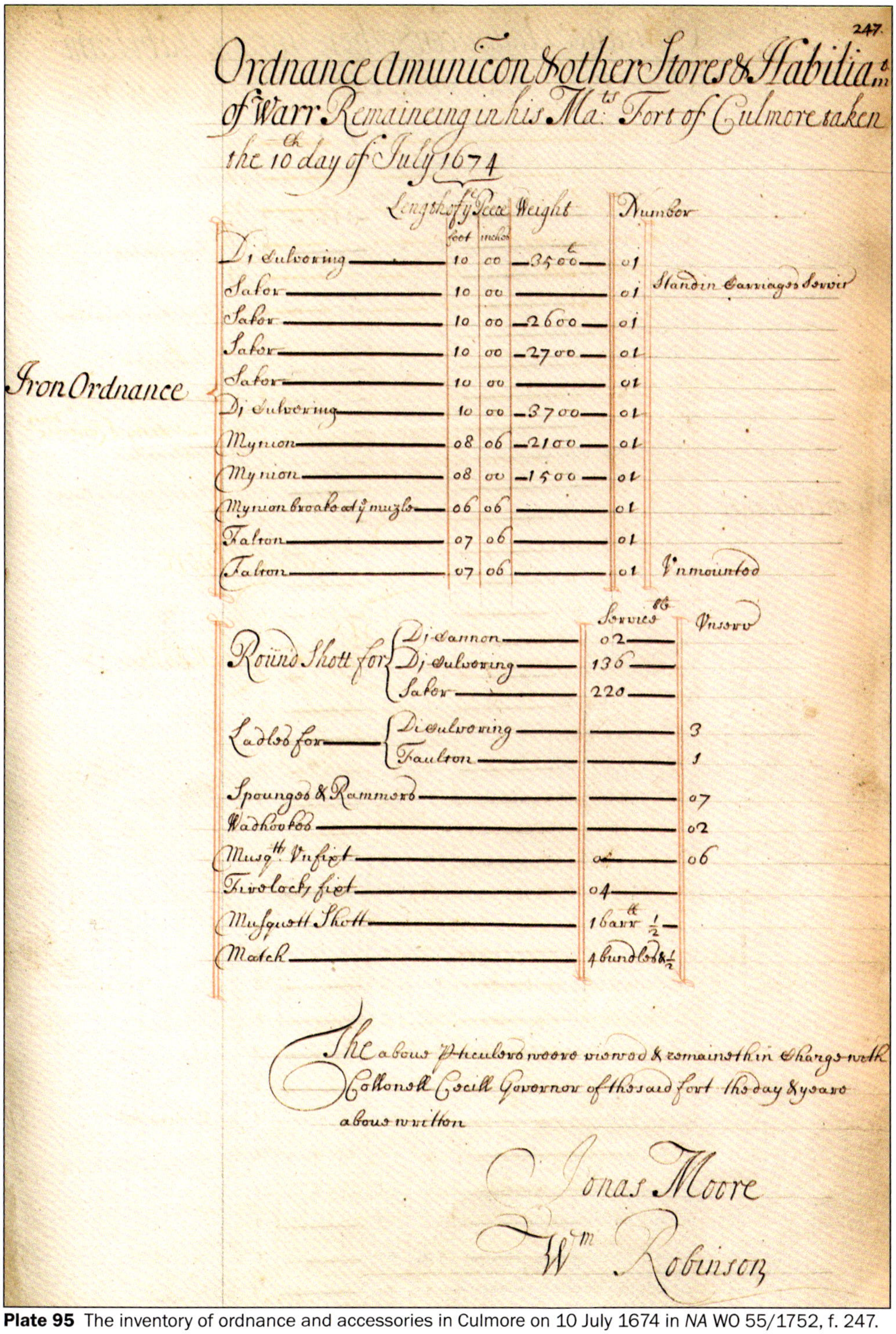

Appendix A – Contemporary Documents Relating to the Londonderry Ordnance

Ordnance Amunicon & other Stores & Habilim[ts] of Warr: Remaineing in his Ma[ts] Fort of Culmore taken the 10th day of July 1674

		Length of y[e] Peece		Weight	Number	
		feet	inches			
Iron Ordnance	D[i] Culvering	10	00	3500	01	
	Saker	10	00		01	Standin Carriages Servis:
	Saker	10	00	2600	01	
	Saker	10	00	2700	01	
	Saker	10	00		01	
	D[i] Culvering	10	00	3700	01	
	Mynion	08	06	2100	01	
	Mynion	08	00	1500	01	
	Mynion broake at y[e] muzle	06	06		01	
	Falcon		07	06	01	
	Falcon		07	06	01	Vnmounted

		Servis:ble	Vnserv:ble
Round Shott for	D[i] Cannon	02	
	D[i] Culvering	136	
	Saker	220	
Ladles for	D[i] Culvering		3
	Faulcon		1
Sponges & Rammers			07
Wadhookes			02
Musq[tt] vn fixt		04	06
Fire locks fixt		04	
Musquett Shott		1 barr ½	
Match		4 bundles & ½	

The above P[ar]ticulers weere viewed & remainsth in Charge with Collonell Cecill Governour of the said fort the day & yeare above written

Jonas Moore
W[m] Robinson

Plate 95 The inventory of ordnance and accessories in Culmore on 10 July 1674 in NA WO 55/1752, f. 247.

A14.2b Ordnance Amunicon and other Stores & Habiliam[ts] of Warr Remaineing in his Ma:[ts] Fort of Culmore Taken the 10th day of July 1674 (Plate 95: *NA* WO 55/1752, f. 247).

		Length of y[e] Peece feet inches		Weight	Number	
Iron Ordnance	Di Culvering	10	00	– 3500[li] –	01	
	Saker	10	00	–	01	Standin Carriages Servic[bl]
	Saker	10	00	– 2600 –	01	
	Saker	10	00	– 2700 –	01	
	Saker	10	00	–	01	
	Di Culvering	10	00	– 3700 –	01	
	Mynion	08	06	– 2100 –	01	
	Mynion	08	00	– 1500 –	01	
	Mynion broake at y[e] Muzle	06	06	–	01	
	Falcon	07	06	–	01	
	Falcon	07	06	–	01	Unmounted

			Serv[bl]	Unserv[bl]
Round Shott for	{	Di Cannon	62	
		Di Culvering	431	
		Saker	077	
Ladles for	{	Di Culvering	–	3
		Faulcon	–	1
Standing and Rammers			–	07
Wadhookes			–	02

The aforesaid particulars were viewed and remaineth in charge wth Collonell Cecil Governor of the said Fort London[derry] the Day and yeare above written. (Jonas Moore / W. Robinson)

A14.3 Ordnance Armes and Ammunition remaining in these stores of Londonderry and Culmore the 25th of March 1684 (*Ormond MSS* I, 393–394, *Carte MSS* 66, ff 440–441).

	In Londonderry	Length	Weight	Number	Notes
Iron Ordnance	Demy Culvering	10: –	33:3:–	1	Standing carriage defective
	Demy Culvering	10: –	35:3: –	1	Standing carriage defective
	Demy Culvering	10: –	36: –:–	1	Standing carriage – the wheels new
	Demy Culvering	10: –	35:2: –	1	Standing carriage serviceable
	Demy Culvering	10: –	34: –:14	1	Standing carriage serviceable
	Demy Culvering	8: –	26: –:–	1	Standing carriages defective
	Demy Culvering	10: –	36: –:14	1	Standing carriages defective
	Demy Culvering	10: –	35:2:14	1	Standing carriage serviceable
	Demy Culvering	9: –	30:1: –	1	Standing carriage defective
	Demy Culvering	10: –	36: –:14	1	Standing carriage serviceable
	Saker honeycombed and clogged	10: –	20: –:–	1	Standing carriage defective
	Saker	9: –	25: –:–	1	Standing carriage – the wheels new
	Saker	9: –	22:2: –	1	Standing carriage serviceable
	Saker cutt off at the muzzle	7:3	21:2: –	1	Standing carriage serviceable
	Mynion	7:6	16: –:–	1	Standing carriage serviceable
	Mynion	7:6	16: –:14	1	Standing carriage serviceable
	Falcon	7:4	10: –:–	1	Standing carriage serviceable
	Falcon	3:8	:482	1	Standing carriage – the wheels defective
	Falcon	3:8	:472	1	Standing carriage – the wheels defective
	Falconet blown and unserviceable	5:3	:700 per est	1	Standing carriage serviceable

Continued over ▶

Appendix A – Contemporary Documents Relating to the Londonderry Ordnance

A14.3 Continued.

	In Culmore Fort	Length	Weight		Number	Notes
Brass ordnance	Three pounder cutts	2:3	190ˡⁱ 190ˡⁱ 188ˡⁱ 187ˡⁱ		4	Standing carriage serviceable
	Falconet cut	1:11	84ˡⁱ Est		1	Standing carriage serviceable
	Falconett cutts	1:11	84ˡⁱ Est		3	Standing carriage serviceable
Iron	Demy Culvering	9:10	3700		1	
	Demy Culvering	9:10	3700		1	
	Saker	9:10	2700		1	
	Saker	9:10	27 cwt		1	
	Saker	9:10	2700		1	
	Saker	9:10	27 cwt Est		1	
	Mynion	8:7	2100		1	
	Mynion	8: –	2100		1	
	Mynion broken at the muzzle	6:6	14 cwt per est		1	
	Falcon	7:6	12 cwt per est		1	
	Falcon	7:4	12 cwt per est		1	

	Round shot	
In Derry	For demy culvering	431
	For saker	77
In Culmore	For demy cannon	4
	For demy culvering	172
	For saker	180
	Stone shot in Derry for culvering	62

	Serviceable	Repairable	Unserviceable
Powder	31 barrels 36lb		1
Gynn for mounting guns, with 3 brasse sheaves and an old rope		1	
Ladles for saker and falcon			2
In Culmore			
Rammers and spunges			4
Wadd hookes			1
Rings for carriages			7

A15 A REPORT BY COLONEL WILLIAM LEGGE[11] ON LONDONDERRY

This Citty is Strongly seated by the great River of Lough foyle compassing the same on three sydes making a Goodly Capacious and Safe Haven. That ground to the landward is Marrish [=marsh] and with small cost may be cutt to bring the water quite round the towne. It is walled with a good Stone wall, Rampired and well Flankered in Good Repair, the Defects nothing considerable, save the want of Platformes upon the Bullwarkes.

The Towne is built upon a Steepe Rising Ground from the Haven on the highest part whereof (the whole length of the Towne from the Key) is their Church and Churchyard Joyning to the City Walls, of which the Late Usurpers made a Kinde of Cittadell Including the Church and part of the Churchyard, makeing the Steeple the Magazine. Here are some Twenty and odd Iron gunnes, serviceable in themselves, but all dismounted.

I found here the foot Company of Coll: Gorges the Governor and half of the foot Company of the Lo: Massarine the other halfe being at Antrim 50 miles distant from hence. The greatest part of the Inhabitants of Derry are Scotts as is all the country here abouts, indeed all Ulster over.

I moved to the Magistrates for Repairing the few defects, especially the Antient Storehouse (being a place very convenient for the Magazine) making Platformes for the Cannon and Mounting the same upon Carriages, the Gunnes having upon them the Markes and Armes of the Severall Companyes of London. I delivered an Estimate of the Charge to the Mayor, the repairing of the Store house he undertook and the Demolishing of some poor Cottages upon the walls, but the rest he must recommend to his Master in London.

The Towne is considerable for its strength and situation itt lyes upon a Noble Haven without Barrier or Lett twenty miles from the Sea into which Ships of great burden may enter without danger the same River flowing and being Navigable many miles further into the Land, but the people not Industrious nor well accomodated to make use of ye Conveniences ye place affords them.

Six foot Companies and 2 Troopes of Horse will be a good garrison in this Towne wch well ordered will have an Influence upon all of those Northerne parts of Ulster preserve ye poore and oblidg the people to Obedience; and those Troopes will be of farre greater use in this place, than as now disperst in privat villiages to preserve private Interests.

I was very much in wonder to see a place soe Commodiously seated for Trade and Navigation without a Seaman (only one man for a Pylotte) not soe much as a Fisherman inhabiting the same, nor one boate belonging to ye place save the Ferry which Carry horses cross the River. The greate defect here is the Inhabitants who are a very odd and meane mixture of people.

Culmore Castle lies three miles distant, down the River from this place. A Triangular work well designed in these times to command the Channel, the River running in form of a halfe moone about it and a Bogge on the Land Side. In y^e Late troubles there was a Large work begunn, to take in the grounde lying betweene y^e Bogge and Castle wch may containe 3 or 4 Acres of Land, but this worke was never finished, and my advice was to Demolish what was raised. Here is neither Store of cannon mounted. There is an Estabmishm^t of $19^s : 4^d$ per day for a Capt; a Gunner and tenn Warders; there are now to these two files of Musquetteers if Sr Francis Howards Company, the rest lying at Strabane the housing and wall much impaired, but if mended in time will Cost little and this I conceive the Cittizens of Londonderry obliged unto.

Extracted from a set of proposals dated of 12 July 1682 for the rationalisation of garrisons in Ireland (*in Carte MSS* 66, ff 408–409, undated, with another copy being dated 1662 in *NA* WO 55/1752, ff 153–158. Legge's comments on Londonderry and Culmore are contained in ff 154–156.)

A16.1 Abstract from *An Estimate of the Charge for repair of Magazines and Storehouses in the several Forts and Garrisons of Ireland*, dating to 1663 (*Carte MSS 54, ff 591–594*).

f. 594v	
Culmore ffort	
Platformes for 10 Gunnes to be mended	20 : 00 : 00
Ships carriages for 10 guns	30 : 00 : 00
Londonderry	
The Storehouse in the Citty is uncovered and the ffloors and walls defective, the Reparacon thereof will come to	160 : 00 : 00
Platformes new and to be repaired for 28 guns	60 : 00 : 00
Ships carriages for 28 Gunnes	84 : 00 : 00

A16.2 Abstract from *An Estimate of the Charge for putting into repair his Majesty's chief Fortifications & places of strength throughout Ireland*, dated October 1677 (*Carte MSS 59, ff 633–637*).

f. 636r		
Londonderry		
The walls in the Citty are in goode repaire kept at the Citty's charge, but there is wanting stone Platformes in 6 Bastions w^{ch}: comes to	60 l : –: –	
Standing carriages for 20 Gunns	130 l : –: –	} 340 l : –: –
The storehouse to be roofed and covered, 2 new Floors, stayers, doors windows	150 l : –: –	
Culmore		
The Bastions being small will not admit of		
Standing carriages therefore must be supplied With 10 shipp carriages for ye fort comes to	30 l : –: –	
Platformes wanting in two bastions	10 l : –: –	} 420 l : –: –
A magazine to be built in the Crown works	300 l : –: –	
A powder house in ye fort	80 l : –: –	

A17 EXTRACTS FROM THE DERRY CORPORATION MINUTES

Minutes of the Common Council of the City of Londonderry start in 1673 and run to 1686 (*Derry Corporation* I, 1673–1686), earlier records probably having been lost in the fire of 1668. There is then a hiatus, with records resuming in late 1689. Again, presumably those of the intervening years did not survive the Siege of that year. There are only a few entries for the earlier period relating to ordnance, and all but one relate to an attempt to retrieve cannon removed from the City by Sir Charles Coote, presumably after the Siege of 1649 and before the start of his campaigning in Connaught in 1651 (p. 118).

Derry Corporation

f. 18 – 1 July 1675

> *Ordered, that the gun carriages within this City be speedily repaired, and raised where they need, at the charge of the Chamber; And Mr John Burridge and Mr William Kyle by this Court appointed and Desired to assist Mr William Turkey in the oversight thereof.*
>
> *Ordered that a peticon be prepared to the Lord Lieutenant when it shall please God he shall returne from England, concerning the bras gunnes now at Galway and Slego [Sligo] belonging to this City.*

f. 28 – 2 September 1676

> *Also ordered, that a Petition be drawne by this said Comittee, to the Lord Lieu^t of this Kingdome, for leave to bring our bras gunnes from Galway and Slego, to this City, which were carried thither, in the time of the late warre.*

f. 91 – 5 April, 1682

> *Also from Geo. Phillips esq^r Govourno^r to Mr Major concerning three bras guns belonging to this City and Mr Willm Smyths*

answere thereunto in Mr Majors absence being read, Mr Smyths answere was approved of and left wth him.

f. 93 – 22 June 1682

Upon a motion concerning one bras Demy Canon sent from this Guarison by Sr Charles Coote then Comander in chiefe of ye parliamts forces in Ulster to some other part of this Kingdome, & now supposed to be in Kingsale [Kinsale] as carried thither from Galway by information of Wm Robison esqr, And one bras Culverin, and one bras faulcon now at Slego, as this Court is informed, Mr Mogridge and Mr Chamberlain now appointed to prepare a ltr to George Phillips esqr against Tuesday next.

Notes to Appendix A

1 This word is almost obliterated and cannot be read with certainty. One possibility is 'mariner', but in view of the London Port Book reference (p. 106), the more likely reading is 'merchant'.

2 'Mr Secretary Calvert' was Sir George Calvert, later Lord Baltimore, Clerk to the Privy Council and Secretary of State. We are most grateful to the late Bob Hunter for his kind assistance in transcribing this document.

3 The 'Windebank' who signed the licence was Francis Windebank, at this time a Clerk of the Signet, who later became Secretary of State and was knighted.

4 Formerly Miscellaneous Papers, Box 181, Bundle vi. A transcript of this manuscript is held in the Public Record Office of Northern Ireland, MS T/640/16. This information came to light late in the project and it has not been possible to research possible London documentary evidence in the London Metropolitan Archives as this institution was closed to the public between the discovery and the publication deadline. We are most grateful to Sarah Joy Maddeaux, National Archives of Scotland for assistance in locating the original and other documents in the collections there.

5 Rests for firearms.

6 Wadmore (1902, 276) wrote that *Londonderry had been fortified with culverins and sakers given by the Companies, some of which still remain on the city walls. It appears by the Renter Warden's accounts that the Skinners purchased a gun for £25 from the Hon. East India Company; that it weighed over 18 cwt., and that a further sum of £11 was paid for sending it by ship to Londonderry.*
However, there is no trace of any payment for shipping in the accounts for 1641–1642, or subsequent years and, given his error over the weight of the gun, it is likely that he mistook the payment of £11 8s 6d as shipping costs. Shipping was certainly only a minor cost to the Merchant Taylors and Vintners, being included with other goods and services in totals of 21s 6d and £3 11s 0d respectively. We are most grateful to Colm Hasson and Annesley Malley for drawing this reference to our attention.

7 They also decided (*ibid.*) to donate £200 to provide '*Generall Reliefe to Ireland*' with a down payment of £50, the remainder to follow within three months.

8 The Tylers and Bricklayers are not, in fact, mentioned at all.

9 We are most grateful to Guy Wilson for providing us with a transcript of the Londonderry section.

10 There appears to be an error of recording here – see A11 above.

11 William Legge was a veteran Royalist officer who rose to be Lieutenant-General of the Ordnance under Charles II.

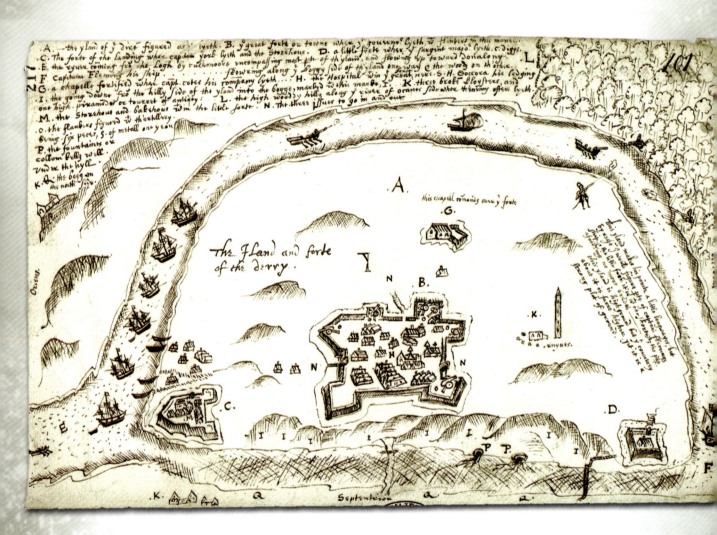

APPENDIX B
The Siting of the Derry Magazine in 1566

It is quite possible that a very early example of defences using angular bastions in Ireland can be found in the defences thrown up by the garrison established by Sir Henry Sidney as part of his campaign against Shane O'Neill. On 12 October 1566, Sidney joined up at Derry with forces under the command of Colonel Edward Randolph, Lieutenant of the Ordnance. He established a fortified base at Derry, stating in his memoirs (Brady 2002, 45) that

> . . . I left Tyrone and entered Tirconnell, where I found that renowned and worthy Colonel Mr Edward Randolph, with a regiment of seven hundred soldiers full well captained, chosen and appointed . . . There of an old church I made a new fort and being furnished with men, munition and victual, I left the colonel with his regiment in it and marched through Tirconnell . . .

After a winter of privation and sickness, and the death of Randolph in action against the forces of Shane O'Neill on 15 November 1566, the end came on 21 April 1567, when a fire that started in a smithy spread to the powder magazine (*Cal. SPI* 1507-1573, 332, 12 May 1567). The resulting catastrophic explosion killed at least thirty soldiers and injured many others, including Captain Gourley of the arquebusiers, who was struck by flying debris and lost a leg as a result. Questions were asked as to the possibility of 're-edifying the Derry' (*ibid.* 333, 12 May 1567) and, although it is possible that an attempt to reinforce the garrison and repair the defences was contemplated, the survivors abandoned the site, leaving Derry unfortified until the arrival of Sir Henry Docwra.

Catastrophic accidents involving gunpowder were by no means uncommon (pp 39*ff*), but since the English at Derry had placed their magazine on consecrated ground, the story naturally grew that the explosion was the result of divine intervention. One of those who repeated the folk-legend was Philip O'Sullivan Beare, writing sometime before 1621 (Byrne 1903, 4–5).

> *English heretics having landed in this town* [Derry], *they, against the wish and command of O'Donnell, expel the priests and monks, invade the holy churches, and in one church place for safe keeping gunpowder, leaden bullets, tow-match, guns, pikes, and other munition at war. In other churches they performed the heretical rites of Luther, left nothing undefiled by their wickedness . . . St. Columba (it is supposed) did not long delay the punishment of this sin. The natives confidently assert that a wolf of huge size and with bristling hair coming boldly out of the nearest wood to the town and entering the Iron barriers, emitting from his mouth a great number of sparks, such as fly from a red hot iron when it is struck, proceeded to the place in which the powder was stored and spitting out sparks set fire to powder and church. I will not take upon myself to vouch for the truth of this story: upon fancie and long-standing tradition let it rest. This which is admitted by all, I may assert, viz., that the gunpowder suddenly took fire, the English who were in the church were burnt up, and those who were patrolling round the church were struck with burning tiles and killed; those who fled to neighbouring houses or into the adjoining lake were killed by pursuing tiles, some of which were thrown five hundred paces from the town.*

Lacy (1988, 393) concurs with the general view that Sidney used the building known as the *Tempall Mór* as the nucleus of his camp, and for his magazine. The main problem with this identification is that the structure supposedly was all but roofless and derelict by 1469, and a roofless building is not the best of places in which to store hygroscopic powder in an Ulster autumn, especially when planning hostilities against the locals.[1] We must take account of two details in the account of O'Sullivan Beare, where he says that priests and monks were driven out and that the English performed the 'heretical rites of Luther in other churches'. Further, he suggested that casualties were caused by 'burning tiles' flung out by the blast, suggesting that the structure used for the magazine was indeed roofed. Other ecclesiastical buildings on the site included the *Dubreclés*, probably the original monastic church of Derry, and 'a ruined chapel or house of nuns' which Lacy (*ibid*. 394) notes as mentioned in inquisitions between 1603 and 1609. This latter is of particular interest because it is on the highest part of what was then the 'island' of Derry and for this reason was fortified in 1600 by Docwra in addition to the main works which he erected (p. 66). Docwra chose his main area for fortifications on high ground (*Docwra* 44), but also added an outwork

> . . . *a litle aboue, where the walls of an old Cathedrall church were yet standing, to evert annother for our future safetie & retreate vnto upon all occasions.*

Plate 96 The 'chapel' shown on *NA* SP 63/207, pt VI, no. 84/1. The legend over the image reads 'This chapell comandz over ye forte'. In the main text, against 'G' is found '. . . a chapelle fortified where capt. Cotes his company lyeth'.

At position 'G' on the 1600 plan of Derry (see Plate 45) is a simple structure, but by comparison with other conventions on the map, one to which has been added a single bastion at one end and some form of earthwork surrounding it (Plate 96).[2]

Docwra's comment that these defences, on what was the highest part of the land, would act as a refuge in time of difficulty is interesting. It is surely to be expected that an experienced soldier such as Randolph would have dictated the location for the Derry base, especially in view of the fact that it was Sidney's intention to take a significant proportion of the joint force to campaign elsewhere. Randolph thus knew that he and his troops were there for the duration, and would have been most careful to choose the best ground for a garrison that would have to remain anchored in hostile territory. Further, if Lacy is correct in his assessment that both *Tempall Mór* and *Dubreclés* were at best dilapidated in 1566 and that the 'ruined chapel or house of nuns' was, in fact the *ecclesia cathedrali Derensi* (Lacy 1988, 394) in 1590, then we can perhaps draw the strands together. A functioning church would certainly have been roofed over and serviced by priests, possibly also monks and this would seem to make this structure the most likely candidate to have been the first fortification.

O'Sullivan Beare noted particularly the deaths and injuries caused by flying 'tiles' both close to the church and wider afield, and it is hard to believe that comparatively flimsy wooden shingles would have done much damage at '500 paces'. Lacy (*ibid*. 393) mentions the possibility that *Tempall Mór* had been stone roofed, but notes that at a projected width of 13.7m, it was nearly three times the width of the oldest known stone-roofed structure in Ireland. However, while comparative scales on older maps are at best subjective, the 'old church' would seem to have been significantly smaller than either *Tempall Mór* or *Dubreclés*. One should also observe that Docwra noted 'a Quarrie of stone and slatt we found hard at hand' (*Docwra* 44), confirming that an adequate supply of building stone and roofing slate was available to the Irish builders of the ecclesiastical structures. On balance, therefore, it is not unlikely that Sidney and Randolph placed their magazine in a stone-built church with a slate roof, in other words the 'old church'.

The forces at Derry included at least 300 'harqubusiers' (*Cal. SPI* 1509–1573, 307–308, 5 June 1566), and a memorandum of 29 June 1566 (*ibid*. 307) recorded plans to send quantities of powder and match to the garrison. They also had a culverin (p. 81), which would have required mounting effectively. On 10 November, an order was given to the Ordnance Office to send from the Tower, amongst other supplies, seven lasts (1 last = 2400lb or 1089kg) of corn powder (*NA* SP 63/18 f. 82) to be supplied in double-casked barrels and shipped via Bristol.[3] It is not unreasonable to suggest that this consignment would not have reached Derry any earlier than around the end of December given the time of year amongst other things. In fact, probably in January 1567, it was noted that the garrison was short of munitions 'and furniture such as is wanting for the service at Derry . . . small tents meet for the camp.' (*ibid.* 326, January[?] 1567), while on 13 January 1567, Randolph's successor Colonel Edward St. Low[4] petitioned Dublin for more troops and a reduction in the price of victuals for the garrison (*ibid.* 324, 13 January 1567).

It is, of course, pure speculation, but if the seven lasts of powder did arrive after St. Low's appeal, it would have meant that from, say, the start of February until the fateful day of the explosion, there was some 7.62 metric tonnes of powder to be accounted for. If we allow that each of three hundred arquebusiers would have been issued with some 700gm of powder each at any one time, then this would amount to around 210kg per issue. However, although we have no figures, we do know that sickness was rife and that there was significant attrition amongst all forces, and it is likely that by February 1567 any issue would have been smaller. Finally, the months of February to March seem to have been relatively quiet, with no major action having been recorded, so that there would not have been the need for a constant topping up of individual stocks. Thus, it would seem quite possible that on 15 April 1567, the magazine could have been storing at least half of the original consignment or perhaps more. Allowing for the sort of spoilage noted in Chapter 2 (p. 38), giving perhaps ten per cent or more of 'unserviceable' stock, we could still be looking at the detonation of some 3 metric tonnes of corn powder. The force of any explosion will be most acute on the weakest part of a structure, and in this case it would have been the roof. And had the roof been of slate, then we may easily imagine the lethal impact of shards flung outwards by the blast over a wide radius.

Notes to Appendix B

1 However, in 1532 in the *Betha Colaim Chille*, Manus O'Donnell referred to the church incidentally. He did not mention the roof, but the sense would seem to imply (but not definitely) an operational church (Lacey 1998, 47). Further, Lacy (1997) has argued for the existence of a *turas* or local pilgrimage leading to *Tempall Mór* from the area of modern Shipquay Place as a part of a renewal at Derry which, overall, certainly would have involved at least some degree of restoration work. We are most grateful to Dr. Brian Lacey for drawing these points to our attention.

2 A similar structure, but without any sign of earthworks, is shown in the same position on *NA* MPF 1/335-1 (Plate 50), while another version of Plate 47, dating to 1600 and reproduced by McGurk (2006, 63, Fig. 3) indicates a building surrounded by outworks.

3 *A proporcion of Powder and other munitions to be conveyed to Mr Randolph to Bristol and from there to Dyrie uppon Loch ffoyle within the Realme of Ireland . . .*

4 Also spelled Saintloo or St Loo.

BIBLIOGRAPHY

Abbreviations

BL = The British Library, London.
CLA = The City of London Archives
HMC = The Historic Manuscripts Commission.
ICR = Ipswich County Record Office.
NA = The National Archives, London.
NAS = The National Archives of Scotland, Edinburgh.
NLI = The National Library of Ireland, Dublin
TCD = Trinity College Dublin.

Primary Sources

A

AFM = O'Donovan, J. ed. (1856) *Annals of the Kingdom of Ireland by the Four Masters*. Vol. VI (reprinted Dublin 1990, De Búrca Rare Books).

APC = *Acts of the Privy Council*. London (HMSO).

APC Colonial = *Acts of the Privy Council, Colonial Series*, Vol. I, *1613–1680*. Hereford (HMSO).

A Light to the Blind = Brendan Clifford int. (1990) *Derry and the Boyne by Nicholas Plunkett [extracts]*. Belfast (Belfast Historical and Educational Society), 75–128.

Art Military = *The Third Part of the Principles of the Art Military Practised in the Warres of the United Provinces... Written and composed by Captaine Henry Hexham...* Rotterdam 1642 (2nd edition, corrected and emended, printed by John Moxon).

Art of War = Boyle, Roger, Earl of Orrery (1677) *A Treatise of the Art of War: dedicated to the Kings most Excellent Majesty*. London.

Ash Journal = 'A Circumstantial Journal of the Siege of Londonderry by Captain Thomas Ash' in Witherow, T. ed. (1888) *Two Diaries of Derry in 1689*. Londonderry (William Gailey).

A true relation of such passages and proceedings of the Army of Dublin in the Kingdome of Ireland as hath happened from the seventh of July to this present shewing how unprovided the Rebels are of powder... London, August 3rd, 1642. British Library, Thomason Tracts E108[46].

B

Barbers CM = *Court Minutes of the Worshipful Company of Barber Surgeons*. Vol. 5 (1621–1651), Guildhall Library, London, MS 05257 (on microfilm).

Blacksmiths CM = *Court Minutes of the Worshipful Company of Blacksmiths*. Vol. 5 (1639–1648), Guildhall Library London, MS 02881/5.

Blacksmiths AC = *Worshipful Company of Blacksmiths, Warden's Accounts*. Vol. 4 (1625–1646), Guildhall Library London, MS 02883/4.

C

Cal. Pat. Close Rolls = ed. Morrin, J. (1863) *Calendar of Patent and Close Rolls of Chancery in Ireland*. Vol. I, 1861, Dublin (Alex. Thom and Sons), Vol. II, 1862, London (Longman).

Cal. SP Colonial = *Calendar of State Papers, Colonial Series*, London.

Cal. SPD = *Calendar of State papers, Domestic Series*. London.

Cal. SPI = *Calendar of State Papers Ireland*. London.

Cal. SP Venetian = *Calendar of State Papers Venetian*. London.

Carew MSS = Calendar of the Carew Manuscripts preserved in the Archiepiscopal Library at Lambeth, 1589–1600. eds J.S. Brewer and W. Bullen, London 1869 (Longmans, Green and Co.).

Carte MSS = *The Manuscript Collection of Thomas Carte*, Bodleian Library, Oxford.

Carter MS = *Documents relating to the Ulster Plantation from the records of the Goldsmiths' Company... compiled by Henry Carter*. Goldsmiths' Hall, London, MS B.393/1645.

Certaine Waies = Whithorne, Peter (1588) *Certaine Waies for the ordering of Souldiours in battelray... Gathered & set foorth by Peter Whithorne* London (Imprinted at London by Thomas East: for John Wright).

Clothworkers AC = The Worshipful Company of Clothworkers Quarter and Renter Wardens' Accounts (1639–1649), CL/D/5/8, Clothworkers Hall, London.

Clothworkers CO = The Worshipful Company of Clothworkers Court Orders H (1639–1649), CL/B/1/8, Clothworkers Hall, London.

Clothworkers IA = The Worshipful Company of Clothworkers Irish Estate Survey Accounts 1620–1671, Estates/Irish/D/1/1, Clothworkers Hall, London.

Commons J. = Journal of the House of Commons.

Commons J. Ireland = *The Journals of the House of Commons of the Kingdom of Ireland*, Vol. I (May 18th 1613–August 7th, 1666), Dublin (George Grierson) 1796.

Compleat Gunner = *The Compleat Gunner in Three Parts translated out of Casimir, Diego, Uffano, Hexham and other authors*. London 1672 (reprint by S.R. Publishers Ltd., Wakefield, 1971).

Continuation = *Plans of the principal towns, forts and harbours in Ireland... for Mr. Tindal's continuation of Mr. Rapin's History*, 1751. BL Maps 10920.(1.) and K Top 51.55.

Cutlers CR = *Court Minutes of the Worshipful Company of Cutlers of London*. Vol. 1 (1602–1670), Guildhall Library, London, MS 07151 (on microfilm).

D

De Re Metallica = Hoover, H.C. and Hoover, L.H. eds and trans. (1950) *Georgius Agricola De Re Metallica*. New York (Dover Publications).

Derry Corporation = *Londonderry Corporation Minutes*. Vol. 1 (1673–1704), Derry City Council, Heritage and Museum Service, Archive Collection CC/1.

Docwra = Kelly, W.P. ed. (2003) *Docwra's Derry*. Belfast (Ulster Historical Foundation).

Doe Castle = *A true copy of a letter sent from Doe Castle in Ireland, from an Irish rebell, to Dunkerke. And from thence sent to London, by a well-wisher to the advancement of the Protestant religion. As also a copy of the league which the captaines of London-Derry have entred into, for the keeping thereof, and the county adjoyning.* London 1643 (Printed for William Hope). British Library, Thomason Tracts E.84[46].

Drapers MR = The Worshipful Company of Drapers Minutes and Records for 1640–1667, Drapers' Hall, London, shelfmark MB14.

E

Englands Defence = Englands defence, a treatise concerning invasion . . . exhibited in writing to the Right Honourable Robert Dudley, Earl of Leicester, a little before the Spanish Invasion, in the year 1588 by Thomas Diggs Muster-Master General of all of Her Majesty's Forces in the Low Countries to which is now added, an account of such stores of war and other materials as are requisite . . . collected by Thomas Adamson, Master Gunner of his Majesty's Train of Artillery, Anno 1673 . . . London 1680 (Printed for F. Haley).

Epitome = Joseph Moxon *An epitome of the whole art of war. In two parts. The first of military discipline . . . The second of fortification and gunnery, which shews the principles and practice . . . used . . . at the late sieges of Athlone, Galoway, Limerick, etc.* London 1692 (printed for J. Moxon).

Execrable Irish Rebellion = Borlase, E. (1662) *The History of the Execrable Irish Rebellion . . .* London (Robert Clavell).

Extracts = Another Extract of more Letters sent out of Ireland, Informing the condition of the Kingdome as it now stands. London (Printed by George Miller, Blackfriars) August 26th, 1643. British Library, Thomason Tracts E.65[34].

F

Finch Journal = A true relation of the twenty weeks siege of London derry, by the Scotch, Irish, and dis-affected English . . . Related in two letters from Captaine Henry Finch, one of the Captains of London derry, and one of the Aldermen of the city. To his friend in London. London 1649 (Printed by R.I. for S.G. and A.W. and are to bee sold at the Exchange, and at Westminster). British Library Thomason Tracts, E.573[4].

Fishmongers AC = Worshipful Company of Fishmongers Prime Wardens' Account Book. Vol. 1 (1636–1658), Guildhall Library, London, MS 05561.

Fishmongers CR = Worshipful Company of Fishmongers Court Minute Books Vol. 3 (1631–1646), Guildhall Library, London, MS 05570.

Fleet Diary = 'Richards' Diary of the Fleet' in Witherow, T. ed. (1888) *Two Diaries of Derry in 1689.* Londonderry (William Gailey).

G

Goldsmiths CM = Court Minutes of the Worshipful Company of Goldsmiths 1639–1642, held at Goldsmiths' Hall, London, MS 1539/B39.

Good and bad Newes from Ireland. July 13th, 1642. British Library Thomason Tracts, E.155[7].

Good News = Good News from London-Derry in Ireland being a full and true relation of a Great and Signal Victory . . . June 5th. 1689. London (Printed for J. Williams, in Fleet Street).

Griffin = Newes from London-derry in Ireland: or, A true and sad relation of the deplorable and lamentable estate of London-derry, which is much distressed by reason of the Rebels neare approaches unto it, and the menaces and treats they daily send unto them, to make them deliver up their city. Also how they burnt the towne of Strabam, with many people in it. Related in a letter from one Mr William Griffin, to one Mr Iames Humphry of Stuke in Berkshire, Gent. Febr. 20. 1641. London 1642 (Printed for William Ley). British Library, Thomason Tracts E.136[25].

Grocers AC = Worshipful Company of Grocers Wardens' Accounts Vol. 7 (1579–1592), Vol. 8 (1592–1601), Vol. 9 (1601–1611), Guildhall Library, London, MS 11571.

Grocers CM = Worshipful Company of Grocers Court Minute Books Vol. 3 (1616–1639), Vol. 4 (1640–1668), Guildhall Library, London, MS 11588.

Gunner = Norton, Robert (1628) *The Gunner, shewing the whole Practise of Artillerie: with all the appurtenances thereunto belonging. Together with the making of extra-ordinary artificiall fireworkes, as well for pleasure and triumphes, as for warre and seruice. Written by Robert Norton, one of his Maiesties gunners and enginiers.* London (A[gustine] M[athewes] for Humphrey Robinson. To be sold at the three Pidgeons in Paules-Churchyard).

Gunners Dialogue = Norton, Robert (1628) *The Gunners Dialogue with the Art of great Artillery.* London (printed for John Tap).

Gunners Glasse = Eldred, William (1646) *The Gunners Glasse.* London (printed by T. Forcet for Robert Boydel).

Gunnery = Nye, Nathaniel (1670) *The Art of Gunnery.* London (printed for William Leak at the sign of the Crown in Fleetstreet).

H

Haberdashers CM = Worshipful Company of Haberdashers Court of Assistants Minute Books. Vol. 1 (1582/3–1652), Guildhall Library, London, MS 15842.

Hennessy Archive = Unpublished drawings, manuscripts and photographs in the archive of the late N. St John Hennessy, held by the National Museum of Ireland, Dublin.

HMC Franciscans = Historical Manuscripts Commission (1906) *Report on the Franciscan manuscripts preserved at the convent, Merchant's Quay, Dublin.* Dublin (HMSO, John Falconer).

Holmes = Letter from George Holmes to William Fleming at Coniston Hall, November 16th, 1689. Historical Manuscripts Commission. Twelfth Report, Appendix Part VII, 264–265.

I

Inniskilling-men = Hamilton, A. (1690) *A true relation of the actions of the Inniskilling-men, from the first taking up of arms in December 1688.* London (reprinted 2001, Castlepoint Press, Dalbeattie, Scotland).

IOR = India Office Records, Court Minutes of the East India Company, British Library.

Ireland's Lamentation = Ireland's Lamentation for the late Destructive Cessation or, A Trap to catch Protestants. Written by Lieutenant Colonell Chidly Coote.

London, March 1643 (Printed by R.C. for H.S.). British Library, Thomason Tracts E.35[4].

Irish Rebellion = Sir John Temple *The Irish Rebellion or, an History of the Beginnings and first progress of the General Rebellion raised within the Kingdom of Ireland upon the three and twentieth day of October, 1641*. Dublin (1724 edition).

Ironmongers AC = *Worshipful Company of Ironmongers 'Registers'* (*Wardens' Accounts*) Vol. 5 (1634–1651), Guildhall Library, London, MS 16988 (on microfilm).

Ironmongers CM = *Worshipful Company of Ironmongers Court Minute Books*. Vol. 4 (1629–1646), Guildhall Library, London, MS 16967 (on microfilm).

J

Jacobite Narrative = Gilbert, J.T. ed. (1892) *A Jacobite Narrative of the War in Ireland 1688–1691*. Dublin (Joseph Dollard).

L

Lawson = *A true relation of Severall Acts, Passages and Proceedings, done, undertaken, suffered and performed, by Captaine Robert Lawson, now one of the Sheriffes of the City and County of London-Derry, upon and since the first beginning of the great and generall Rebellion in Ireland, in severall parts and places within the Province of Ulster*. London 1643.

Letters and Papers = Hogan, J. ed. (1936) *Letters and Papers relating to the Irish Rebellion between 1642–46*. Dublin (Stationery Office).

Letter from Dublin = *A letter from Dublin giving an account of the Siege of Londonderry... 12th June 1689* in J. Somers (1809) *A collection of scarce... Tracts...* Vol. 11, London, 411–415.

Lords J. = *Journal of the House of Lords*. London.

M

Mackenzie = Killen, W.D. ed. (1861) *Mackenzie's Memorials of the Siege of Derry Including His Narrative and its Vindication*. Belfast (C. Aitchison).

Mackenzie Narrative = *A Narrative of the Siege of Londonderry, or the late Memorable Transactions of that City...* London 1690 (Printed for the Author, and are to be Sold by *Richard Baldwin* in the *Old Baily*).

Memoires = Jean Thomas, Ingenieur *Memoires Touchant La Fortification de Londonderry*. British Library K Top LIV 32C (undated).

Memorable Passages = *A iournall of the most memorable passages in Ireland. Especially that victorious battell at Munster, beginning the 25. of August 1642. and continued. Wherein is related the siege of Ardmore Castle; together with a true and perfect description of the famous battell of Liscarroll. Written by a worthy gentleman, who was present at both these services*. London 1642 (Printed for T. S., October 19th 1642). British Library, Thomason Tracts E.123[15].

Mercers AC = *Worshipful Company of Mercers Second Wardens' Accounts* 1638–1648, held at the Mercers Hall, London, MS shelf 149.

Mercers CM = *Worshipful Company of Mercers Acts of Court* 1641–1645, held at the Mercers Hall, London, MS shelf 64.

Merchant Taylors AC = *Worshipful Company of Merchant Taylors Master and Wardens' Account Books*. Vol. 18 (1641–1644), Guildhall Library, London, MS 24048 Vol.18.

Merchant Taylors CM = *Worshipful Company of Merchant Taylors Court Minutes*. Vol. 6 (1620–1636), Vol. 7 (1637–1654), Guildhall Library, London, MS 34010.

Merchant Taylors Freemen = *List of Freemen of the Merchant Taylors Company 1530–1928*. Guildhall Library, London, MS 34037, 3 Vols.

Mervyn = Mervyn, Sir Audley (1642) *An exact relation of all such occurrences as have happened in the severall counties... in the north of Ireland, since the beginning of this horrid, bloody, and unparaleld rebellion there, begun in October last: In all humility presented to the Honorable House of Commons in England by Lieutenant Collonel Audley Mervyn the 4 of June 1642*. London (Printed for The Downes and William Bladen). British Library, Thomason Tracts E.149[34].

Mitchelburne = Mitchelburne, Colonel John (1708) *Ireland Preserv'd: or the Siege of London-Derry. Together with the troubles of the North. Written by the then Governor (J. Michelburne). [A tragi-comedy, in two parts, each in five acts and in prose.]*. London (2nd edition).

N

NA = National Archive, Kew, London. E 190 = *Records of the Exchequer, Port Books*, MPF and MPHH = Maps and Plans, WO = *War Office Records*, SP 14, SP16 = State Papers Domestic (on microfilm), SP 39 = *Signet Office, Kings Bills* 1567–1645, SP 63 = State Papers Relating to Ireland (on microfilm).

Négociations = J. Hogan ed. (1934 and 1958) *Négociations de M. Le Comte d'Avaux en Irelande 1689–90*. 2 vols. Dublin (Irish Manuscripts Commission). *Négociations supp.* = Vol. 2.

Newes from the North of Ireland = Winter, R. (1643) *Newes from the North of Ireland: of the monethly atchievements of the forces in the city of London Derry... untill November, 1642*. London (reprinted Derry 1929, Londonderry Sentinel).

O

Ormond MSS = *The Manuscripts of the Marquis of Ormond preserved at the Castle, Kilkenny*. London (H.M.S.O.).

OS Londonderry = Colby, T. (1837) *Ordnance Survey of the County of Londonderry, I*. Dublin (Hodges and Smith).

P

Phillips MSS = Chart, D. A. ed. (1928) *Londonderry and the London Companies 1609–1629 being a survey and other documents presented to King Charles I by Sir Thomas Phillips*. Belfast (H.M.S.O).

Pirotechnia = Gnudi, M.T. and Smith, C.S. eds and trans. (1942) *The Pirotechnia of Vannoccio Biringuccio*. New York (reprint of 1942 original edition, Basic Books Inc.).

Proceedings of the Scottish Army = *A true relation of the proceedings of the Scottish army now in Ireland, by three letters*. London 1642. British Library, Thomason Tracts E.149[12].

R

Remarkable Occurrences = An Account of the most Remarkable Occurrences relating to London-Derry. With a relation of the signal Defeat given to the French and Irish Papists, May 5 1689. London (Printed for Richard Baldwin, near the Black Bull in the Old-Baily).

S

Skinners AC = Worshipful Company of Skinners Receipts and Payments Vol. 6 (1617–1646), Guildhall Library, London, MS 30727.

Salters CM = Worshipful Company of Salters Court Minutes (1627–1684), Salters Hall, London, MS C1/1.

Sea Grammar = Goell, K. ed. (1970) *A Sea Grammar by John Smith*. London (Michael Joseph).

Skinners Apprentices = Worshipful Company of Skinners Apprentices and Freedoms Vol. 1, 1496–1602, Vol. 2, 1601–1694, Guildhall Library, London, MS 30719.

Skinners CR = Worshipful Company of Skinners Court Book Vol. 3 (1617–1651), Guildhall Library, London, MS 30708.

Strafford = The Papers of Thomas Wentworth. Sheffield Archives, Sheffield.

T

Transactions = A true relation of the transactions between Sir Charls Coot Kt, Lord President of Connaught in Ireland and Owen-Roe-O-Neal. August 28, 1649. British Library, Thomason Tracts E.571[33].

Travaux de Mars = Manneson Mallet, Alain (1696) *Les Travaux de Mars*. La Haye (Adrian Moetjens).

Treatise = Moretti, Tomaso *A Treatist of Artillery: or, Great Ordnance . . . Translated into English . . . by Jonas Moore, junior*. London 1673 (printed by William Godbid).

True and Breife Account = A true and breife account of the services done by the seaven regiments and troopes raised in the kingdome of Ireland . . . by Sir Robert Stewart. Historical Manuscripts Commission, Twelfth Report, Appendix, Part II, 297–302.

True and Impartial Account = A True and Impartial Account of the most Material Passages in Ireland, since December 1688. With a particular relation of the Forces of Londonderry; being taken from the notes of a Gentleman who was eye-witness to most of the actions mention'd therein [i.e. Captain Joseph Bennett] . . . To which is added a description and map of Londonderry, etc. London 1689 (printed for John Amery).

True Newes = True newes from Ireland, or, The state of Dublin as it stood 27 of December. London 1641 (Printed for F.C. and J.W.).

True Relation = A true relation of the twenty weeks Siege of London-Derry by the Scotch, Irish and Dis-affected English . . . related in two Letters from Captaine Henry Finch . . . London, September 11th 1649. British Library, Thomason Tracts E573[4].

V

Vintners AC = The Worshipful Company of Vintners Wardens' Accounts. Vol. 3 (1617–1636), Vol. 4 (1636–1658), Guildhall Library, London, MS 15333.

Vintners CM = The Worshipful Company of Vintners Court Minute Books Vol. 4 (1639–1659), Guildhall Library, London, MS 15201.

W

Walker = George Walker (1689) *A True Account of the Siege of London-Derry*. London (Printed for Robert Clavel and Ralph Simpson).

A Sermon preached before the Garrison of London-Derry = Whittle, Reverend Seth (1689) *A Sermon preached before the Garrison of London-Derry in the Extremity of the Siege*. Edinburgh.

WPB = Woolwich Proof Books, Royal Armouries Library, Leeds.

Secondary Sources

A

Angus, H.T. (1976) *Cast Iron: Physical and Engineering Properties*. London (2nd edition, Butterworths).

Anon. (1825) *Tavern Anecdotes including the origin of signs and reminiscences of taverns, coffee houses, clubs &c &c*. London (W. Cole, Newgate Street).

Anon. – initials L.H.H. (1875) 'Explosions of gunpowder magazines by lightning', *Notes and Queries* s5–III, 114–115.

Appleby, J.C. (1992) *A Calendar of Material Relating to Ireland from the High Court of Admiralty Examinations 1536–1641*. Dublin (Irish Manuscripts Commission).

B

Bara, J.L. (1985) 'Russian artillery: the political and commercial background of the 18th century Anglo-Russian relationship and its results', *Arms Collecting* 23(2), 43–49.

Baraclough, K.C and Kerr, J.A. (1976) 'Steel from 100 years ago', *J. Hist. Met. Soc.* 10(2), 70–76.

Bailey, A.R. and Samuels, L.E. (1976) *Foundry Metallography*. Betchworth (Metallurgical Services Ltd.).

Balasubramaniam R. and Brown R.R. (forthcoming) *The Cannons of Mehrangarh Fort, Jodhpur, India*.

Barnard, T. (1993) '1641: A bibliographical essay', in ed. B. Mac Cuarta 1993, 173–186.

Barter Bailey, S. (1991) 'Information relating to the operation of the early cast-iron gun industry from a manuscript account book in the collection of the Royal Armouries', *J. Ordnance Soc.* 3, 11–23.

— (2000) *Prince Rupert's Patent Guns*. Leeds.

— (2003) 'Early attempts to control the export of cast-iron guns and the market on Tower Hill', *J. Ordnance Soc.* 15, 53–70.

Bartlett, R. and Jeffrey, K. eds (1996) *A Military History of Ireland*. Cambridge (University Press).

Beaver, S.H. (1951) 'Coke manufacture in Great Britain: A Study in Industrial Geography', *Inst. Brit. Geographers Trans. and Papers* 17, 133–148.

Bennett, E. (1970) *The Worshipful Company of Wheelwrights of the City of London 1670–1970*. Newton Abbot (David and Charles).

Björkenstam, N. Fernheden, K., Magnusson, G. and Serning, I. eds (1985) *Medieval Iron in Society*

Stockholm (Jernkontoret and Riksantikvarieämbetet: *Jernkontorets Forskning* H 34).
Black, J. (2002) *European Warfare, 1494–1660*. London (Routledge).
Blackmore, H.L. (1976) *The Armouries at the Tower of London, I Ordnance*. London (HMSO).
Bound, M. ed. (1995) *The Archaeology of Ships of War*. Oswestry (The International Maritime Archaeology Series Vol. I).
— ed. (1998) *Excavating Ships of War*. Oswestry (The International Maritime Archaeology Series Vol. II).
— and Gosset, P. (1998) 'The *'Dragon'* in ed. M. Bound 1998, 149–158.
Boyns, T. ed. (1997) *The Steel Industry. I – the Iron Era pre-1870*. London (Tauris).
Bradley, I. (1975) *A History of Machine Tools*. Hemel Hempstead (Model and Allied Publications Ltd.).
Brady, C. ed. (2002) *A Viceroy's Vindication? Sir Henry Sidney's Memoir of Service in Ireland, 1556–78*. Cork (University Press).
Braid, D. (1991) 'Gunmaking in North America in the 18th century: Henry Foxall and the transfer of John Wilkinson's technology to the U.S.A.', *J. Ordnance Soc.* 3, 77–86.
Brenner, R. (1993) *Merchants and Revolution: Commercial Change, Political Conflict, and London's Overseas Traders, 1550–1653*. Princeton, New Jersey (Princeton University Press).
Brinck, N. (1996) 'The Wreck at Terschelling', *Ordnance Soc. Newsletter* 34, 8–10.
— (2004) 'Coats of arms on guns of the Dutch Admiralties', *J. Ordnance Soc.* 16, 43–56.
— (2005) 'Identification of the marks of the Dutch auxiliary maritime forces in the 17th and 18th centuries', *J. Ordnance Soc.* 17, 39–48.
Brookfield, C.M. (1941) 'Cannon on Florida Reefs Solve Mystery of Sunken Ship', *National Geographic*, December 1941, 807–824.
Brown, R.R. (1988) 'The Woolwich proof registers 1780–1781', *Int. J. Nautical Archaeol.* 17, 105–111.
— (1989) 'Identifying 18th-century trunnion marks on British iron guns: a discussion', *Int. J. Nautical Archaeol.* 18(4), 321–329.
— (1990a) 'TJ: An unknown trunnion mark', *Ordnance Soc, Newsletter* 10, 9.
— (1990b) 'F-SOLID: A suggested solution', *Ordnance Soc. Newsletter* 11, 1–2.
— (1990c) 'Guns carried on East Indiamen, 1600–1800', *Int. J. Nautical Archaeol.* 19(1). 17–22.
— (1995) 'Arming the East Indiamen', in ed. M. Bound 1995, 114–119.
— (2000) 'Gunfounding and watercolourists: The Board of Ordnance's patronage of artists in the 18th century', *Royal Armouries Yearbook* 4, 102–112.
— (2001) 'Thomas Westerne: the great ironmonger', *J. Ordnance Soc.* 13, 39–54.
— (2004a) 'The thundering cannon: guns for the English navy in the 17th century', in eds G. Groenendijk et al. 2004, 122–133.
— (2004b) 'The Ordnance Records: Thomas Browne', *Wealden Iron Research Group Bull.* 24 (second series), 16-25.
— (2005) 'John Brown, gunfounder to the King Part 1', *Wealden Iron Research Group Bull.* 25 (second series), 36–61.
Buchanan, B. (2005) '"The Art and Mystery of Making Gunpowder": The English Experience in the seventeenth and eighteenth centuries', in eds B.D. Steele and T. Dorland 2005, 233–274.
Buckley, J. (1910) 'Report of Sir Josias Bodley on some Ulster fortresses in 1608', *Ulster J. Archaeol.* 16 (second series), 61–64.
Butler, D.S. and Tebbutt, C.F. (1975) 'A Wealden cannon-boring bar', *Post-Med. Archaeol.* 9, 38–41.
Bull, S. (1990) 'Pearls from the dungheap: English saltpetre production 1590–1640, *J. Ordnance Soc.* 2, 5–10.
Byrne, M.J. ed. (1903) *Ireland Under Elizabeth: a Portion of the History of Ireland... by Don Philip O'Sullivan Beare*. Dublin (Sealy, Bryers and Walker).

C

Callister, W. D.(2007) *Materials Science and Engineering: An Introduction*, New Jersey (7th edition, John Wiley and Sons).
Canny, N. (1997) 'Religion, politics and the Irish rising of 1641', in eds J. Devlin and R. Fanning 1997, 40–71.
Caruana, A.B. (1994) *The History of English Sea Ordnance 1523–1875: Vol. 1–The Age of Evolution 1523–1715*. Rotherfield (Jean Boudriot Publications).
Carlton, C. (1992) *Going to the Wars*. London (BCA).
— (1998) 'Civilians', in eds J. Kenyon and J. Ohlmeyer 1998, 272–305.
Casway, J.I. (1984) *Owen Roe O'Neill and the Struggle for Catholic Ireland*. Philadelphia (University of Pennsylvania Press).
Chatterji, S.K. (2001) *Vintage Guns of India*. New Delhi.
Chaudhuri, K.N. (1965) *The English East India Company. The study of an early joint-stock company 1600–1640*. London (Frank Cass and Co. Ltd.).
Cipolla, C.M. (1965) *Guns, Sails and Empire*. London (Minerva Press).
Clarke, N. (1975) 'Water pipes or cannon?', *J. Broseley Hist. Soc.* 3, 8.
— (1984) '"As others see us": Contemporary opinion of John Wilkinson and his achievements', *J. Broseley Hist. Soc.* 12, 4–7.
Cleere, H. and Crossley, D. (1995) *The Iron Industry of the Weald*. Cardiff (2nd edition, Merton Priory Press).
Coates, W.H., Young, A.S. and Snow, V.F. eds (1982) *The Private Journals of the Long Parliament, 3 January to 5 March 1642*. New Haven (Yale University Press).
Craddock, P. and Lang, J. (2005) 'Charles Dawson's cast-iron statuette: the authentication of iron antiquities and possible coal-smelting in Roman Britain', *J. Hist. Met. Soc.* 39(1), 32–44.
Cranstone, D. (1991) 'Isaac Wilkinson at Backbarrow', *Hist. Metallurgy* 25(2), 87–91.
Crossley, D.W. (1972) 'A 16th-century Wealden blast furnace: a report on excavations at Panningridge, Sussex, 1964–1970', *Post-Med. Archaeol.* 6, 42–68.

— (1975) 'Cannon-manufacture at Pippingford, Sussex: the excavation of two iron furnaces of *c.* 1717', *Post-Med. Archaeol.* 9, 1–37.

— (1997) 'The management of a sixteenth-century ironworks', in ed. T. Boyns 1997, 55–70.

Curl, J.S. (1986) *The Londonderry Plantation 1609–1914.* Chichester (Phillimore and Co.).

— (2000) *The Honourable The Irish Society and the plantation of Ulster, 1608–2000: a history and critique: the City of London and the colonisation of County Londonderry in the Province of Ulster in Ireland.* Chichester (Phillimore and Co. Ltd.).

D

Dale, T.C. (1931) *The inhabitants of London in 1638 : edited from Ms. 272 in the Lambeth palace library.* London (Society of Genealogists).

Dawson, F. (2004) 'The Quarrels of the Brothers Wilkinson', *J. Broseley Hist. Soc.* 26, 2–27.

Day, T. (2000) 'The failure of Inverythan Bridge, 1882', *J. Railway and Canal Hist. Soc.* 33(6), 404–415.

Devlin, J. and Fanning, R. eds (1997) *Religion and rebellion: papers read before the 22nd Irish Conference of Historians, held at University College Dublin, 18–22 May 1995.* Dublin (University College Dublin Press).

Dickinson, H.W. (1914) *John Wilkinson, Iron Master.* Ulverston.

— (1958) 'The steam-engine to 1830', in eds C. Singer *et al.* 1958, 168–198.

Duffy, C. (1979) *Siege Warfare: The Fortress in the Early Modern World.* London (Routledge).

Dwyer, P. ed. (1893) *The Siege of Londonderry in 1689, as set forth in the literary remains of Colonel The Reverend George Walker D.D.* London (Elliot Stock).

E

Edwards, P. (2000) *Dealing in Death: the Arms Trade and the British Civil Wars, 1638–52.* Stroud, Glos. (Sutton Publishing).

Edwards, S. (undated) *Children of the Weald.* Tonbridge.

Ellis, S.G (1996) 'The Tudors and the origins of the modern Irish states: a standing army', in eds T. Bartlett and K. Jeffrey 1996, 116–135.

Eltis, D. (1998) *The Military Revolution in Sixteenth-Century Europe.* London (I.B. Tauris).

F

Falls, C. (1950) *Elizabeth's Irish Wars.* London.

Farrow, G.W.E. (1984) 'Iron gun-founding in the mid 17th century. The winter blowings at Horsmonden 1656 and 1659', *Hist. Metallurgy* 18(2), 109–111.

ffoulkes, C. (1937) *The Gunfounders of England.* Cambridge (University Press: reprint 1969, George Shumway, York PA).

Ferguson, W.S. (2005) *Maps & Views of Derry 1600–1914, a catalogue.* Dublin (Royal Irish Academy).

Firth, C.H. ed. (1895) *Papers relating to Thomas Wentworth, First Earl of Strafford from the MSS of Dr. William Knowler. The Camden Miscellany* IX (London, The Camden Society).

Fissell, M.C. (1994) *The Bishops' Wars: Charles I's campaigns against Scotland 1638–1640.* Cambridge (Cambridge University Press).

— (2001) *English Warfare 1511–1642.* London (Routledge).

Flanagan, L.N.W. (1988) *Ireland's Armada Legacy.* London (Gill and MacMillan).

Furgol, E.M. (2003) *A Regimental History of the Covenanting Armies 1639–1651.* Edinburgh (John Donald).

G

Gentles, I. (1998) 'The Civil Wars in England', in eds J. Kenyon and J. Ohlmeyer 1998, 103–155.

Gilbert, J.T. ed. (1879) *A contemporary history of affairs in Ireland from 1641–1652.* 3 Vols. Dublin (Irish Archaeological Society).

— ed. (1882) *History of the Irish Confederation and the War in Ireland 1641–1643.* 7 Vols, Dublin (M.H. Gill and Son).

Gilmour, B. (2000) 'Dutch composite ordnance of the early 17th century', *Royal Armouries Yearbook* 5, 85–106.

Green, J.N. (1980) 'The armament from the *Batavia*', *Int. J. Nautical Archaeol.* 9(1), 43–51.

— (1986) 'The survey and identification of the English East India Company ship *Trial* (1622)', *Int. J. Nautical Archaeol.* 15, 195–204.

— (1989) *The loss of the Verenigde Oostindisch Compagnie Retourschip* Batavia, *Western Australia 1629. An excavation report and catalogue of artefacts.* Oxford (*British Archaeological Reports*, International Series 489).

Grenter, S. (1992) 'Bersham Ironworks Excavations: 1987–1990 Interim Report', *Industrial Archaeol. Rev.* XIV, 177–192.

Groenendijk, G., de Gryse, P., Staat, D. and Bronder, H. eds (2004) *A farewell to arms: studies on the history of arms and armour.* Delft (Legermuseum/Army Museum).

Guilmartin J.F. (1982) 'The cannon of the *Batavia* and the *Sacramento*: early modern cannon founding reconsidered', *Int. J. Nautical Archaeol.* 11(2), 133–144.

— (2003) *Gunpowder and Galleys: changing technology and Mediterranean warfare at sea in the 16th century.* London (revised edition Conway Maritime Press).

H

Hale, J.R. (1983) *Renaissance War Studies.* London (Hambledon Press).

— (1985) *War and Society in Renaissance Europe 1450–1620.* London (Fontana).

Hall, A.R. (1952) *Ballistics in the Seventeenth Century.* Cambridge (The University Press).

Hall, B.S. (1997) *Weapons and Warfare in Renaissance Europe.* Baltimore (The John Hopkins University Press).

Harkness, D.W. and O'Dowd, M. eds (1981) *The Town in Ireland.* Belfast (The Appletree Press).

Harris, G.G. ed. (1983) *Trinity House of Deptford Transactions, 1609–1635.* London (London Record Society Publications no. 19).

Hayes-McCoy, G.A. (1969) *Irish Battles: A Military History of Ireland.* Belfast (Appletree Press).

— (1976) 'Tudor conquest and counter-reformation', in eds T. Moody *et al.* 1976, 94–141.

Hazlett, H. (1938) *A History of the Military Forces Operating in Ireland, 1641–1649.* 2 Vols, Belfast (unpublished Ph.D. thesis, The Queen's University of Belfast).

Hennessy, N. St J. (1995) 'Crimean-war guns in Ireland', *Irish Sword*, XIX(78), 333–343.

— (1996) 'Russian guns in Ireland', *J. Ordnance Soc.* 8, 27–44.

Hildred, A. (2003) 'A gunner's rule from the *Mary Rose*', *J. Ordnance Soc.* 15, 29–40.

Hughes, B.P. (1969) *British Smooth-Bore Artillery: The Muzzle Loading Artillery of the 18th and 19th centuries.* London (Arms and Armour Press).

Hunter, R.J. (1975a) 'Carew's Survey of Ulster, 1611: the 'Voluntary Works'', *Ulster J. Archaeol.* 38, 81–82.

— (1975b) *Plantations in Ulster, c. 1600–41.* Belfast (HMSO for the Public Record Office of Northern Ireland).

— (1981) 'Ulster Plantation Towns 1609–1641', in eds D.W. Harkness and M. O'Dowd 1981, 55–80.

— (2004) 'Sir George Paulet', *Dictionary of National Biography* (Oxford University Press).

Hutton, R. and Reeves, W. (1998) 'Sieges and Fortifications', in eds J. Kenyon and J. Ohlmeyer 1998, 195–233.

Huxley, G. (1959) *Endymion Porter, the Life of a Courtier.* London (Chatto and Windus).

I

Irish Society of the New Plantation in Ulster (1822) *A concise view of the origin, constitution and proceedings of the Honourable Society of the governor and assistants of London : of the New Plantation in Ulster, within the realm of Ireland, commonly called the Irish Society, compiled principally from their records.* London (Gye and Balne).

J

Jackson, M. and de Beer, C. (1973) *Eighteenth Century Gunfounding.* Newton Abbot (David and Charles).

James, W. (1837) *The Naval History of Great Britain . . . in six volumes.* London (Richard Bentley).

Johnson, B.L.C. (1977) 'The Foley partnerships: the iron industry at the end of the charcoal era', in ed. T. Boyns 1997, 120–138.

Johnson, D.N. (1976) 'A contemporary plan of the siege of Caher Castle, 1599, and some additional remarks', *Irish Sword* 12 (1975–1976), 109–115.

K

Kearney, H.F. (1989) *Strafford in Ireland 1633–41: a study in absolutism.* Cambridge (Cambridge University Press, 2nd edition).

Kelleher, C. (2004) *The Duncannon Wreck: a seventeenth-century ship in Waterford Harbour.* Dublin (Archaeol. Ireland Heritage Guide No. 26).

Kelly, J. (2004) *Gunpowder: Alchemy, Bombards and Pyrotechnics.* New York (Basic Books).

Kelly, W. P. (2001a) 'The forgotten siege of Derry, March-August 1649', in ed. W.P. Kelly 2001, 31– 52.

— (2003) *Docwra's Derry: A narration of events in north-west Ulster 1600–1604.* Belfast (Ulster Historical Foundation).

— ed. (2001b) *The Sieges of Derry.* Dublin (Four Courts Press).

Kelsey, F.W. ed. and trans. (1925) *De Jure Belli ac Pacis Libri Tres by Hugo Grotius.* Vol. II, Translation. Oxford (Clarendon Press).

Kennedy, J. (1971) *Isle of Devils: Bermuda under the Somers Island Company, 1609–85.* London (Collins).

Kenyon, J. and Ohlmeyer, J. eds (1998) *The Civil Wars: A Military History of England, Scotland and Ireland 1638–1660.* Oxford (University Press).

Kerrigan, P. (1996) *Castles and Fortifications in Ireland 1485–1945.* Cork (The Collins Press).

Kew, G. ed. (1998) *The Irish Sections of Fynes Moryson's Unpublished Itinerary.* Dublin (Irish Manuscripts Commission).

Knowler, W. (1739) *The Earl of Strafford's letters and despatches, with an essay towards his life by Sir G. Radcliffe.* 2 Vols, London.

L

Lacy, B. (1983) *Archaeological Survey of County Donegal.* Lifford (Donegal County Council).

— (1988) 'The development of Derry *c.* 600 to *c.* 1600', in eds G. Mac Niocaill and P.F. Wallace 1988, 378–396.

— (1990) *Siege City: The story of Derry and Londonderry.* Belfast (Blackstaff Press).

— (1997) 'A lost Columban *turas* in Derry', *Donegal Annual* 49(1), 39–41.

— ed. (1998) *Manus O'Donnell: The Life of Colum Cille.* Dublin (Four Courts Press).

Lake, D. (2003) 'Today Broseley – Tomorrow the World', *J. Brosely Local Hist. Soc.* 25, 5–15.

Latham, R.E. (1965) *Revised Medieval Latin Word-List from British and Irish Sources.* Oxford (Oxford University Press).

Lathom, R. and Matthews, W. (1970) *The Diary of Samuel Pepys.* Vol. 2, London (Bell).

Lenihan, P. (2001) *Confederate Catholics at War 1641–49.* Cork (Cork University Press).

— ed. (2001) *Conquest and Resistance. War in Seventeenth-Century Ireland.* Leiden (Brill).

Lennon, C. (1988) 'The great explosion in Dublin, 1597', *Dublin Hist. Rec.* XLII, 7–20.

Lewis, M.A. (1961) *Armada Guns: A Comparative Study of English and Spanish Armaments* London (Allen and Unwin).

L'Hour, M., Long, L. and Reith, E. (1989) *Le Mauritius.* Grenoble (Casterman).

Lindley, K.J. (1997) *Popular Politics and Religion in Civil War London.* Aldershot (Scholar Press).

Loeber, R. (1979) 'Biographical Dictionary of Engineers in Ireland, 1600–1730', *Irish Sword* 13 (1977–1979), 30–44, 106–122, 230–255, 283–314.

— and Parker, G. (1995) 'The military revolution in seventeenth-century Ireland', in ed. J. Ohlmeyer 1995, 66–88.

Logue, P. and O'Neill, J. (2006) 'Excavations at Bishop's Street Without: 17th century conflict archaeology in Derry City', *J. Conflict Archaeol.* 2(1), 49–75.

Lucy, G. ed. (1989) *Lord Macauley on Londonderry, Aughrim, Enniskillen and the Boyne.* Lurgan (The Ulster Society).

M

McCracken, E. (1957) 'Charcoal-burning ironworks in seventeenth and eighteenth century Ireland', *Ulster J. Archaeol.* 20, 123–138.

— (1965) 'Supplementary list of charcoal-burning ironworks', *Ulster J. Archaeol.* 28, 132–136.

Mac Cuarta, B. ed. (1993) *Ulster 1641 – Aspects of the Rising.* Belfast (Institute of Irish Studies, The Queen's University).

McConnell, D. (1988) *British Smooth-Bore Artillery: a Technological Study.* Canada (National Historic Parks and Sites).

McGurk, J. (1997) *The Elizabethan Conquest of Ireland: The 1590s Crisis.* Manchester (Manchester University Press).

— (2006a) *Sir Henry Docwra 1564–1631: Derry's Second Founder.* Dublin (Four Courts Press).

— (2006b) 'Garrison life in Derry, 1600–1603', *Irish Sword* XXV(100), 149–180.

McKenny, K. (2005) *The Laggan Army in Ireland 1640–1685.* Dublin (Four Courts Press).

McNeill, T.E. (1981) *Carrickfergus Castle.* Belfast (HMSO: Northern Ireland Archaeological Monographs No. 1).

Mac Niocaill, G. and Wallace, P.F. eds (1988) *Keimelia: Studies in Medieval Archaeology and History in Memory of Tom Delaney.* Galway (University Press).

Maguire, W.A. (2000) *A Century in Focus.* Belfast (Appletree Press).

Mallet, R. (1856) *On the Physical Conditions Involved in the Construction of Artillery, with an Investigation of the Relative and Absolute Values of the Materials Principally Involved and of Some Hitherto Unexplained Causes of the Destruction of Cannon in Service.* London (Longman, Brown, Green, Longmans and Roberts).

Martin, C. J. M. (2004) 'An Iron Bastard Minion Drake Extraordinary by John Browne from the Pinnace *Swan* (1641–53)', *Int. J. Nautical Archaeol.* 33, 79–95.

Meehan, J. (1907) 'The arms of the O'Rourkes: a metal casting from County Leitrim 17th-century foundries', *J. Roy. Soc. Antiq. Ireland* 36, 123–142.

Miller, D. (1996) 'Non-professional soldiery', in eds T. Bartlett and K. Jeffrey 1996, 315–334.

Milligan, C.D. (1951) *History of the Siege of Londonderry 1689.* Londonderry (Carter Publications, Belfast).

— (1996) *The walls of Derry, their building, defending and preserving.* Lurgan (Ulster Society: reprint of edition of 1948–1950, Londonderry).

Moody, T.W. (1939) *The Londonderry Plantation 1609–41.* Belfast (William Mullen and Son).

Morrogh, H. (1941) 'The metallography of inclusions in cast irons and pig irons', *J. Iron and Steel Inst.* 143(1), 207–253.

Mortensen, M. (1999) *Dansk Artilleri Indtil 1600.* Copenhagen.

Mulloy, S. ed. (1984) *Franco-Irish Correspondence, December 1688–February 1692.* III Vols, Dublin (Irish Manuscripts Commission).

Murray, R.H. ed. (1912) *The Journal of John Stevens, containing a brief account of the war in Ireland 1689–1691.* Oxford (Clarendon Press).

Murtagh, H. (1996) 'Irish soldiers abroad 1600–1800', in eds T. Bartlett and K. Jeffrey 1996, 294–314.

— (2003) 'Jacobite artillery, 1689–91', *Irish Sword* XXIII(94), 383–400.

Murphy, S. (2001) 'The technology of casting cannon', *J. Ordnance Soc.* 13, 73–96.

O

O'Brien, G. ed. (1999) *Derry and Londonderry. History and society.* Dublin (Geography Publications).

Ohlmeyer, J.H. (1996a) 'The wars of religion 1603–1660', in eds T. Bartlett and K. Jeffrey 1996, 160–187.

— (1996b) 'Strafford and the 'Londonderry Business'', in ed. J.F. Meritt 1996, 209–229.

— ed. (1995) *Ireland from Independence to Occupation 1641–1660.* Cambridge (University Press).

De hÓir, S. (1983) 'Guns in Medieval and Tudor Ireland', *Irish Sword* 15 (1982–1983), 76–88.

Oldham, N., M. Palmer and Tyson, J. (1993) 'The Erme Estuary, Devon, historic wreck site 1991–3, *Int. J. Nautical Archaeol.* 22, 323–330.

Ó Siochrú, M. (1999) *Confederate Ireland, 1642–1649.* Dublin (Four Courts Press).

P

Peck, L.L. (1990) *Court Patronage and Corruption in Early Stuart England.* Boston (Unwin Hyman).

Pepper, S. and Adams, N. (1986) *Firearms and Fortifications: Military Architecture and Siege Warfare in Sixteenth-Century Siena.* Chicago (The University of Chicago Press).

Perceval-Maxwell, M. (1994) *The Outbreak of the Irish Rebellion of 1641.* Dublin (Gill and McMillan).

Percy, J. (1864) *Metallurgy.* London (John Murray: 1984 facsimile edition, De Archaeologische Pers Nederland, Eindhoven).

Powell, J.R. (1962) *The Navy in the English Civil War.* London (Archon Books).

Puype, J.P. (1991) 'Guns and their handling at sea in the 17th century: a Dutch point of view', *J. Ordnance Soc.* 2, 11–23.

— and van der Hoeven, M. eds (1996) *The Arsenal of the World: The Dutch Arms Trade in the Seventeenth Century.* Amsterdam (Batavian Lion International).

R

Reid, J.S. (1853) *History of the Presbyterian Church in Ireland.* III Vols., second edition, London (Whittaker and Co.).

Riden, P. (1990) *The Butterley Company 1790–1830.* Derby Record Society.

Roberts, K. (2005) *Cromwell's War Machine: The New Model Army 1645–1660.* Barnsley, Yorks (Pen and Sword).

Roberts, M. (1995) 'The Military Revolution, 1560–1660', in ed. C.J. Rogers 1995, 13–35 (originally published in Roberts, M. (1967) *Essays in Swedish Military History*. pp 195–225, Minneapolis).

Rogers, C.J. ed. (1995) *The Military Revolution Debate. Readings on the Military Transformation of Early Modern Europe*. Oxford (Westview Press).

Roth, R. (1995) 'The reporting of ordnance: the guns from the *Mauritius*, a casebook study', in ed. M. Bound 1995, 120–130.

Rostoker, W. (1986) 'Troubles with cast iron cannon', *Archaeomaterials* 1(1), 69–90.

Rothrock, G.A. trans. (1968) *A Manual of Siegecraft and Fortification by Sebastien Le Prestre de Vauban*. Ann Arbor (University of Michigan Press).

S

Schafer, R.G. (1997) 'Genesis and structure of the Foley 'Ironworks in Partnership' of 1692', in ed. T. Boyns 1997, 101–119.

Schubert, H.R. (1957) *History of the British Iron and Steel Industry from c. 450 BC to AD 1775*. London (Routledge and Kegan Paul).

Scott, B.G. (1976) 'Remanent metal structures in corrosion products from an early mediaeval iron knife', *Irish Archaeol. Res. Forum* III(2), 61-64.

— (1985) 'The blast-furnace in Ireland: a failed industry', in eds N. Björkenstam *et al.* 1985, 286–296.

— (1991) *Early Irish Ironworking*. Belfast (Ulster Museum).

— (forthcoming) 'Some notes on the production of ordnance in Ireland in the earlier 17th century'.

Simmons, J.J. (1991) 'Replication of early 16th century shot-mould tongs', J. Ordnance Soc. 3, 5–10.

Simms, H. (1997) 'Violence in County Armagh, 1641', in ed. B. Mac Cuarta 1997, 123–138.

Simpson, R. (1847) *The Annals of Derry*. Limavady (North West Books: 1987 reprint, Londonderry).

Singer, C., Holmyard, E.J., Hall, A.R. and Williams, T.I. eds (1958) *A History of Technology: Vol. IV The Industrial Revolution c 1750 to c 1850*. Oxford (Clarendon Press).

Smith, R.D. (1991) 'Early cast-iron guns with particular reference to guns on the Isle of Man', *J. Ordnance Soc.* 3, 25–46.

— (2001) 'A carriage and cast-iron cannon at Windsor Castle', *J. Ordnance Soc.* 13, 25–38.

Snow, V.F. and Young, A.S. eds (1987) *The Private Journals of the Long Parliament, 7 March to 1 June 1642*. New Haven (Yale University Press).

Soldon, N.C. (1998) *John Wilkinson 1728–1808: English Ironmaster and Inventor*. Lampeter (Studies in British History 49).

Sténuit, R. (1974) *Treasures of the Armada*. London (Cardinal).

Stevenson, D. (1973) *The Scottish Revolution 1637–44*. Newton Abbott (David and Charles).

— (1981) *Scottish Covenanters and Irish Confederates*. Belfast (Ulster Historical Foundation).

Steele, B.D. and Dorland, T. eds (2005) *The Heirs of Archimedes: Science and the Art of War through the Age of Enlightenment*. Cambridge, Mass. (MIT Press).

Straker, E. (1931) *Wealden Iron*. Newton Abbott (David and Charles: reprint of the 1931 edition published by G. Bell and Sons).

T

Teesdale, E.B. (1991) *Gunfounding in the Weald in the sixteenth century*. London (Royal Armouries Monograph 2).

Thomas, A. (1999) 'Londonderry and Coleraine: walled towns, epitome or exception', in ed. G. O'Brien 1999, 259–277.

— (2005) *Derry-Londonderry: Irish Historic Towns Atlas no. 15*. Dublin (Royal Irish Academy).

The Tojhusmuseum (1971) *The Cannon Hall*. Copenhagen.

Tomalin, C. (2003) *Samuel Pepys, The Unequalled Self*. London (Penguin).

Tomlinson, H.C. (1974) 'Place and profit: an examination of the Ordnance Office, 1660–1714', *Trans. Roy. Hist. Soc.* 25 (5th series), 55–75.

Trollope, C. (2002) 'The design and evolution of English cast-iron guns from 1543 to 1660', *J. Ordnance Soc.* 14, 51–64.

— (2007) 'The design and evolution of English cast-iron guns: 1660 to 1725', *J. Ordnance Soc.* 17, 49–58.

Tylecote, R.F. (1972) 'Ores, slags and metal from Panningridge', in D. Crossley 1972, 66–68).

— (1975) 'Ore, slag and cast iron', in D. Crossley 1975, 35–37.

— (1986) *The Prehistory of Metallurgy in the British Isles*. London (The Institute of Metals).

Tyler, D. (2006) 'Gainsborough, Humphrey', *Dictionary of National Biography* (Oxford University Press).

Tyler, L.G. (1892) 'Pedigree of a Representative Virginia Planter', *William and Mary Quarterly Historical Papers* 1(2), 80–88.

V

Vere, R.T. (1943) *The House of Gregory*. Dublin (Richview Press).

Verhoeven, P.J.C. and Brown, R.R. (forthcoming) 'The Dragon Gun of Karatsu'.

W

Wadmore, J.F. (1902) *Some Account of the Worshipful Company of Skinners of London*. London (Blades, East and Blades).

Wayman, M.L., Lang, J. and Michaelson, C. (2004) 'The metallurgy of Chinese cast-iron statuary', *J. Hist. Met. Soc.* 38(1), 10–23.

van Wakeren, A I. (1996) 'English cast-iron guns: a Dutch trade 1609–1640', in eds J. P. Puype and M. van der Hoeven 1996, 28–35.

Walton, S.A. (2003) 'The Bishopsgate Artillery Garden and the first English Ordnance school', *J. Ordnance Soc.* 15, 41–52.

Wedgwood, C.V. (1961) *Thomas Wentworth First Earl of Strafford 1593–1641*. London (Jonathan Cape).

Wheeler, S. (1995) 'Four armies in Ireland', in ed. J. Ohlmeyer 1995, 43–65.

White, L. Jr (1962) *Mediaeval Technology and Social Change*. Oxford (Clarendon Press).

Williams, A.L. (2001) 'Bersham ironworks and John Wilkinson, gunfounder', *J. Ordnance Soc.* 13, 55–62.

Wilson, G.M. (1988) 'The Commonwealth Gun', *Int. J. Nautical Archaeol.* 17, 87–99.

Willeboordse, A. (2008) 'Een kanon van de koningin: Een 16de-eeuwse mignonte Sluis', *Appeltjes van Meetjesland. Jaarboek Heemkundig Genootschap Meetjesland*, 60 (2008).

Wingood A. J. (1982) '*Sea Venture*. An interim report on an early 17th century shipwreck lost in 1609' *Int. J. Nautical Archaeol.* 11, 333–347.

Woodhead, J.R. (1966) The Rulers of London 1660–1689: A biographical record of the Aldermen and Common Councilmen of the City of London. London (London and Middlesex Archaeological Society).

Worssam, B.C. and Gibson-Hill, J. (1976) 'Analyses of Wealden iron ores', *J. Hist Met. Soc.* 10(2), 77–82.

Y

Young, W.R. (1932) *Fighters of Derry: their deeds and descendants. Being a chronicle of events in Ireland during the revolutionary period, 1688–1691*. London (Eyre and Spottiswood).

INDEX

Aickin, Joseph, see *Londerias*
Arcana, Francisco 141
Arms trade 153, 199, 200
Artillery, see Ordnance
Ash, Captain Thomas xx, xxi, 39, 85, 86, 91, 92, 93, 97, 117
Ashon, Sir Arthur 29
Avaux, Jean-Antoine, Comte d' 47, 57, 88, 96

Bagenal, Sir Henry 39, 82, 142, 143
Baker, Captain John 72, 101, 105, 135, 212, 213
Baker, Governor Henry 79, 92
Bateman, Sir Robert 121
Battles and sieges
    Aughrim, Co. Galway xix, 31
    Blackwater Fort, Co. Armagh 16, 30, 39, 43, 47
    Benburb, Co. Tyrone 31, 83
    Caher, Co. Tipperary 59, 176
    Carrigans, Co. Donegal 83, 95
    Charlemont, Co. Armagh 49, 58, 81, 95, 118, 133
    Charles Fort, Co. Londonderry 39, 84, 99, 109, 118
    Clones, Co. Monaghan 82
    Drogheda, Co. Louth 29, 30, 63, 64, 81
    Duncannon, Co. Wexford xx, 42, 57, 68, 155
    Enagh, Co. Donegal 64
    Glenmaquin, Co. Donegal 82
    Harry Avery's Castle, Co. Tyrone 64
    Kilrush, Co. Kildare 41, 57
    Kinsale, Co. Cork 28, 41
    Limerick, Co. Limerick 12, 25, 27, 31, 32, 40, 42, 50, 52, 57, 58, 60, 77
    Liscarrol, Co. Cork 51
    Londonderry 1649 39, 83–84
    Londonderry 1689 xix–xxi, 1, 30, 40, 43–44, 50–51, 67, 69, 75–77, 79, 81, 83–85, 91, 93–96, 127, 132
    Maynooth, Co. Kildare 63
    New Buildings, Co. Londonderry 109
    Portlester Castle, Co. Westmeath 51
    Ross, Co. Wexford 43
    Scarrifhollis, Co. Donegal 95
    Yellow Ford, Co. Armagh 30, 39, 82
Bennett, Captain Joseph xxi, 67, 85, 88, 89, 90, 92
Benson, Peter xix, 72
Bermuda colony xxi, 128, 129, 135, 142
Betson, Captain John 212, 213
Bingham, Sir Richard 27, 29
Bishop's Wars 27, 32
Bodley, Sir Josias 60, 71, 72, 105, 107
Borgard, Colonel Albert 54, 139, 143, 148
Boulton, Matthew and Watt, James 204, 206, 209
Boyle, Roger, Earl of Orrery 44, 55
Burlamachi, Phillip 33, 200
Burt Castle, Co. Donegal 28–29, 99
Butler, James, Duke of Ormond 25, 27, 52, 76, 77, 79, 94, 95, 96, 99, 122
Butterly Company 164

Calvert, Sir George 211, 230
Cannon, see Ordnance
Carrickfergus Castle, Co. Antrim xxii, 25, 50, 97, 99, 103, 118, 119, 120, 122, 132, 133
Cast iron
    casting xxi, 33
    chemical composition of 179–181
    corrosion of 8, 184
    graphite forms 189
    hardness 190, 197
    porosity 182
    specific gravity 187–188, 196
Charcoal 32, 37, 38, 40, 53, 54, 55, 206
Charles Fort, Co. Cork 118, 132
Chester, port of 31, 105, 131, 205, 213
Chichester, Sir Arthur 38
Citadel, construction of
    in Ireland 77
    in Londonderry 69, 76, 77–79, 80, 95, 96, 223
Coalbrookdale, Shropshire 205
Colby, Col. Thomas 1, 9
Collins, George 48
Coote, Sir Charles Jnr, first Earl of Mountrath xx, 27, 40, 83, 84, 95, 96, 105, 109, 118, 229, 230
Cordwell, Samuel 48, 58
Covell, Francis 107, 128
Covell, Thomas 107, 132, 135, 212
Covert, Sir Humphrey 50, 66, 103
Cromwell, Henry 77
Cromwell, Oliver 29, 30, 32, 40, 52, 63, 67
Culmore Castle, Co. Londonderry xx, 10, 15, 31, 44, 45, 50, 58, 67, 69, 70, 71, 76, 77, 81, 83, 84, 85, 89, 92, 93, 96, 97, 99, 100, 101, 102, 105–106, 107, 108, 109, 110–112, 117, 118, 119, 128, 131, 132, 135, 148, 163, 166, 169, 176, 194

Docwra, Sir Henry xvii, xix, xx, 10, 29, 38, 39, 40, 50, 52, 60, 64, 65, 66, 68, 69, 70, 71, 73, 81, 82, 94, 99, 101, 102, 103, 105, 108, 139
Doddington, Sir Edward xix, 72
Dumbarton Castle, Dunbartonshire 119
Dunalong, Co. Londonderry xx, 10, 69, 70, 71, 91, 99, 101, 102, 105
Dutch East India Company (VOC) 142, 150, 155

Elagh Castle, Co. Donegal 69
English East India Company 54, 55, 57, 99, 106, 123, 126, 130, 133, 150, 155, 199, 201, 203, 209, 212, 218, 230
Evelyn family 38, 41, 48, 106, 212

Felgate family
    Erasmus 128, 134, 135
    John 134
    Robert 134–135
    Thomas 134
    Tobias 122, 129, 135
    William xxi, 57, 100, 106, 107, 113, 122, 124, 125, 126, 127, 128–130, 135, 136, 212, 214, 215, 218, 219, 220, 221, 222
Ferrers, Samuel 123, 124, 126, 127, 130, 136, 155, 159, 215, 217, 220, 221, 222
Finch, Captain Henry xxi, 39, 56, 83, 84, 109, 114, 118, 132
Foley, Thomas 130, 137, 201, 209
Fortifications
    bastions for artillery 13, 16, 25, 28, 44, 63, 64–65, 69, 70, 72, 73, 75, 76, 77, 81, 85, 92, 94
    breastwork 63, 93
    gabion (blind) 67, 91, 92
    rampier 29, 64, 66, 67, 72, 79
    ravelin 79–80, 95
    trace italienne 65
Frere, Thomas 129, 130, 134, 136

Gainsborough, Thomas and Humphrey 205, 209
Gold and silver refining 37, 55
Goodwin, Robert 126, 217, 218, 221
Gorges, Colonel John 77, 79, 96, 115, 228
Gregory, Captains Robert and George 88, 89, 96
Griffin, William 119
Gun carriages
    building 16–18, 21–22
    construction of wheels 18–21
    illustrations of 2, 3, 4, 9, 13, 14, 15, 16, 17, 18, 22, 23
    reconstructions of xx, 12
    types of 12
Gun foundries
    Ashburnham, Kent 153
    Ballynakill, Co. Laois 33, 44, 49

Index

Bersham, Wales xix, 163, 164, 165, 166, 167, 179, 193, 205, 207
Brenchley /Horsmonden, Kent 9, 33, 136, 142, 146, 147, 148, 199, 202, 203, 204
Cappoquin, Co. Waterford 33, 34, 44, 53
Carron Works, Falkirk, Stirlingshire 207
Kilrea, Co. Londonderry 44
Lisfinny, Co. Waterford 33, 34
Maresfield, Sussex 152, 153, 199
Mayfield, Sussex 153
Mountrath, Co. Laois 33
Pippingford, Sussex 179
Pounsley, Sussex 153
Scarlets, Kent 179, 199
Gunfounders
 Aynscombe, Steven 153, 201, 203
 Blacknall, Richard 33, 53–54, 201, 209
 Boyle, Sir Richard, first Earl of Cork 33, 34, 44, 53–54, 55, 145, 159, 201
 Browne dynasty xvii, xix, 10, 32, 48, 106, 195, 199–204, 209
  George 201, 204
  John I xvii, 9, 33, 34, 49, 53, 106, 159, 193, 196, 199, 200, 201, 202, 203, 204, 209
  John II 202
  Thomas 142–143
 Coote, Sir Charles Snr 27, 33, 201
 Crowe, Sir Sackville 53, 152, 201, 203, 209
 Fawcett, William 169
 Hogge, Ralph 199
 Johnson, Cornelius 199
 Johnson dynasty 140
 Johnson, John 140, 199
 Johnson, Thomas xvii, 10, 139, 140, 142, 193, 195, 199–200
 Owen, John and Thomas 141, 143
 Phillips, Richard and John 142, 199
 Pitt, Richard and Thomas 53
 Polhill, Richard 142
 Relf family 153
 Wilkinson, John 163, 164, 165, 166, 167, 168, 169, 170, 175, 179, 193, 195, 199, 204–208, 209
Gunfounding
 boring out 34, 36
 casting xvii, 10, 33, 34, 44, 53, 54
 mould making 33
Gunners
 accuracy of 50–51, 64, 84, 85
 Beech, John 50, 60
 Brewton, Thomas 50
 Cave, Thomas 50, 60
 Eldred, William 50, 60, 75, 76
 Elyot, Thomas 48
 Hexham, Henry 44
 Holland, William 60
 Horne, Thomas 50, 60
 Norton, Robert 12, 13, 30, 33, 34, 38, 42, 44, 50, 54, 59, 75, 90
 Nye, Nathaniel 38
 Poterchelo, Martin 25
 Redworth, John 50
 Smith, John 33, 34, 37, 45, 59, 97
 St George, Richard 60
 Watson, Captain Alexander 50, 88
 wages of 77
 Whithorn, Peter 55
 Williams, William 60
Gunners' accessories 44–47
 cases of plate 44
 dispart 50, 60
 gabion (blind) 67, 91–92
 gin, gynne 44, 102, 108
 ladle 44, 45, 46, 102
 linstock 47, 59
 pricker 44
 quadrant 50, 51
 ramrod 45, 47
 rule 47
 searcher 37, 46, 59
 shot gauge 47
 sponge 9, 45, 46
 wadhook, worm 45, 102
Gunpowder
 cartridges 44, 59
 composition of 54
 corned 38, 39, 58, 102, 103, 104, 107
 deflagration of 39, 55
 explosions of xx, 39, 40, 55–56, 69
 impact on warfare in ireland 27, 30
 imports of 40, 41
 manufacture of 37, 38, 42, 55, 58
 mills 40
 price of 57, 103
 'repairing', 'renewing' 38
 serpentine 38, 39
 shortages of 41, 57, 58
Gurney, Sir Richard 120, 121, 213–214, 217, 218, 220

Higgins, Dr Daniel 40, 42, 57
Hill, Sir George 170, 172, 176
Hoey, Lawrence 42
Holmes, Captain George 92, 95, 97
Horton, John 107, 109, 212

Ireton, Henry 52, 95
Irish Rebellion xviii, 30, 32, 42, 53, 58, 60, 72, 73, 76, 81, 99, 118, 120, 126, 154
Irish Society, see Plantation of Ulster

Laggan Army 27, 29, 82
Lalloe, La Lalloe, Nicholas 40, 57, 68
Legge, Co. William 66, 76, 77, 95, 228, 230
Leslie, Sir Alexander 29
Lifford, Co. Donegal xx, 10, 65, 69, 71, 72, 99, 101, 102
London, City of
 Arms of 105, 153
 Minor Companies
  Bakers 218
  Barber-Surgeons 219
  Blacksmiths 121
  Brewers 121, 219
  Carpenters 219
  Coachmakers 127, 128, 131, 137
  Coopers 219
  Cutlers 219
  Girdlers 218
  Pewterers 121, 219
  Scriveners 219
  Stationers 218
  Tylers and Bricklayers 220, 230
 Tower of xx, 48, 49, 58, 129, 130, 136, 212
 Worshipful Company of
  Clothworkers 113, 121, 122, 123, 125, 126, 129, 130, 133, 213, 221–222
  Drapers 15, 59, 74, 123, 124, 126, 127, 133, 160, 216, 219, 223
  Fishmongers xx, 24–25, 81, 122, 123, 124, 126, 133, 154, 156, 216–217, 218, 223
  Goldsmiths 37, 55, 101, 217–218, 223
  Grocers 5, 22, 24–25, 45, 46, 56, 106, 213, 215, 219, 223
  Haberdashers 101, 213
  Ironmongers 46, 214, 219–220, 223
  Mercers 1, 24, 25–25, 84, 214, 223
  Merchant Taylors 24–25, 37, 55, 106, 108, 213, 218–219, 230
  Salters 24, 38, 213, 219–220, 223
  Skinners 100, 107, 217, 218
  Vintners 24–25, 46, 213, 217, 218, 219, 220–221, 223, 230
Londerias xxi, 85, 88, 91, 97
Lundy, Colonel Robert 67, 80

Maculloch, Captain Archibald 79, 89, 90
MacKenzie, Reverend John xxi, 86, 89, 90, 91, 92

247

Mallet, Robert 187, 195, 196
Millhall, Kent 49
Mitchelburne, Governor John xxi, 79, 80, 91, 96
Monro, General Robert 29, 83
Mortars 40, 44, 51, 52, 85, 86, 93, 95, 97
Mountney, Richard 106, 212

Neville, Captain Thomas 79, 80

O'Doherty, Sir Cahir 69, 71, 81, 100, 101, 131
O'Neill, Hugh 28, 31, 40, 69
O'Neill, Owen Roe 27, 29, 51, 53, 82
O'Neill, Sir Phelim 57, 58, 81, 82, 118
O'Neill, Shane 27, 81
Office of Ordnance, Board of Ordnance
   Artificers
      Banks, Matthew 25, 130
      Bateman, Thomas and descendents 124, 125, 126, 127–128, 131, 134, 215, 221
      Franklin, William 49, 124, 125, 130, 214, 219, 220, 221
      Hancock, Anthony 84, 126, 127
      Hedland, John 142
      Hodgkins, Thomas 127, 134
      Hopkins, Martin 142
      Horton, John 107, 109, 130, 212
      Pitt, John 25, 124, 126, 128, 130–131, 134, 137, 215
      Preston, Abraham 124, 125, 127, 154, 215, 219, 221
      Smeaton, William 142
      Tate, Lewis 109, 134
      Wheatley, William 107
   in England xx, 14, 25, 32, 43, 44, 47, 48, 49, 60, 84, 107
   in Ireland xxi, 30, 34, 48, 54, 66
   Master of the Ordnance 48, 59, 76
      Bourchier, Sir George 40
      Carew, Sir George 30–31, 37–38, 81, 100, 103
      Caulfield, Sir Tobias 31, 37, 109, 191
      St John, Sir Oliver 101
      Travers, Sir John 48
      Wingfield, Jacques 60
Ordnance
   'brass' xx, 112, 114, 115, 116, 117, 118, 121, 132, 141, 147, 148, 179, 202, 209
   bursting in use 39, 49, 54, 60, 92, 207
   Carronade, Carron works 25
   casting flaws in 10, 34, 37, 46
   casting technology see Gunfounding
   City of London shield on 194
   conservation program xvii, 7–12
   cost of 106, 109
   Crimean War xix
   effects of in battle 43, 59
   evidence for firing xx, 194–196
   finds from barrels 8, 12
   founders' marks on 9, 10
   home bored 8
   honeycombed 34, 37, 45, 46, 54, 59
   in Britain
      Churchill House Museum, Hereford 156, 158
      Deal Castle, Kent 150
      Fort Amhurst, Kent 169
      Fort Nelson, Portsmouth, Hampshire 140, 150
      Manx Museum, Isle of Man 150
      Windsor Castle 13–14, 157, 158
   in Ireland
      Armagh City, Co. Armagh 173–174
      Ballymullan Barracks, Tralee, Co. Kerry 148–149
      Belfast, Ulster Museum 141, 169
      Caher Castle, Co. Tipperary 176
      Carrickfergus Castle, Co. Antrim 139, 148
      Duncannon Fort, Co. Wexford 155
      Lisburn, Co. Antrim 174–175
      Newry, Co. Down 173–174
      Portumna Castle, Co. Galway 31
      Youghal, Co. Cork 41, 145, 148, 149, 159
   in other countries
      America, Florida 147
      Ascension Island 169
      Australia xxi, 132, 147, 150, 172
      Austria, Vienna 169
      Canada, Bay View, Novia Scotia 169
      Canada, Fort York, Toronto 141, 155
      Canada, Kingston, Ontario 166, 167–168, 175–176
      China, Forbidden City, Beijing 150
      Denmark, Copenhagen 150
      Holland, off Terschelling 147, 148, 150, 154, 158
      India, Mehrangarh Fort, Jodhpur 142, 147, 150, 158
      Japan, Karatsu Castle 140
      Latvia, Riga 150
      Mozambique xxi, 169
      Portugal, Lisbon 140
      St Kitts, Brimstone Fort 150
      Spain, Madrid 169
   leather 53
   locations of the restored cannon xviii, 24
   marks on 9
   mortars 40, 44, 51, 52, 85, 85, 93, 95, 97
   multiple gun 132
   'nealed and turned' 131, 195
   neglect of 1, 84, 96
   number at Londonderry in 1689 xx, 85, 99
   platforms for 75, 76, 83, 84, 101, 105, 107, 108
   proofing of 33, 49, 54, 106
   recoil of 12, 13, 14
   rose-and-crown emblem 4, 9, 10, 101
   salvage of 30, 31, 53
   sent by the City of London to Culmore Castle 105–107, 211–213
   sent to Londonderry by the London Companies 213–222
   terminology xiii–xv
   use of as street furniture 4, 99

Paulet, Sir George 100, 131
Pepys, Samuel 59, 130
Petty, George 212
Phillips, Captain Thomas 67, 77, 78, 79, 95, 97, 132
Phillips, Sir Thomas 15, 66, 73, 74, 75, 77, 100, 104, 107, 108, 109
Pierson, Richard 130, 134, 136, 202, 209
Plantation of Ulster xvii, xix, xx, 15, 54, 69, 72, 81, 99–101, 105, 107, 108, 109, 120, 121, 122, 131, 168
Pointis, Jean-Bernard-Louis Desjean, Sieur de 86, 96
Porter, Endymion 41, 57
Portumna Castle, Co. Galway, cannon at 31
Povey, Francis 34
Proby, Peter 72, 101, 107
Pynnar, Nicholas 72, 73, 94, 101, 105, 107

Randolph, Randolfe, Colonel Edward 48, 81, 94, 103
Rastall, John 40, 42, 57
Raven, Thomas 15, 73, 74, 79, 80
Richards, Colonel 93, 97
Roaring Meg xx, 1, 2, 3, 4, 7, 10, 11, 12, 37, 81, 143, 156, 157, 186, 190
Roose, John 106, 212
Rose, Levan de 131
Rose, Roose, Roger 105–106, 131, 148, 211, 212

Rosen, General Conrad de 47, 85, 86
Rowley, Hugh 176
Rowley, John 75

Sacheverell, Francis 49
St Leger, Sir William 27, 120
Saltpetre 32, 37, 38–39, 41–43, 47, 54, 55, 57, 58
Shannon, William 167–168, 175–176
Ships
   Avondster 155
   Batavia 132, 147, 150
   Bennett 133
   Blessing 155
   Charity 122, 130, 133
   Confidence 31
   Eighth Whelp 133
   Fortune 129
   Gennett 105
   Grace 105
   Great Lewis 155
   Greyhound 92
   Guyance 142
   Hoche 170, 172
   Isaac 135
   James 128, 135
   Mare Scourge 199
   Mary Rose 39, 56, 142, 208
   May fflower 212–213
   Mauritius 140, 142, 150, 209
   Popinjay 31
   Sea Venture 142
   Seventh Whelp 39, 56
   Sovereign of the Seas 14
   Supply 135
   Swan 147, 155
   Trial 147, 150
   Victory 207
   William and Joan 106
Shot
   canister 43, 59, 60, 91, 97
   chain 43–44, 91
   composite lead and brick 90–91
   heated 43, 91
   price of
   stone 58, 59, 114, 116
   windage 25, 47, 59
Sidney, Sir Henry 66, 69, 81, 94
Spanish Armada 59
   vessels
      Duquesa Santa Anna 52, 150
      Girona 31, 59
      La Trinidad Valancera 30, 47, 59
   cannon recovered from 30, 31
   gunners' accessories from 47
Springham, Mathias 72, 101, 107
Stevens, John 86
Stewart, Sir Robert 29, 82, 83, 110, 119
Stewart, Sir William 29, 122, 133
Stilgoe, Mr 125, 126, 127, 222
Strabane, Co. Tyrone xx, 31, 69, 72, 88, 89, 94, 99, 101, 110, 228

Strafford, Earl of, see Wentworth, Sir Thomas
Stuart, James, first Duke of Richmond 110, 113, 119, 133
Sulphur 37, 41, 54, 57

Temple, Sir John 42, 58
Thomas, Engineer Jean 67, 68, 78, 96
Thomson, Maurice 129
Tone, Wolfe 170
Trip, Elias 200
Tucker, William 129
Turvill, Turville, Edmond 106, 131, 132, 211, 212

Vauban, Seigneur Sebastien Le Prestre 67, 86, 93, 94
Vaughan, Sir John 72, 122
Virginia Plantation xxi, 100, 128, 129, 134, 135

Wabion, Thomas 73–74, 94
Wadding, Fr Luke 41, 53
Walker, Reverend George xx, xxi, 84, 85, 88, 89, 90, 91, 92, 93, 96, 97, 132
Wandesford, Sir Christopher xx, 109, 120, 133
Webb, Captain William 77, 95
Wentworth, Sir Thomas, Earl of Strafford xx, 33, 41, 44, 49, 57, 109, 120, 133
Westerne, Thomas 134
Windebank, Francis 211, 230
Winter, Reverend Richard xxi, 72, 113, 118, 121, 123, 156, 218